全人教育英语专业本科教材系列

总顾问　刘润清

U1015823

汉英翻译教程

A Coursebook on Chinese-English Translation

总主编　文　旭

主　编　肖开容　罗　天

副主编　李　智　孟凡君　杨　洁

编写人员（按章节排序）

杨　洁　罗　天　肖开容　朱晓烽

刘　黎　孟凡君　李奉栖　李　智

中国人民大学出版社

·北京·

总 序

教育作为一种社会现象，自人类社会产生之日起就出现了。在人类社会的发展过程中，人类积累了经验和知识，而将这些经验和知识传递给下一代的活动就是教育的雏形。随着人类知识和经验的不断丰富，教育活动也不断发展和完善，逐渐成为一种组织严密、培养人的正规社会活动。教育的重要性是无与伦比的，之所谓“建国君民，教学为先”就是这个道理。今天几乎没有人会否认迪斯累利 (Disraeli) 在 1874 年所说的话：“一个国家的命运取决于这个国家的人民的教育。”外语教育作为教育的一个重要组成部分，在人类的教育中扮演着十分重要的角色。外语教育如何在我国的教育中发挥自己的作用，落实立德树人根本任务，这是我们所有外语学人必须关注的问题。我国的外语教育有一百多年的历史，取得了辉煌的成就，但如何进一步提升外语教育的质量，这是当今外语教育的核心问题，也是外语教育改革的一个永恒主题。英语专业教育如何提升自己的质量，到底希望培养什么样的学生，怎样才能实现这些希望，这是我们英语专业教师必须思考的问题，也是英语专业教育改革的核心问题。把英语作为专业外语来学习，这是新时代的需求，既是个人的需要，更是国家语言战略规划的需要。

《国家中长期教育改革和发展规划纲要 (2010—2020 年)》明确指出，要“适应国家经济社会对外开放的要求，培养大批具有国际视野、通晓国际规则、能够参与国际事务和国际竞争的国际化人才”。要培养既通晓相关专业知识又熟练掌握外语的优秀人才，我国的外语教育责无旁贷。英语专业是我国高等教育的重要组成部分，其专业化、特色化非常明显。我们组织编写这套“全人教育英语专业本科教材系列”，其目的就是为了彰显英语专业教育的特色，满足我国英语专业教育的多元需求。在编写之前，我们研究了多种国内外现行的英语专业教科书，咨询资深专家学者，进行了充分的调研和需求分析，确定了本套教材的编写理念和编写方案，最终本套教材才得以与广大师生见面。

一、编写依据

1. 政策依据

“全人教育英语专业本科教材系列”编写的政策依据是《国家中长期教育改革和发展规划纲要

(2010—2020年)》《教育部关于全面提高高等教育质量的若干意见》(教高【2012】4号)以及新颁布的《外国语言文学类教学质量国家标准》。在编写过程中我们充分考虑到新时代我国英语专业教育的现状，并力求体现当代英语专业教育的本质、特征、目标和任务，贯彻为实现目标所倡导的外语教育理念、教学原则、教学模式、教学过程、教学方法和教学评价，着力服务并促进我国英语专业教育改革，提升英语专业教育的质量，更好地提高英语专业学生的英语水平、跨文化交际能力和综合素质，促进学生的全面发展。

2. 理论依据

本套教材编写的理论依据主要是教育学、心理学、语言学、认知神经科学等学科的理论和原则。其教育学依据主要是“全人教育理论”(holistic education)，主张“教单科、育全人，教外语、育全人”的外语教育理念；其心理学依据主要是多元智能理论，强调英语学习的特殊性，把听、说、读、写、译等基本技能与学生的多元智能有机地结合起来；其语言学依据主要是应用语言学和教育语言学，尤其是终身学习理论下的体验学习、自主学习、合作学习、泛在学习、深度学习以及适应性学习；其认知神经科学依据主要是全脑教育，认知神经科学有助于我们理解人脑的共同之处与个体差异，有助于英语教学的因材施教，人脑具有可塑性，只要学生拥有信心、自尊和动机，外语学习随时都可以成功。

3. 实践依据

本套教材的编写是在广泛调研的基础上进行的。针对我国英语专业学生的英语水平和学习情况，并参照英汉语言文化的差异，系统地培养和提高学生的语言意识和文化意识，提高他们的英语水平、跨文化交际能力和国际视野。我们在编写前对国内多所院校的英语专业教学的实际情况进行了需求分析，与专家学者、教师、学生开展了广泛的交流，同时也吸收了国内外同类优质教材的宝贵经验以及英语专业教材编写的经验。此外，本套教材的编写还认真参考了《义务教育英语课程标准》(2011年版)和《高中英语新课程标准》，充分考虑了英语专业教学与中学英语的合理衔接，内容编排也考虑了大学生的认知特点和情感因素。

二、教材特色

记不清楚是谁说过这样一句话：“教育是民族的根本；教科书是教育的根本。”由此可见教科书的重要性。现代社会教科书在学校教育中的地位是双重的：一方面，互联网时代学生获得信息的渠道快捷而方便，慕课(MOOC)、私播课(SPOC)等也冲击着高校课堂，传统教科书的权威性已受到极大的挑战；另一方面，教科书仍然是课程的中心和学校教育的重要载体，教科书的地位同时得到教育主管部门和教师的强化。当今我国英语专业教育改革的不断深化，给教科书的内容、使用和外部环境都带来了很多变化。教科书要与时俱进，编写新教材就势在必行。

“全人教育英语专业本科教材系列”正是在上述背景下应运而生的。本套教材以《外国语言文学类教学质量国家标准》为指导，以教育学、心理学、语言学、学习科学、认知神经科学等学科为理论依据，以培养学生的英语应用能力及跨文化交际能力为核心，以促进学生的全面发展为目标，针对我国英语专业教育的现状以及学生的心理、生理和认知特点，主要突出以下特色：

1. 倡导“教单科、育全人，教外语、育全人”的全人教育理念

“全人教育英语专业本科教材系列”编写的主要理念是“教单科、育全人，教外语、育全人”的全人教育，即以“终身学习和终身发展”的育人、发展人、提高人的综合素质为核心的教育模式。这一模式体现了人本主义的基本思想：学习就是成为一个和谐而完善的人。也就是要把学生培养成为有道德、有知识、有能力、和谐发展的“完人”。我们虽然教的是英语专业，注重学生的基本知识和基本技能，但培育的是一个完整的人。所以，在英语专业教学中决不能忽视对人的培养，要帮助学生树立正确的人生观、价值观和世界观，教育学生认知、认同和践行社会主义核心价值观。联合国教科文组织和国际教育发展委员会编著的《学会生存——教育世界的今天和明天》中就特别强调要“培养完人”(2009:192)，“把一个人在体力、智力、情绪、伦理各方面的因素综合起来，使他成为一个完善的人，这就是对教育基本目的的一个广义的界说”(2009:195)。

2. 围绕“教育的四大支柱”，突显体验学习、自主学习和深度学习

全人教育特别重视人生的经验和体验学习。本套教材的编写始终围绕四种基本的学习能力进行安排，即教育的四大支柱：学会认知 (learning to know)、学会做事 (learning to do)、学会共同生活 (learning to live together) 以及学会生存 (learning to be)。教材的编写始终把语言知识、语言技能、学习能力和学习策略等融入教材内容中，通过任务、活动及练习的设置引导学生体验学习和自主学习；通过“体验”“模仿”“合作”等学习方式，丰富学生的百科知识，提高他们的英语应用能力和自主学习能力。

3. 强调批判性思维能力的培养

本套教材秉承一个重要的主张，即教育的真正目的就是让人不断地提出问题和思索问题。据说，美国天赋教育的“童子功”入门第一招就是培养学生的批判性阅读行为，第二招就是培养批判性聆听技巧。而批判性思维能力的培养成了各个高校课程设计围绕的核心。培养学生的批判性思维能力，这是全人教育的重要主张之一。本套教材非常注重培养学生的批判性思维能力和创新思维能力，在教材设计的任务、活动和练习中，引导学生对问题进行批判性思考，展示自身作为读者或参与者的理解和评价，提出问题、分析问题和解决问题。

4. 强调英语的工具性与人文性的结合

学校教育的最终目标就是发展学生的能力。本套教材的编写充分注重工具性和人文性的结合。除了帮助学生掌握英语这一交流工具外，即提高学生英语听、说、读、写、译的能力以及跨文化交际能力，还特别强调英语教育的人文性，把以人为本、弘扬人的价值作为英语专业教育的另一核心，注重学生的综合素质培养和全面发展。在教材中我们充分挖掘英语专业课程丰富的人文内涵，把社

会主义核心价值观有机地融入各类教材中，以知促行，以行促知，学以致用，在潜移默化中培育学生的爱国情怀。

5. 体现实用性与趣味性的有机统一

本套教材在内容的选择、练习的设计等方面都体现了新时代的特点和要求，遵循我国英语专业大学生的情感因素和认知特点，重视学生的兴趣和需求以激发他们的求知欲望，让他们变“要我学”为“我要学”，从而使他们在主动学习丰富多彩的教材内容的过程中提升英语水平和综合素质。各类教材题材丰富，内容生动有趣，语言地道，文笔优美，体现了趣味性和实用性的有机统一。

6. 融中西文化为一体，注重培养国际化视野

斯宾塞有一个著名的问题：什么知识最有价值？这一问题的背后实际上蕴含着这样的核心问题：谁的知识最有价值？用谁的文化去教育学生？在这些问题上，教科书起到很重要的作用。因此，本套教材特别注重培养学生对中国传统文化的认知与意识，注重培养和提高学生使用英语介绍中国文化的能力。教材融入中西文化，在选材方面重视本土问题和国际问题、中西对比等问题，帮助学生了解国际惯例、规则和形势。既培养学生的跨文化意识，又提升其跨文化交际能力，同时培养其国际化视野。

三、编写团队

本套教材的编写有一个强大的团队。顾问为我国著名外语教育专家、北京外国语大学博士生导师刘润清教授，总主编为西南大学博士生导师文旭教授，参加编写的主要有（排名不分先后）：西南大学、北京理工大学、华中科技大学、东北大学、内蒙古大学、河南大学、贵州大学、上海海事大学、西南政法大学、山西大学、广州大学、湖南科技大学、华南师范大学、陕西师范大学、西北师范大学、四川师范大学、贵州师范大学、云南师范大学、广西师范大学、海南师范大学、西华师范大学、重庆师范大学、重庆交通大学、重庆理工大学、重庆邮电大学、浙江理工大学 、沈阳工业大学、西南石油大学、新疆师范大学、青海师范大学、北京信息科技大学、长江师范学院、中国海洋大学、中国石油大学、济南大学、四川农业大学、长沙理工大学、四川文理学院等多所高校的英语专业教师，他们长期从事英语专业教学工作，具有丰富的英语教学经验和教材编写经验，确保了教材的水平和质量。

本套教材的编写凝聚了许多专家学者和教师的经验和智慧，从内容到形式都有不少新的尝试与探索。在此，对为本套教材的编写和出版付出辛勤劳动的所有专家、老师表示衷心的感谢。对于共同研发并出版此套教材的中国人民大学出版社外语分社表示诚挚的谢意。诚然，由于时间仓促、水平有限，不足之处在所难免。我们会虚心听取大家的意见和批评，并在未来的教学中使之日臻完善。

全人教育英语专业本科教材系列编委会

2018 年 8 月

前言

一、编写理念

作为“全人教育英语专业本科教材系列”之一,《汉英翻译教程》以《外国语言文学类教学质量国家标准》和全人教育思想为指导,在总体设计、结构编排、内容编写等方面注重经典性、人文性、知识性的结合，突出输入与输出、理解与转换、忠实性与可接受性、文化传播与文化调适等翻译思维的培养，强化学生英语表达的准确性、规范性意识和汉英翻译中的写作思维训练，通过阅读欣赏、模仿实战、总结拓展等翻译训练过程，培养学生以国际视野和规范英语表达中国文化的能力。

1. 注重经典性、人文性、知识性

首先是经典性，选材以中国文学和文化经典著作为主，古今结合，集合名家、名作和名译，力求体现中国文化精髓，涵盖文学、文化、历史、哲学、思想等领域。选材内容偏重人文性，目标是通过本教材的教学内容培养学生的审美意识、文化意识和思想意识。知识性体现在不同文体和知识领域的编排。每章围绕一个文体或主题，引导学生了解相关背景知识，熟悉文体知识和领域知识。选材还力求体现翻译的创造性，多数篇章提供 2 ～ 3 个译本，让学生体会不同译者基于不同理解、针对不同目标和不同读者提供的多种译法。

2. 突出多种翻译思维能力的培养

我们认为，汉英翻译与英汉翻译能力的培养既有相通之处，也有不同之处。在汉英翻译教学中，要培养恰当的翻译思维能力，处理好以下几种能力之间的关系：一是输入与输出能力。在汉英翻译教学中，由于英语是外语，英语表达能力是决定学生汉英翻译水平的关键因素。因此，我们主张在汉英翻译教学中着重加强英语表达输入，既包括对英语基本词汇、句法、语篇知识的输入，也包括对中国文化核心术语、概念和思想的权威英语表达方式的输入。因此，本教材通过阅读欣赏、翻译热身、翻译实战、译文荟萃等多个板块，提供多种原文和译文，使本教材成为一种资源性教材，方便学生在学习中获得大量语言输入，从而增强输出能力。二是理解与转换能力。不管是英汉翻译还是汉英翻译，理解都是翻译转换的基础，在教学中应妥善处理理解能力和转换能力的关系，避免过于偏重技巧讲解而忽略了理解能力的培养。本教材主张将文本阅读和理解训练放在前面，将技巧训练放在文本阅读和翻译练习之后，作为翻译实践后的总结与归纳。三是忠实原文与确保译文可接受性的能力。中英语言文化差异导致译文的忠实性与可接受性之间存在矛盾。本教材主张从不同的文体和主题出发处理忠实性与可接受性之间的问题，章节编排以文体和主题为主线，在每一种文体和主题内讨论文体特点、表达特点和翻译策略。四是文化传播与文化调适的能力。在忠实原文和保证译文可接受性的基础上，本教材主张汉英翻译应在准确、完整传播中国文化和与西方文化的接轨和适应中找到恰当的平衡。

3. 强调规范性意识与写作思维

在长期的教学中，我们发现很多学生对汉英翻译存在一些误解，其中之一便是简单地将翻译看作语言转换活动，或者机械地寻找语言对应，造成死译、硬译或者中式英语译文。其主要原因在于学生过于重视翻译中的语言转换，对英语表达的规范性重视不够，或者英语规范表达能力不够。本教材编写组认为，汉英翻译教学的一个重要目标是培养学生用规范、准确、恰当的英语表达中国文化的能力。因此，本教材选取大量中国文化经典作品的多种译文，目的在于引导学生深入理解中国文化，积累规范、地道的英语表达，学会用准确的英语来表达中国思想和文化。同时，我们主张在汉英翻译教学中突出英语写作意识和英语写作能力培养，强调以英语写作思维从事汉英翻译，即在对汉语篇章理解的基础上，重点思考如何用规范、准确的英语，创造性地“写出”汉语原文的信息或思想，而非机械地进行字词转换。为此，我们选取了经典的文学作品、思想性较强的典籍作品作为翻译训练材料，而不是以孤立的句子和翻译技巧为主要训练内容。

4. 优化翻译教学流程

较为传统的翻译教学流程主要包括：技巧讲解、技巧训练（以句子为主）、课后训练（包括句子和篇章）、练习讲评。这种教学流程存在一些不足，包括：案例缺乏语境和整体性、难以培养学生的文体意识、不注重主题知识和概念的理解等。

本教材主张以下教学流程：阅读欣赏和模仿译文、总结翻译思路和方法、巩固和拓展翻译能力。具体操作程序为：（1）在每单元开始，学生课前完成一个篇章原文和译文的阅读赏析，然后模仿所阅读的译文做翻译热身练习；（2）课堂上教师组织讨论，进一步对译文进行赏析，并解决学生翻译热身练习中遇到的问题；（3）基于阅读欣赏和翻译热身练习，教师进行翻译理论、策略和方法的讲解和讨论；（4）学生课后进行翻译实战练习，巩固翻译技能；（5）课后通过译文荟萃进行拓展学习，通过翻译家介绍了解翻译历史与文化，参照补充资源进行自主学习。

本教材所编排的教学内容体现以下几个特点：一是注重整体性。以段落、篇章为单位，有上下文语境，翻译策略和方法融于语篇中，避免单独以句子为单位。二是注重文体特点与主题知识。每单元的翻译策略和方法紧贴单元主题，每种文体有特点介绍，对每个主题给出一定数量的核心概念及其英语表达。三是发挥学生的主动性和参与性。减少教师讲解的比重，主张学生探究型学习，将课外学习与课堂教学、教师讲授和学生讨论相结合。四是注重教师使用上的灵活性。本教材以文体和主题为线索，提供的材料既可以作为教师课堂教学材料，也可以作为学生课外学习的材料。教师也可以围绕单元主题自选材料，还可以借助补充资源搜集材料作为补充。五是教学方式的多样化。教材编排的内容和所选教学材料既适合做课堂讲授，也方便教师开展课堂分组讨论、小组报告以及课外自主学习等。

二、教材结构

本教材按照文体类型和话题内容编排，共八章十六个单元，每章两个单元。第一至六章按文体或主题划分，涵盖散文、小说、诗歌、哲理故事、历史和哲学六个主题。第七、八两章侧重应用翻译，包括发言与演讲、政府文件、宣传与介绍、公示语。

每单元包括七个部分：阅读欣赏、翻译热身、翻译技巧、翻译实战、译文荟萃、翻译家、补充资源。

（1）阅读欣赏：提供汉语原文一篇，英语译文一个或多个，目的是让学生在课前自学，熟悉该文体或主题的特点和英译思路。（2）翻译热身：提供汉语原文一篇，供学生课前或课堂上做热身练习，英语译文作为参考答案另附。（3）翻译技巧：结合本单元的文体特点和主题介绍翻译思路和方法，主要包括以下内容：一是本单元文体特点或文本类型特点及英译要点，二是相关的汉语句法或篇章特点及翻译要点。总体上尽量体现主题相关性和以本单元所选语篇材料为基础的原则。（4）翻译实战：提供汉语原文一篇，供学生课后练习，英语译文作为参考答案另附。（5）译文荟萃：提供与本单元主题相关的译文集锦，包括短语或术语的翻译、经典句子翻译、段落或篇章翻译。句子、段落或篇章翻译以多译本对照为主。（6）翻译家：每单元介绍一位相关领域的中外著名翻译家，旨在帮助学生通过阅读翻译家生平、翻译成果和翻译思想，了解翻译历史和文化，激发翻译学习的兴趣。（7）补充资源：提供学生课外进一步学习的翻译著作、教材、著名译本、工具书、参考书、辅助资料、语料库、电子资源和网站资源，便于学生开展拓展学习。

三、编写分工

2014 年 4 月，在西南大学外国语学院召开了“全人教育英语专业本科教材系列”编写座谈会，在总主编文旭教授的指导下，翻译教材编写组确定了以文体和主题为主线、以篇章为单位、以案例为主体的翻译教程编写思路，由肖开容拟定了教材结构和纲领，该纲领在杨朝军和程树华编写、2015 年出版的《英汉翻译教程》中得到了体现和检验。《汉英翻译教程》延续了这一编写思路，并结合汉英翻译教学的特点，在结构编排和选材方面做了调整，更加突出古今结合的编写思路。

本教程由西南大学、重庆交通大学、重庆师范大学、西南政法大学、贵州大学五所大学的八位编写人员共同完成。全书的整体框架、章节结构和编写思路由肖开容拟定，罗天对编写思路和原则提出了重要的参考意见，编写组全体成员多次就教材的编写理念、思路、结构和选材进行了讨论。八位编写人员完成了各章的选材和编写工作，具体分工为：杨洁（第一章　散文翻译）、罗天（第

二章　小说翻译）、肖开容（第三章　诗歌翻译）、朱晓烽（第四章　哲理故事翻译）、刘黎（第五章　历史翻译）、孟凡君（第六章　哲学翻译）、李奉栖（第七章　应用翻译（一））、李智（第八章　应用翻译（二））。

教材初稿完成后，编写组对全书进行了多次修改和校阅，力求准确。然而，由于编写时间和编者水平所限，本教材或有不足之处，诚望各位专家学者和教材使用者提出宝贵意见，以便进一步修订完善。

本教材练习配有参考答案，读者可登录中国人民大学出版社主页 http:www.crup.com.cn，搜索本书后下载，或与 010–62512737、010–62515580、huangt@crup.com.cn、wangxw@crup.com.cn 联系索取相关教学资源。

编者

2018 年 9 月

目 录
Contents

第一章 散文翻译

第二章 小说翻译

第三章 诗歌翻译

第四章 哲理故事翻译

第五章 历史翻译

第八章　应用翻译（二）

Chapter 1

第一章　散文翻译

第一单元　中国现代散文

第二单元　中国古代散文

第一单元　中国现代散文

1.1 阅读欣赏:《落花生》

【说明】对照原文阅读译文，对比三个译文的异同，体会不同译者对原文句式的处理技巧以及对原文微妙情感的处理效果。

简介:《落花生》是中国现代著名小说家、散文家、“五四”时期新文学运动先驱者之一许地山（1894 年—1941 年）的一篇散文。该文着重讲述了一家人过花生收获节的经过，通过对花生好处的谈论，揭示了花生不图虚名、默默奉献的品格，说明人要做有用的人，不要做只讲体面而对别人没有好处的人，表达了作者扎扎实实做人的思想情感。面对这篇借物喻人的经典叙事散文，译者该怎样传达它的意境呢？下面我们就来对比欣赏一下刘士聪、张培基以及杨宪益、戴乃迭等国内外翻译名家是如何处理的。

落　花　生

许地山

我们屋后有半亩隙地。母亲说:“让它荒芜着怪可惜，既然你们那么爱吃花生，就辟来做花生园罢。”我们几姊弟和几个小丫头都很喜欢——买种的买种，动土的动土，灌园的灌园，过不了几个月，居然收获了！

母亲说:“今年我们可以做一个收获节，也请你们爹爹来尝尝我们的新花生，如何？”我们都答应了。母亲把花生做成好几样的食品，还吩咐这节期要在园里底茅亭举行。

那晚上的天色不大好，可是爹爹也到来，实在很难得！爹爹说："你们爱吃花生么？"

我们都争着答应："爱！"

"谁能把花生的好处说出来？"

姊姊说："花生的气味很美。"

哥哥说："花生可以制油。"

我说："无论何等人都可以用贱价买它来吃；都喜欢吃它。这就是它的好处。"

爹爹说："花生的用处固然很多，但有一样是很可贵的。这小小的豆不像那好看的苹果、桃子、石榴，把它们底果实悬在枝上，鲜红嫩绿的颜色，令人一望而发生羡慕的心。他只把果子埋在地底，等到成熟，才容人把他挖出来。你们偶然看见一棵花生瑟缩地长在地上，不能立刻辨出它有没有果实，非得等到你接触他才能知道。"

我们都说："是的。"母亲也点点头。爹爹接下去说："所以你们要像花生，因为他是有用的，不是伟大、好看的东西。"我说："那么，人要做有用的人，不要做伟大、体面的人了。"爹爹说："这是我对于你们的希望。"

我们谈到夜阑才散，所有花生食品虽然没有了，然而父亲的话现在还印在我心版上。

译文一

The Peanut

At the back of our house there was half a *mu* of unused land. "It's a pity to let it lie idle like that," Mother said. "Since you all enjoy eating peanuts, let us open it up and make it a peanut garden." At that my brother, sister and I were all delighted and so were the young housemaids. And then some went to buy seeds, some began to dig up the ground and others watered it and, in a couple of months, we had a harvest!

"Let us have a party tonight to celebrate," Mother suggested, "and ask Dad to join us for a taste of our fresh peanuts. What do you say?" We all agreed, of course. Mother cooked the peanuts in a variety of styles and told us to go to the thatched pavilion in the garden for the celebration.

The weather was not very good that night but, to our great delight, Father came all the same.

"Do you like peanuts?" Father asked.

"Yes!" We all answered eagerly.

"But who can tell me what the peanut is good for?"

"It is very delicious to eat," my sister took the lead.

"It is good for making oil," my brother followed.

"It is inexpensive," I said. "Almost everyone can afford it and everyone enjoys eating it. I think this is what it is good for."

"Peanut is good for many things," Father said, "but there is one thing that is particularly good about it. Unlike apples, peaches and pomegranates that display their fruits up in the air, attracting you with their beautiful colors, peanut buries its fruit in the earth. It does not show itself until you dig it out when it is ripe and, unless you dig it out, you can't tell it bears fruit or not just by its frail stem quivering above ground."

"That's true," we all said and Mother nodded her assent, too. "So you should try to be like the peanut," Father went on, "because it is useful, though not great or attractive."

"Do you mean," I asked, "we should learn to be useful but not seek to be great or attractive?"

"Yes," Father said. "This is what I expect of you."

We stayed up late that night, eating all the peanuts Mother had cooked for us. But Father's words remained vivid in my memory till this day.（刘士聪 译）

译文二

Peanuts

Behind our house there lay half a mou vacant land. Mother said: "It's a pity to let it lay waste. Since you all like to eat peanuts so very much, why not plant some here?" That exhilarated us children and our servant girls as well, and soon we started buying seeds, ploughing the land and watering the plants. We gathered in a good harvest just after a couple of months!

Mother said, "How about giving a party this evening to celebrate the harvest and inviting your Daddy to have a taste of our newly-harvested peanuts?" We all agreed. Mother made quite a few varieties of goodies out of the peanuts, and told us that the party would be held in the thatched pavilion on the peanut plot.

It looked like rain that evening, yet, to our great joy, Father came nevertheless. "Do you like peanuts?" asked father.

"Yes, we do!" we vied in giving the answer.

"Which of you could name the good things in peanuts?"

"Peanuts taste good," said my elder sister.

"Peanuts produce edible oil," said my elder sister.

"Peanuts are so cheap," said I, "that anyone can afford to eat them. Peanuts are everyone's favourite.

That's why we call peanuts good."

"It's true that peanuts have many uses," said Father, "but they're most beloved in one respect. Unlike nice-looking apples, peaches, and pomegranates, which hang their fruit on branches and win people's admiration with their brilliant colours, tiny little peanuts bury themselves underground and remain unearthed until they're ripe. When you come upon a peanut plant lying curled up on the ground, you can never immediately tell whether or not it bears any nuts until you touch them."

"That's true," we said in unison. Mother also nodded. "So you must take after peanuts," Father continued, "because they're useful though not great and nice-looking."

"Then you mean one should be useful rather than great and nice-looking," I said.

"That's what I expect of you," Father concluded.

We kept chatting until the party broke up late at night. Today, though nothing is left of the goodies made of peanuts, Father's words remain engraved in my mind.（张培基　译）

译文三

The Peanut

Behind our house there was a patch of land. "It would be a pity to let it go wild," said Mother. "I suggest that since you are all so fond of peanuts you should grow some there."

We children and the little maidservants were all delighted. Some of us bought seeds, some dug up the plot and others watered it. In just a few months we had a harvest.

Mother said, "Let's have a harvest festival tonight and invite your father to taste our fresh peanuts."

We all agreed. Mother made a variety of dishes using our peanuts and instructed that the festival should be held in the thatched pavilion in the garden.

The weather was not very good that evening, but even Father put in an appearance, which was a rare event.

"Do you all like peanuts?" asked Father.

"Yes!" we all clamoured to reply.

"Who can tell me what's good about peanuts?"

"They taste good," said older sister.

"They can be made into oil," said older brother.

"Everybody can afford to buy them, whoever they might be, and everyone likes them. That's what's good about peanuts," said I.

Father said, "In fact the peanut has many uses, but the most valuable thing about this little nut is this: it's not like the apple, peach or pomegranate, flaunting their bright, beautiful fruits on their branches for all to see and admire. The peanut lies buried in the soil, waiting until it is ripe before letting people dig it up. If ever you come across a shy peanut plant you cannot immediately tell whether or not it has any nuts. You have to find them to be certain."

We all agreed with this and Mother nodded her head too. Father continued, "So you should all try to be like the peanut, because it is neither grand nor beautiful, but useful."

"Does that mean that people should try to be useful rather than famous or great?" I asked.

"That is what I hope of you all," Father replied.

We talked late into the night before dispersing. Although we ate all the peanuts that evening, Father's words still remain embedded in my mind.（杨宪益、戴乃迭　译）

1.2 翻译热身：《风筝》

【说明】 翻译下面的文字，然后将自己的译文与所提供的参考译文对比，体会其中的差异。

简介：《风筝》是我国著名文学家、中国现代文学奠基人鲁迅先生所撰写的一篇回忆性散文。该文写于1925年，鲁迅先生时年44岁，生活的经历和思想的深广使鲁迅先生对过往的事情进行了深沉的思索和深刻的反省。文章以风筝为引线，对“我”粗暴对待小弟、扼杀弟弟玩的天性的言行作了深刻的反思，同时又对小弟深受虐杀，却不仅认为我是对的，且无任何怨恨而倍感悲哀。善于解剖自己的鲁迅先生通过对这一事件的反思，引发了一个令人深思的问题，那就是，我们应该如何保护孩子的天性，如何让孩子在自由的天地中自由地生活和成长。文章包含强烈的自我谴责意味，充满着对封建宗族制度摧残儿童的罪恶的控诉，其语调是沉重的，情绪是悲哀的。《风筝》是鲁迅先生很有影响力的一篇散文，纽约出版的《亚洲》杂志（英文版）曾在1936年9月将其作为鲁迅先生的代表作品之一推荐给世界读者。

风　　筝（节选）

鲁迅

北京的冬季，地上还有积雪，灰黑色的秃树枝丫叉于晴朗的天空中，而远处有一二风筝浮动，在我是一种惊异和悲哀。

故乡的风筝时节，是春二月，倘听到沙沙的风轮声，仰头便能看见一个淡墨色的蟹风筝或嫩蓝色的蜈蚣风筝。还有寂寞的瓦片风筝，没有风轮，又放得很低，伶仃地显出憔悴可怜模样。但此时地上的杨柳已经发芽，早的山桃也多吐蕾，和孩子们的天上的点缀相照应，打成一片春日的温和。我现在在哪里呢？四面都还是严冬的肃杀，而久经诀别的故乡的久经逝去的春天，却就在这天空中荡漾了。

但我是向来不爱放风筝的，不但不爱，并且嫌恶它，因为我以为这是没出息孩子所做的玩艺。和我相反的是我的小兄弟，他那时大概十岁内外罢，多病，瘦得不堪，然而最喜欢风筝，自己买不起，我又不许放，他只得张着小嘴，呆看着空中出神，有时至于小半日。远处的蟹风筝突然落下来了，他惊呼；两个瓦片风筝的缠绕解开了，他高兴得跳跃。他的这些，在我看来都是笑柄，可鄙的。

1.3 翻译技巧：现代散文英译

1.3.1 中国现代散文的特点

作为文学体裁之一的中国现代散文自“五四”新文化运动后开始异军突起，在中国文学界和思想界起着启蒙和先锋作用，成绩斐然。现代散文由于受到西方文学观念的影响，它在继承传统的同时从内容到形式都发生了根本性蜕变，形成了自己鲜明的特征。

一是作品中往往透露出作者鲜明的个性。中国现代散文在发展历程中，涌现出一大批独具个性的散文家，他们既受到多年民族文化的熏陶，又吸收了外来文化的精华，他们的创作中处处有“我”的存在——“我”的思想，“我”的灵魂，“我”的人格，“我”的情感。鲁迅的散文风格多样，简约冷峻；周作人的散文平和恬淡；冰心的散文歌颂母爱、童真和自然美，形成了独特的“冰心体”。还有朱自清、林语堂、刘半农、俞平伯、梁遇春、何其芳等一大批散文作家，他们的散文或儒雅闲趣，或含蓄蕴藉，或坦露胸襟，或清丽典雅，或绮丽缠绵，或机智幽默，在各自的作品中，作家们都留下了自己鲜明的自我形象。郁达夫曾明确指出“现代散文之最大特征，是每一个作家的每一篇散文里所表现的个性，比从前的任何散文都来得强烈。”瞿秋白也曾说过：“我愿意突出个性，印取自己的思潮。”巴金在总结自己的散文创作时说：“我的任何一篇散文里面都有我自己。”

二是题材广泛，意境独特。由于新思想、新文化的冲击，散文已不再固守“文以载道”的规范，大到国家大事、日月星辰，小到日常生活中的家长里短以及地方风习、山水湖光、往事漫忆、感想述怀、读书心得等均可入题，正所谓“宇宙之大，苍蝇之微，皆可取材”（林语堂语）。散文不重题材，却注重意境，因此意境的有无和高低也就成了文章的审美标准以及能否永葆艺术魅力的试金石。中国现代散文作为“五四”新思潮、新观念沐浴下的产物，作为散文家内心情感的记录，擅长把握内在的情感节奏，用空灵的语言进行主观抒写，以“淡而有味”的艺术境界建构着与小说、诗歌和戏剧不同的纯美的精神空间，形成了自己多样的意境体系，如鲁迅多关注中国历史和对国民性的深刻剖析，其作品意境宏伟壮阔；周作人多关注人与自身、人与大自然的关系，其作品意境恬淡优美；许地山、丰子恺则把宗教感悟和人生哲理糅合在一起，注重精神层面的升华。

三是语言自然，韵味十足。散文的语言要平易自然，不事琢磨，以本色为重，看上去随意拈来，意到笔就，没有任何笔凿的痕迹。刘半农主张“以手写口”“心手相应”，朱自清则提出“谈话风”要求，他们都强调语言应是作家的思想、感情、气质、文化素养和美学趣味的自然表现。不同的作家，其语言风格也是各臻其妙，富于个性，或绚丽多彩，或朴素清新，或精工典雅，或诙谐幽默，然又无不简洁凝练，韵味十足。冰心的散文，语言清丽典雅，凝练而富于表现力，简洁又饱含诗意。朱自清的散文遣词造句上精益求精，既讲究辞藻的修饰，又重视口语的赏心悦目，文而不涩，美而不俗。周作人的散文则不同于朱自清的绚丽纤巧，也不同于冰心的精致秀丽，而是善于将白话口语、文言古语和外来欧化语杂糅调和，酿成一种“简单味”和“涩味”相结合的语言风格，平淡自然，不重藻饰，简洁流畅，令人回味无穷。总之，中国现代散文发展的历史并不长，但对于中国现代文学的发展却起到了推波助澜的作用，也影响着后来散文的发展。

1.3.2 中国现代散文的英译思路

常见的现代散文多以叙事和写景为主，但不论叙事还是写景，都离不开一个“情”字。情随景生，景随情移，一切景语皆情语。散文之所以美，美就美在它的情真意切，它是作者直抒胸臆的结果，是作者自然情感的真实流露。它体现在文字表达上往往不加雕饰，不施铅华，朴实、自然、流畅、平实。因此，散文翻译也只有围绕“真”“情”“美”三个字才能准确、传神。这就要求译者首先要充分理解作者表现在原文中的这份真情，并通过恰当的语言手段将这份真情充分地再现在译文中，力求译文在意义、形式、趣味、情调等方面与原文具有内在的一致性。如“叶子出水很高，像亭亭的舞女的裙。”此句与前句“曲曲折折的荷塘上面，弥望的是田田的叶子。”合并翻译为：“All over this winding stretch of water, what meets the eye is a silken field of leaves, reaching rather high above the surface, like the skirts of dancing girls in all their grace.”原文为明喻，译文也为明喻。再如第五段的第一句：“月光如流水一般，静静地泻在这一片叶子和花上”中，原文用明喻，把月光比作流水，而译文则用暗喻，译为“The moon sheds her liquid light silently over the leaves and flowers.”，而且原句中，“泻”这一动词的表述非常传神，形象生动地描写了月光照射在叶子和花上的情形，耐人寻味。译文中用了动词短语 shed over，over 一词将月光这种由上而下倾泻的情形表现得恰到好处，形成了与原文一样的动态美。“叶子和花仿佛在牛乳中洗过一样；又像笼罩着轻纱的梦。”与前面一句合译为：“The moon sheds her liquid light silently over the leaves and flowers, which, in the floating transparency of a bluish haze from the pond, look as if they had just been bathed in milk, or like a dream wrapped in a gauzy hood.”。直译原文中的明喻“仿佛”和“又像”，使原文传达的意境表现出来。“月光是隔了树照过来的，高处丛生的灌木，落下参差的斑驳的黑影，峭楞楞如鬼一般；弯弯的杨柳的稀疏的倩影，却又像是画在荷叶上。”“The moonlight is streaming down through the foliage, casting bushy shadows on the ground from high above, dark and checkered, like an army of ghosts; whereas the benign figures of the drooping willows, here and there, look like paintings on the lotus leaves.”“如鬼一般”“又像是画在荷叶上”这两处比喻，译文中也都同样采用比喻手法进行翻译。“杨柳稀疏的倩影”译为 benign figures，使用了比拟的修辞手法，与原文互相呼应，表达非常自然。也就是说，在英译中国现代散文时，译者不但要传达出原文的语流、节奏和句子结构等语义信息，更应着重传达原文的艺术神韵，只有这样才能把原文中所蕴含的“情”充分表达出来，从而使目标读者在读译文时可以获得和原文读者读原文时同样的语义和美学的双重享受。

1.4 翻译实战：《泥土的微笑》

【说明】 请根据文末的提示将下列短文翻译为英语。

简介：栖云是《读者》杂志的签约作家，著有散文集《幸福的柴门》（吉林人民出版社）、《在指缝间歌唱》（中国青年出版社）等。其散文《幸福的柴门》《敬重卑微》《月亮的脸笑在掌心》等传播十分广泛。《幸福的柴门》《敬重卑微》等还被选入了中小学语文教材。栖云的《泥土的微笑》这篇散文语言朴素，生活气息浓郁，不庸俗，翻译时要把握住这样一个特点。

泥土①的微笑

栖云

我在花园里种满了芬芳的玫瑰花，远远望去，像一片燃烧的晚霞。我想等朋友来做客的时候，让他们携带些玫瑰回家。② 我相信朋友捧着火红的玫瑰渐渐走远的背影，一定能点燃易感的情怀。有一天，一位非常要好的女友来探望我，我知道她平素最喜欢花花草草了，临别时我说，采一束玫瑰点缀你的闺房，保证十里飘香。③

女友轻轻跨进花园，东闻闻，西嗅嗅，神采飞扬，就是不肯采摘。我说没关系，多的是，我又不是花店的老板，不会靠玫瑰赚钱的。说完我就举起剪刀准备献美。女友急忙拦住，高声叫着不可不可。

这么美丽的玫瑰剪下来，让人心疼。她抓紧我的袖子叮咛：千万不能剪啊，玫瑰是泥土的微笑，谁忍心杀戮美得醉人的微笑？

我的灵魂悚然一惊，丑陋的泥土，卑微的泥土，朴素的泥土，因为玫瑰，露出了惊艳一笑。因为这一笑，让人爱惜非常。④

一个朋友在拍卖会上有幸购得一个花瓶，花瓶细颈大肚，碎花蓝白调子，流光溢彩，从造型到色彩，整个如唐朝盛世的化身，雍容，华贵，高傲，悠闲，目空一切。⑤朋友请我们大家观赏。奇怪的是每一个参观者都小心谨慎，生怕碰坏这盛唐的宝贝。其实不过是一撮泥土，经过窑烧才千修百炼成瓷中经典。

江南的紫砂壶玲珑剔透，泥人张的彩塑令人拍案叫绝，它们不都是泥土的微笑吗？弥足珍贵。即使曾丑陋，即使曾卑微，即使曾朴素，同样让人肃然起敬。

我懂得了，即使再平凡的人，也没有理由被埋没，只要努力活出色彩，一定叫人刮目相看。⑥

翻译提示

1. 如何理解①处的“泥土”？
2. 请注意②这句话的说话方式：我……玫瑰花，（我或者人们）远远望去，（玫瑰）像一片……，我……让他们……。在这一句中，叙事的角度是不断变化的。想一想，在英文中该如何处理？
3. ③中的“十里”是指实际的距离吗？
4. ④⑤这两句话之间该如何衔接才能显得自然？
5. 如何理解句⑥“只要努力活出色彩，一定叫人刮目相看”？

1.5 译文荟萃

1. 短语翻译

1) 叙事性散文 narrative prose
2) 抒情性散文 lyric prose
3) 哲理性散文 philosophical prose
4) 说理性（议论性）散文 argumentative prose
5) 写景性（描写性）散文 descriptive prose

6) 形散神不散 loose in form but concentrated in idea / wide in subject matter but concentrated in idea

7) 意境深远 be magnificently conceived / far-reaching artistic conception

8) 包罗万象 all-inclusive / all-embracing

9) 诗情画意 poetic effect / poetic illusion

10) 签约作家 signed writer

11) 乡土散文 prose works of localism

12) 文章题材 subject matter / theme

13) 文学体裁 literary genre

14) 画龙点睛之笔 something added to bring out the crucial point / a finishing touch

15) 借景抒情 take advantage of a scene to express one's emotions

16) 触景生情 The scene evoked one's memories of the past. / The scene stirs up one's past memories. / The scene touches a chord in one's heart.

17) 情景交融 with the scenery depicted and the emotions expressed in perfect harmony

18) 直抒胸臆 free expression of one's feeling / to express one's feeling directly

19) 简洁流畅 concise and fluent

20) 埋伏笔 making a foreshadowing

2. 句子翻译

1) 北宋时期的文学家周敦颐称："莲花出淤泥而不染，是花中君子。"

Zhou Dunyi, a writer of the Northern Song Dynasty, declared that "The lotus flower, emerging unstained from the filth, is the gentleman among flowers."

2) 袁世凯去世那天，消息一传进紫禁城，人人都像碰上了大喜事。太监们奔走相告。

The news of Yuan Shikai's death was received with great rejoicing in the Forbidden City. The eunuchs rushed hither and thither spreading the news.

3) 不经风雨，长不成大树；不经百炼，难以成好钢。

Without braving strom and wind, a sapling cannot grow into a tall tree; without being toughened and hardened repeatedly, iron cannot be tempered into good steel. / An accomplished man must stand the hardest of hardships.

4) 不经一番寒彻骨，哪有梅花扑鼻香。

It is severe cold that brings forth the fragrance of plums. / No pains, no gains.

5) 我看了她这种单纯的态度，心里忽而起了一种不可思议的感情。

Her simplicity touched me but at the same time an unthinkable notion swept over me.

6) 不怕不识货，就怕货比货。

The worth of a thing is shown through comparison.

7) 中国有句老话叫“酒逢知己千杯少”。

“Even a thousand cups of wine are not too many when one drinks with a close friend,” runs one traditional Chinese saying.

8) 昆明市是云南省省会，地处云贵高原中部，冬无严寒，夏无酷暑，四季如春，花开似锦，一向有花城之称。

As the provincial capital of Yunnan, Kunming, which is situated at/in the central part of the Yunnan-Guizhou Plateau, is known as a city of flowers with its warm weather and flowers in all seasons of a year.

9) 刚进大学时，陌生的环境，陌生的人群，甚至连宿舍楼下的磁卡电话也是陌生的。

译文 1：When I was a freshman at university, everything seemed new to me: the environment, the crowd of people, and the magnetic card telephone booth below our dormitory building.

译文 2：As a freshman at university, I felt I was surrounded by the new environment, the new people, and even the magnetic card telephone booth below our dormitory building was new to me.

译文 3：At the very beginning of my university life, I felt I was in a new environment, among the new people, and even the magnetic card telephone booth below our dormitory building was new to me.

10) 培养一个人才真是不容易。俗话说：一年树谷，十年树木，百年树人。

It costs a lot to produce a qualified professional. As the saying goes, it takes a year to grow crops and ten years to grow trees but a hundred years to rear people.

11) 只要我们的政策是得人心的，中华民族伟大复兴的中国梦就一定可以实现。

The Chinese dream of national rejuvenation can be surely achieved, provided that our policies have the great support of the people.

12) 今年是鸡年，是我的本命年，据说得穿红内裤辟邪。

It is the Year of the Rooster. It is also my animal year. It is said that I have to wear red underpants to avoid / counteract evil spirits.

13) 人家是醋罐子，她是醋缸、醋瓮。

If other women are jealous, she’s a hundred times so.

14) 北京是一座生机勃勃、充满活力、古老风貌和现代风格相融合的城市，每年都吸引成千上万的国内外游客。

Beijing, a vigorous, dynamic city where the old and the new intermingle, remains a magnet for visitors from inside and outside China/ at home and abroad.

15) 你还在想让他来帮你呀，恐怕到时黄花菜都凉了哦。

Are you still expecting his help? It will be too late when he comes, I am afraid.

16) 孔子是中国第一个教育家，毕生从事教学和古代典籍整理，并提出了许多重要的教育原则和有效的教学方法。

Confucius was China's first educator, engaging in teaching and editing ancient classics all his life. He put forward many important educational principles and effective teaching methods.

17) 科学是老老实实的学问，来不得半点虚假，需要付出艰巨的劳动。

Science means honest, solid knowledge, allowing not an iota of falsehood, and it involves herculean efforts and grueling toil.

18) 他们是普通到不能再普通的人，日子也平淡到不能再平淡。

They are the most ordinary of the ordinary run of the people, who live their lives in the most ordinary way.

19) 有人说，做人难，做名人更难。

It is said that to live the life of an ordinary person is difficult and that it is even more difficult to live as a celebrity.

20) 学无止境，一生的时间都嫌太短，所以古人皓首穷经，头发白了还是在继续做研究，不过在这样的研究中确是有浓厚的趣味。

Art is long, life is short. That is why some of our ancients continued to study even when they were hoaryheaded. They were, of course, motivated by an enormous interest in their studies.

3. 段落翻译

1) 曲曲折折的荷塘上面，弥望的是田田的叶子。叶子出水很高，像亭亭的舞女的裙。层层的叶子中间，零星地点缀着些白花，有袅娜地开着的，有羞涩地打着朵儿的；正如一粒粒的明珠，又如碧天里的星星，又如刚出浴的美人。微风过处，送来缕缕清香，仿佛远处高楼上渺茫的歌声似的。这时候叶子与花也有一丝的颤动，像闪电般，霎时传过荷塘的那边去了。叶子本是肩并肩密密地挨着的，这便宛然有了一道凝碧的波痕。叶子底下是脉脉的流水，遮住了，不能见一些颜色；而叶子却更见风致了。（朱自清 《荷塘月色》）

All over this winding stretch of water, what meets the eye is a silken field of leaves, reaching rather high above the surface, like the skirts of dancing girls in all their grace. Here and there, layers of leaves are dotted with white lotus blossoms, some in demure bloom, others in shy bud, like scattering pearls, or twinkling stars, or beauties just out of the bath. A breeze stirs, sending over breaths of fragrance, like faint singing drifting from a distant building. At this moment, a tiny thrill shoots through the leaves and flowers, like a streak of lightning, straight across the forest of lotuses. The leaves, which have been standing shoulder to shoulder, are caught trembling in an emerald heave of the pond. Underneath, the exquisite water is covered from view, and none can tell its color; yet the leaves on top project themselves all the more attractively.（朱纯深 译）

2) 月光如流水一般，静静地泻在这一片叶子和花上。薄薄的青雾浮起在荷塘里。叶子和花仿佛在牛乳中洗过一样，又像笼着轻纱的梦。虽然是满月，天上却有一层淡淡的云，所以不能朗照；但我以为这恰是到了好处——酣眠固不可少，小睡也别有风味的。月光是隔了树照过来的，高处丛生的灌木，落下参差的斑驳的黑影，峭楞楞如鬼一般；弯弯的杨柳的稀疏的倩影，却又像是画在荷叶上。塘中的月色并不均匀；但光与影有着和谐的旋律，如梵婀玲上奏着的名曲。（朱自清 《荷塘月色》）

The moon sheds her liquid light silently over the leaves and flowers, which, in the floating transparency of a bluish haze from the pond, look as if they had just been bathed in milk, or like a dream wrapped in a gauzy hood. Although it is a full moon, shining through a film of clouds, the light is not at its brightest; it is, however, just right for me — a profound sleep is indispensable, yet a snatched doze also has a savor of its own. The moonlight is streaming down through the foliage, casting bushy shadows on the ground from high above, dark and checkered, like an army of ghosts; whereas the benign figures of the drooping willows, here and there, look like paintings on the lotus leaves. The moonlight is not spread evenly over the pond, but rather in a harmonious rhythm of light and shade, like a famous melody played on a violin.（朱纯深 译）

3) 荷塘的四面，远远近近，高高低低都是树，而杨柳最多。这些树将一片荷塘重重围住，只在小路一旁，漏着几段空隙，像是特为月光留下的。树色一例是阴阴的，乍看像一团烟雾；但杨柳的丰姿，便在烟雾里也辨得出。树梢上隐隐约约的是一带远山，只有些大意罢了。树缝里也漏着一两点路灯光，没精打采的，是渴睡人的眼。这时候最热闹的，要数树上的蝉声与水里的蛙声，但热闹是它们的，我什么也没有。（朱自清 《荷塘月色》）

Around the pond, far and near, high and low, are trees. Most of them are willows. Only on the path side can two or three gaps be seen through the heavy fringe, as if specially reserved for the moon. The shadowy shapes of the leafage at first sight seem diffused into a mass of mist, against which, however, the charm of those willow trees is still discernible. Over the trees appear some distant mountains, but merely in sketchy silhouette. Through the branches are also a couple of lamps, as listless as sleepy eyes. The most lively creatures here, for the moment, must be the cicadas in the trees and the frogs in the pond. But the liveliness is theirs, I have nothing.（朱纯深 译）

4) 咬着小鸟，猫一头跑进厨房，又一头跑到西屋。我不敢紧追，怕它更咬紧了，可又不能不追。虽然看不见小鸟的头部，我还没忘了那个眼神。那个预知生命危险的眼神。那个眼神与我的好心中间隔着一只小白猫。来回跑了几次，我不追了。追上也没用了，我想，小鸟至少已半死了。猫又进了厨房，我愣了一会儿，赶紧的又追了去；那两个黑豆眼仿佛在我心内睁着呢。（老舍《小麻雀》）

With my eyes fixed on the bird, I watch the kitten run first to the kitchen and then to the west room. I know I must not press too hard after her, but I have to follow her in case she tightens her jaws. Though I cannot see the bird's head, its look, the look with anticipated danger in its eyes, is still vivid in my mind.（刘士聪　译）

5) 小猫没再扑它，只试着用小脚碰它。它随着击碰倾侧，头不动，眼不动，还呆呆地注视着地上。但求它能活着，它就决不反抗。可是并非全无勇气，它是在猫的面前不动！我轻轻地过去，把猫抓住。将猫放在门外，小鸟还没动。我双手把它捧起来。它确是没受了多大的伤，虽然胸上落了点毛。它看了我一眼！（老舍　《小麻雀》）

The kitten makes no more attempts to attack. She only tries to touch it with her little paws. As the kitten touches it, it tilts from side to side, its head undisturbed and its eyes looking blank at the floor. It will not fight back so long as there is a chance of survival. But the bird has not lost all of its courage; it responds this way only to the kitten. I go over light-footed, pick up the kitten and put her outside the door, and the sparrow remains where it is. When I pick it up in my hands I find it is not seriously injured, though some fluff has come off its chest. It throws a look at me.（刘士聪　译）

6) 若是有个人冷不丁地出来问你：天津卫出嘛？要答不上话碴儿，你还真被人家问“闷儿”了。天津卫这地方，大马路上不种五谷杂粮，小胡同里不长瓜果梨桃，满城几十万人口，几十万张嘴巴睁开眼睛就要吃要喝，就算天津卫有九条河流横穿而过，即使这九条大河里游满了鱼虾螃蟹，连河岸边的青蛙一起捉来下锅，恐怕也喂不饱这几十万张肚皮。所以，君不见日日夜夜火车轮船不停地往天津运大米白面，城乡公路车拉肩担又不停地往天津送蔬菜瓜果。就这么着，天津爷们儿还吵闹着嘛也买不到，大把的钞票攥在手心里愣花不出去。（林希　《天津闲人》）

If someone throws a question to you: What does Tianjin produce? If you are unable to give an answer, you may feel completely flummoxed. The city of Tianjin produces neither grain nor fruit, and with a population of several hundred thousand, it would be difficult to feed all the residents, even if the place were endowed with nine rivers teemed with fish and shrimps, and even if all the frogs in the river were killed for food. No wonder trains and ships carry rice and flour to Tianjin non-stop, day and night, and all roads to the city are congested with truckloads and cartloads of vegetables and fruits. Even so, Tianjin folks still obstreperously complain that there is absolutely nothing to buy, and there is simply no way to spend the huge lumps of cash they are holding.（孙艺风　译）

7) 说顺听的吧，天津卫出秀才，出圣人。有人说瞎掰，你天津卫千多年没出过一个状元，到清朝政府废除科举，天津卫就没一个人上过金榜，所以直到如今天津的文庙不能开正门，你说寒碜不寒碜。其实天津不出状元是因为天津离京城太近，想考状元的早早搬迁进京城住去了，中了状元甩京腔他也不承认自家是天津人，白喝了天津卫的海河水，白吃了这许多年的煎饼馃子，这叫不厚道。再说天津爷们儿从来没把状元看得有什么了不起，好汉子讲的是独霸一方，状元郎不就是给皇帝老子作驸马吗？没劲，认皇后作丈母娘，这姑爷准不好当。（林希 《天津闲人》）

So let me start by saying something flattering. Tianjin produces scholars and sages. Some may say this is sheer twaddle. Over a thousand years, Tianjin hasn't produced a Number One Scholar. Up to the time when the Qing government abolished the imperial examination system, not a single person from Tianjin had ever found his name on the list of successful examination candidates. So even today due to this disgrace the Confucian Temple in Tianjin can't open its main gate. Isn't it humiliating? But the reason for it can be ascribed to Tianjin's geographical proximity to Beijing. Those who wanted to take the examination would move there at their earliest convenience, and those who passed the examination would acquire a Beijing accent and refuse to acknowledge their Tianjin origin, with no credit being given to the fact that they had been raised in this city. Years of feeding them plainly went down the drain. How ungrateful! But then, no one in Tianjin cared much about scholars. If you were a big shot of the day, you had your own territory to rule. What was so special about Number One Scholar? You might end up being the emperor's son-in-law, which could hardly be fun. It wasn't exactly exciting either to have the empress as your mother-in-law.（孙艺风 译）

8) 说不中听的话，天津卫出混混，出青皮。有这么回事没有？有。这用不着捂着瞒着，天津混混有帮有派，打起架来不要命，最能耐的叫“叠”了，一双胳膊抱住脑袋，曲膝弓背侧躺在地上，任你乱棍齐下，血肉横飞，打烂了这边，再翻过身来让你打那边，不许喊叫，不许出声，不许咬牙，不许皱眉头。为什么要这样打人？为什么要这样挨打？说不清缘由，这叫天津气派，后来时兴新潮词汇，叫作“天津情结”。（林希 《天津闲人》）

To put it bluntly, Tianjin produces good-for-nothing loafers and hooligans. Is that so? Oh, yes. There is no need to say less than the truthful. Tianjin hooligans, organized and grouped, would risk their necks in scrimmages. Their most peculiar practice is called "folding" while holding your head in your arms, you lie on your side with knees bent, and no matter how unsparingly they bludgeon you, with blood gushing and spouting in every direction, you are not supposed to scream, or even utter a sound. In addition, you should neither clench your teeth nor frown. When one side of your body is thoroughly battered, you turn around to expose the other side. Why beat people like this? And why do the victims put up with this? No particular reason. Maybe this is Tianjin style. Or to use a trendy phrase, it is the "Tianjin complex."（孙艺风 译）

9) 不逢北国之秋，已将近十余年了。在南方每年到了秋天，总要想起陶然亭的芦花，钓鱼台的柳影，西山的虫唱，玉泉的夜月，潭柘寺的钟声。在北平即使不出门去吧，就是在皇城人海之中，租人家一椽破屋来住着，早晨起来，泡一碗浓茶，向院子一坐，你也能看得到很高很高的碧绿的天色，听得到青天下驯鸽的飞声。从槐树叶底，朝东细数着一丝一丝漏下来的日光，或在破壁腰中，静对着像喇叭似的牵牛花（朝荣）的蓝朵，自然而然地也能够感觉到十分的秋意。说到了牵牛花，我以为以蓝色或白色者为佳，紫黑色次之，淡红色最下。最好，还要在牵牛花底，教长着几根疏疏落落的尖细且长的秋草，使作陪衬。（郁达夫 《故都的秋》）

It is more than a decade since I last saw autumn in North. When I am in the South, the arrival of each autumn will put me in mind of Peiping's Tao Ran Ting with its reed catkins, Diao Yu Tai with its shady willow trees, Western Hills with their chirping insects, Yu Quan Shan Mountain on a moonlight evening and Tan Zhe Si with its reverbrating bell. Suppose you put up in a humble rented house inside the bustling imperial city, you can, on getting up at dawn, sit in your courtyard sipping a cup of strong tea, leisurely watch the high azure skies and listen to pigeons circling overhead. Saunter eastward under locust trees to closely observe streaks of sunlight filtering through their foliage, or quietly watch the trumpet-shaped blue flowers of morning glories climbing half way up a dilapidated wall, and an intense feeling of autumn will of itself well up inside you. As to morning glories, I like their blue or white flowers best, dark purple ones second best, and pink ones third best. It will be most desirable to have them set off by some tall thin grass planted underneath here and there.（张培基 译）

10) 北方的果树，到秋天，也是一种奇景。第一是枣子树，屋角，墙头，茅房边上，灶房门口，它都会一株株地长大起来。像橄榄又像鸽蛋似的这枣子颗儿，在小椭圆形的细叶中间，显出淡绿微黄的颜色的时候，正是秋的全盛时期，等枣树叶落，枣子红完，西北风就要起来了，北方便是沙尘灰土的世界，只有这枣子、柿子、葡萄，成熟到八九分的七八月之交，是北国的清秋的佳日，是一年之中最好也没有的 Golden Days。（郁达夫 《故都的秋》）

Fruit trees in the North also make a wonderful sight in autumn. Take jujube tree for example. They grow everywhere — around the corner of a house, at the foot of a wall, by the side of a latrine or outside a kitchen door. It is at the height of autumn that jujubes, shaped like dates or pigeon eggs, make their appearance in a light yellowish-green amongst tiny elliptic leaves. By the time when they have turned ruddy and the leaves fallen, the north-westerly wind will begin to reign supreme and make a dusty world of the North. Only at the turn of July and August when jujubes, persimmons, grapes are 80–90 percent ripe will the North have the best of autumn — the golden days in a year.（张培基 译）

1.6 翻译家：朱纯深

朱纯深是福建莆田人，长年从事与翻译相关的研究、教学和实践活动，是我国著名翻译家和翻译理论家。1966 年，正在莆田二中读初二的他时逢学校停课而失学。1969 年 12 月，他随父母下放莆田白沙公社，后转为知青插队当地。但他并没有就此放弃读书学习。在父亲的指导下，他找来当时的中学和大学教材，通过将英语课文翻译为中文再回译为英文的方式来自学中英文并练习翻译。1974 年底，他因为母亲退休补员进入当地中学任教英语。1978 年春，他以英语差一分满分的成绩考入福建师范大学外语系英文专业本科 77 级，又于 1979 年考入该系首届硕士研究生班，师从许崇信教授攻读文学翻译。1982 年硕士毕业后留校任教翻译，1987 年底赴英国诺丁汉大学为英文系访问学者，1989 年获英国国家和诺丁汉大学双份奖学金转读该系博士，先后师从 Prof. Walter Nash 和 Prof. Michael McCarthy，从文体学、功能语言学和语言哲学的角度研究翻译中的意义结构与呈现。1993 年博士毕业后任职新加坡国立大学，教授翻译。1998 年始于香港城市大学任教翻译并指导翻译专业硕士和博士研究生，2015 年转系讲授与中国文学相关的课程，故先后为中文翻译及语言学系和中文及历史学系教授。2017 年朱纯深自香港城市大学退休，随即获聘香港中文大学（深圳）人文社科学院翻译学教授，并继续兼任北京外国语大学客座教授、香港浸会大学翻译学中心荣誉研究员、《中国翻译》和 *ITT*（*The Journal of Interpreter and Translator Trainer*）编委。他对翻译的研究兴趣涵盖了语言学理论、文学与诗学理论以及机器辅助翻译教学的研发等，研究论文自 1986 年起先后发表于《中国翻译》、*British Journal of Aesthetics*、*META*、*Target*、*Multilingua*、*TTR*、*Journal of Pragmatics*、*ITT* 等学刊，并于 2000 年、2001 年和 2006 年三次获得宋淇翻译研究纪念奖。

朱纯深的学术活动以研究为主，多以英文论文发表，部分翻译为中文后主要见于《翻译探微——语言 · 文本 · 诗学》（台北书林，2001 年；南京译林，2008 年）一书。他的译作虽然不多，但多与研究相关，形成研究与实践的互动相长。早年翻译的《短篇小说写作指南》（辽宁教育，1998 年）为其硕士论文的主要参考书之一；后来翻译的双语版王尔德的《自深深处》（南京译林，2008 年、

2015 年）以及 2017 年的《夜莺与玫瑰：王尔德童话与短篇小说全集》（浙江文艺）是他从事机器辅助翻译教学平台研发的语料来源之一；2004 年的中国古典诗词英译今译双语版选集《古意新声 · 品赏本》（湖北教育）是基于他诗歌翻译研究的综合实践；其他如朱自清的散文《匆匆》、《荷塘月色》和梁实秋的《读画》以及新加坡的一些华语新诗，则旨在探索翻译中音、形、义在文本和文体层面的互动效果。朱纯深的汉英翻译同他的英汉翻译和研究写作一样，重质不重量，求深不求广。因此，每个翻译作品都是语言与诗学的精心实验。将文学翻译实践的经验与理论思考结合，使他得以提出“隐喻连贯”“意象聚焦”等概念来审视中国诗学“境界全出”这一经典命题，探讨意境怎么

"出"、如何"全"等问题。实践与理论双栖的学术积淀，加上多年习练太极拳的感悟，令他在2016年通过追溯太极推手所体现的道家"气"的哲学，融合孟子"浩然之气"及"以意逆志"的论述、本雅明的"纯语言"概念、巴什拉的诗学和海德格尔的语言观，独辟蹊径地提出以"舍己"地倾听语言来达致互补互济的能量转化这一翻译的阴阳诗学。针对中国译界争论不休的"信、达、雅"问题，他也根据自己对功能和文本语言学的研究，提出独到的见解。他主张实事求是地看待严复的"信、达、雅"三字理论，避免功利地将严复对自己翻译的经验总结与反思当成评价翻译的通用标准，反而忽视了它足以成为描述翻译过程真实性、可达性以及适当性的分析框架这一理论意义。总之，朱纯深的翻译实践和研究体现了他始终秉持的理念：翻译的最大价值在于令人类可以"管窥一豹"地了解自身和他者文化的共性和个性，翻译研究的终极意义在于提供一个独特的新视角，促进人类对自己、对世界的理解。

1.7 补充资源

参考书目

张培基. 英译中国现代散文选（1—3）. 上海：上海外语教育出版社，2007.
张培基. 英译中国现代散文选（4）. 上海：上海外语教育出版社，2012.
黄源深，徐凯，周小进. 英汉散文比较赏析. 北京：高等教育出版社，2011.
杨扬，朱希祥. 中文读写教程（第1册）. 上海：上海外语教育出版社，2010.
乔萍，瞿淑蓉，宋洪玮. 散文佳作108篇. 南京：译林出版社，2002.
居祖纯. 高级汉英语篇翻译. 北京：清华大学出版社，2000.

网络资源

散文网：https://www.sanwen.net
中国散文网：http://www.cnprose.com

第二单元　中国古代散文

2.1 阅读欣赏：《岳阳楼记》

【说明】对照原文阅读译文，比较三个译文的异同，体会不同译者对原文句式的处理技巧以及对原文微妙情感的处理效果。

简介：《岳阳楼记》是北宋文学家范仲淹应好友巴陵郡太守滕子京之请，于北宋庆历六年（公元 1046 年）9 月 15 日为重修岳阳楼所写。滕子京是被诬陷擅自动用官钱而被贬的，范仲淹正是借作记之机，含蓄规劝他要“不以物喜，不以己悲”，试图以自己“先天下之忧而忧，后天下之乐而乐”的济世情怀和乐观精神感染老友。文章通过对洞庭湖的侧面描写来衬托岳阳楼，超越了单纯写山水楼观的局限，将自然界的晦明变化、风雨阴晴和“迁客骚人”的“览物之情”结合起来写，从而将全文的重心放到了纵议政治理想方面，扩大了文章的境界。

岳阳楼记

范仲淹

庆历四年春，滕子京谪守巴陵郡。越明年，政通人和，百废具兴。乃重修岳阳楼，增其旧制，刻唐贤今人诗赋于其上。属予作文以记之。

予观夫巴陵胜状，在洞庭一湖。衔远山，吞长江，浩浩汤汤，横无际涯；朝晖夕阴，气象万千。此则岳阳楼之大观也。前人之述备矣。然则北通巫峡，南极潇湘，迁客骚人，多会于此，览物之情，得无异乎？

若夫霪雨霏霏，连月不开，阴风怒号，浊浪排空；日星隐曜，山岳潜形；商旅不行，樯倾楫摧；薄暮冥冥，虎啸猿啼。登斯楼也，则有去国怀乡，忧谗畏讥，满目萧然，感极而悲者矣！

至若春和景明，波澜不惊，上下天光，一碧万顷；沙鸥翔集，锦鳞游泳；岸芷汀兰，郁郁青青。而或长烟一空，皓月千里，浮光跃金，静影沉璧；渔歌互答，此乐何极！登斯楼也，则有心旷神怡，宠辱偕忘，把酒临风，其喜洋洋者矣。

嗟夫！予尝求古仁人之心，或异二者之为，何哉？不以物喜，不以己悲；居庙堂之高，则忧其民；处江湖之远，则忧其君。是进亦忧，退亦忧。然则何时而乐耶？其必曰："先天下之忧而忧，后天下之乐而乐"欤？噫！微斯人，吾谁与归！

时六年九月十五日。

译文一

In the spring of the fourth year of the Qingli period (the year 1044), Teng Zijing was banished from the capital to be governor of Baling Prefecture. After he had governed the district for a year, the administration became efficient, the people became united, and all things that had fallen into disrepair were given a new lease of life. Then he restored Yueyang Pavilion, adding new splendour to the original structure and having inscribed on it poems by famous men of the Tang Dynasty as well as the present time. And he asked me to write an essay to commemorate this.

Now I have found that the finest sights of Baling are concentrated in the region of Lake Dongting. Dongting, nibbling at the distant hills and gulping down the Yangzi River, strikes all beholders as vast and infinite, presenting a scene of boundless variety; and this is the superb view from Yueyang Pavilion. All this has been described in full by writers of earlier ages. However, since the lake is linked with Wu Gorge in the north and extends to the rivers Xiao and Xiang in the south, many exiles and wandering poets gather here, and their reactions to these sights vary greatly.

During a period of incessant rain, when a spell of bad weather continues for more than a month, when louring winds bellow angrily, tumultuous waves hurl themselves against the sky, the sun and stars hide their light, hills and mountains disappear, merchants have to halt in their travels, masts collapse and oars splinter, the day darkens and the roars of tigers and howls of monkeys are heard, if men come to this pavilion with a longing for home in their hearts or nursing a feeling of bitterness because of taunts and slander, they may find the sight depressing and fall prey to agitation or despair.

But during mild and bright spring weather, when the waves are unruffled and the azure translucence above and below stretches before your eyes for myriads of *li*, when the water-birds fly down to congregate on the sands and fish with scales like glimmering silk disport themselves in the water, when the iris and orchids on the banks grow luxuriant and green; or when dusk falls over this vast expanse and bright moonlight casts its light a thousand *li*, when the rolling waves glitter like gold and silent shadows in the water glimmer like jade, and the fishermen sing to each other for sheer joy, then men coming up to this pavilion may feel complete freedom of heart and ease of spirit, forgetting every worldly gain or setback to hold their winecups in the breeze in absolute elation, delighted with life.

But again when I consider the men of old who possessed true humanity, they seem to have responded quite differently. The reason, perhaps, may be this: Natural beauty was not enough to make them happy, nor their own situation enough to make them sad. When such men are high in the government or at court, their first concern is for the people; when they retire to distant streams and lakes, their first concern is for their sovereign. Thus they worry both when in office and when in retirement. When, then, can they enjoy themselves in life? No doubt they are concerned before anyone else and enjoy themselves only after everyone else finds enjoyment. Surely these are the men in whose footsteps I should follow!

[The time is: the 15th day of the 9th month, the 6th year.]（杨宪益、戴乃迭 译）

译文二

In the spring of the fourth year of the Qingli period, Teng Zijing was relegated to the position of the prefect of Baling. The following year witnessed a great change there in terms of the smooth conduct of government and the harmonious human relations as well as the resumption of a great many neglected undertakings. Thus Yueyang Pavilion was rebuilt on a scale larger than before and was graced with the inscriptions of the poems and rhythmic prose of the Tang and contemporary celebrities. I was requested to write something to mark the event.

In my view, the grandeur of Baling lies only in Lake Dongting, which looks as if it were holding in its mouth the distant mountains and gulping down the Yangtze River. Boundless and marvelous, it presents in the morning sunshine and the evening twilight a most gorgeous spectacle. This is the general view from the pavilion, already described in full by our predecessors. However, since the lake connects with the Wu Gorge in the north and ends at the Xiao and Xiang rivers in the south, many demoted or banished officials and literati often gather here. Can there be no shades of difference in their feelings when admiring the scenery?

If the continuous drizzle does not let up for several months on end, one can hear the bleak wind howling and see the turbid waves surging to the sky. The brilliance of the sun and the stars are eclipsed and the shapes of the mountains and hills become obscured. The merchants and travellers are stopped on their way, staying in boats with declined masts and broken oars, while the light being so dim at dusk, one can fancy tigers' roars and monkeys' gibbers. So the ascent to the pavilion is associated with the nostalgia in exile and the fear of slanders and taunts. Confronted with such disconsolate scenes, one is apt to be moved to the extreme and feel much saddened.

As for the days when spring weather is mild and sunny, nature is lit with a bright smile, and the waves being halcyon, the sky and the lake are tinged with the same hue, making up an infinitely huge canvas of light blue, on which white gulls are hovering in bevies and fish shimmering with silvery scales. And the lake shores adorned with irises and sandbars dotted with orchids are all enshrouded in a sweet and lush green. Sometimes the broad firmament is clear of all mist, a bright moon shines over the vast lake gleaming with a golden glow, and the moon's reflection in the watery mirror reminds one of a sunken jade. And then the fishermen's songs are heard to be echoing one another. What an unbounded joy! In such a case, ascent to the pavilion gives one a broadened mind and eased heart, with credit and discredit both forgotten. Holding a wine cup in the wind, one is overflowing with happiness.

Oh, I have tried to probe the souls of the noble ancients. Their feelings might differ from the above two. Why? Because they were not glad of things adventitious, or sad for the sake of themselves. Positioned high at court, they worried about the people. Banished to remote regions, they worried about their sovereign. Thus they were carefree in neither case. Then, at what time would they feel happy? They were sure to say: "Worry before all others have worried, rejoice after all others have rejoiced." Who should I emulate, if not people of this type?（谢百魁　译）

译文三

In the spring of the fourth year of Qingli[1], Teng Zijing[2] was exiled to Baling Prefecture[3] to be the prefect there. In the second year of his office, because of his excellent administration, people lived in peace and contentment, and all previous neglected matters were taken care of. The Yueyang Tower was renovated and enlarged, and inscribed on its wall were the poetry and the rhymed prose of learned men of the Tang and the present dynasty. I was invited to record this restoration effort in writing.

The beauty of Baling centers round the Dongting Lake, which holds the mountain ranges in the distance and swallows the water of the Yangtze River. It is so vast and mighty that it seems boundless. Dazzling in the morning sun and fading in the gray evening mist, it affords a myriad of scenes. This is the magnificent view that the Yueyang Tower commands, of which many descriptions have been written. This beautiful scenic spot is linked with the Wu Gorge in the north and the Xiao and Xiang Rivers in the south. Exiled officials and poets often gather here. How could there be no difference in their feelings?

In the rainy season, an unbroken spell of wet weather lasts for months. Chilly winds howl and turbid waves surge sky-high. The sun and the stars lose their luster, and the mountain ranges are scarcely visible. Merchants and travelers have to put off their voyage, for the masts of the ships have collapsed and their oars broken. It is dark towards evening, and the roaring of tigers and the cry of monkeys can be heard. At such a time anyone ascending the tower will be filled with nostalgia for the imperial court and his home as well as fears of calumny and derision against him. Around him is a scene of desolation. Emotions well up in him so strong that he feels pain at heart.

In springtime it is warm and the sun is bright. The Lake is tranquil and it merges with the azure sky into a vast expanse of blue. The water-birds are playing, some fluttering in the sky, some gathering together on the sandbars. Fishes of varied hues are swimming merrily in the water. The sweet-smelling grass by the banks and the faintly scented orchids on the sandy beaches are lush and green. Sometimes, when the mist over the Lake vanishes, the glorious moon shines over the vast land, its brightness glistening with golden light on the lake. The reflection of the moon is like a piece of jade in the depths of the water. The fishermen's songs chime in with each other. How delightful they are! On ascending the Tower at such a time, one will feel spiritual uplift, caring for neither glory nor shame. With a cup of wine in the gentle breeze, he will enjoy the greatest happiness in life!

Ah! I have tried to study the minds of people of lofty ideals in ancient times. Perhaps they were different from the people I mentioned above. Why is this? The reason is that they were not thrown into ecstasies over their success, nor felt depressed over their failures. When they were in high positions at court, they were concerned about people. When they were in remote places, they were concerned about their emperor. They worried when they got promoted or when they were sent into exile. Then, when were they happy? They would say: "To be the first in the country to worry about the affairs of the state and the last to enjoy oneself." Alas! Who else should I seek company with save them?（罗经国　译）

[1] Qingli was the title of Emperor Renzong's reign of the Song Dynasty.

[2] Teng Zijing was Fan Zhongyan's friend.

[3] Baling Prefecture was Yuezhou Prefecture, now Yueyang City in Hunan Province where the Yueyang Tower is located.

2.2 翻译热身：《醉翁亭记》

【说明】 翻译下面的文字，然后将自己的译文与所提供的参考译文对比，体会其中的差异。

简介：《醉翁亭记》作于宋仁宗庆历六年（公元 1046 年），当时欧阳修正任滁州太守。庆历五年，欧阳修被贬官到滁州，被贬之前曾任太常丞知谏院、右正言知制诰、河北都转运按察使等职。在滁州，欧阳修实行宽简政治，发展生产，使当地人过上了平和安定的生活，年丰物阜，而且又有一片令人陶醉的山水，这使得欧阳修感到无比快慰。但当时整个北宋王朝却是政治昏暗，奸邪当道，一些有志改革图强的人纷纷受到打击，眼睁睁地看着国家积弊不能消除，衰亡景象日益增长，这又不能不使他感到沉重的忧虑和痛苦。《醉翁亭记》正是他当时心情的真实写照。

醉翁亭记

欧阳修

环滁皆山也。其西南诸峰，林壑尤美，望之蔚然而深秀者，琅琊也。山行六七里，渐闻水声潺潺，而泻出于两峰之间者，酿泉也。峰回路转，有亭翼然临于泉上者，醉翁亭也。作亭者谁？山之僧曰智仙也。名之者谁？太守自谓也。太守与客来饮于此，饮少辄醉，而年又最高，故自号曰醉翁也。醉翁之意不在酒，在乎山水之间也。山水之乐，得之心而寓之酒也。

若夫日出而林霏开，云归而岩穴暝，晦明变化者，山间之朝暮也。野芳发而幽香，佳木秀而繁阴，风霜高洁，水落而石出者，山间之四时也。朝而往，暮而归，四时之景不同，而乐亦无穷也。

至于负者歌于途，行者休于树，前者呼，后者应，伛偻提携，往来而不绝者，滁人游也。临溪而渔，溪深而鱼肥。酿泉为酒，泉香而酒洌；山肴野蔌，杂然而前陈者，太守宴也。宴酣之乐，非丝非竹，射者中，弈者胜，觥筹交错，起坐而喧哗者，众宾欢也。苍颜白发，颓然乎其间者，太守醉也。

已而，夕阳在山，人影散乱，太守归而宾客从也。树林阴翳，鸣声上下，游人去而禽鸟乐也。然而禽鸟知山林之乐，而不知人之乐；人知从太守游而乐，而不知太守之乐其乐也。醉能同其乐，醒能述以文者，太守也。太守谓谁？庐陵欧阳修也。

2.3 翻译技巧：古代散文英译

2.3.1 中国古代散文的特点

“散文”一词作为文体之义最晚在 12 世纪的南宋时代已经出现在典籍中。朱熹说：“若散文，则山谷大不及后山。”此后，“散文”这一概念多次在宋元人的文学理论中出现。此时的散文是与骈体文相对应而出现的一个概念，亦即散体之意，是“古文”的另一种表达方式。学界现在所说的“中国古代散文”就是指文章，是与诗歌相对应的中国古代文学的另一大类文体。可以说，“中国古代散文”这一概念，实质上是以现代意义的“散文”概念返视中国古代作品而形成的。因此，我们对于古代散文范畴的界定也只能是一种现代意义上的界定，是基于对散文文体作历史流变考察的基础之上的。

中国古代文论将散文的特点概括为不押韵和句式的散化，似乎散文在形式上更为自由随意，能够信笔写来，不拘一格。其实，一篇好的散文，总是对结构极为讲究，因为结构是表现主题、展现精妙构思的重要手段。我国古代散文家们历来十分关注作品的谋篇布局，王充在《论衡·超奇篇》中说：“能精思著文，连接篇章者，为鸿儒”，清人李渔在《闲情偶寄》中也曾说“至于结构二字，则在引商刻羽之先，拈韵抽毫之始。如造物之赋形，当其精血初凝，胞胎未就，先为制定全形，使点血而具五官百骸之势。倘先无成局，而由顶及踵，逐段滋生，则人之一生，当有无数断续之痕，而血气为之中阻矣。”因此，历代的文学家们对散文结构总是仔细琢磨，反复推敲，使之随人事物象、主观情感的变化而千差万别，多姿多彩：或成文自然，一气呵成；或波澜起伏，引人入胜；或移步换景，层层递进，不一而足。中国古代散文始终以“散”为特色，结构形式层出不穷、类别繁多，行文自如、仪态万千。不过，散文笔法虽散，却贵在凝练，普遍注重结构的一脉贯通，上下一气，并于法度规范中灵动多变，推陈出新，既增添了散文的精巧玲珑之美，也丰富了散文的结构形式，使得中国古代散文呈现出一些鲜明的基本特征。首先是形散神聚。如欧阳修的《醉翁亭记》，几乎一句一事，散不可收，但文章紧紧抓住了他的感受“乐”，融贯于字字句句之中，是“形散神聚”的典范之作。其次，中国古代散文讲究结构的谨严完整，首尾圆合。完整的结构应是整体的浑圆，中国古代散文自形成之始，就不断追求周严完整、井然有序，即对文章的各部分要合理安排与布局，使之成为线条清晰、首尾圆合的有机整体。其实，从某种角度看，散文结构不仅是形式的问题，还是作者行文思路的一种体现。

2.3.2 中国古代散文的英译思路

与中国现代散文相比较，中国古代散文的叙事、写景要言不烦，给人一种点到为止的感觉。所以，尽管古代散文也始终围绕一个“情”字展开，但在句法上显得简约、精练。古代散文的这种语言艺术造就了古代无以数计的精美名篇，从先秦的诸子散文到两汉的辞赋，从六朝的骈文到“唐宋八大家”，从明代的“公安派”到清代“桐城派”，简直就是一条奔腾跌宕、激扬迂回的散文的长河，或纵横捭阖，气势恢宏；或精雕细琢，玲珑剔透；或豪壮奔放，激情横溢；或清新婉约，自然淳朴，犹如群星璀璨。如“衔远山，吞长江，浩浩汤汤，横无际涯；朝晖夕阴，气象万千”；“环滁皆山也。其西南诸峰，林壑尤美，望之蔚然而深秀者，琅琊也”；“武陵人捕鱼为业。缘溪行，忘路之远近”。

古代散文的语言紧凑而简练，意思的表达却完备而深刻。句中无余字，篇中无剩言。如陶渊明的《桃花源记》，文章开头只用“晋太元中，武陵人捕鱼为业。缘溪行，忘路之远近”。仅十九字，就写清了故事发生的时间、人物和开端。第二段描写桃花源的景色，只用一百多字就勾画出了一幅极其动人的场景。从桃花源的土地、屋舍，一直写到男女老少的衣着以及他们的精神状态，写得层层深入，次序井然，无一句多余的话。写山里人见到渔人，问他从何而来，只用了“具答之”三个字，就写出了渔人讲述经过的全部答话。渔人见太守说起桃花源的情状，也只用了“诣太守，说如此”。“如此”两字，表达了渔人在桃花源里的一切见闻。语言的提炼、遣词用语都恰到好处，表现了作者高超的语言概括能力。

对于这种简约、精练句子，我们首先得把他们翻译成恰当的现代汉语，并在适当的地方根据语境对相关内容加以补充，然后在此基础上翻译成得体的英文。换句话说，中国古代散文的英译实际上需要经历把古文翻译成白话文和把白话文译成英文这两道基本工序。如：“衔远山，吞长江，浩浩汤汤，横无际涯；朝晖夕阴，气象万千”一句，我们根据语境加以补充后以现代汉语形式表达出来就是：洞庭湖衔接远山，吞纳长江，水势浩荡，无边无际。早晚天气阴晴不定，景象千变万化。由此可以翻译成：The Dongting Lake holds the mountain ranges in the distance and swallows the water of the Yangtze River. It is so vast and mighty that it seems boundless. Dazzling in the morning sun and fading in the gray evening mist, it affords a myriad of scenes。再如，“其西南诸峰，林壑尤美，望之蔚然而深秀者，琅琊也”，这一句根据语境加以适当补充后翻译成现代汉语就是：滁州这个地方群山环绕。它西南边的那几座山峰，树林和山谷尤其优美。远处，那一眼望去树木茂盛，又幽深又秀丽的，是琅琊山。翻译成英文就是：The district of Chu is enclosed all around by hills, of which those in the southwest boast the most lovely forests and dales. In the distance, densely wooded and possessed of a rugged beauty, is Mount Langya.

其次，中国古代散文中的很多名篇佳作辞藻对仗，骈散结合，强调音韵，讲究修辞，文字微言精义，韵律优美动人，富有节奏和韵律，读起来朗朗上口，令人荡气回肠。这些文字和韵律承载着中国的文学精髓，因此，对节奏和韵律的把握也是中国散文英译需要加以考虑的重要因素。如《醉翁亭记》中，作者借描写醉翁亭的自然美景和太守宴游的热闹场面，表达了寄情山水、与民同乐的思想。除了内容精彩、意境高远之外，该文之所以为世人传诵，原因之一就是它讲究节奏韵律，读来朗朗上口，如：大量运用骈偶句并夹有散句，骈散结合，整齐中有变化，音调读来铿锵有序；“而”字反复出现，回环往复，充满了旋律感；等等。例如：“临溪而渔，溪深而鱼肥，酿泉为酒，泉香而酒洌，山肴野蔌，杂然而前陈者，太守宴也。”原文四字格、五字格、六字格相互对比，回环往复；中间四个“而”字、两个“溪”字、“泉”字、“酒”字以及同音字“渔”和“鱼”交替重复，构成了韵律上的和谐；此外，“……者……也”判断句的运用，诵读起来韵律十足，给人以美的享受。怎样把原文体现的韵律转换到译文中呢？试看以下三位名家的译文：

杨宪益译本：There the governor gives a feast... The fish are freshly caught from the stream, and since the stream is deep the fish are fat; the wine is brewed with spring water, and since the spring is sweet the wine is superb.

罗经国译本：Some are fishing by the creek where the water is deep and the fish are big. The water itself is faintly scented and the wine brewed from it is crystal clear... edible mountain herbs.

Herbert A. Giles 译本：A cast in the stream, and a fine fish taken from some spot where the eddying pools begin to deepen; a draught of cool wine from the fountain; and a few such dishes of meats and fruits... constitute the Governor's feast.

杨译本模仿原文的句法，把原文前四个四字格和五字格小句翻译成语序相互对应的、格律整体的四音部和五音部，再现了原文的格律美。罗译本前两个小句的翻译与原文的结构相似，后两个小句则打破原文的句法结构，重新组织句法，把“泉香而酒冽”翻译成两个并列主句，把“酿泉为酒”以后置定语的形式依附在第二个并列主句的主语后面，构成三个重音节奏。而在“泉香”句的翻译中，加一个 faintly，巧妙地构成了三个重音节奏，与后一个“酒冽”句的翻译构成重音节奏数量相同的结构，也同样补偿了译文的节奏感。Giles 译本全面打破了原文句法，看似没有韵律可言，但是跨越小句的范围，从整句话来看，他还是在韵律方面做出了一定程度的补偿。“A cast..., and a fine fish...; a draught of cool wine...; and a few such dishes of meats and fruits... constitute the Governor's feast.”四个以单词“A”开头的短语，重复出现，构成排比，同样给读者一种韵律节奏感。三则译文的共同点是，都注意到了原文节奏韵律的转换；不同的是，转换的方式不同。杨译本模仿原文的句法和节奏；罗译本对原文部分句法做出改变，但同样以英文特有的轻重音节、节奏、韵律加以补偿；Giles 译本完全打破原文句法，重新组织英语句子，在更大的范围内做出韵律上的补偿。

此外，春秋战国的百家争鸣，诸子峰起，造就了一大批兼及史学家、思想家、哲学家的文学家，也造就了一个辉煌的散文时代。《春秋》《左传》《国语》《战国策》，语言以事论史，长于说理。《春秋》更是“微言大义”，寓褒贬于字里行间，开创了“春秋笔法”。诸子散文纵横捭阖，语言中蕴含着对大千世界、万物兴灭、国家盛衰、苍茫人生的思索，对真的内涵、善的本质、美的意义的探求，具有深刻的思想性和哲理内涵。《论语》虽然是一部语录体散文，但其语言中不乏令人深思、耐人寻味的理趣，如：“子曰：‘岁寒然后知松柏之后凋也’”。这句话原喻立场坚定、意志坚强的人，才能够经得起艰苦危难的严峻考验，但由于取象贴切、语言精警，看似平易晓物，却有极深的内蕴。类似的语句在《论语》中比比皆是，如“为政以德，譬如北辰，居其所而众星共之”。“子在川上曰：‘逝者如斯夫，不舍昼夜’，“三人行，必有我师焉”。“后生可畏，焉知来者之不如今也”。“学而时习之，温故而知新”。这些句子，辞约义丰，具有以有限表无限，含蓄无穷之妙，寓深刻的哲理于常见的事物之中，理性的内容消解于感性的形象之中，有限转为无限，真善美和谐统一，引人深思，给人启迪。先秦诸子散文语言的魅力，在于哲学的思辨与真切感情的融合，通过生动的语言艺术，把哲理化为深永的理趣，平凡中渗透着高妙，深邃的哲理中流溢着生活的情趣。读之回肠荡气；思之，余味无穷。先秦散文长于说理，富于哲理的语言艺术极大地影响了后世散文，唐宋的古文运动就是复先秦散文之古。在“唐宋八大家”的散文中，无论是政治色彩很浓的政论散文，还是记事写景、抒情议论的游记散文，往往说古道今，纵横驰论，以犀利的文辞、格言式的语句，显见思想的锋芒，道出社会人生的哲理。如苏轼为人称道的《策论》，从容说理，以古道今。语言力透纸背，意蕴深刻。在对历史和现实生活深刻洞悉之后，从中抽绎出看似平凡其实很不平凡的社会和人生的道理。韩愈的《师说》、柳宗元的《捕蛇者说》、欧阳修的《醉翁亭记》、王安石的《游褒禅山记》、苏辙的《六国论》、曾巩的《墨池记》，都以其意蕴深刻的说理语言，道出令人深思的哲理。“唐宋八大家”散文的说理语言，凝聚着对人生和社会的思考，对真善美的探讨，哲理的思辨也在字里行间表露出来，是理性精神的真实记录和准确表现，洋溢着时代的气息，呈现出鲜明的个性特色和独特的语言艺术风格。因此，对于中国古代散文的翻译，译者在把握其言简意赅特点的同时，还要把蕴含在其中的“微言大义”表现出来。如“师者，所以传道授业解惑也”（A teacher is one who can propagate the doctrine, impart professional knowledge and resolve doubts.）；“人非生而知之者，孰能无惑？”（Since no one is born omniscient, who can claim to have no doubts?）；“士穷乃见节义”（A person manifests moral integrity and fidelity only when he is in poverty.）。这就要求译者不仅要有丰富的相关知识储备，还必须对生活有较深的感悟。只有这样，才能理解原文作者富含哲理的“微言大义”，并使之在译文中得以正确传达。

2.4 翻译实战：《桃花源记》

【说明】根据文末的提示，将下列短文翻译为英语。

简介：《桃花源记》是东晋文人陶渊明的代表作之一，是《桃花源诗》的序言，选自《陶渊明集》。本文借武陵渔人发现桃花源的经过，用虚实结合、层层设疑和浪漫主义的笔法虚构了一个人人劳作、没有剥削、没有压迫、社会安定、民风淳朴的理想社会。文章寄托了作者的社会理想，反映了广大人民的意愿，表达了作者对理想的桃花源生活的向往以及对动乱和黑暗的现实生活的不满。

桃花源记

陶渊明

晋太元中，武陵人①捕鱼为业。缘溪行，忘路之远近。②忽逢桃花林，夹岸数百步，中无杂树，芳草鲜美，落英缤纷；渔人甚异之。复前行，欲穷其林。林尽水源，便得一山。山有小口，仿佛若有光，便舍船，从口入。初极狭，才通人③；复行数十步，豁然开朗。土地平旷，屋舍俨然。有良田美池，桑竹之属，阡陌交通，鸡犬相闻。其中往来种作，男女衣着，悉如外人；黄发垂髫④，并怡然自乐。

见渔人，乃大惊，问所从来；具答之。便要还家，设酒、杀鸡、作食。村中闻有此人，咸来问讯。⑤自云：先世避秦时乱，率妻子邑人来此绝境，不复出焉；遂与外人间隔。问今是何世？乃不知有汉，无论魏、晋！此人一一为具言所闻，皆叹惋。余人各复延至其家，皆出酒食，停数日，辞去。此中人语云："不足为外人道也。"

既出，得其船，便扶向路，处处志之。及郡下，诣太守，说如此。太守即遣人随其往，寻向所志，遂迷不复得路。南阳刘子骥，高尚士也，闻之，欣然规往，未果，寻病终。后遂无问津者。

翻译提示

1. 如何理解①处"武陵人"？是指所有的武陵人吗？
2. ②处的这句话与第一句话如何衔接才显得自然？
3. ③处"才通人"中的"才"是我们通常意义上的"刚刚开始"的意思吗？如：昨天才来；现在才懂得这个道理。
4. ④处"黄发垂髫"指的是什么？
5. 如何理解句⑤"村中闻有此人，咸来问讯"中的"问讯"二字？

2.5 译文荟萃

1. 短语翻译

1) 妄自菲薄 belittle oneself / humble oneself / having an undue sense of inferiority
2) 作奸犯科 to violate the law and commit crimes
3) 兴复汉室 to rejuvenate the Han Dynasty
4) 咨诹善道，察纳雅言 to judge judiciously and accept good advice
5) 以孝治天下 to rule the country on the principle of filial piety
6) 落叶缤纷 peach petals falling in riotous profusion
7) 怡然自得 to be happy and pleased with oneself /to be happy and contented
8) 闲静少言 to bc quiet and does not talk much
9) 好读书，不求甚解 reading casually without a need for thorough understanding

10) 忘怀得失，以此自终 spending one's life in a way of disregarding personal gains and losses

11) 著文自娱 writing essays to amuse oneself

12) 不慕荣利 coveting no fame or wealth

13) 物华天宝 with the products being nature's jewels

14) 钟鸣鼎食之家 a family of great affluence

15) 时运不济 a life full of frustrations

16)《陋室铭》"An Epigraph in Praise of My Humble Home"

17)《陈情表》"A Letter to His Majesty"

18)《滕王阁序》"A Tribute to King Teng's Tower"

19)《秋声赋》"Ode to the Sound of Autumn"

20)《捕蛇者说》"The Snake Catcher"

2. 句子翻译

1) 先帝创业未半而中道崩殂。

Our late king passed away before the great undertaking founded by him was only half accomplished.

2) 诚宜开张圣听，以光先帝遗德，恢弘志士之气。

It is advisable that Your Majesty should listen extensively to the counsels of officials in order to carry on the late king's lofty virtues, and heighten the morale of people with high aspirations.

3) 亲贤臣，远小人，此先汉所以兴隆也。

To be close to the virtuous and able officials and keep away from the vile and mean persons was the reason that the Western Han Dynasty was prosperous.

4) 臣本布衣，躬耕于南阳，苟全性命于乱世，不求闻达于诸侯。

I was originally a commoner who had to wear clothes made of hemp, and tilled land in Nanyang. I merely managed to survive in times of turbulence and had no intention of seeking fame and position from princes.

5) 永和九年，岁在癸丑，暮春之初，会于会稽山阴之兰亭，修禊事也。

At the beginning of the late spring in the ninth year of Yonghe, that is, the year of Guichou according to the lunar calendar, a group of learned scholars gathered at the Orchid Pavillion in the Shanyin County of Kuaiji Prefecture to celebrate the festival of Xi (paying homage to the water god).

6) 先生不知何许人也，亦不详其姓氏。

Nobody knows where he came from or what his family name was.

7) 勿以恶小而为之，勿以善小而不为。

Do not commit a bad deed because it is small, and do not fail to do a good deed because it is small.

8) 物极必反

When something has reached its extreme, it starts to develop in the opposite direction. / Too much of one thing is good for nothing. / Things turn into their opposites when they reach the extreme.

9) 物以类聚，人以群分。

Things of the same kind come together and people of the same kind seek out each other's company. / Birds of a feather flock together.

10) 唯公则生明，唯廉则生威。

Judgments should only be made with an impartial mind; true authority only attaches to upright officials.

11) 落霞与孤鹜齐飞，秋水共长天一色。

A solitary wild duck flies alongside the multi-colored sunset clouds, and the autumn is merged with the boundless sky into one hue.

12) 山不在高，有仙则名；水不在深，有龙则灵。

A mountain needn't be high;

It is famous so long as there is a deity on it.

A lake needn't be deep;

It has supernatural power so long as there is a dragon in it.

13) 师者，所以传道授业解惑也。

A teacher is one who can propagate the doctrine, impart professional knowledge and resolve doubts.

14) 人非生而知之者，孰能无惑？

Since no one is born omniscient, who can claim to have no doubts?

15) 呜呼！士穷乃见节义。

Alas! A person manifests moral integrity and fidelity only when he is in poverty.

16) 永州之野产异蛇，黑质而白章，触草木，尽死。

In the wilderness of Yongzhou there exists a kind of snake with black skin marked with white stripes. Any plant dies upon its touch and anyone bitten by it is doomed to death.

17) 事不目见耳闻，而臆断其有无，可乎？

Is it right for one to assume that something exists without seeing or hearing it on one's own?

18) 黄冈之地多竹，大者如椽。竹工破之，刳去其节，用代陶瓦。比屋皆然，以其价廉而工省也。

The district of Huanggang abounds in bamboos, the largest as big as rafters. Bamboo workers split the stems and slice off the knots, and the bamboo is used in place of earthen tiles. All the buildings here are roofed with these bamboo titles because they are cheap and save labour.

19) 四年之间，奔走不暇；未知明年又在何处，岂惧竹楼之易朽乎！

The last four years have seen me incessantly on the move, and I have no idea where I shall be next year. Why, then, should I worry because this Bamboo Pavilion may not last?

20) 君侯不以富贵而骄之，寒贱而忽之，则三千之中有毛遂。

If wealth and power do not make you proud, nor do poverty and low station incite your prejudice, it is natural that there is no lack of a talented and brave man like Mao Sui among your followers.

3. 段落翻译

1) 嗟乎！时运不齐，命途多舛。冯唐易老，李广难封。屈贾谊于长沙，非无圣主；窜梁鸿于海曲，岂乏明时？所赖君子见机，达人知命。老当益壮，宁移白首之心？穷且益坚，不坠青云之志。酌贪泉而觉爽，处涸辙以犹欢。北海虽赊，扶摇可接；东隅已逝，桑榆非晚。孟尝高洁，空余报国之情；阮籍猖狂，岂效穷途之哭！（王勃 《滕王阁序》）

Alas, the caprice of fortune,
The path of which is filled with obstacles.
The talented Feng Tang soon grew old and remained unknown;
Li Guang was not enfeoffed despite his brave campaigns.
When Jia Yi was a mere tutor to the Prince of Changsha,
It was not a time without a good ruler.
When Liang Hong sought refuge on a remote shore.
It was not in a period of turmoil.
Nevertheless, the superior man can discern
What Fate has in store,
And the man of great understanding
Accepts his Destiny.
His resolution is the stronger despite his old age;
He will not change because his hair is turning grey.
His determination is greater in times of adversity,
He would be refreshed and remain uncorrupted
Though he drinks from the Spring of Avarice;
And he would maintain a happy state
Even if he were in straitened circumstances.

Though the North Sea is remote,
It can be reached with the help of the wind.
The rays of dawn
Have disappeared from the east,
But it is not too late
Even if the stars Sang and Yu are already here.
We admire the patriotic Meng Chang
Who cherished his noble aspirations in vain.
How can we follow the unruly Ruan Ji,
Who wailed at the road's end?（T.C. Lai & Monica Lai　译）

2) 太行、王屋二山，方七百里，高万仞，本在冀州之南，河阳之北。北山愚公者，年且九十，面山而居。(《愚公移山》)

The two mountains Taihang (in Shanxi) and Wangwu cover a territory of seven hundred square *li*, and are ten thousand cubits high. They were formerly situated in the south of Chichow and north of Hoyang. Old Man Fool of the North Mountain was about ninety years old and he lived in a house facing the mountain.（林语堂　译）

3) 子城西北隅，雉堞圮毁，蓁莽荒秽，因作小楼二间，与月波楼通。远吞山光，平挹江濑，幽阒辽夐，不可具状。夏宜急雨，有瀑布声；冬宜密雪，有碎玉声。宜鼓琴，琴调虚畅；宜咏诗，诗韵清绝；宜围棋，子声丁丁然；宜投壶，矢声铮铮然；皆竹楼之所助也。(王禹偁 《黄冈竹楼记》)

At the northwest corner of my city the walls had crumbled, the ground was overgrown with brambles, the place wild and dirty; so I had a small two-roomed pavilion constructed there, linking it with the Moon Wave Pavilion. It affords a view of the distant hills and dips at the shallows of the river below. The quiet seclusion there defies description. This pavilion is delightful during a sudden summer shower, when rain beats on the roof like a waterfall; it is equally delightful during heavy snow in winter, when the snow tinkles on the roof like jade. The pavilion is a good place for strumming a lyre, for the echo is smooth and mellow; it is a good place for chanting poetry too, for the recitation rings out fine and clear; it is a good place for playing draughts and hearing the sound made by draughtsmen on the board, or for playing cottabus and hearing the thud of arrows dropping into the pot; for all these sounds are brought out to the best advantage in the Bamboo Pavilion.（杨宪益、戴乃迭　译）

4) 公退之暇，被鹤氅衣，戴华阳巾，手执《周易》一卷，焚香默坐，消遣世虑。江山之外，第见风帆沙鸟，烟云竹树而已。待其酒力醒，茶烟歇，送夕阳，迎素月，亦谪居之胜概也。彼齐云、落星，高则高矣；井干、丽谯，华则华矣；止于贮妓女，藏歌舞，非骚人之事，吾所不取。(王

禹偁《黄冈竹楼记》）

In leisure moments after my official duties I put on a priestly gown and cap, take up the *Book of Change* and sit there in silence with incense burning to banish mundane cares. So, beside the river and hills, I watch the sails in the wind, the birds on the sand, the mist and clouds, the bamboos and trees, and when I recover from the effects of wine, when my tea stops bubbling on the stove, I bid goodbye to the setting sun and welcome the rising of the white moon. Such are my pleasures in exile. Pavilion famed in history like the Cloud Reaching Pavilion, the Fallen Star Pavilion, the Well Frame Pavilion and the Splendid Pavilion, may have been superbly imposing and magnificent; but they served solely to entertain sing-song girls and dancers, a pastime hardly suited to a man of letters, and this is not my way.（杨宪益、戴乃迭 译）

2.6 翻译家：刘士聪

刘士聪是南开大学教授、博士生导师，我国著名翻译家。他一直从事翻译实践、翻译教学与翻译研究工作，系《中国翻译》编委，《英语世界》顾问，曾任南开大学外国语学院首任院长。刘士聪出版有编译《英汉·汉英美文翻译与鉴赏》《英语经典散文翻译与赏析》，主编《红楼译评——〈红楼梦〉翻译研究论文集》。他的翻译著作有：英译作品 *Confucius*（《孔子》）、*Lao Zi*（《老子》）、*The Recluse*（《听画》）、*The Broad Sworder*（《扬子江摇篮曲》）；汉译作品《钢琴师》（*The Pianist*）、《红色的英勇标志》（*The Red Badge of Courage*）（与谷启楠合译）、《皇帝的孩子》（*The Emperor's Children*）等，以及一些短篇小说和散文英译。此外，还有一些论述翻译的短评与文章。

在《汉英·英汉美文翻译与鉴赏》“序言”里，刘士聪提出“文学作品的翻译，是语言艺术，其至高境界是再现原文的韵味。译作的‘韵味’就是原作的艺术内涵通过译文准确而富有文采的语言表达时所蕴含的艺术感染力，这种艺术感染力能引起读者的美感共鸣。”并指出，“散文的韵味，主要体现在三个方面”：“声响与节奏”、“意境与氛围”和“个性化的话语方式”，使“韵味”之说具体化且可操作。

刘士聪的译文用词讲究、行文流畅，注重简洁、生动而忠实地传达原作意蕴，形神兼备，深受读者喜欢。在多年的翻译和教学实践中，他体会到：读书，特别是阅读文学经典，对译者的成长特别重要。他认为，培养译者有多种途径：学习翻译教科书、跟老师学、向译者请教、参加进修班或研讨会等，但最重要的是自己读书，阅读汉语和英语的经典文学著作，在书籍的海洋里、在阅读的过程中，去体会和领悟语言的美感和力量。他指出，语言不仅是表达思想和感情的媒介，语言更是艺术。语言艺术的美感和力量在文学作品中有突出表现，文学作品是语言的宝库，是取之不尽、用之不竭的语言源泉。一个译者最终是否成功，取决于他是否读了书、读了多少，是否感悟到语言之美和语言的力量。他认为，读书培养人的语言修养和审美修养，同时培养

人的人文修养。一个人的修养在深层次上影响他的语言，即他的表达方式，这二者有机地统一在一个人的身上。因此，他认为，正在学习翻译并有志将来做一个译者的人，必须重视读书，真正地下工夫读书，因为好的译家，同好的作家一样，无一例外的都是爱读书，且读书多的人。

关于什么样的语言是好的语言，刘士聪认为，好的语言是自然、朴素、简洁的语言。所谓“自然”，就是不做作，按照事理的本真叙述、描写；所谓“朴素”，就是不卖弄，实事求是地说，实事求是地写；所谓“简洁”，就是有一说一，有二说二，不说多余的话。其实，越是“自然、朴素、简洁”的语言，越是有美感，越是有力量。对于译者，这是很高的要求，要把自己的语言修炼到这个程度，需矢志不渝地朝着这个目标终生努力。

2.7 补充资源

参考书目

林语堂，译 . 诸子百家（英、汉）. 北京：外语教学与研究出版社，2015.
林语堂，译 . 明清小品（上、中、下；英、汉）. 北京：外语教学与研究出版社，2015.
林语堂，译 . 晋唐心印（英、汉）. 北京：外语教学与研究出版社，2015.
顾伟列，朱希祥 . 中文读写教程 . 上海：上海外语教育出版社，2009.
庄绎传 . 译海一粟：汉英翻译九百例 . 北京：外语教学与研究出版社，2015.

网络资源

中国古典文学网：http://www.gudianwenxue.com
古典文学网：http://www.gudwx.com/default.aspx
China Knowledge: http://www.chinaknowledge.de/index.html

Chapter 2

第二章 小说翻译

- 第三单元 中国现代小说
- 第四单元 中国古代小说

第三单元　中国现代小说

3.1 阅读欣赏：《阿Q正传》

【说明】阅读下列小说及译文，体会中国现代小说的特点及英译思路。

简介：《阿Q正传》是鲁迅于1921年底创作的一部小说，共分《序》《优胜记略》《续优胜记略》《恋爱的悲剧》《生计问题》等九章。小说以辛亥革命前后的中国农村为背景，描述了未庄流浪雇农阿Q的人生经历，塑造了一个从物质到精神都受到严重戕害的农民形象。他生活在社会最底层，受尽压迫和屈辱，但他不能正视自己被压迫的悲惨地位，反而自我安慰，即使是在受到污辱甚至要被杀头的情况下，他也以为自己是精神上的"胜利者"。小说有力地批判了当时中国社会的封建、保守、庸俗、腐败等特点，深刻地揭示了旧中国人民的生活场景及其在水深火热之中的病态。

阿Q正传（节选）

鲁迅

阿Q"先前阔"，见识高，而且"真能做"，本来几乎是一个"完人"了，但可惜他体质上还有一些缺点。最恼人的是在他头皮上，颇有几处不知起于何时的癞疮疤。这虽然也在他身上，而看阿Q的意思，倒也似乎以为不足贵的，因为他讳说"癞"以及一切近于"赖"的音，后来推而广之，"光"也讳，"亮"也讳，再后来，连"灯""烛"都讳了。一犯讳，不问有心与无心，阿Q便全疤通红的发起怒来，估量了对手，口讷的他便骂，气力小的他便打；然而不知怎么一回事，总还是阿Q吃亏的时候多。于是他渐渐的变换了方针，大抵改为怒目而视了。

谁知道阿Q采用怒目主义之后，未庄的闲人们便愈喜欢玩笑他。一见面，他们便假作吃惊地说："哙，亮起来了。"

阿Q照例的发了怒，他怒目而视了。

"原来有保险灯在这里！"他们并不怕。

阿Q没有法，只得另外想出报复的话来：

"你还不配……"这时候，又仿佛在他头上的是一种高尚的光荣的癞头疮，并非平常的癞头疮了；但上文说过，阿Q是有见识的，他立刻知道和"犯忌"有点抵触，便不再往底下说。

闲人还不完，只撩他，于是终而至于打。阿Q在形式上打败了，被人揪住黄辫子，在壁上碰了四五个响头，闲人这才心满意足的得胜的走了，阿Q站了一刻，心里想，"我总算被儿子打了，现在的世界真不像样……"于是也心满意足的得胜的走了。

阿Q想在心里的，后来每每说出口来，所以凡是和阿Q玩笑的人们，几乎全知道他有这一种精神上的胜利法，此后每逢揪住他黄辫子的时候，人就先一着对他说：

"阿Q，这不是儿子打老子，是人打畜生。自己说：人打畜生！"

阿Q两只手都捏住了自己的辫根，歪着头，说道：

"打虫豸，好不好？我是虫豸——还不放么？"

但虽然是虫豸，闲人也并不放，仍旧在就近什么地方给他碰了五六个响头，这才心满意足的得胜的走了，他以为阿Q这回可遭了瘟。然而不到十秒钟，阿Q也心满意足的得胜的走了，他觉得他是第一个能够自轻自贱的人，除了"自轻自贱"不算外，余下的就是"第一个"。状元不也是"第一个"么？"你算是什么东西"呢？！

The True Story of Ah Q

(Excerpt)

Ah Q who "used to be much better off," who was a man of the world and "a good worker," would have been almost the perfect man had it nor been for a few unfortunate physical blemishes. The most annoying were some places on his scalp where in the past, at some uncertain date, shiny ringworm scars had appeared. Although these were on his own head, apparently Ah Q did not consider them as altogether honourable, for he refrained from using the word "ringworm" or any words that sounded anything like it. Later he improved on this, making "bright" and "light" forbidden words, while later still even "lamp" and "candle" were taboo. Whenever this taboo was disregarded, whether intentionally or not, Ah Q would fly into a rage, his ringworm scars turning scarlet. He would look over the offender, and if it were someone weak in repartee he would curse him, while if it were a poor fighter he would hit him. Yet, curiously enough, it was usually Ah Q who was worsted in these encounters, until finally he adopted new tactics, contenting himself in general with a furious glare.

It so happened, however, that after Ah Q had taken to using this furious glare, the idlers in Weichuang grew even more fond of making jokes at his expense. As soon as they saw him they would pretend to give a start, and say:

"Look! It's lighting up."

Ah Q would rise to the bait as usual, and glare furiously.

"So there is a paraffin lamp here," they would continue, not in the least intimidated.

Ah Q could do nothing but rack his brains for some retort: "You don't even deserve…" At this juncture it seemed as if the scars on his scalp were noble and honourable, not just ordinary ringworm scars. However, as we said above, Ah Q was a man of the world: He knew at once that he had neatly broken the "taboo" and refrained from saying any more.

If the idlers were still not satisfied, but continued to bait him, they would in the end come to blows. Then only after Ah Q had, to all appearances, been defeated, had his brownish pigtail pulled and his head bumped against the wall four or five times, would the idlers walk away, satisfied at having won. Ah Q would stand there for a second, thinking to himself, "It is as if I were beaten by my son. What is the world coming to nowadays…" Thereupon he too would walk away, satisfied at having won.

Whatever Ah Q thought he was sure to tell people later; thus almost all who made fun of Ah Q knew that he had this means of winning a psychological victory. So after this anyone who pulled or twisted his brown pigtail would forestall him by saying: "Ah Q, this is not a son beating his father, it is a man beating a beast. Let's hear you say it: A man beating a beast!"

Then Ah Q, clutching at the root of his pigtail, his head on one side, would say: "Beating an insect — how about that? I am an insect — now will you let me go?"

But although he was an insect the idlers would not let him go until they had knocked his head five or six times against something nearby, according to their custom, after which they would walk away satisfied that they had won, confident that this time Ah Q was done for. In less than ten seconds, however, Ah Q would walk away also satisfied that he had won, thinking that he was the "foremost self-belittler," and that after subtracting "self-belittler" what remained was "foremost." Was not the highest successful candidate in the official examination also the "foremost"? "And who do you think you are anyway?"（杨宪益、戴乃迭 译）

3.2 翻译热身:《围城》

【说明】 参照"阅读欣赏"部分的译文和翻译思路，将下列小说选段翻译为英语。

简介:《围城》是钱钟书所著的长篇小说，1947年首次出版。这是中国现代文学史上一部风格独特的讽刺小说，主要描写20世纪20至40年代知识分子的群相，被誉为"新儒林外史"。《围城》是钱钟书"锱铢积累"写成。小说不以明确的故事线索、激烈的情节冲突见长，而有绝佳的言语表达。可以说,《围城》把语言运用到了登峰造极的境界。字里行间处处透露着机智与幽默，精言妙语是这部小说的最成功之处，是最值得赏析的地方，也是本书的一大特色。

围　城（节选）

钱钟书

苏小姐领了个二十左右的娇小女孩子出来，介绍道:"这是我表妹唐晓芙。"唐小姐妩媚端正的圆脸，有两个浅酒涡。天生着一般女人要花钱费时、调脂和粉来仿造的好脸色，新鲜得使人见了忘掉口渴而又觉嘴馋，仿佛是好水果。她眼睛并不顶大，可是灵活温柔，反衬得许多女人的大眼睛只像政治家讲的大话，大而无当。古典学者看她说笑时露出的好牙齿，会诧异为什么古今中外诗人，都甘心变成女人头插的钗，腰束的带，身体睡的席，甚至脚下践踏的鞋，可是从没想到化作她的牙刷。她头发没烫，眉毛不镊，口红也没有擦，似乎安心遵守天生的限止，不要弥补造化的缺陷。总而言之，唐小姐是摩登文明社会里那桩罕物——一个真正的女孩子。有许多都市女孩子已经是装模做样的早熟女人，算不得孩子；有许多女孩子只是浑沌痴顽的无性别孩子，还说不上女人。方鸿渐立刻想在她心上造个好印象。唐小姐尊称他为"同学老前辈"，他抗议道:"这可不成！你叫我'前辈'，我已经觉得像史前原人的遗骸了。你何必又加上'老'字？我们不幸生得太早，没福气跟你同时同学，这是恨事。你再叫我'前辈'，就是有意提醒我是老大过时的人，太残忍了！"

唐小姐道:"方先生真会挑眼！算我错了，'老'字先取消。"苏小姐同时活泼地说:"不羞！还要咱们像船上那些人叫你'小方'么？晓芙，不用理他。他不受抬举，干脆什么都不叫他。"

方鸿渐看唐小姐不笑的时候，脸上还依恋着笑意，像音乐停止后袅袅空中的余音。许多女人会笑得这样甜，但她们的笑容只是面部肌肉柔软操，仿佛有教练在喊口令:"一！"忽然满脸堆笑，"二！"忽然笑不知去向，只余个空脸，像电影开映前的布幕。他找话出跟她讲，问她进的什么系。苏小姐不许她说，说:"让他猜。"

3.3 翻译技巧：小说翻译

小说是四大文学体裁之一。它描绘生活事件，塑造人物形象，展开作品主题，表达作者的思想感情，从而艺术地概括和表现社会生活。

小说的三要素是：生动的人物形象、完整的故事情节和具体的环境描写。小说一般描写人物故事，塑造多种多样的人物形象。小说中人物的对话是否具有鲜明的个性，每个人物是否具有独特的语言风格，是衡量小说水平的一个重要标准。小说情节一般包括开端、发展、高潮和结局四部分，有的还包括序幕和尾声。环境包括自然环境和社会环境。

在翻译小说时，译者要克服不同语言在词汇、语法、构句、修辞以及思维方式、民族文化等方面的异同，不仅要再现原著的意义，而且要再现原著的艺术意境、风格特征、情感、韵味，充分传达原文的文学意象与艺术美感。翻译时，需要仔细分析小说的人物形象、性格、故事情节、环境气氛等多种因素，采取恰当的翻译技巧和策略，采用贴切、生动、传神的语言，努力再现与原著相契合的艺术意境。

翻译汉语小说的时候，需要特别注意小说的以下几个特点：生动形象的语言、个性化的人物、广泛运用的修辞格、复杂多变的句式等。下面我们将选取几部中国名著的片段译文进行分析和探讨。

一、生动形象的语言

小说在描绘环境或叙述故事情节时，往往都用生动、活泼、形象的语言进行具体而细腻的描写，从而刻画出栩栩如生的人物，再现场景中的各种细节，渲染情绪，能给读者一种身临其境的感觉，使人读后印象深刻。在用词上，往往表现出用词准确、多用形容词和副词进行修饰等特征。因此在翻译小说时，要准确选择所用词语，提升表现力。

例 (1)：（贾政）一面引人出来，转过山坡，穿花度柳，抚石依泉，过了荼蘼架，入木香棚，越牡丹亭，度芍药圃，到蔷院，傍芭蕉土房里盘旋曲折，忽闻水声潺潺，出于石洞，上则萝薜倒垂，下则落花浮荡。

译文： He led them out of the “village” and round the foot of the hill! Through flowers and foliage,
By rock and rivulet,
Past rose-crowned pergolas and rose-twined trellises,
Through small pavilions,
Embowered in peonies,
Where scent of sweet-briers stole,
Or pliant plantains waved —

Until they came to a place where a musical murmur of water issued from a cave in the rock. The cave was half-veiled by a green curtain of creeper, and the water was starred with bobbing blossoms.

原文如诗的语言使一幅美丽的图画呼之欲出。译文的措辞和韵律也做到了这一点，读后使人如闻其声，如临其境。特别是 stole、waved 译得十分生动又忠于原文。

二、个性化的人物

个性化是小说的重要特性。小说往往从外貌、动作、语言、心理等方面对人物进行多层次的刻画，把人物的政治面貌、社会地位、性格特征，以及生活与语言习惯等描绘得惟妙惟肖。

（1）语言描写

例如，个性化的语言是塑造人物形象的一个重要手段。作家常常会让笔下的人物通过本人之口来表现自己的个性，所谓“只闻其声，便识其人”。不同的人物语言往往折射出人物迥异的身份、年龄、职业、地位、教养、性格等。尤其在角色众多的小说中，有的人物语言可能非常文雅，有的会十分浅显，有的则使用方言和俚语，还有的十分粗俗。言为心声，人物的语言对话无疑是对其自身形象最佳的诠释。

翻译小说时，译者要揣摩人物各自的语言和对话特点，生动地展现形形色色的人物的个性。在某种意义上说，原作的艺术风格能否在译作中得以体现，在一定程度上取决于译者对人物的语言处理是否得当。

例 (2)：（第十一回）凤姐与尤氏谈论秦可卿的病情：凤姐听了，眼圈儿红了一会子，方说道：“‘天有不测风云，人有旦夕祸福’，这点年纪，倘或因这病上有个长短，人生在世，还有什么趣儿呢！”

译文： Xi Feng's eyes became moist and for a moment she was too overcome to speak. “I know ‘the weather and human life are both unpredictable,’” she said at last, “but she's only a child still. If anything should happen to her as a result of this illness, I think all the fun would go out of life!”（David Hawks 译）

《红楼梦》是中国文学园地百花丛中的一朵奇葩，它塑造了众多独特鲜明的人物。书中的主要角色，如贾宝玉、林黛玉、薛宝钗、王熙凤、刘姥姥等都栩栩如生，如在眼前。如《红楼梦》中的刘姥姥，初进贾府时，听说王熙凤答应把丫头们做衣服的二十两银子给她时说道：“俗话说的：‘瘦死的骆驼比马大’，凭他怎样，你老拔根寒毛比我们的腰还粗呢……”对比贾府里面出身上等社会和家庭、有身份的女子来说，这样的言辞显得很粗俗，但却能生动地表现出刘姥姥的性格特点，符合她的地位和身份，虽然有些滑稽可笑，但却有点儿可爱，值得同情。霍克思运用灵心妙手，将之妥帖地译成合乎惯用法的地道英文。

例 (3)： 北静王见他语言清朗，谈吐有致，一面又向贾政笑道：“令郎真乃龙驹凤雏，非小王在世翁前唐突，将来‘雏凤清于老凤声’，未可量也。”贾政赔笑道：“犬子岂敢谬承金奖，赖藩郡余恩，果如所言，亦荫生辈之幸矣。”（《红楼梦》第十五回）

译文 1: The clarity and fluency of Bao Yu's answers made the Prince turn to observe to Chia Cheng, “Your son is truly a dragon's colt or young phoenix. May I venture to predict that in time to come this young phoenix may even surpass the old one?"

"My worthless son does not deserve such a high praise," rejoined Chia Cheng hurriedly with a courteous smile. "If thanks to the grace of Your Highness such proves the case, that will be our good fortune."（杨宪益、戴乃迭 译）

译文 2：Delighted that everything Bao-yu said was so clear and to the point, the prince observed to Jia Zheng that "the young phoenix was worthy of his sire." "I trust I shall not offend you by saying so to your face," he said, "but I venture to prophesy that this fledgling of yours will one day 'sing sweeter than the parent bird.'"

Jia Zheng smiled politely. "My son is doubtless unworthy of the compliment. Your Highness is good enough to pay him. If, thanks to your encouragement, he turns out as you say, we shall count ourselves truly fortunate."（David Hawkes 译）

本例是《红楼梦》中贾政与北静王的一段对话。中国文化讲究尊人抑己，北静王虽身为王爷，为体现自己的教养，他在贾政面前使用了"小王""唐突"等词以示自谦，并称贾宝玉为"令郎""龙驹凤雏"，称贾政为"世翁"；而贾政也收敛了往日贾府里的那种威风，用了"犬子""萌生辈"等词来自贬。

在翻译上述自谦词及敬语时，杨译用 May I venture、My worthless son、the grace of Your Highness 以及所增 courteous 等词；霍译用 doubtless unworthy、Your Highness 等词；这些词语均比较确切地体现了讲话人的自谦和对对方的敬重，反映了人物身份地位以及为人处世的态度。特别是贾政平日在奴才面前盛气凌人，但在对地位比自己高的北静王面前，却又极尽卑躬屈膝之能事，一副虚伪的奴才相栩栩如生地呈现在译语读者面前。

例 (4)：李逵听了大怒道，"教你咬我鸟！晁宋两位哥哥将令，干我屁事！"（《水浒传》第五十二回）

译文 1："You can eat my prick," roared Li Kui,"I was carrying out the orders of brothers Chao and Song! It hadn't a tooting fart to do with me!"（沙博里 译）

译文 2：Li K'uei heard this and he was filled with a great anger and he cried,"And you would — you would — would you — My elder brothers bade me do what I did, and what has it to do with my hide?"（赛珍珠 译）

为逼引朱仝上梁山，李逵在晁宋两位头领的授意下，斧劈小衙内，朱仝气愤之下要杀了李逵，李逵为自己的行为有了这番辩解。作者施耐庵用"鸟""屁"等粗俗语，将李逵粗鲁的个性披露得淋漓尽致，也将其觉得憋屈的气愤之情表现无遗。译文 1 中，沙博理用 prick 这一粗俗讳语直译出"鸟"，用 tooting fart（响屁）直译出"屁"，这样英文读者就有可能领略到李逵粗俗的个性和气愤的心情。而译文 2 中，赛珍珠省译了这两个粗俗词，而用"you would — you would — would you"来表现李逵的气愤。这样一来，在译文读者眼里，李逵仿佛就成了一个言语文明有礼，气愤起来说不出话的文雅书生，自然与施耐庵塑造的李逵形象差距太大，没能传译出原文人物的个性。

（2）肖像描写

小说中人物形象塑造最常用的写作手法便是肖像描写，即通过描写人物的容貌、衣饰及姿态等外部特征来刻画人物形象，形神兼备地表现人物的思想性格。翻译时要特别注意这些起关键作用的细节描写，运用不同的翻译策略，精确地再现人物形象。

例 (5)：孔乙己是站着喝酒而穿长衫的唯一的人。他身材很高大；青白脸色，皱纹间时常夹些伤痕；一部乱蓬蓬的花白的胡子。穿的虽然是长衫，可是又脏又破，似乎十多年没有补，也没有洗。他对人说话，总是满口之乎者也，教人半懂不懂的。（鲁迅 《孔乙己》）

译文：Kong Yiji was the only long-gowned customer who used to drink his wine standing. A big, pallid man whose wrinkled face often bore scars, he had a large, unkempt and grizzled beard. And although he wore a long gown it was dirty and tattered. It had not by the look of it been washed or mended for ten years or more. He used so many archaisms in his speech that half of it was barely intelligible.（杨宪益、戴乃迭 译）

孔乙己是近代文学巨匠鲁迅所著的同名短篇小说中的人物形象。小说描写了孔乙己在封建腐朽思想和科举制度的毒害下，精神上迂腐不堪、麻木不仁，生活上四体不勤、穷困潦倒，最后被封建地主阶级所吞噬的悲惨形象，具有强烈的反封建意义。通过孔乙己这一人物形象，鲁迅深刻揭露了当时科举制度对知识分子精神的毒害和封建制度“吃人”的本质。本例中的人物外貌描写，着墨不多，但是处处皆有所指。译文中，杨宪益、戴乃迭用 the only long-gowned customer 来翻译“穿长衫的唯一的”人，一方面准确地反映长衫所代表的是孔乙己所自诩的封建知识分子形象，另一方面 customer 一词体现了小说的叙事者和孔乙己之间的人物关系。犹如，将“伤痕”译为 scars，忠实地反映出孔乙己被人嘲笑奚落的悲惨经历，“乱蓬蓬的花白的胡子”译为 unkempt and grizzled beard，则生动地描绘出了孔乙己四体不勤的形象。

（3）动作描写

人物形象刻画也离不开动作描写。动作描写涉及使用精心挑选的动词，摹写人物在不同场景中的一系列动作、行为，能较为动态地折射出人物的性格特点。翻译时，需在译入语中找到等值的富有表现力的动词。

例 (6)：华大妈在枕头底掏了半天，掏出一包洋钱，交给老栓。老栓接了，抖抖的装入衣袋，又在外面按了两下，便点上灯笼，吹熄灯盏，走向里屋去了。（鲁迅 《药》）

译文：After some fumbling under the pillow his wife produced a packet of silver dollars which she handed over. Old Chuan pocketed it nervously, patted his pocket twice, then lighting a paper lantern and blowing out the lamp went into the inner room.（杨宪益、戴乃迭 译）

这一段是描写老栓准备去买“药”的情形。鲁迅先生通过运用了一系列形象生动的词语，如

“掏”“按”等字，表现了华大妈老夫妇俩省吃俭用的习惯，而译文用了 fumbling、pocketed、patted 等词也将原文中老栓充满希望地去买“药”的心理刻画得细腻生动而传神。

（4）心理描写

心理描写通过对人物内心世界的直接叙述，反映人物的喜怒哀乐等情感状态和变化，展示人物的心灵和性格特征，也能对人物形象的塑造产生至关重要的影响。翻译时应注意人物的身份与个性，以适当的语气、语调来传递人物的心理状况，忠实传达原作人物的心理情感，准确再现作者对特定人物的审美评价和情感态度。下面是《红楼梦》第二十四章的一个片段和杨宪益的译文。

例 (7)： 这里林黛玉见宝玉去了，又听见众姊妹也不在房，自己闷闷的。正欲回房，刚走到梨香院墙角上，只听见笛韵悠扬，歌声婉转。林黛玉便知那十二个女孩子演习戏文呢。只是林黛玉素习不大喜看戏文，便不留心，只管往前走。偶然两句吹到耳内，明明白白，一字不落，唱道是：“原来姹紫嫣红开遍，似这般都付与断井残垣。”林黛玉听了，倒也十分感慨缠绵，便止住步侧耳细听，又听唱道是：“良辰美景奈何天，赏心乐事谁家院。”听了这两句，不觉点头自叹，心下自思道：“原来戏上也有好文章，可惜世人只知看戏，未必能领略这其中的趣味。”想毕，又后悔不该胡想，耽误了听曲子。又侧耳时，只听唱道：“则为你如花美眷，似水流年……”林黛玉听了这两句，不觉心动神摇。又见道：“你在幽闺自怜”等句，亦发如醉如痴，站立不住，便一蹲身坐在一块山子石上，细嚼“如花美眷，似水流年”八个字的滋味。忽又想起前日见古人诗中有“水流花谢两无情”之句，再又词中有“流水落花春去也，天上人间”之句，又兼方才所见《西厢记》中“花落水流红，闲愁万种”之句，都一时想起来，凑聚在一处，仔细忖度，不觉心痛神痴，眼中落泪。

译文： With Pao-yu gone and the other girls all out too, Tai-yu did not know what to do and decided to go back to her own room. As she rounded the corner of Pear Fragrance Court where the twelve actresses were rehearsing, she heard sweet fluting and singing over the wall. Normally the words of operas made little appeal to her, so she did not listen carefully; but now as she proceeded on her way two lines carried to her distinctly:

“What a riot of brilliant purple and tender crimson,

Among the ruined wells and crumbling walls.

Strangely touched by this, she stopped to listen. The singer went on:

What an enchanting sight on this fine morning.

But who is there that takes delight in the spring?”

Tai-yu nodded and sighed.

“So there are fine lines in these operas,” she thought. “What a pity that people just care for the spectacle without understanding the meaning.”

Then, sorry to have missed a stanza through her preoccupation, she listened again and heard:

“For you are as fair as a flower

And youth is slipping away like flowing water."
Tai-yu's heart missed a beat. And the next line:
"Alone you sit in your secluded chamber"
Affected her so much that she sank down on a rock to ponder the words.
"For you are as fair as a flower
And youth is slipping away like flowing water."
They reminded her of a line in an old poem:
"Water flows and flowers fall, knowing no pity."
And the lines form another poem:
"Spring departs with the flowing water and fallen blossom,
Far, far away as the heaven from the world of men."
She compared this with the lines she had just read in *The Western Camber*:
"Flowers fall, the water flows red,
Grief is infinite."
As she brooded over the meaning of all these verses, her heart ached and tears coursed down her cheeks.

曹雪芹笔下的林黛玉多才多艺，通晓中国古典文学艺术，但是却体弱多病、多愁善感。原文细致入微地刻画了她有一天走到大观园的梨香院墙角旁，偶然听到了贾府戏班子演奏的曲子，心生触动，黯然神伤，继而泪下的心理过程。杨译忠实地再现了林黛玉心理情感的变化过程：例如，用"Strangely touched by this, she stopped to listen"翻译"十分感慨缠绵，便止住步侧耳细听"，然后用 nodded and sighed 对应"点头自叹，心下自思"，用语贴切自然。接着，译文用地道的英语表达"Tai-yu's heart missed a beat"翻译"怦然心动"。再后来，译文使用"Affected her so much that she sank down on a rock to ponder the words"来反映黛玉被诗句触动心弦，瘫坐在石头上，陷入沉思的过程。最后，黛玉思绪万千，仔细忖度，不觉心痛神痴，眼中落泪，译文则化为"As she brooded over the meaning of all these verses, her heart ached and tears coursed down her cheeks"，简练而生动。

三、修辞格的广泛运用

小说常常大量使用修辞格，其中尤以拟人、比喻、讽刺、夸张、双关为多。这些修辞一般都具有形式独特新颖、内容形象生动、功能丰富鲜明等特点。例如《围城》是学贯中西的大学者钱钟书先生所著的长篇小说，他以犀利幽默的手笔描绘了国难时期各个阶层的众生相，尤其是知识分子的窘境，书中包含大量新颖奇特的修辞方法，如灵活用典、奇特比喻、滑稽类比、夸张、多语混用等。

由于中西语言和文化的差异，修辞格的翻译往往比较棘手。在翻译的过程中，译者首先要保证内容准确，其次应尽量体现原文效果，最后要力争表达形式妥当。

（1）比喻

比喻有明喻和暗喻两种。明喻使用“像”“如”“一样”等词语，表明了本体和喻体之间的关系。而暗喻则没有直接明示本体和喻体之间的关系，赋予读者更广阔的想象及阐释空间。

例 (8)：忠厚老实人的恶毒，像饭里的沙砾或者出骨鱼片里未净的刺，会给人一种不期待的伤痛。

译文：The viciousness of a kind, simple-hearted soul, like gritty sand in rice or splinters in a deboned fish, can give a person unexpected pain.

例 (9)：这一张文凭，仿佛有亚当、夏娃下身那片叶子的功用，可以遮盖包丑；小小一方纸能把一个人的空疏、寡陋、愚笨都掩藏起来。（钱钟书 《围城》）

译文：This diploma, it seemed, would function the same as Adam and Eve's fig leaf. It could hide a person's shame and wrap up his disgrace. This tiny square of paper could cover his shallowness, ignorance and stupidity.（珍妮·凯利和茅国权合译）

珍妮·凯利和茅国权合译的英译《围城》大都采用直译的方法，并在翻译隐喻时保全了原文中的比喻修辞格，向译文读者展示了钱钟书写作时的幽默风趣。

例 (10)：“我们新吃过女人的亏，都是惊弓之鸟，看见女人影子就怕了。”

译文：“Having recently been jilted by women, we are like birds afraid of the bow; we're frightened even by a woman's shadow.”

这些绝妙的比喻将一出人间闹剧刻画得入木三分，嘲笑中含着辛涩，表现了钱钟书先生的机巧犀利、博喻多讽的幽默风格，译文也做到了忠实贴切。

（2）夸张

例 (11)：方鸿渐恨不得把苏小姐瘦身体里任何一根骨头都捏成石灰粉。

译文：Fang wished he could have crushed every bone in Miss Su's thin body to lime powder.

（3）幽默

《围城》以其幽默诙谐的语言风格深受读者的喜爱。幽默不仅深化了小说的主题，而且营造了喜剧气氛，是小说不朽艺术魅力的源泉所在。

例 (12)：以后飞机接连光顾，大有绝世佳人一顾倾城，再顾倾国的风度。（钱钟书 《围城》）

译文：Later, the planes kept coming in much the same manner as the peerless beauty whose first glance could conquer a city and second glance could vanquish an empire*.

(Note: An expression which describes superlative beauty; it is equivalent to Helen of Troy in Western literature.)（珍妮·凯利、茅国权 译）

本例描写抗日战争时期日本飞机轰炸上海附近一个小城市的情况，以戏谑的口吻点出战争的严酷，体现了原文幽默、讽刺的风格。日本飞机被比作“绝世佳人”，飞机频频轰炸被比作“佳人的顾盼”，而它们的“光顾”使城市毁于一旦，无辜百姓遭殃。原文用表面上的轻松幽默抒发胸中的愤懑，这种风格要传译出来却非易事。译者把“绝世佳人”译作 peerless beauty，意在形成 peerless 和 glance 的联系，而且还加上注释 equivalent to Helen of Troy in Western literature，帮助译文读者理解原文的语用意义。这样，译者把汉语所表达的思维内容准确地用英语重新表达出来，译出了语言信息，也译出了原作的风格和神韵。

综上所述，小说翻译时要注意“传神达意”，较为准确地翻译小说的风格。应特别关注叙述语言、人物形象、修辞方法等几方面。

3.4 翻译实战：《生死疲劳》

【说明】参照“阅读欣赏”、“翻译热身”和小说翻译思路，将下列小说选段翻译为英语。

简介：《生死疲劳》是莫言的代表作之一，曾获得第二届红楼梦奖和第一届美国纽曼华语文学奖。小说讲述了一个被冤杀的地主西门闹经历了六道轮回，变成驴、牛、猪、狗、猴，最后终于又转生为一个患有不可治愈的先天性疾病的大头婴儿；他滔滔不绝地讲述着他身为畜生时的种种奇特感受，以及西门闹一家和农民蓝解放一家半个多世纪生死疲劳的悲欢故事。小说透过各种动物的眼睛，观照了 1950 年到 2000 年这五十多年来中国乡村社会的庞杂喧哗、充满苦难的蜕变历史。围绕着土地这个沉重的话题，阐释了农民与土地的种种关系，并透过生死轮回的艺术图像，展示了新中国成立以来中国农民的生活和他们顽强、乐观、坚韧的精神。

生死疲劳（节选）

莫言

第二章　西门闹行善救蓝脸　白迎春多情抚驴孤

那时候我可谓少年得志。连年丰收，佃户交租踊跃，粮仓里大囤满小囤流。六畜兴旺，家养的黑骡马竟然下了双驹。这可是奇迹，传说中有，现实中少见。来我家看双驹的乡民络绎不绝，恭维的话不绝于耳。家里准备了茉莉花茶和绿炮台烟卷招待乡亲。村里的半大小子黄瞳偷了一包烟卷，被人拧着耳朵拖到我面前。这小子黄头发黄面皮，黄眼珠子滴溜溜转，似乎满肚子坏心眼儿。我挥手放了他，还送他一包茶叶，让他带回家给他爹喝。他爹黄天发是忠厚老实人，做一手好豆腐，是我的佃户，种着我五亩靠河的肥田，想不到他竟生养出这么一个混混儿子。后来黄天发送来一挑子能用秤钩子挂起来的老豆腐，赔情的话说了两箩筐，我又让太太送他二尺青直贡呢，让他回家做双新鞋过年。黄瞳啊黄瞳，就冲着我跟你爹多少年的交情，你也不该用土枪崩了我啊。我自然知道你是听人之命，但你完全可以对准我的胸膛开枪，给我留下个囫囵尸身啊！你这忘恩负义的杂种啊！

我西门闹堂堂正正，豁达大度，人人敬仰。接手家业时虽逢乱世，既要应付游击队，又要应付黄皮子，但我的家业还是在几年内翻番增值，良田新置一百亩，大牲口由四匹变成八匹，新拴了一辆胶皮轱辘大车，长工由两人变成四人，丫环由一个变成两个，还新添了两个置办饭食的老妈子。就是在这样的情景之下，我从关帝庙前，把冻得只有一口游气的蓝脸抱了回来。那天我是早起捡粪，说来你不会相信，我虽是高密东北乡第一的大富户，但一直保持着劳动的习惯。三月扶犁，四月播种，五月割麦，六月栽瓜，七月锄豆，八月杀麻，九月掐谷，十月翻地，寒冬腊月里我也不恋热炕头，天麻麻亮就撅着个粪筐子去捡狗屎。乡间流传着我因起得太早错把石头当狗屎捡回来的笑话，那是他们胡说，我鼻子灵敏，大老远就能嗅到狗屎的气味。一个地主，如果对狗屎没有感情，算不上个好地主。

3.5 译文荟萃

1. 短语与术语翻译

长篇小说 full-length novel

中篇小说 novella

短篇小说 novelette/short story

惊险小说 fictional thriller

侦探小说 detective story

科幻小说 science fiction

惊险小说 horror fiction

书信体小说 epistolary novel

爱情小说 romance novel

人物 character

塑造人物形象 characterization

主人公 protagonist/hero/heroine

故事情节 plot

环境 settings

悬念 suspense

内心独白 soliloquy

2. 句子翻译

1) 他（赵辛嵋）身大而心不大，像个空心大萝卜。在小学里，他是同学们玩笑的目标，因为这样庞大的箭垛子，放冷箭没有不中的道理。（钱钟书 《围城》）

译文：In grade school he was the butt of his classmates' jokes; for with such a large target, no shot could ever miss the mark.

2) 开目四视，见席上双烛青焰莹莹，光缩如豆，毛骨悚然，通体寒栗。（沈复 《浮生六记》）

译文：I opened my eyes again and looked around and saw the two candle-lights burning low on the table as small as little peas. It gave me a goose-flesh and I shuddered all over.（林语堂 译）

3) 黛玉三步两步转过床后，出后院而去。（曹雪芹 《红楼梦》）

译文 1：She bounded round to the back of the bed, slipping into the rear courtyard.（霍克思 译）

译文 2：She slipped past his bed and out through the back court.（杨宪益、戴乃迭 译）

4) 宝玉听了，登时发作起痴狂病来，摘了那玉，就狠命摔去，骂道：……（曹雪芹 《红楼梦》第三回）

译文 1：This sent Bao-yu off instantly into one of his mad fits. Snatching the jade from the neck he hurled it violently on the floor as if to smash it and began abusing it passionately...（霍克思 译）

译文 2：This instantly threw Baoyu into one of his frenzies. Tearing off the jade he flung it on the ground... he stormed...（杨宪益、戴乃迭 译）

5) 她整日紧闭了嘴唇，头上带着大家以为耻辱的记号的那伤痕，默默的跑街，扫地，洗菜，淘米。（鲁迅 《祝福》）

译文：All day long she kept her lips tightly closed, bearing on her head the scar considered by everyone as a badge of shame, while she shopped, swept the floor, washed the vegetables and prepared the rice in silence.

6) 他一手擎着烟卷，一只手扶着酒杯，似笑非笑的向我说。（鲁迅 《在酒楼上》）

译文 1：He said with a wan smile, holding his cigarette aloft with one hand and grasping his winecup with the other.

译文 2：Holding his cigarette in one hand and the winecup in the other, he spoke with a bitter smile.

7) 沉默只一瞬间，癞头疮忽而发一声喊，拔步就跑；其余的也都笑着嚷着跑出去了。（《长明灯》）

译文 1：The silence lasts only an instant before it is broken by Scabby Scalp, who suddenly lets out a yell, breaks into a run, and heads for the gate. The other children run out too, shouting and laughing as they go.

译文 2：After a second's silence, Scabby Head rushed off with a shout, and laughing and shouting, the others raced after him.

8) 太太，我们见得多了：回头人出嫁，哭喊的也有，说要寻死觅活的也有，抬到男家闹得拜不成天地的也有，连花烛都砸了的也有。（鲁迅 《祝福》）

译文：We go-betweens see life, madam. Some widows sob and shout when they remarry; some threaten to kill themselves; some refuse to go through the ceremony of bowing to heaven and earth after they've been carried to the man's house; some even smash the wedding candlesticks.

9) 老栓也向那边看，却只见一堆人的后背；颈项都伸得很长，仿佛许多鸭，被无形的手捏住了的，向上提着。（鲁迅 《药》）

译文 1：Big-bolt also looks toward the intersection but can see nothing except the backs of the crowd.

Their necks are stretched out long, like ducks whose heads have been grabbed and pulled upward by an invisible hand.

译文 2：Old Shuan looked in that direction too, but could only see people's backs. Craning their necks as far as they would go, they looked like so many ducks, held and lifted by some invisible hand.

3. 段落翻译

1) 那时恰是暗夜，一队兵，一队团丁，一队警察，五个侦探，悄悄地到了未庄，乘昏暗围住土谷祠，正对门架好机关枪；然而阿 Q 不冲出。许多时没有动静，把总焦急起来了，悬了二十千的赏，才有两个团丁冒了险，逾墙进去，里应外合，一拥而入，将阿 Q 抓出来；直待擒出祠外面的机关枪附近，他才有些清醒了。（鲁迅 《阿 Q 正传》）

译文 1：It happened to be a dark night. A squad of soldiers, a squad of militia, a squad of police, and five secret servicemen made their way quietly to Weizhuang and, after posting a machine-gun opposite the entrance, under cover of darkness surrounded the Tutelary God's Temple. But Ah Q did not bolt for it. For a long time nothing stirred till the captain, losing patience, offered a reward of twenty thousand cash. Only then did two militiamen summon up courage to jump over the wall and enter. With their co-operation the others rushed in and dragged Ah Q out. But not until he had been carried out of the temple to somewhere near the machine-gun did he begin to wake up to what was happening.（杨宪益、戴乃迭 译）

译文 2：In the dark night a company of soldiers, a company of militia, a company of police, and five spies quietly made their way to Weizhuang and under cover of darkness, surrounded Tugu Temple. They put up a machine gun directly facing the door; but still Ah Q did not rush out. When there was no movement for a long time, the captain, being highly excited, offered a reward of twenty thousand dollars, and it was not until then that two of the local militia took the risk, climbed over the wall, and entered. Thus, working from within and from without, the whole mass crowded in and extracted Ah Q, but not until he had been dragged out of Tugu temple and brought near the machine gun did he become slightly awakened.

2) 阿 Q 又很自尊，所有未庄的居民，全不在他的眼睛里，甚而至于对于两位“文童”也有以为不值一笑的神情。夫文童者，将来恐怕要变秀才者也；赵太爷，钱太爷大受居民的尊敬，除有钱之外，就因为都是文童的爹爹，而阿 Q 在精神上独不表格外的崇奉，他想：我的儿子会阔得多啦！加以进了几回城，阿 Q 自然更自负，然而他又很鄙薄城里人，譬如用三尺长三寸宽的木板做成的凳子，未庄叫“长凳”，他也叫“长凳”，城里人却叫“条凳”，他想：这是错的，可笑！油煎大头鱼，未庄都加上半寸长的葱叶，城里却加上切细的葱丝，他想：这也是错的，可笑！然而未庄人真是不见世面的可笑的乡下人呵，他们没有见过城里的煎鱼！

译文：Since he thought so well of himself, Ah Q considered the other villagers simply beneath his notice. He went so far with this that he even looked down his nose at the village's two Young Literati. He didn't realize, of course, that up there in the rarefied world of scholar-officialdom those whom one doth Young Literati name can darn well get to be those whom one must Budding Talents proclaim — if you don't keep an eye on them. That's why Older Master Qian and Old Master Zhao were so all-fired respected in the village: they were daddies to those two Young Literati — and rich to boot. Ah Q, however, was less than impressed. "My son's gonna be a lot richer." On top of that, Ah Q had been to town a couple of times and that made him even more full of himself. Yet he could be contemptuous of townsfolk too. For instance, Wei Villagers called a seat made from a three-foot plank a longbench and so did Ah Q, but the townsfolk called it a stickbench. "That's not right, that's flatass dumb!" he thought to himself. And how about fish? When frying bigheads, Wei Villagers would toss chopped scallions into the pan, but the townsfolk always used shredded ones. "That's not right, that's flatass stupid!" he thought to himself. "On the other hand, I gotta remember that next to me, Wei Villagers are just a bunch of hicks. They've never even seen how bigheads are fried in town."（W. A. 莱尔　译）

4. 篇章选段翻译

简介：《三体》是刘慈欣创作的系列长篇科幻小说，由《三体》（2006 年 5 月起在《科幻世界》杂志上连载）、《三体Ⅱ·黑暗森林》（2008 年 5 月首次出版）、《三体Ⅲ·死神永生》（2010 年 11 月出版）组成。《三体》经过刘宇昆翻译后，于 2015 年获得了第 73 届雨果奖（Hugo Award）最佳长篇小说奖。《三体》讲述了地球人类文明和三体文明的信息交流、生死搏杀及两个文明在宇宙中的兴衰历程。

三　体（节选）

刘慈欣

两个质子

审问者：在宏观世界，两个质子就等于什么都没有——即使是一个细菌的一根毛发，也包含着几十亿个质子。这有什么意义？

叶文洁：它是一把锁。

审问者：锁？锁什么？

叶文洁：锁死人类的科学，在三体舰队到达前的四个半世纪，因为这两个质子的存在，人类的科学将不可能有任何重大进展。据传伊文斯说过这样的话：两个质子到达地球之日，就是人类科学死亡之时。

审问者：这未免太离奇了吧，怎么做到呢？

叶文洁：不知道，我真的不知道。在三体文明眼中，我们可能连野蛮人都算不上，只是一堆虫子。

汪淼和丁仪走出作战中心时已近午夜，他们刚刚监听了上面的对话。

"你相信叶文洁说的吗？"汪淼问。

"你呢，信吗？"

"最近有些事情确实太不可思议了，但，用两个质子锁死全人类的科学？这也……"

"首先注意一点：三体文明从半人马座三星向地球发射了两个质子，竟都到达了地球！从四光年外？这也瞄得太准了，漫长的途中有数不清的干扰，星际尘埃什么的，太阳系和地球都在运动中，这比从冥王星上开枪击中这里的一只蚊子都准确，真是个不可思议的射手。"

听到"射手"一词，汪淼的心不由紧了一下。"这说明什么？"

"不知道。在你的印象中，质子、中子和电子这样的微观粒子，是个什么样子？"

"几乎是一个点，当然这个点是有结构的。"

"很幸运，我印象中的图像比你要真实些。"丁仪说着，把手中抽尽的烟蒂扔向远处，"看那什么？"他指着落到地上的烟蒂问。

"香烟过滤嘴。"

"很好，从这个距离看那个小东西，是什么？"

"差不多也就是一个点。"

"对。"丁仪走过去把过滤嘴拾起来，在汪淼眼皮底下将它撕开，露出里面已由白变黄的海绵丝，汪淼闻到了一股焦油味。丁仪接着说，"你看，就这么个小玩意儿，它的吸附面积如果展开来，有一间客厅那么大。"他说着一扬手又将过滤嘴扔掉，"抽烟斗吗？"

"我什么烟都不抽了。"

"烟斗使用另一种更高级的过滤芯，三块钱一个，直径与香烟过滤嘴差不多，但比它长些，是一个装着活性炭的小纸筒，把里面的活性炭倒出来，也就是一小撮像老鼠屎似的黑炭粒，但它们内部微孔构成的吸附面积，展开来有一个网球场这么大，这就是活性炭具有超强吸附性的原因。"

"你想说什么？"汪淼很注意地听着。

"过滤嘴中的海绵或活性炭是三维体，它们的吸附面则是二维的，由此可见，一个微小的高维结构可以存贮何等巨量的低维结构。但在宏观世界，高维空间对低维空间的容纳也就到此为止了，因为上帝很吝啬，在创世大爆炸中只给了宏观宇宙三个维度。但这不等于更高的维度不存在，有多达八个维度被禁锢在微观中，加上宏观的三维，在基本粒子中，存在着十一维的空间。"

"那又如何？"

"我只想说明以下的事实：在宇宙间，一个技术文明等级的重要标志，是它能够控制和使用的微观维度。对于基本粒子的一线使用，从我们那些长毛裸体的祖先在山洞中生起篝火时就开始了，对化学反应的控制，就是在一维层次上操控微观粒子。当然，这种控制也是从低级到高级，从篝火到后来的蒸汽机，再到后来的发电机；现在，人类对微观粒子一维控制的水平已达到了顶峰，有了计算机，也有了你们的纳米材料。但这一切，都局限于对微观维度的一维控制，在宇宙间一个更高级的文明看来，篝火和计算机、纳米材料等等是没有本质区别的，同属于一个层次，这也是他们仍将人类看成虫子的原因——遗憾的是，他们是对的。”

Two Protons

Interrogator: At the macroscopic level, two protons are nothing. Even a single cilium on a bacterium would include several billion protons. What's the point?

Ye: They're a lock.

Interrogator: A lock? What are they locking?

Ye: They are sealing off the progress of human science. Because of the existence of these two protons, humanity will not be able to make any important scientific developments during the four and a half centuries until the arrival of the Trisolaran Fleet. Evans once said that the day of arrival of the two protons was also the day that human science died.

Interrogator: That's too fantastic. How can that be?

Ye: I don't know. I really don't know. In the eyes of Trisolaran civilization, we're probably not even primitive savages. We might be mere bugs.

It was near midnight by the time Wang Miao and Ding Yi walked out of the Battle Command Center. They had been invited to listen to Ye's interrogation due to Wang's involvement in the case and Ding Ye's connection to Ye's daughter.

"Do you believe what Ye Wenjie said?" Wang asked.

"Do you?"

"Many things that have happened recently are incredible. But for two protons to block all progress of human science? That seems..."

"Let's focus on one thing first. The Trisolarans were able to shoot two protons at the Earth from four light-years away and they both reached the target! That accuracy is incredible! There are numerous obstacles between there and here: interstellar dust, for example. And both the solar system and the Earth are moving. It would require more precision than shooting a mosquito here from Pluto. The shooter is beyond imagination."

Wang's heart clenched when he heard "shooter." "What do you think this means?"

"I don't know. In your impression, what do subatomic particles such as neutrons and protons look like?"

"They would just look like a point. Though the point has internal structure."

"Luckily, the image in my head is more realistic than yours." As Ding spoke, he tossed his cigarette butt away. "What do you think that is?" He pointed at the butt.

"A cigarette filter."

"Good. Looking at that tiny thing from this distance, how would you describe it?"

"It's practically just a point."

"Right." Ding walked over and picked up the butt. In front of Wang's eyes he tore it open and revealed the yellowed spongy material inside. Wang smelled burnt tar. Ding continued, "Look, if you spread this little thing open, the adsorbent surface area can be as large as a living room." He tossed the filter away. "Do you smoke pipes?"

"I no longer smoke anything."

"Pipes use another type of more advanced filter. You can get one for three yuan. The diameter is about the same as a cigarette filter, but it's longer: a small paper tube filled with active charcoal. If you take out all the active charcoal, it will look like a little pile of black particles, like mouse droppings. But added together, the adsorbent surface formed by the tiny holes inside is as large as a tennis court. This is why active charcoal is so adsorbent."

"What are you trying to say?" Wang asked, listening intently.

"The sponge or active charcoal inside a filter is three-dimensional. Their adsorbent surfaces, however, are two-dimensional. Thus, you can see how a tiny high-dimensional structure can contain a huge low-dimensional structure. But at the macroscopic level, this is about the limit of the ability for high-dimensional space to contain low-dimensional space. Because God was stingy, during the Big Bang He only provided the macroscopic world with three spatial dimensions, plus the dimension of time. But this doesn't mean that higher dimensions don't exist. Up to seven additional dimensions are locked within the micro scale, or, more precisely, within the quantum realm. And added to the four dimensions at the macro scale, fundamental particles exist within an eleven-dimensional space-time."

"So what?"

"I just want to point out this fact: In the universe, an important mark of a civilization's technological advancement is its ability to control and make use of micro dimensions. Making use of fundamental particles without taking advantage of the micro dimensions is something that our naked, hairy ancestors already began back when they lit bonfires within caves. Controlling chemical reactions is just manipulating micro particles without regard to the micro dimensions. Of course, this control also progressed from crude to advanced: from bonfires to steam engines, and then generators. Now, the ability for humans to manipulate micro particles at the macro level has reached a peak: We have computers and nanomaterials. But all of that is accomplished without unlocking the many micro dimensions. From the perspective of a more advanced civilization in the universe, bonfires and computers and nanomaterials are not fundamentally different. They all belong to the same level. That's also why they still think of humans as mere bugs. Unfortunately, I think they're right."（刘宇昆　译）

3.6 翻译家：葛浩文

葛浩文（Howard Goldblatt）是美国圣母大学亚洲研究中心教授，从事中国文学、文化研究教学 30 多年。葛浩文 1961 年于美国长滩州立大学本科毕业，20 世纪 60 年代在中国台湾地区服役期间学习了汉语，1971 年于旧金山州立大学硕士毕业，1974 年于印第安纳大学博士毕业。

葛浩文是美国当代著名的翻译家，一生致力于翻译中国文学，其翻译出版的第一部中国小说是张洁的《沉重的翅膀》，并荣获第二届茅盾文学奖，深受鼓舞。随后 30 多年来，葛浩文先后将萧红、陈若曦、白先勇、李昂、张洁、杨绛、冯骥才、古华、贾平凹、辛锐、刘恒、苏童、老鬼、王朔、莫言、虹影、阿来、朱天文、朱天心、姜戎等 20 几位中国现当代最著名作家及其 50 多部中国现当代文学作品推向了海外。葛浩文翻译中国作品多，涉及作家广，翻译风格多样，已经成了海外汉学界最重要的翻译家，为中国文学在海外的传播和影响做出了不可估量的贡献。

葛浩文是翻译莫言作品最多的英语译者。他陆续将莫言的《红高粱》《红高粱家族》《天堂蒜薹之歌》《酒国》《师傅越来越幽默》《丰乳肥臀》《生死疲劳》等作品带入西方世界。经由其译笔走向世界的中国作家莫言，终于在 2012 年 10 月 12 日荣获全球瞩目的诺贝尔文学奖。此后，葛浩文又翻译、出版了莫言的小说《四十一炮》和《檀香刑》。

葛浩文不仅译品数量众多、选材精准，而且翻译功力深厚、文学性强。他每推出一部新译，都能在报刊媒体上引起众多关注、评论和赞誉。因为其巨大的翻译贡献，葛浩文先后获得美国文学翻译家协会"年度翻译奖"(National Translation Award)、"古根海姆基金"(Guggenheim Fellowship)、"中华图书特殊贡献奖"等荣誉。经其翻译的作品也多次斩获"曼氏亚洲文学奖"(Man Asian Literary Prize)、"纽曼华语文学奖"(Newman Prize for Chinese Literature) 等奖项。

葛浩文认为："我并不认为翻译是一种次要的艺术，我热爱翻译。我喜欢读中文，我喜欢用英语写作。我热爱这个事业的挑战性、模糊性及不确定性。""我做翻译就是这样，一定要不停地翻，一旦没事干，没货了，没有小说翻了，恐怕就要归西了。"葛浩文多年来笔耕不辍的翻译，让众多西方读者了解了中国当代的社会生活状况，为中国文学走向世界，促进不同文化之间的交流搭起了

一座桥梁。他在翻译活动中始终保持谨慎的态度。对他来说，翻译永远意味着“未完成”，他对自己的译稿总是不满意，通常都会修改四五遍以上才定稿。在翻译前，他还会花很多时间搜集关于原作的资料及相关评论。翻译时，他会与原作者通信或打电话，就原作中的文字难点、文化背景、富有地方色彩的表达等提问。他不辞劳苦，绞尽脑汁，一字一句煞费苦心。在翻译《北京娃娃》时，小说中有一段高中“礼仪口诀”，全是四字押韵:“坐姿端正，两腿莫翘，站立挺拔，收腹立腰”之类，葛先生反复推敲，力图翻译成同样整齐押韵的英文短语。细微之处，他都能仔细琢磨，其严肃认真的态度可见一斑。正如他自己所言:“我葛浩文做翻译一点也不马虎。我不马虎的。”

在葛浩文看来，在翻译这一跨文化交流活动中，译者要履行“人类精神的使者”这一身份赋予他们的职责，促进文化之间的交流。在《我为什么痛恨韦利》(“Why I Hate Arthur Waley”)一文中，他批评韦利一味讨好目的语读者，使翻译起不到促进文化交流的作用。他指出，翻译的作用之一，是要从外来文化引进新的想法，而新的想法必须靠新的语言来表达。如果一味地用熟悉的语句替换陌生概念，则将永远在旧思维里打转。

对于翻译中的原作和译作的关系问题，葛浩文认为:“我喜欢既要创作，又要忠实，甚至两者之间不可避免的折中。”即翻译不仅要求译者的“忠实”，又要求他们的“创造”，译者需要很好地处理两者的关系。在《狼图腾》英文版首发仪式上葛浩文把作家比作鱼，译者是虾，认为虾是配角。他提出，译者“必须尊重原著”，他们“最大的导师就是文本”。为了在最大限度上不偏离原文作者的意图，翻译中遇到的疑问，葛先生都会尽力与作家联系，进行沟通。

葛浩文认为，原文词汇进入译文后可以得到更为丰富的表述。比如“磕头”的翻译。他说虽然 kowtow 一词已进入英语词汇，但“磕头”这一动作所表达的或尊敬或惧怕或悔恨或感激等微妙的心理是西方读者所不易捕捉的，这就要求译者细心揣摩其中暗含的意味加以准确处理，而不能一概简单地译作 kowtow。又如阿来的《尘埃落定》中经常出现的一个感叹词“天哪”。从字面上看，英语中同“天哪”意思接近的词应该是 Heavens，但把所有的“天哪”统统翻成 Heavens 显然不能保证每一处都贴切。因此，他将不同人物口中的“天哪”翻译成不同词汇，如 Aicaramba、Achdulieber、Mamamia、Oy gevalt、Merde。在他看来，这些非英语感叹词要比 Heavens 来得更传神。这一手段看似不忠，实则使原文语言的意义在新的文化语境里获得重生，达到另一层次的忠实。

3.7 补充资源

参考书目

老舍等. 中国现代名家短篇小说选（汉英对照）. 沙博理等，译. 北京：外文出版社，2002.
鲁迅. 鲁迅小说选（汉英对照）. 杨宪益，戴乃迭，译. 北京：外文出版社，2000.
沈从文. 边城（插图本，新版）. 杨宪益，戴乃迭，译. 南京：译林出版社，2017.
鲁迅. 阿 Q 正传（中英对照版）. 杨宪益，戴乃迭，译. 香港：香港中文大学出版社，2002.
辛红娟. 文学翻译读本. 南京：南京大学出版社，2012.
胡谷明. 篇章修辞与小说翻译. 上海：上海译文出版社，2004.
张保红. 文学翻译. 北京：外语教学与研究出版社，2010.
胡显耀，李力. 高级文学翻译. 北京：外语教学与研究出版社，2009.
魏清光. 汉英翻译教程（文学篇）. 北京：外文出版社，2008.

网络资源

中国现代文学研究网：http://www.modernchineseliterature.net/

http://www.timeoutbeijing.com/features/Books_Film-Book_Features/36426/The-best-Chinese-fiction-books-of-the-last-century.html

中国汉英平行语料库大世界：http://corpus.usx.edu.cn/

BCC 汉英对照语料库：http://bcc.blcu.edu.cn/bi/cid/31

英译小说网：https://www.novelall.com

第四单元　中国古代小说

4.1 阅读欣赏：《聊斋志异》

【说明】 阅读下列小说原文及译文，体会中国古代小说的文体特点及翻译思路。

简介：《聊斋志异》是中国清朝著名小说家蒲松龄创作的文言短篇小说集。《聊斋志异》的意思是在书房里记录奇异的故事。全书共有短篇小说490多篇。它们或者揭露封建统治的黑暗，或者抨击科举制度的腐朽，或者反抗封建礼教的束缚，具有丰富深刻的思想内容。

聊斋志异（节选）

蒲松龄

崂山道士

邑有王生，行七，故家子。少慕道，闻崂山多仙人，负笈往游。登一顶，有观宇，甚幽。一道士坐蒲团上，素发垂领，而神观爽迈。叩而与语，理甚玄妙。请师之。道士曰："恐娇惰不能作苦。"答言："能之。"其门人甚众，薄暮毕集。王俱与稽首，遂留观中。

凌晨，道士呼王去，授以斧，使随众采樵。王谨受教。过月馀，手足重茧，不堪其苦，阴有归志。

一夕归，见二人与师共酌，日已暮，尚无灯烛。师乃剪纸如镜，粘壁间。俄顷，月明辉室，光鉴毫芒。诸门人环听奔走。一客曰："良宵胜乐，不可不同。"乃于案上取壶酒，分赉诸徒，且嘱尽醉。王自思：七八人，壶酒何能遍给？遂各觅盎盂，竞饮先釂，惟恐樽尽；而往复挹注，竟不少减。心奇之。俄一客曰："蒙赐月明之照，乃尔寂饮。何不呼嫦娥来？"乃以箸掷月中。见一美人，自光中出，初不盈尺；至地，遂与人等。纤腰秀项，翩翩作“霓裳舞”。已而歌曰：“仙仙乎，而还乎，而幽我于广寒乎！”其声清越，烈如箫管。歌毕，盘旋而起，跃登几上，惊顾之间，已复为箸。三人大笑。又一客曰：“今宵最乐，然不胜酒力矣。其饯我于月宫可乎？”三人移席，渐入月中。众视三人，坐月中饮，须眉毕见，如影之在镜中。移时，月渐暗；门人然烛来，则道士独坐而客杳矣。几上肴核尚故。壁上月，纸圆如镜而已。道士问众：“饮足乎？”曰：“足矣。”“足宜早寝，勿误樵苏。”众诺而退。王窃忻慕，归念遂息。

又一月，苦不可忍，而道士并不传教一术。心不能待，辞曰：“弟子数百里受业仙师，纵不能得长生术，或小有传习，亦可慰求教之心；今阅两三月，不过早樵而暮归。弟子在家，未谙此苦。”道士笑曰：“我固谓不能作苦，今果然。明早当遣汝行。”王曰：“弟子操作多日，师略授小技，此来为不负也。”道士问：“何术之求。”王曰：“每见师行处，墙壁所不能隔，但得此法足矣。”道士笑而允之。乃传以诀，令自咒毕，呼曰：“入之！”王面墙不敢入。又曰：“试入之。”王果从容入，及墙而阻。道士曰：“俯首骤入，勿逡巡！”王果去墙数步，奔而入；及墙，虚若无物；回视，果在墙外矣。大喜，入谢。道士曰：“归宜洁持，否则不验。”遂助资斧遣之归。

抵家，自诩遇仙，坚壁所不能阻。妻不信。王效其作为，去墙数尺，奔而入，头触硬壁，蓦然而踣。妻扶视之，额上坟起，如巨卵焉。妻揶揄之。王惭忿，骂老道士之无良而已。

The Taoist Priest of Lao-Shan

There lived in our village a Mr. Wang, the seventh son in an old family. This gentleman had a penchant for the Taoist religion; and hearing that at Lao-shan there were plenty of Immortals, he shouldered his knapsack and went off for a tour thither. Ascending a peak of the mountain he reached a secluded monastery, where he found a priest sitting on a rush mat, with long hair flowing over his neck, and a pleasant expression on his face. Making a low bow, Wang addressed him thus: “Mysterious indeed is the doctrine: I pray you, Sir, instruct me therein.” “Delicately nurtured and wanting in energy as you are,” replied the priest, “I fear you could not support the fatigue.” “Try me,” said Wang. So when the disciples, who were very many in number, collected together at dusk, Wang joined them in making obeisance to the priest, and remained with them in the monastery.

Very early next morning the priest summoned Wang, and giving him a hatchet sent him out with the others to cut firewood. Wang respectfully obeyed, continuing to work for over a month until his hands and feet were so swollen and blistered that he secretly meditated returning home.

One evening when he came back he found two strangers sitting drinking with his master. It being already dark, and no lamp or candles having been brought in, the old priest took some scissors and cut out a circular piece of paper like a mirror, which he proceeded to stick against the wall. Immediately it became a dazzling moon, by the light of which you could have seen a hair or a beard of com.

The disciples all came crowding round to wait upon them, but one of the strangers said, “On a festive occasion like this we ought ail to enjoy ourselves together.” Accordingly he took a kettle of wine from the table and presented it to the disciples, bidding them drink each his fill; whereupon our friend Wang began to wonder how seven or eight of them could all be served out of a single kettle. The disciples, too, rushed about in search of cups, each struggling to get the first drink for fear the wine should be exhausted. Nevertheless, all the candidates failed to empty the kettle, at which they were very much astonished, when suddenly one of the strangers said, “You have given us a fine bright moon; but it's dull work drinking by ourselves. Why not call Ch‘ang-ngo to join us?” He then seized a chopstick and threw it into the moon, whereupon a lovely girl stepped forth from its beams. At first she was only a foot high, but on reaching the ground lengthened to the ordinary size of woman. She had a slender waist and a beautiful neck, and went most gracefully through the Red Garment figure. When this was finished she sang the following words:

“Ye fairies! Ye fairies! I'm coming back soon,

Too lonely and cold is my home in the moon.”

Her voice was clear and well sustained, ringing like the notes of a flageolet, and when she had concluded her song she pirouetted round and jumped up on the table, where, with every eye fixed in astonishment upon her, she once more became a chopstick.

The three friends laughed loudly, and one of them said, “We are very jolly tonight, but I have hardly room for any more wine. Will you drink a parting glass with me in the palace of the moon?” They then took up the table and walked into the moon, where they could be seen drinking so plainly that their eyebrows and beards appeared like reflections in a looking-glass. By-and-by the moon became obscured; and when the disciples brought a lighted candle they found the priest sitting in the dark alone. The viands, however, were still upon the table and the mirror-like piece of paper on the wall. “Have you all had enough to drink?” asked the priest; to which they answered that they had. “In that case,” said he, “you had better get to bed, so as not to be behind-hand with your wood-cutting in the morning.” So they all went off, and among them Wang, who was delighted at what he had seen, and thought no more of returning home.

But after a time he could not stand it any longer; and as the priest taught him no magical arts he determined not to wait, but went to him and said, “Sir, I have travelled many long miles for the benefit of your instruction. If you will not teach me the secret of Immortality, let me at any rate learn some trifling trick, and thus soothe my cravings for a knowledge of your art. I have now been here two or three months, doing nothing but chop firewood, out in the morning and back at night, work to which I was never accustomed in my own home.” “Did I not tell you,” replied the priest, “that you would never support the fatigue? Tomorrow I will start you on your way home." "Sir," said Wang, "I have worked for you a long time. Teach me some small art, that my coming here may not have been wholly in vain." "What art?" asked the priest. "Well," answered Wang, "I have noticed that whenever you walk about anywhere, walls and so on are no obstacle to you. Teach me this, and I'll be satisfied." The priest laughingly assented, and taught Wang a formula which he bade him recite. When he had done so he told him to walk through the wall; but Wang, seeing the wall in front of him, didn't like to walk at it. As, however, the priest bade him try, he walked quietly up to it and was there stopped. The priest here called out, "Don't go so slowly. Put your head down and rush at it." So Wang stepped back a few paces and went at it full speed; and the wall yielding to him as he passed, in a moment he found himself outside. Delighted at this, he went in to thank the priest, who told him to be careful in the use of his power, or otherwise there would be no response, handing him at the same time some money for his expenses on the way.

When Wang got home, he went about bragging of his Taoist friends and his contempt for walls in general; but as his wife disbelieved his story, he set about going through the performance as before. Stepping back from the wall, he rushed at it full speed with his head down; but coming in contact with the hard bricks, finished up in a heap on the floor. His wife picked him up and found he had a bump on his forehead as big as a large egg, at which she roared with laughter; but Wang was overwhelmed with rage and shame, and cursed the old priest for his base ingratitude. (Herbert A. Giles 译)

4.2 翻译热身:《三国演义》

【说明】 参照“阅读欣赏”的译文思路，将下列小说选段翻译为英语。

简介:《三国演义》是中国古典四大名著之一，中国第一部长篇章回体历史演义小说，作者为元末明初的小说家罗贯中。《三国演义》描写了从东汉末年到西晋初年之间近百年的历史风云，以描写战争为主，展示了一幅东汉末年的群雄割据混战的历史画卷，描绘了魏、蜀、吴三国之间的政治、军事斗争，司马炎最终一统三国，建立晋朝的故事。小说反映了三国时代各类社会斗争与矛盾，并概括了这一时代的历史巨变，塑造了一群叱咤风云的三国英雄人物。全书可大致分为黄巾起义、董卓之乱、群雄逐鹿、三国鼎立、三国归晋五大部分。《三国演义》在世界广为翻译和传播。

三国演义（节选）

罗贯中

第一回　宴桃园豪杰三结义　斩黄巾英雄首立功

那人不甚好读书；性宽和，寡言语，喜怒不形于色；素有大志，专好结交天下豪杰；生得身长七尺五寸，两耳垂肩，双手过膝，目能自顾其耳，面如冠玉，唇若涂脂；中山靖王刘胜之后，汉景帝阁下玄孙：姓刘，名备，字玄德。昔刘胜之子刘贞，汉武时封涿鹿亭侯，后坐酎金失侯，因此遗这一枝在涿县。玄德祖刘雄，父刘弘。弘曾举孝廉，亦尝作吏，早丧。玄德幼孤，事母至孝；家贫，贩屦织席为业。家住本县楼桑村。其家之东南，有一大桑树，高五丈余，遥望之，童童如车盖。相者云："此家必出贵人。"玄德幼时，与乡中小儿戏于树下，曰："我为天子，当乘此车盖。"叔父刘元起奇其言，曰："此儿非常人也！"因见玄德家贫，常资给之。年十五岁，母使游学，尝师事郑玄、卢植，与公孙瓒等为友。及刘焉发榜招军时，玄德年已二十八岁矣。

当日见了榜文，慨然长叹。随后一人厉声言曰："大丈夫不与国家出力，何故长叹？"玄德回视其人：身长八尺，豹头环眼，燕颔虎须，声若巨雷，势如奔马。玄德见他形貌异常，问其姓名。其人曰："某姓张，名飞，字翼德。世居涿郡，颇有庄田，卖酒屠猪，专好结交天下豪杰。恰才见公看榜而叹，故此相问。"玄德曰："我本汉室宗亲，姓刘，名备。今闻黄巾倡乱，有志欲破贼安民;恨力不能，故长叹耳。"飞曰："吾颇有资财，当招募乡勇，与公同举大事，如何？"玄德甚喜，遂与同入村店中饮酒。正饮间，见一大汉，推着一辆车子，到店门首歇了；入店坐下，便唤酒保："快斟酒来吃，我待赶入城去投军。"玄德看其人：身长九尺，髯长二尺；面如重枣，唇若涂脂；丹凤眼，卧蚕眉：相貌堂堂，威风凛凛。玄德就邀他同坐，叩其姓名。其人曰："吾姓关，名羽，字长生，后改云长，河东解良人也。因本处势豪倚势凌人，被吾杀了；逃难江湖，五六年矣。今闻此处招军破贼，特来应募。"玄德遂以己志告之。云长大喜。同到张飞庄上，共议大事。

4.3 翻译技巧：汉语无主句和流水句的翻译

4.3.1 汉语无主句的翻译

汉语的无主句是指只有谓语部分，没有主语部分的句子。无主句，并非是主语省略，而是句子按约定俗成不出现主语，或者是无须主语句子的意义也一样完整。无主句在汉语成语、口语中大量出现，是汉语所特有的句型。可是，英语句子大都有主语。因此，翻译汉语无主句时，为了符合英语语法的规范，可采用以下几种方法。

(一) 补充主语

汉语中有些无主句泛指性很强，类似警句格言，大多数不用主语，然而译成英文时却需要补上适当的主语，以符合英文的表达习惯，照顾英语重形合的特点。所补充主语多为泛指代词或名词（we, one, you）。有些情况下，为了增强表现力，也可以采用非人称主语。

例 (1)：不入虎穴，焉得虎子。

How can you catch tiger cubs without entering the tiger's den?

例 (2)：别和他说话才好。若和他说话，不是呆话，就是疯话。（曹雪芹 《红楼梦》）

We mustn't talk to him. If we do, he talks like a fool or a lunatic.（杨宪益、戴乃迭 译）

例 (3)：勤俭持家，修桥补路，乐善好施。（莫言 《生死疲劳》）

I was a good and thrifty family man. I repaired bridges and roads and was charitable to all.（Howard Goldblatt 译）

例 (4)：卵石上粘着一缕缕布条和肮脏的毛发，散发着浓重的血腥。（莫言 《生死疲劳》）

Dirty clumps of hair and strips of cloth sticking to the stones gave off a disagreeable blood stench.

例 (5)：少欲无为，身心自在。（莫言 《生死疲劳》）

Few desires and inaction bring peace to the mind.（Howard Goldblatt 译）

例 (6)：在咀嚼中，在吞咽中，又使我体验到了一种纯驴的快乐。（莫言 《生死疲劳》）

The chewing and swallowing imbue me with an unadulterated sense of donkey delight.（Howard Goldblatt 译）

例 (7)：连夜雨雪，一点星光都看不见。

It had been snowing all night, not a single star in sight.

例 (8)：不经一事，不长一智。

译文 1：You can't gain knowledge without practice.

译文 2：Wisdom comes from experience.

(二) 译成被动句

某些表示事物存在、出现，表示要求、规定的无主句，可以译成被动句。如果没有必要交代动作的发出者，或者没有办法指明动作的发出者，或者为了强调动作的接受者，通常可以译成被动句。

例 (9)：封面上印着一个猎人的像。

The figure of a hunter was printed on the cover of the book.

例 (10)：屋内悄无一人，只听见钟在滴答滴答地走。

No one was in the room, only the ticking of a clock could be heard.

例 (11)：一时间，我家院子里六畜兴旺，人头攒动，一派热闹景象。（莫言 《生死疲劳》）

Within minutes, the yard was filled with farm animals and the bobbing heads of their owners, bringing the place alive.（Howard Goldblatt 译）

例 (12)： 要开发中国广阔的西部地区，需要处理好经济发展和人口控制的关系。

译文 1： The relationship between the economic growth and population control should be handled properly to develop the vast western areas in China.（被动句）

译文 2： To develop the vast western areas in China, we should handle properly the relationship between the economic growth and population control.（增添主语）

（三）译成 there be 结构

例 (13)： 无水则无鱼。

Without water there would be no fish.

例 (14)： 那天下了很大的雪，房屋、树木、街道都被遮盖，白茫茫一片。（莫言《生死疲劳》）

There was so much snow that the buildings, trees, and streets were buried, nothing but white.（Howard Goldblatt 译）

例 (15)： 黎明时分，有众多奇异现象，不早起何能看到？（莫言《生死疲劳》）

At that early hour, there were all sorts of strange and mysterious rarities — the only way you could see them is to get up early.（Howard Goldblatt 译）

（四）译为倒装句

例 (16)： 在游廊的最左端，靠近一道门，却坐有一位将近三十岁的男子。

Close by a door at the extreme left of the veranda sat a man of about thirty.

例 (17)： 街角躺着一个病得很重的老人。

There lies at the corner of the street an old man who is seriously ill.

例 (18)： 从远处偶尔传来枪声。

From the distance came occasional shots.

例 (19)： 随着一声吼叫，呼地从树林里窜出一只狮子来。

Following the roar, out rushed a lion from among the bushes.

例 (20)： 只有承认多样性，才有利于全人类的发展和进步。

Only by recognizing this diversity can we help promote the development and progress of mankind.

例 (21)： 在船边，离他头很近，开着几朵紫色的水莲。

Just outside the port-hole and very close to his head bloomed many purple lilies.

（五）译成祈使句

当汉语无主句表示请求、命令、号召、口号等时，可采取英语祈使句译出。

例 (22)： 以其人之道，还治其人之身。

Deal with a man as he deals with you.

例 (23)： 为建设一个现代化的社会主义强国而奋斗。

Strive to build a modern powerful socialist country!

例 (24)： 不要攀折花木。

Don't pick the flowers.

例 (25)："去取驴血来啊！"（莫言 《生死疲劳》）

"Go get some donkey blood."（Howard Goldblatt 译）

例 (26)：不要再单干，不要闹独立，不要顽固不化，不要充当挡路的石头。（莫言 《生死疲劳》）

Stop working for yourself; end your quest for independence. Stop being head-strong, an obstructionist.（Howard Goldblatt 译）

（六）译成"it + be...+ to"结构

例 (27)： 在当今社会上，学好英语十分重要。

It is extremely important to have a good command of English in society today.

例 (28)： 要促进不同文明对话，推动解决贫困落后、社会不公等问题，消除恐怖主义产生的根源。

It is essential to promote inter-civilization dialogue, earnestly tackle such problems as poverty, backwardness and social injustice, and remove the soil that breeds terrorism.

4.3.2 汉语流水句的翻译

在翻译汉语的小句、短句、流水句时，往往需要重构其逻辑关系，利用英语的从属结构，使之符合英文多繁复的特点。在具体翻译过程中，可以采用以下步骤：首先，补充省略部分，重建逻辑关系；其次，分译为汉语小句或者短语；最后，调整从属结构，优化句子结构。

例 (1)： 须臾茶毕，早已设下杯盘，那美酒佳肴自不必说。（曹雪芹 《红楼梦》）

Soon they had finished their tea and sat down to a collection of choice wine and delicacies.（杨宪益、戴乃迭 译）

本例中，各小句有一定的联系，第一句和第二句存在时间先后次序，第三句可理解为对第二句的说明。翻译时，如果依照原文顺序逐次译出，就会显得语义较散，上下文不连贯。译文彻底打破了原句的结构，沿用上文的主语 they，将主语统一，这样上下文连贯，句式紧凑。

例 (2)： 到了济南府，进得城来，家家泉水，户户垂柳，比那江南风景，觉得更为有趣。（刘鹗 《老残游记》）

When he reached Jinan and entered the city, there were flowing streams by every house and willow trees by every door, which delighted him even more than the sceneary of the south.（杨宪益、戴乃迭 译）

原文 5 个小句，其中较多零句，有的缺少主语，有的缺少宾语。补充如下：①（他）到了济南府；②（他）进得城来；③家家泉水；④户户垂柳；⑤比那江南风景，（他）觉得（济南府的风景）更为有趣。可以分译为：① He reached Jinan, ② He entered the city of Jinan, ③ Streams are flowing by every house, ④ Willows are standing by every door, ⑤ He found out that the sceneary of Jinan is more interesting and beautiful than that of the South。然后根据英语多长句，多从属结构的特点，该句可以调整优化。

例 (3)：那十一个厢禁军，担子又重，无有一个稍轻，天气热了行不得，见着林子，便要去歇息。杨志赶着催促要行。如若停住，轻则痛骂，重则藤条鞭打，逼赶要行。（施耐庵 《水浒传》）

The eleven guards were all carrying heavy loads and the weather was hot. Walking was a severe effort. Whenever they saw a grove they wanted to rest, but Yang Zhi drove them on. If they halted, the least he did was curse them, and often he flogged them with his switch, forcing them to continue.

本例中有 3 个句子，前后两个都是流水句。译文采取了拆句翻译的方法，较为逼真地反映了原文的节奏感。同时，根据英文重形合的特点，补充了句内的主语和句间的连词。

例 (4)：当时街坊上家家箫管，户户弦歌，当头一轮明月，飞彩凝辉，二人愈添豪兴，酒到杯干。（曹雪芹 《红楼梦》）

The sound of flutes and strings could be heard from all the houses in the neighborhood; everywhere was singing; and overhead the bright moon shone in full splendor. The two men became very merry and drained cup after cup.（杨宪益、戴乃迭 译）

此例中各小句之间语义比较松散，无法找到一个统领 4 个小句的 S-V 结构，译者将其断为四个小句按原文的顺序译出，各小句都有自己的 S-V 结构，意义得以准确传达。毕竟，这样的句子在英语中不多见，而且各小句多为简单句，主语转换频繁，语势上不连贯。

例 (5)：譬如说，当我们正在旅游胜地享受假期，却忽然接到老板的电话，告诉我们客户或工作方面出了麻烦——现代便捷先进工具在此刻显示出了它狰狞、阴郁的面容——搞得人一下子兴趣全无，接下来的休闲只能徒有其表，因为心里已是火烧火燎了。

For example, during our vacation at a scenic spot, we get informed of troubles with our clients or in the workplace via a sudden call from the boss. At that moment, viciousness and gloom find expression in the modern, convenient and advanced devices. This ruined our good mood right away and we can't enjoy the sightseeing at all because we have become very distracted and anxious.

原文有 5 个小句，为典型的流水句式。其主要分句如下：①当我们正在旅游胜地享受假期；②（我们）却忽然接到老板的电话；③（老板）告诉我们客户或工作方面出了麻烦；④现代便捷先进的工具在此刻显示出了它狰狞、阴郁的面容；⑤（这种情况）搞得人一下子兴趣全无；⑥接下来（我们）的休闲只能徒有其表；⑦因为（我们）心里已是火烧火燎了。可以分译为① When we are spending our vacation in a scenic spot, ② We receive a sudden phone call from out boss, ③ a sudden call from the boss informs us of the troubles with our clients or in the workplace, ④ At that moment, the modern, convenient and advanced devices show their viciousness and gloom appearance, ⑤ This makes us lose our interest in sightseeing, ⑥ during the rest of time, we cannot enjoy the tour at all, ⑦ because we are irritated and frustrated。随后，恰当运用英语形合手段按语义层次进行结构重组，能使译文符合英语聚集型句式的特点。

例 (6)： 忽信步至一山环水旋、茂林深竹之处，隐隐的有座庙宇，门巷倾颓，墙垣朽败，门前有额，题着“智通寺”三字，门旁有一副旧破的对联，曰……（曹雪芹 《红楼梦》）

He came to luxuriant woods and bamboo groves set among hills and interlaced by streams, with a temple half hidden among the foliage. The entrance was in ruins, the walls were crumbling. A placard above the gate bore the inscription: Temple of Perspicacity. And flanking the gate were two mouldering boards with the couplet...（杨宪益、戴乃迭 译）

本例中，译者使用了三种翻译方法。首先，按原序译成英语中的独立句，增加必要的连接词，如 and 等。其次，将小句“山环水旋”译为分词短语，用以修饰 woods and bamboo groves。还有，译者用介词短语 with a temple half hidden among the foliage 来译“隐隐的有座庙宇”，挂靠在第一个小句上，精练传神。

4.4 翻译实战：《水浒传》

【说明】 参照“阅读欣赏”、“翻译热身”和小说翻译思路，将下列小说选段翻译为英语。

简介：《水浒传》是中国四大名著之一，小说描写了北宋末年朝政腐败，官府无道，民不聊生，许多正直善良的人被迫奋起反抗，最终 108 位好汉在梁山聚义，但随后宋江对朝廷的投降使得一场轰轰烈烈的农民起义走向失败的故事。全书以农民起义的发生、发展过程为主线，通过各个英雄被逼上梁山的不同经历，描写出他们由个体觉醒到走上小规模联合反抗，到发展为盛大的农民起义队伍的全过程。小说塑造了农民起义领袖的群体形象，深刻反映出北宋末年的政治状况和社会矛盾，揭示了起义的社会根源，歌颂了起义英雄的反抗斗争和他们的社会理想，也具体揭示了起义失败的内在历史原因。《水浒传》流传极广，脍炙人口，对中国乃至东亚的叙事文学都有极其深远的影响，在世界上有英、日、德、俄、法等多个语言的翻译版本。

水 浒 传（节选）

施耐庵

第三回 史大郎夜走华阴县 鲁提辖拳打镇关西

郑屠右手拿刀，左手便来要揪鲁达；被这鲁提辖就势按住左手，赶将入去，望小腹上只一脚，腾地倒在当街上。鲁达再入一步，踏住胸脯，提着醋钵儿大小拳头，看着这郑屠道："洒家始投老种经略相公，做到关西五路廉访使，也不枉了叫做镇关西！你是个卖肉的操刀屠户，狗一般的人，也叫做镇关西！你如何强骗了金翠莲？"扑的只一拳，正打在鼻子上，打得鲜血迸流，鼻子歪在半边，却便似开了个油酱铺：咸的、酸的、辣的，一发都滚出来。郑屠挣不起来，那把尖刀也丢在一边，口里只叫："打得好！"鲁达骂道："直娘贼！还敢应口！"提起拳头来就眼眶际眉梢只一拳，打得眼棱缝裂，乌珠迸出，也似开了个彩帛铺的：红的、黑的、绛的，都绽将出来。两边看的人惧怕鲁提辖，谁敢向前来劝？郑屠当不过，讨饶。鲁达喝道："咄！你是个破落户！若只和俺硬到底，洒家便饶你了！你如今对俺讨饶，洒家偏不饶你！"又只一拳，太阳上正着，却似做了一个全堂水陆的道场：磬儿、钹儿、铙儿一齐响。鲁达看时，只见郑屠挺在地上，口里只有出的气，没了入的气，动弹不得。鲁提辖假意道："你这厮诈死，洒家再打！"只见面皮渐渐的变了。鲁达寻思道："俺只指望打这厮一顿，不想三拳真个打死了他。洒家须吃官司，又没人送饭，不如及早撒开。"拔步便走，回头着郑屠尸道："你诈死！洒家和你慢慢理会！"一头骂，一头大踏步去了。街坊邻舍并郑屠的火家，谁敢向前来拦他？

鲁提辖回到下处，急急卷了些衣服盘缠，细软银两；但是旧衣粗重都弃了；提了一条齐眉短棒，奔出南门，一道烟走了。

4.5 译文荟萃

1. 短语与术语翻译

贵妃 Imperial Consort
亭榭栏杆 pavilions and balustrades
堆石为垣 stone walls
幽尼佛寺 a temple secluded in the hills
亭台轩馆 pavilions and lodges
长廊曲洞 long covered walks, meandering grottoes
方厦圆亭 square mansions and round kiosks
全真道士 Taoist priests of the Perfect Truth Sect
荣国公 the Duke of Rongguo
清堂茅舍 quiet lodges and thatched huts
编花为牖 pergolas of flowers
女道丹房 a convent
达摩庵 Dharma Convent

无量寿佛 Buddha of Infinite Longevity

“富贵长春”宫缎 Imperial satin with designs signifying wealth, nobility and eternal youth

“福寿绵长”宫绸 Imperial silk with designs signifying good fortune and long life

雕梁画栋 carved beams and painted pillars/carved and painted beams and rafters

2. 句子翻译

1) 张飞大怒，睁圆环眼，咬碎钢牙，滚鞍下马，径入馆驿，把门人那里阻挡得住。(《三国演义》)

This provoked the irascible and half intoxicated Zhang Fei to fury. His eyes opened wide until they became circles; he ground his teeth; in a moment he was off his steed, had forced his way past the scared doorkeepers into the building,

2) 且说孙坚飞奔洛阳，遥望火焰冲天，黑烟铺地，二三百里，并无鸡犬人烟。

Sun Jian hastened to the late capital which was still in flames. When he arrived, dense smoke hung all over it and spread for miles around. No living thing, not a fowl, or a dog, or a human being, remained.

3) 忽见草坡左侧转出个少年将军，飞马挺枪，直取文丑，公孙瓒扒上坡去，看那少年：生得身长八尺，浓眉大眼，阔面重颐，威风凛凛，与文丑大战五六十合，胜负未分。

Then suddenly came out from the shelter of a grassy mound on the left a general of youthful mien, but sitting his steed bravely and holding a sturdy spear. He rode directly at Wen Chou, and Gongsun Zan crawled up the slope to look on. The new warrior was of middle height with bushy eyebrows and large eyes, a broad face and a heavy jowl, a youth of commanding presence. The two exchanged some fifty bouts and yet neither had the advantage.

4) 言未绝，只见一位少年将军，面如冠玉，眼若流星，虎体猿臂，彪腹狼腰；手执长枪，坐骑骏马，从阵中飞出。

Hardly were the words spoken when there came out a youth general with a clear, white complexion as jade, eyes like shooting stars, lithe of body and strong of limb. He was armed with a long spear and bestrode an excellent steed.

5) 两马相交，忽然狂风大作，飞沙走石，两军皆乱，各自收兵。

But just as the two horses met, a hurricane burst over the spot, and the flying dust and pebbles threw both sides into the utmost confusion.

6) 正中间坐着那个娘娘，手托着香腮，双眸滴泪，果然是：玉容娇嫩，美貌妖娆。

The queen sat in the middle with her fragrant cheeks in her hands and tears pouring from both of her eyes. Indeed, she had a beautiful face so soft and charming, a bewitching countenance so fair.

7) 老孙因为闹天宫，偷了仙丹，盗了蟠桃，窃了御酒，被小圣二郎擒住，押在斗牛宫前，众天神把老孙斧剁锤敲，刀砍剑刺，火烧雷打，也不曾损动分毫。

When I was captured by the Little Sage for wrecking the Heavenly Palace, stealing the pills of immortality and the heavenly peaches, and filching the imperial wine, I was marched to a place outside the Dipper and Bull Palace, where all the gods of Heaven hacked at me with axes, hit me with maces, cut at me with swords, stabbed at me with daggers, tried to burn me with lightning, and pounded me with thunder; but none of it hurt me in the slightest.

8) 三藏又恐怕他捎断了，口中又念起来，他依旧生痛，痛得竖蜻蜓，翻筋斗，耳红面赤，眼胀身麻。

Sanzang, again frightened that he would snap it, started to recite the spell once more. The pain was so bad this time that Monkey stood on his head, turned somersaults, and went red in the face and ears. His eyes were popping and his body went numb.

9) 那妖精那容分说，抖擞身躯，依前弄法，鼻口内喷烟冒火，举钢叉就刺八戒。

The demon did not allow any more argument but summoned up her spirits and used the same magic as before to breathe out smoke and fire as she thrust at Pig with her steel trident.

10) 八戒害怕，急抽身往草里一钻，也管不得荆针棘刺，也顾不得刮破头疼，战兢兢的，在草里听着梆声。

This so terrified Pig that he fled as fast as he could into the undergrowth, not caring that brambles and thorns were tearing his head. He sat there trembling and listening out for the sound of the cudgel.

3. 段落翻译

红 楼 梦（节选）

曹雪芹

第三回 金陵城起复贾雨村 荣国府收养林黛玉

那女学生原不忍离亲而去，无奈他外祖母必欲其往，且兼如海说："汝父年已半百，再无续室之意，且汝多病，年又极小，上无亲母教养，下无姊妹扶持。今去依傍外祖母及舅氏姊妹，正好减我内顾之忧，如何不去？"黛玉听了，方洒泪拜别，随了奶娘及荣府中几个老妇登舟而去。雨村另有船只，带了两个小童，依附黛玉而行。

一日到了京都，雨村先整了衣冠，带着童仆，拿了宗侄的名帖至荣府门上投了。

彼时贾政已看了妹丈之书，即忙请入相会。见雨村像貌魁伟，言谈不俗，且这贾政最喜的是读书人，礼贤下士。拯溺救危，大有祖风，况又系妹丈致意，因此优待雨村，更又不同。便极力帮助，题奏之日，谋了个复职。不上两月，便选了金陵应天府，辞了贾政，择日到任去了，不在话下。

且说黛玉自那日弃舟登岸时，便有荣府打发轿子并拉行李车辆伺候。这黛玉尝听得母亲说，他外祖母家与别人家不同。他近日所见的这几个三等的仆妇，吃穿用度已是不凡，何况今至其家，都要步步留心，时时在意，不要多说一句话，不可多行一步路，恐被人耻笑了去。

自上了轿，进了城，从纱窗中瞧了一瞧，其街市之繁华，人烟之阜盛，自非别处可比。又行了半日，忽见街北蹲着两个大石狮子，三间兽头大门，门前列坐着十来个华冠丽服之人，正门不开，只东西两角门有人出入。正门之上有一匾，匾上大书“敕造宁国府”五个大字。黛玉想道：“这是外祖的长房了。”又往西不远，照样也是三间大门，方是“荣国府”。却不进正门，只由西角门而进。轿子抬着走了一箭之远，将转弯时便歇了轿，后面的婆子也都下来了，另换了四个眉目秀洁的十七八岁的小厮上来，抬着轿子，众婆子步下跟随。至一垂花门前落下，那小厮俱肃然退出，众婆子上前打起轿帘，扶黛玉下了轿。黛玉扶着婆子的手进了垂花门，两边是超手游廊，正中是穿堂，当地放着一个紫檀架子大理石屏风。转过屏风，小小三间厅房，厅后便是正房大院。正面五间上房，皆是雕梁画栋，两边穿山游廊厢房，挂着各色鹦鹉画眉等雀鸟。台阶上坐着几个穿红着绿的丫头，一见他们来了，都笑迎上来道：“刚才老太太还念诵呢！可巧就来了。”于是三四人争着打帘子，一面听得人说：“林姑娘来了。”

译文一

A Dream of Red Mansions

Chapter 3

Lin Ru-hai Recommends a Tutor to His Brother-in-law
The Lady Dowager Sends for Her Motherless Granddaughter

His pupil Daiyu, who had just got over her illness, could hardly bear to leave her father, but she had to comply with the wishes of her grandmother.

“I am nearly fifty and don’t intend to marry again,” Ruhai told her, “You’re young and delicate, with no mother to take care of you, no sister or brother to look after you. If you go to stay with your grandmother and uncles’ girls, that will take a great load off my mind. How can you refuse?” So parting from him in a flood of tears, she embarked with her nurse and some elderly maid-servants from the Rong Mansion, followed by Yucun and two pages in another junk.

In due course they reached the capital and entered the city. Yucun spruced himself up and went with his pages to the gate of the Rong Mansion, where he handed in his visiting-card on which he had styled himself Jia Zheng’s “nephew.” Jia Zheng, who had received his brother-in-law’s letter, lost no time in asking him in. Yucun cut an impressive figure and was by no means vulgar in his conversation. Since Jia Zheng was well-disposed to scholars and, like his grandfather before him, delighted in honouring worthy men of letters and helping those in distress, and since moreover his brother-in-law had recommended Yucun, he treated him uncommonly well and did all in his power to help him. The same day that he presented a petition to the throne Yucun was rehabilitated and ordered to await an appointment. In less than two months he was sent to Jinling to fill the vacated post of prefect of Yingtian. Taking leave of Jia Zheng he chose a day to proceed to his new post. But no more of this.

To return to Daiyu. When she disembarked, a sedan-chair from the Rong Mansion and carts for her luggage were waiting in readiness. She had heard a great deal from her mother about the magnificence of her grandmother's home; and during the last few days she had been impressed by the food, costumes and behaviour of the relatively low-ranking attendants escorting her. She must watch her step in her new home, she decided, be on guard every moment and weigh every word, so as not to be laughed at for any foolish blunder. As she was carried into the city she peeped out through the gauze window of the chair at the bustle in the streets and the crowds of people, the like of which she had never seen before.

After what seemed a long time they came to a street with two huge stone lions crouching on the north side, flanking a great triple gate with beast-head knockers, in front of which ten or more men in smart livery were sitting. The central gate was shut, but people were passing in and out of the smaller side gates. On a board above the main gate was written in large characters: Ningguo Mansion Built at Imperial Command.

Daiyu realized that this must be where the elder branch of her grandmother's family lived.

A little further to the west they came to another imposing triple gate. This was the Rong Mansion. Instead of going through the main gate, they entered by the smaller one on the west. The bearers carried the chair a bow-shot further, then set it down at a turning and withdrew. The maid-servants behind Daiyu had now alighted and were proceeding on foot. Three or four smartly dressed lads of seventeen or eighteen picked up the chair and, followed by the maids, carried it to a gate decorated with overhanging flowery patterns carved in wood. There the bearers withdrew, the maids raised the curtain of the chair, helped Daiyu out and supported her through the gate.

Inside, verandahs on both sides led to a three-roomed entrance hall in the middle of which stood a screen of marble in a red sandalwood frame. The hall gave access to the large court of the main building. In front were five rooms with carved beams and painted pillars, and on either side were rooms with covered passageways. Cages of brilliantly coloured parrots, thrushes and other birds hung under the eaves of the verandahs.

Several maids dressed in red and green rose from the terrace and hurried to greet them with smiles.

"The old lady was just talking about you," they cried. "and here you are." Three or four of them ran to raise the door curtain, and a voice could be heard announcing, "Miss Lin is here."（杨宪益、戴乃迭　译）

译文二

The Story of the Stone

Chapter 3

Lin Ru-hai Recommends a Private Tutor to His Brother-in-law
And Old Lady Jia Extends a Compassionate Welcome to the Motherless Child

At first his little pupil could not be persuaded to part from her father; but her grandmother was insistent that she should go, and Ru-hai added his own reasons.

"I'm half a century old now, my dear, and I have no intention of taking a second wife; so there will be no one here to act as a mother to you. It isn't, either, as if you had sisters who could help to take care of you. You know how often you are poorly. And you are still very young. It would be a great weight off my mind to know that you had your Grandmother Jia and your uncles' girls to fall back on. I really think you ought to go."

After this Dai-yu could only take a tearful leave of her father and go down to the boat with her nurse and the old women from the Rong Mansion who had been sent to fetch her. There was a separate boat for Yu-cun and a couple of servant-boys to wait on him, and he too now embarked in the capacity of Dai-yu's escort.

In due course they arrived in the capital, and Yu-cun, dressed in his best and with the two servant-boys at his heels, betook himself to the gate of the Rong Mansion and handed in his visiting-card, on which he had been careful to prefix the word "kinsman" to his own name. By this time Jia Zheng had already seen his brother-in-law's letter, and accorded him an interview without delay.

Yu-cun's imposing looks and cultivated speech made an excellent impression on Jia Zheng, who was in any case always well-disposed towards scholars, and preserved much of his grandfather's affability with men of letters and readiness to help them in any sort of trouble or distress. And since his own inclinations were in this case reinforced by his brother-in-law's strong recommendation, the treatment he extended to Yu-cun was exceptionally favourable. He exerted himself on his behalf to such good effect that on the very day his petition was presented Yu-cun's reinstatement was approved, and before two months were out he was appointed to the magistracy of Ying-tian-fu in Nanking. Thither, having chosen a suitable day on which to commence his journey, and having first taken his leave of Jia Zheng, he now repaired to take up his duties.

But of him, for the time being, no more.

On the day of her arrival in the capital, Dai-yu stepped ashore to find covered chairs from the Rong Mansion for her and her women and a cart for the luggage ready waiting on the quay.

She had often heard her mother say that her Grandmother Jia's home was not like other people's houses. The servants she had been in contact with during the past few days were comparatively low-ranking ones in the domestic hierarchy, yet the food they ate, the clothes they wore, and everything about them was quite out of the ordinary. Dai-yu tried to imagine what the people who employed these superior beings must be like. When she arrived at their house she would have to watch every step she took and weigh every word she said, for if she put a foot wrong they would surely laugh her to scorn.

Dai-yu got into her chair and was soon carried through the city walls. Peeping through the gauze panel which served as a window, she could see streets and buildings more rich and elegant and throngs of people more lively and numerous than she had ever seen in her life before. After being carried for what seemed a very great length of time, she saw, on the north front of the east-west street through which they were passing, two great stone lions crouched one on each side of a triple gateway whose doors were embellished with animal-heads. In front of the gateway ten or so splendidly dressed flunkeys sat in a row. The centre of the three gates was closed, but people were going in and out of the two side ones. There was a board above the centre gate on which were written in large characters the words:

NING-GUO HOUSE
Founded and Constructed by
Imperial Command

Dai-yu realized that this must be where the elder branch of her grandmother's family lived. The chair proceeded some distance more down the street and presently there was another triple gate, this time with the legend

RONG-GUO HOUSE

above it.

Ignoring the central gate, her bearers went in by the western entrance and after traversing the distance of a bow-shot inside, half turned a corner and set the chair down. The chairs of her female attendants which were following behind were set down simultaneously and the old women got out. The places of Dai-yu's bearers were taken by four handsome, fresh-faced pages of seventeen or eighteen. They shouldered her chair and, with the old women now following on foot, carried it as far as an ornamental inner gate. There they set it down again and then retired in respectful silence. The old women came forward to the front of the chair, held up the curtain, and helped Dai-yu to get out.

Each hand resting on the outstretched hand of an elderly attendant, Dai-yu passed through the ornamental gate into a courtyard which had balustraded loggias running along its sides and a covered passage-way through the centre. The foreground of the courtyard beyond was partially hidden by a screen of polished marble set in an elaborate red sandalwood frame. Passing round the screen and through a small reception hall beyond it, they entered the large courtyard of the mansion's principal apartments. These were housed in an imposing five-frame building resplendent with carved and painted beams and rafters which faced them across the courtyard. Running along either side of the courtyard were galleries hung with cages containing a variety of different-coloured parrots, cockatoos, white-eyes, and other birds. Some gaily-dressed maids were sitting on the steps of the main building opposite. At the appearance of the visitors they rose to their feet and came forward with smiling faces to welcome them.

"You've come just at the right time! Lady Jia was only this moment asking about you."

Three or four of them ran to lift up the door-curtain, while another of them announced in loud tones, "Miss Lin is here!"（David Hawkes 译）

4.6 翻译家：沙博理

沙博理（Sidney Shapiro, 1915 年—2014 年），华籍美裔犹太人，本名 Sidney Shapiro，汉语名有"博学明理"之意。1915 年 12 月出生于美国纽约，1937 年毕业于圣约翰大学法律系。第二次世界大战期间加入美国陆军服役，退伍后沙博理相继进入哥伦比亚大学和耶鲁大学学习中文和中国历史文化。

1947 年 4 月来到上海，在上海接触了进步的中外人士，由同情转而投身于中国革命，支持中国同志创办进步刊物《人世间》。后结识了中国戏剧家凤子，不久两人喜结连理。1949 年 10 月 1 日，和凤子应邀参加开国大典。他热爱中国和中国文化。沙博理从此定居中国，并以外国专家的身份投身于新中国的建设事业。1963 年经周恩来总理亲自批准，加入中国国籍。

1951 年起沙博理作为外国专家担任翻译和编辑，先后供职于对外文化联络局、外文出版社、《中国画报》杂志社，专事汉英翻译长达 50 年，并自 1983 年以来一直作为全国政协新闻出版委员参与国事。沙博理一生为新中国文学翻译事业和对外文化交流做出了杰出贡献，因此获得"彩虹翻译奖"（1995）、"国际传播终身荣誉奖"（2009）、"'中国因你而美丽'国际友人奖"（2009）、"中国翻译文化终身成就奖"（2010）、"影响世界华人终身成就奖"（2011）等多项荣誉。

沙博理的翻译生涯分为三个阶段。第一个阶段为 1949 年—1966 年，这是沙博理翻译生涯的

“高峰期”。从 1951 年到 1966 年，沙博理翻译的 111 部文学作品以 124 篇署名或匿名的译文形式刊登在《中国文学》(*Chinese Literature*) 上。作品题材主要为红色革命文学，大部分集结修订后以英文小说的形式出版。这一时期的代表作有《新儿女英雄传》(*Daughters and Sons*, 1956)、《林海雪原》(*Tracks in the Snowy Forest*, 1962) 等。《新儿女英雄传》不仅是沙博理翻译的第一部中国小说，也是新中国成立后美国出版的第一部中国小说。

1966 年—1976 年是沙博理翻译生涯的第二个时期。此间，出版了他一生最具影响力的译作《水浒传》(*Outlaws of the Marsh*)，获得极大的赞誉，为他赢得了中国文联授予的最高翻译奖。丹佛大学的伯顿拉费尔教授在 1981 年 8 月 27 日的《亚洲华尔街日报》上发表的文章对该译本给予高度评价：“沙博理先生以他欢快的文笔，让这部在中国几百年来人们十分喜爱的小说读起来非常有趣，他那大胆的译文使小说中的人物栩栩如生。”美国汉学家西里尔·伯奇评价说，沙博理的译文要比原先的旧译本优秀三倍，他的中文知识使这个译本更加准确、直截了当，而它易懂的英文也比旧译本更加优美得体。《水浒传》沙译本准确地向外国读者讲述了故事，同时保留了大部分原汁原味的中国文化。沙博理秉着对翻译艺术的忠实以及对读者的关照，采取异化为主的翻译策略，译本语言可以说是“中国英语”的典型范例，尤其句式层面的汉语文化标记尤为显著。2000 年《水浒传》沙译本被收入外文出版工程《大中华文库》。

1976 年—2014 年是沙博理翻译生涯的第三个阶段。1983 年退休后，沙博理著述颇丰，出版的著作有自传《我的中国》(*My China: The Metamorphosis of a Country and a Man*, 1997)、《四川的经济改革》(*Experiment in Sichuan: a Report on Economic Reform*, 1981) 等。与此同时，他先后整理、编译《中国古代犹太人》等 3 部书。他的翻译代表作有《我的父亲邓小平：“文革”岁月》(*Deng Xiaoping and the Cultural Revolution: A Daughter Recalls the Critical Years*, 2002)。这本书是邓小平之女邓榕亲自委托沙博理翻译。为了再现原作中的历史事件、文化意象，他采取了几种文化翻译策略，如撰写序、跋和专文，以及增减译等，对外推介新时期的中国文学。

沙博理一生都践行着用翻译表达“最真实的中国”的信念。他认为翻译就要把内容和风格二者都表达出来，切记不可逐字直译，允许对形式稍有改动；在风格再现方面，译者除了要透彻了解历史和文化背景、人物的个性和特征、人物生存的自然环境，还得透彻地熟悉外国的对等词语。他逐渐形成了自己“信而不死、活而不乱”的翻译特质。

4.7 补充资源

参考书目

郭著章，黄粉保，毛新耕 . 文言英译教程 . 上海：外语教育出版社，2008.
王宏印 . 中国文化典籍英译 . 北京：外语教学与研究出版社，2009.
汪榕培，王宏 . 翻译专业本科生系列教材：中国典籍英译 . 上海：上海外语教育出版社，2009.
曹雪芹，高鹗 . 红楼梦（汉英对照，共 6 卷）. 杨宪益，戴乃迭，译 . 北京：外文出版社，2006.
曹雪芹，高鹗 . 红楼梦（范圣宇版本校勘，汉英对照）. 闵德福，译 . 上海：上海外语教育出版社，2014.
沈既济等 . 唐代传奇选（汉英对照）. 杨宪益，戴乃迭，译 . 北京：外文出版社，2016.
吴敬梓 . 大中华文库：儒林外史（汉英对照，THE SCHOLARS Ⅰ / Ⅱ / Ⅲ 全 3 册）. 长沙：湖南人民出版社，2011.
施耐庵，罗贯中 . 水浒全传 . 长沙：岳麓书社，1988.
Cao Xueqin. *The Story of the Stone*. Hawks, David (Trans.). London: Penguin Classics, 1974.
Pearl S B. *All Men Are Brothers*. New York: The John Day Company, 1933.
Sidney S. *Outlaws of the Marsh*. Beijing: Foreign Language Press, 1980.

网络资源

https://en.wikipedia.org/wiki/Classic_Chinese_Novels
https://en.wikipedia.org/wiki/Dream_of_the_Red_Chamber
https://en.wikipedia.org/wiki/Water_Margin
https://en.wikipedia.org/wiki/Romance_of_the_Three_Kingdoms
https://en.wikipedia.org/wiki/Journey_to_the_West
https://en.wikipedia.org/wiki/Strange_Stories_from_a_Chinese_Studio
https://en.wikipedia.org/wiki/The_Scholars_(novel)
http://www.innerjourneytothewest.com/english/en-resource.html

第三章　诗歌翻译

Chapter 3

第五单元　中国现代诗歌

第六单元　中国古代诗歌

第五单元　中国现代诗歌

5.1 阅读欣赏：《再别康桥》

【说明】 请欣赏《再别康桥》及两个英译本，领会原诗特点以及翻译思路。

简介:《再别康桥》是中国新月派代表诗人徐志摩的代表作品。1921年，经由狄更生推荐，徐志摩进入康桥大学（现译为“剑桥大学”）皇家学院研习政治经济学。在剑桥求学期间，徐志摩与英国名士交往，广泛涉猎世界名作，接触各种思潮，对其一生产生了深远影响。剑桥的环境不仅塑造了徐志摩的人生观和价值观，而且也触发了他进行文学创作的意念。他在《猛虎集·序文》中说：正是康河的水，开启了诗人的心灵，唤醒了久蛰在他心中的诗人的天命。后来在《吸烟与文化》中，徐志摩富含深情地说：我的眼是康桥教我睁的，我的求知欲是康桥给我拨动的，我的自我意识是康桥给我胚胎的。1922年，在剑桥学习了两年的徐志摩即将回国。回国前夕，他写下了《康桥再会吧》，表达对剑桥的眷恋和不舍。这是“别康桥”组诗的第一首。1928年7月，徐志摩在重访欧洲时再次来到剑桥，勾起无限思念，在11月份归国途中创作了这首脍炙人口的诗篇。该诗最初刊登于1928年12月10日《新月》第1卷10号，后收入《猛虎集》。全诗以轻盈柔和的语言、精巧的形式和富于节奏的音乐感，描绘了流动的画面和美妙的意境，表达了诗人对剑桥的不舍之情，成为徐志摩的经典诗作。

再别康桥

徐志摩

轻轻地我走了，
正如我轻轻地来；
我轻轻地招手，
作别西天的云彩。

那河畔的金柳，
是夕阳中的新娘；
波光里的艳影，
在我的心头荡漾。

软泥上的青荇，
油油的在水底招摇；
在康河的柔波里，
我甘心做一条水草。

那榆荫下的一潭，
不是清泉，是天上的虹，
揉碎在浮藻间，
沉淀着彩虹似的梦。

寻梦？撑一支长篙，
向青草更青处漫溯，
满载一船星辉，
在星辉斑斓里放歌。

但我不能放歌，
悄悄是别离的笙箫；
夏虫也为我沉默，
沉默是今晚的康桥！

悄悄的我走了，
正如我悄悄的来，
我挥一挥衣袖，
不带走一片云彩。

译文一：

On Leaving Cambridge Again

Quietly I leave,
Just as I quietly came;
I quietly wave,
Saying goodbye to the bright clouds of the
western sky.

The river banks' golden willows,
Like brides in a setting sun;
Beautiful shadows in bright waves.
Waving in my heart.

The soft mud's green grasses,
Bright green, waving on the river bottom;
Would I were a blade of water grass,
In the river Cam's gentle waves.

That lake under the Elm shadow,
Not a clear fountain but a rainbow in heaven,
Twisted into floating weeds.
Precipitating rainbow dreams.

Dream searching? Push a long boat pole,
Upstream towards green grass and an even
greener place, a boat filled with starlight,
Let loose a song midst pointed starlight.

But I cannot sing,
It is quiet like a parting Hsiao;
The summer insects are also quiet for me,
Cambridge tonight is silent.

Quietly I leave,
Just as I quietly came;
My sleeves are waving,
Not taking away a single cloud.
（Edward Connynham　译）

译文二：

Second Farewell to Cambridge

Lightly let me leave now,
Lightly as first I came;
Lightly wave farewell
To the western sky aflame.

Golden willows on river path,
A bride in the setting sun:
Her splendor on the stream
In my heart makes ripples run.

Green fronds upon the mud
Below surface lazily sway:
Could I only live as a water plant
Where Cam winds her gentle way!

That pool in the elm tree's shade,
No spring, but a rainbow it seems.
Shattered among the rushes,
Steeped in a rainbow dream.

A dream? To pole with a long pole
Where the green grass greener springs
A punt loaded with starlight,
And in dapple of starlight to sing.

But I have no voice to sing,
Silent the farewell pipe,
The very insects for me are still
And still is Cambridge tonight.

Silently I leave now,
Silent as that first day,
With shakes of sleeve, to carry
Not a wisp of cloud away.
（Cyril Birch　译）

5.2 翻译热身:《断章》

【说明】请将下列现代诗翻译为英语，参照“阅读欣赏”的译文体会中国现代诗的英译思路。

简介:《断章》是“新月派”诗人卞之琳的代表作，创作于1935年10月，是一首精致的哲理诗。该诗原在一首长诗中，但诗人认为全诗令他满意的仅有这四行，于是抽出来独立成章，标题由此而来。卞之琳（1910年—2000年）是中国著名现代诗人、文学评论家、翻译家，“新月派”和现代派代表诗人，1929年就读于北京大学英文系，1930年开始写诗。1936年卞之琳与李广田、何其芳一起出版诗集《汉园集》，被誉为“汉园三诗人”。抗战期间他在各地任教，曾是徐志摩的学生。他早年的诗作大多表现对现实的不满和找不到出路的苦闷，情感抑郁。他的诗想象微妙，笔墨省简，抗战爆发后，诗风变得开阔、明朗。著有诗集《三秋草》《鱼木集》《十年诗草》等。

断　　章

卞之琳

你站在桥上看风景，

看风景的人在楼上看你。
明月装饰了你的窗子，
你装饰了别人的梦。

5.3 翻译技巧：中国现代诗英译

5.3.1 中国现代诗简介

中国现代诗指五四运动以来的诗，其中的主体是新体诗，又称“中国新诗”“中国现代新诗”。中国现代诗包括以白话文写的中国新诗和五四运动以来用中国古典诗歌形式写的诗。以下以中国新诗为主介绍中国现代诗的特点。

1917 年，胡适在《新青年》上发表《文学改良刍议》，反对文言文，提倡白话文，由此引发文学革命。中国现代文学革命首先起于诗歌的“现代化”。同年 2 月，《新青年》刊出胡适的《白话诗八首》，其中一首是在中国现代诗史上具有重要标志意义的诗《蝴蝶》：“两个蝴蝶，双双飞上天。不知为什么，一个忽飞还。剩下那一个，孤单怪可怜。也无心上天，天上太孤单”，这首诗标志着中国现代新诗的诞生。1918 年 1 月，《新青年》发表了胡适、刘半农、沈尹默的 9 首白话新诗，被认为是中国现代诗的正式开端。1920 年 3 月，胡适的《尝试集》出版，成为中国文学史上第一部个人现代诗集，此后更多的诗人开始创作白话诗。从 1917 年至今的一百年中，出现了郭沫若、徐志摩、戴望舒、冯至、卞之琳、艾青、穆旦等著名诗人，留下了《天狗》《再别康桥》《雨巷》《十四行诗》《断章》《我爱这土地》等经典名篇。

中国现代新诗在不同时期有多个流派，重要的流派包括新月派、九叶派、朦胧派等。新月派以 1927 年为界分为前后两个时期。前期自 1926 年开始，以《晨报副刊诗镌》为阵地，主要成员包括闻一多、徐志摩、朱湘、孙大雨等，他们提倡新格律诗，主张以理性节制情感，反对滥情主义和诗的散文化，在理论和实践中探索新诗的格律。其中的重要主张包括闻一多提出的“音乐美、绘画美、建筑美”三美主张。后期的新月派以《新月》月刊和《诗刊》季刊为主要阵地，新加入的诗人有陈梦家、方玮德、卞之琳等。新月派的代表诗作主要有：徐志摩的《沙扬娜拉》《再别康桥》，闻一多的《死水》《静夜》，朱湘的《采莲曲》等。九叶派也称“中国新诗派”。1948 年，曹辛之与穆旦、杜运燮、郑敏等创办了《中国新诗》，标志着“中国新诗派”的诞生，其代表人物为辛笛、穆旦、郑敏、杜运燮、陈敬容、曹辛之、唐祈、唐湜、袁可嘉，1981 年出版了这九位诗人的诗歌合集《九叶集》，“九叶派”由此得名。九叶派诗人大都是校园诗人出身，深受西方现代主义诗歌的影响，在创作中追求现实与艺术、感性与理性的平衡，主张“人的文学”、“人民的文学”和“生命的文学”的综合，探索诗歌表达的“戏剧性”，为中国新诗的探索做出了重要贡献。朦胧派出现于 20 世纪 70

至80年代，代表人物有北岛、舒婷、顾城、江河、海子等。朦胧派诗人大量使用象征的艺术表达方式，使得诗歌的文学意义充满多样性和不明确性，所以被人们称为朦胧诗。许多作品在民间诗歌刊物《今天》上刊载，1985年出版了《朦胧诗选》。朦胧诗改写了以往诗歌单纯描摹现实与图解政策的传统模式，把诗歌作为探求人生的重要方式，代表诗集有《舒婷顾城抒情诗选》《北岛顾城诗选》等，代表诗作有海子的《面朝大海，春暖花开》、舒婷的《祖国啊，我亲爱的祖国》和《致橡树》、顾城的《一代人》和《远与近》、江河的《星星变奏曲》和《纪念碑》、北岛的《回答》和《红帆船》等。

5.3.2　中国现代诗的特点

总体上讲，中国现代诗以白话语言写作，不受旧体诗格律的限制，在形式上追求灵活自由，在内容上主要反映新文化运动以来的科学、民主等现代主题。在初创时期，中国现代诗旨在突破旧体诗形式上的束缚，主张白话俗语入诗，以表现诗人的真实情感为主要内容，其中的典型代表即胡适的《蝴蝶》。新诗的发展受到外国诗歌的影响较大，许多新诗吸收了中国古典诗歌、民歌和外国诗歌的营养，探索出丰富的诗歌表现方法和艺术形式，产生了现实主义、浪漫主义、象征主义等艺术潮流，出现了自由体、新格律体、十四行诗、阶梯式诗、散文诗等形式。

中国现代诗总体上具有以下特点：

一是以抒情和表达生活为主要目的。诗歌的主要功能是抒情，而社会生活则是诗歌内容的主要来源。诗歌是高度凝练、行文短小的文学形式，因此在抒情和表达社会生活时都是以较为概括的形式。同时，诗歌的抒情往往通过意象来实现。所谓意象，就是经过诗人的主观加工、呈现于诗歌中、用以表达诗歌主题或情感的物象。如徐志摩《再别康桥》中的“那河畔的金柳，是夕阳中的新娘”中的“新娘”、“那榆荫下的一潭，不是清泉，是天上的虹”中的“虹”等都是意象的运用。

二是分行排列，讲究形式艺术。诗歌是十分注重形式的艺术，在语言形式和排列方式上以分行排列构成文本。中国现代诗的排列形式主要有：格律体、参差体、阶梯式、回环体等。格律体的特点是诗句长短整齐、节奏一致，每节的行数也相同，如闻一多的《死水》第一节如下：

这是一沟绝望的死水，
清风吹不起半点漪沦。
不如多扔些破铜烂铁，
爽性泼你的剩菜残羹。
……

参差体的诗每行长短和节奏不一致，显得参差不齐，每节的行数也不相同，较为自由，比较典型的如艾青的《大堰河——我的保姆》。阶梯式诗歌借自俄国诗人马雅可夫斯基诗体，诗行的排列有规律地错落成为阶梯型，由此得名，又称楼梯式诗、台阶式诗。参差体式诗的每节前后的诗句排成楼梯状，如贺敬之的《放声歌唱》（节选）：

无边的大海波涛汹涌……
啊，无边的
大海
波涛
汹涌——
生活的浪花在滚滚沸腾……
啊，生活的
浪花
在滚滚
沸腾！
……

回环体诗又称“回文诗”，采用基于汉语特有的语言特点回环往复使用词序的修辞手法，正读、倒读皆能成章或成句，是中国诗歌中一种颇具特色的诗歌艺术形式。现代回环体主要以相同的词语或诗句的反复出现、构成回环旋绕的效果为主，诗句的排列给读者以视觉和听觉的回环冲击，构成明显的标记。较为著名的现代回环体诗有闻一多的《忘掉她》和戴望舒的《雨巷》等，如闻一多的《忘掉她》（节选）：

忘掉她，像一朵忘掉的花——
那朝霞在花瓣上，
那花心的一缕香——
忘掉她，像一朵忘掉的花！
忘掉她，像一朵忘掉的花！
像春风里一出梦，
像梦里的一声钟，
忘掉她，像一朵忘掉的花！
忘掉她，像一朵忘掉的花！
……

三是表现形式上常常采用复沓、铺排等手法，富有节奏感和音乐性。现代诗一方面革新了旧体诗的限制，具有形式自由、内涵开放、韵律自由等特点，也继承了中国传统诗歌“赋、比、兴”等表现手法，在复沓、铺排的运用上更加突出。复沓与铺排的运用使诗人的情感更加充沛地表达出来。复沓又称重叠、重章叠句，指重复使用同一韵母、词语、句子或句群的艺术表现方法。戴望舒的《雨巷》突出地使用了复沓手法，表现出优美的音乐性和浓郁的诗意。其对复沓的使用主要有三种形式：一是首尾“起结复见”的段式复沓，二是贯串“我”与“丁香姑娘”雨巷相遇过程中的词句复沓，三是同韵到底的韵脚复沓。如：

撑着油纸伞，独自
彷徨在悠长、悠长
又寂寥的雨巷
我希望逢着
一个丁香一样地
结着愁怨的姑娘

她是有
丁香一样的颜色
丁香一样的芬芳
丁香一样的忧愁
在雨中哀怨
哀怨又彷徨

……

撑着油纸伞，独自
彷徨在悠长、悠长
又寂寥的雨巷
我希望飘过
一个丁香一样地
结着愁怨的姑娘

该诗的第一节和最后一节完全相同，形成段式复沓。另外，每一节都有词句的复沓。除了首尾两节的“悠长、悠长”，在第 2 ～ 6 节中，诗人用一组镜头（动态的画面），通过大量的词句复沓描绘了“我”与丁香姑娘的“雨巷奇遇”，第 2 ～ 3 节写丁香姑娘现身雨巷，用了三个“丁香一样的”和两个“哀怨”写其容颜。此外，《雨巷》用韵统一，全诗通篇押 ang 韵，每节六行押韵两到三次，而且“雨巷”“姑娘”“芬芳”“惆怅”“眼光”等词也多次出现。总的来说，复沓、铺排的使用大大增强了该诗的意境和音乐性，使之成为中国现代诗歌史上的不朽名篇。

5.3.3 中国现代诗英译思路

美国诗人罗伯特 · 弗罗斯特曾说：“诗者，译之所失也”（Poetry is what gets lost in translation），

意思是诗歌是不可译的，强调诗歌翻译之难，也说明诗歌翻译者需要倍加小心谨慎，总体要求是翻译诗歌须像诗歌。而英国文化派翻译理论家苏珊·巴斯奈特则提出："诗者，译之非所失也；诗者，恰为译之所得也"（Poetry is not what is lost in translation; it is rather what we gain through translation and translators）。这说明，从另一个角度看，诗歌翻译有其必要性和积极作用。对于译者而言，不可译的诗，通过译者的努力加工，反而能得到一首好诗。

综合诗歌翻译实践者和理论家的观点，理想的诗歌翻译应具备以下几个特点：一是译诗须是诗；二是译诗须传达原诗的情绪（或意境）；三是译诗须传达原诗的内容；四是译诗应取原诗的形式。

然而，毕竟中外诗歌存在诸多差异，译诗要完全保留原诗的内容、形式和意境，很难做到。因此，在诗歌翻译中常常需要变通。

（一）中国现代诗英译中的选词

中国古诗有"诗眼"的说法，即诗句中最为出彩的词语或表达，这些词汇或表达常常能创造出鲜明的意象，或蕴含深刻的哲理。中国现代诗同样如此，而且往往通过某些词汇的复沓、重叠、反复出现，增加诗的意境和效果。如徐志摩的《再别康桥》中第一节连用三个"轻轻地"，让读者感受到诗人"像清风一样地来"，又"悄无声息地离开"，招手向西边的云彩作别，颇具意境。前面"翻译热身"所选的两个译本分别以 quietly、lightly 来翻译"轻轻地"，意在传达这种"轻柔、悄无声息"之美，特别与"轻轻地来"和"轻轻地招手"相呼应，表达诗人离别时幽幽的伤感。

一般而言，诗歌翻译中的选词应力求具有诗意，以诗歌语言为最佳，避免使用过于平庸或生活化的词汇，也不宜选用复杂、过于学术性的词汇。译诗选词的最高理想是传神，结合原诗的风格或意境进行选词，做到与原诗风格接近，或者再现原诗的意境为最佳选择。如《再别康桥》两个英译本中的 a blade of water grass（一条水草），a bride in the setting sun（夕阳中的新娘），to pole with a long pole（撑一支长篙），in dapple of starlight（在星辉斑斓里），have no voice to sing（不能放歌），a wisp of cloud（一片云彩）都是比较形象生动、富有诗意的表达。

再如卞之琳的《断章》中"明月装饰了你的窗子，你装饰了别人的梦"，其中"装饰"一词重复出现，呈现出回环与复沓的效果。两个译本分别以 decorate 和 adorn 来翻译。相比较而言，decorate 更多指房屋的装饰、布置或美化，而 adorn 更加抽象，既可指房屋、物品的装饰，也可指为人或其他的抽象事物（如思想）等增加光彩。比较而言，adorn 更适合于这个语境，表达明月增加了窗子的光辉，而"你"又为"别人的梦"增加光彩。

（二）中国现代诗英译中的音美

许渊冲（2010）认为，诗歌翻译应当在不失真的条件下，尽可能传达原诗的"三美"：意美、音美和形美。在许渊冲看来，音美包括押韵、节奏和重复等。翻译家丰华瞻（1978）认为，译诗首先应"上口"，应当能够吟唱，便于背诵，便于流传。中国现代诗英译中的音美主要通过押韵和节奏来实现。

首先是押韵。如果原诗押韵，那么译诗则尽可能押韵。如果原诗不押韵，译诗可采用自由诗来译而不押韵。押韵的译法如《再别康桥》原诗每节 2、4 行押韵，第一节押 ɑi 韵，第二节押 ɑng 韵，第三节押 ɑo 韵，第六节押 iɑo 韵，第四节和第五押相似的韵，第四节 2、4 行末字为 ong 韵和 eng 韵，第五节 2、4 行末字分别为 su、ge，也基本是押韵的。Ryril Birch 的译文参照原文在每一节的 2、4 行押韵，如第一节的 came、aflame; 第二节的 sun、run；第三节的 sway、way；第四节的 seems、dream；第五节的 springs、sing；第六节的 ripe、tonight；最后一节的 day、away。不过，也有人主张译诗不必受此限制，以无韵体来译诗。林语堂在《论译诗》中就指出："凡译诗，可用韵，而普遍来说，还是不用韵妥当。只要文字好，仍有抑扬顿挫，仍可保存风味。"由此可见，如果译诗不用韵，那么更须在文字上下工夫。卞之琳的《断章》原诗没有押韵，叶维廉和杨宪益、戴乃迭的译文也都没有押韵，但依然可算是好的译诗。中国现代诗主张形式自由，不受传统格律的限制，因此翻译时可以通过押韵来增强译诗效果，但若为了押韵而费尽周折、为音害义，还不如不用韵而注重文字的抑扬顿挫和意美效果。

其次是节奏。诗的节奏即每行诗句的顿逗和抑扬的节拍感，就像音乐的节拍和韵律。中国现代诗虽然有自由化、散文化的倾向，但还是常以节奏见长，否则难以叫诗。诗人北岛认为，诗的节奏感源于诗人内在的一种节律。法国诗人菲利普－雅各泰说："诗的节拍必然响应着我所感受到的节拍，无疑，它依循着我的天性去响应，依循着我的内心耳朵的倾向。"中国古诗既要押韵，又讲究平仄关系，因而节奏感更强。中国现代诗中也不乏富有节奏感的例子，如徐志摩的《再别康桥》，每行三顿："轻轻地 / 我 / 走了，正如 / 我 / 轻轻地来。我 / 轻轻地 / 招手，作别 / 西天的 / 云彩。"

翻译现代诗，可以模仿原诗的节奏和音顿。如 Edward Connynham 所译的《再别康桥》第一节，也采用每行三顿：Quietly / I / leave, Just as / I /quietly came; I / quietly / wave, Saying goodbye /to the bright clouds / of the western sky.

再如戴望舒的《雨巷》第一节，短顿与长顿结合，形成优美的音乐感：撑着 / 油纸伞，// 独自 /// 彷徨在 / 悠长，// 悠长 /// 又寂寥的 / 雨巷，我希望 / 逢着 /// 一个 / 丁香一样的 /// 结着愁怨的 / 姑娘。叶维廉的译文节奏也模仿原始的长、短顿：Holding / an oil-paper umbrella, // alone /// I hesitate / in a long, // long, /// Sparse, / quiet alley / in the rain. /// Would that / I encountered /// A girl, // sorrow-laden, /// Like / a lilac.

总之，诗的构成，既有诗意、诗情，又有诗性和音乐之美。英译中国现代诗也需要尽量照顾到诗意、诗情的传达，同时尽可能传达原诗的意境和艺术效果。正如林语堂所说，翻译应力求忠实、通顺、美。或如刘重德所言："不管是译格律诗，还是自由诗，首先必须信于内容，保留原诗意义、意象和意境；其次必须锤炼文字，达如其分；第三必须尽量切合原诗形式。"

5.4 翻译实战：艾青诗选

【说明】参照“阅读欣赏”、“翻译热身”的译文和“翻译技巧”有关中国现代诗的英译思路，从以下两首艾青的诗中选取一首翻译为英语。

（一）《大堰河——我的保姆》

简介：《大堰河——我的保姆》是著名诗人艾青的成名作。1932年，艾青因加入左翼美术家联盟被捕。在狱中，艾青写下了这首著名的诗。艾青小时候被送到一个贫苦农民家里抚养，大堰河便是艾青的乳母。艾青5岁时被领回家开始读书，但是依然被家人冷落，却从乳母大堰河那里感受到了温暖的母爱。在被关押期间，艾青写下了这首饱含深情的诗，成为艾青的代表作，也由此奠定了他在中国现代文学史上的重要地位。

大堰河——我的保姆（节选）

艾青

大堰河，含泪的去了！
同着四十九年的人世生活的凌侮，
同着数不尽的奴隶的凄苦，
同着四块钱的棺材和几束稻草，
同着几尺长方的埋棺材的土地，
同着一手把的纸钱的灰，
大堰河，她含泪的去了。

大堰河，今天，你的乳儿是在狱里，
写着一首呈给你的赞美诗，
呈给你黄土下紫色的灵魂，
呈给你拥抱过我的直伸着的手，
呈给你吻过我的唇，
呈给你泥黑的温柔的脸颜，
呈给你养育了我的乳房，
呈给你的儿子们，我的兄弟们，
呈给大地上一切的，

我的大堰河般的保姆和她们的儿子，
呈给爱我如爱她自己的儿子般的大堰河。

（二）《礁石》

简介：《礁石》是艾青于1954年创作的一首诗。1954年7月，艾青应邀出访智利。在出访期间，诗人写下了这首诗。当时正值新中国社会主义建设伊始，百事待兴，面临种种困难。诗人通过此诗表达了对礁石这种坚韧顽强的生命存在的由衷赞美，亦表达了对正处在种种困扰和挤压中的中国人民的深切鼓舞和激励。

礁　　石

艾青

一个浪，一个浪
无休止地扑过来
每一个浪都在它脚下
被打成碎沫，散开……

它的脸上和身上
像刀砍过的一样
但它依然站在那里
含着微笑，看着海洋……

5.5 译文荟萃

1. 短语翻译

中国现代诗 modern Chinese poetry
白话诗 modern vernacular style of poetry
新月派 Crescent Moon Society
格律诗 metrical poetry
中国湖畔诗派 China Lake Poets
新诗 new poetry
新文化运动 New Culture Movement
朦胧诗人 Misty Poets
自由诗 free verse
押韵 rhyme

意象派 imagism　　象征主义 symbolism
古典主义 classicism　　浪漫主义 romanticism
现实主义 realism　　唯美主义 estheticism

2. 句子翻译

1) 诗必穷而后工。

译文 1：Poetry becomes good only after one becomes poor or unsuccessful.（林语堂　译）

译文 2：Poverty inspires poetry.（张其春　译）

2) 值得回忆的事是生活中的诗。

All that is worth remembering in life is the poetry of it.

3) 诗意盎然的神话传说使人更能忍受散文般平淡无奇的生活。

The poetry of myth helps men to bear the prose of life.

4) 吃一堑，长一智。

A fall into the pit, a gain in your wit.（钱钟书　译）

5) 多少事，从来急；天地转，光阴迫；一万年太久，只争朝夕。

So many deeds cry out to be done, and always urgently; the world rolles on, time presses. Ten thousand years are too long; seize the day, seize the hour!

6) 尽管春天很美，/ 可有时候，/ 我还是想回到从前，/ 回到那白雪飘飘的日子里。（汪国真《人在冬天》）

Spring is beautiful, / Yet at times, / I'd like to go back to the past, / To the days when snowflakes danced in the sky.（蒋隆国　译）

7) 呼喊是爆发的沉默，沉默是无声的召唤。（汪国真　《山高路远》）

Shouting is burst-out silence. And silence is a soundless call.（蒋隆国　译）

8) 没有比脚更长的路，没有比人更高的山。（汪国真　《山高路远》）

No roads are longer than feet. No mountains are higher than human beings.（蒋隆国　译）

9) 我不去想是否能够成功，/ 既然选择了远方，/ 便只顾风雨兼程。（汪国真　《热爱生命》）

译文 1：I don't want to consider, / If I'll be able to succeed. / Since I leave for a faraway place, / I'll do nothing but trek night and day.（蒋隆国　译）

译文 2：I don't want to consider, / If I'll be able to succeed. / Since I've decided to go to a distant place, /I'll try my best to make the trip.

10) 小时候，/ 乡愁是一枚小小的邮票，/ 我在这头，/ 母亲在那头。

长大后，/ 乡愁是一张窄窄的船票，/ 我在这头，新娘在那头。（余光中　《乡愁》）

When I was a child, / Nostagia seemed a small stamp: "Here am I and there my mother."
Then I was a grown-up, / Nostagia became a traveling ticket: "Here am I and there my bride."
（杨钟琰 译）

3. 中国现代诗两首

1) 戴望舒《雨巷》

简介：戴望舒（1905 年—1950 年），浙江余杭人，1932 年赴法国留学，抗战后去香港主编《星岛日报》，曾任《现代》《顶点》诗刊主编，1941 年被日军投入监狱，受伤致残，1949 年任教于华北大学，出版诗集《望舒草》《望舒诗稿》《灾难的岁月》。《雨巷》是戴望舒的成名作，写于 1927 年夏天。该诗通过描写狭窄阴沉的雨巷、在雨巷中徘徊的独行者、像丁香一样的姑娘，含蓄地表达出作者既迷惘感伤又有期待的情怀，并给人一种朦胧而又幽深的美感。也有人把这些意象解读为反映当时黑暗社会的缩影，或者是在革命中失败的人和朦胧的、时有时无的希望。

雨　　巷

戴望舒

撑着油纸伞，独自
彷徨在悠长，悠长
又寂寥的雨巷，
我希望逢着
一个丁香一样的
结着愁怨的姑娘

她是有
丁香一样的颜色
丁香一样的芬芳
丁香一样的忧愁
在雨中哀怨
哀怨又彷徨

她彷徨在这寂寥的雨巷
撑着油纸伞
像我一样
像我一样地
默默彳亍着
冷漠，凄清，又惆怅。

她静默地走近
走近，又投出
太息一般的眼光。
她飘过
像梦一般的，
像梦一般的凄婉迷茫。

像梦中飘过
一枝丁香地，
我身旁飘过这女郎；
她静默地远了，远了，
到了颓圮的篱墙。
走尽这雨巷。

在雨的哀曲里，
消了她的颜色，
散了她的芬芳，
消散了，甚至她的
太息般的眼光，
丁香般的惆怅。

撑着油纸伞，独自
彷徨在悠长，悠长
又寂寥的雨巷，
我希望飘过

一个丁香一样的
结着愁怨的姑娘。

The Alley in the Rain

Holding an oil-paper umbrella, alone
I hesitate in a long, long,
Sparse, quiet alley in the rain.
Would that I encountered
A girl, sorrow-laden,
Like a lilac.

A girl with
Color like the lilac,
Sadness like the lilac,
Pensive in the rain,
Hesitating and pensive.

Hesitating in this sparse, quiet alley in the rain
Holding an oil-paper umbrella,
Like me, like me,
Moving slowly, silently,
Cold, plaintive, melancholy.

She comes quietly closer,
Closer, casts
A glance like a sigh,
And floats past
Like a dream,
Like the misty grief in a dream.

Floating past like a dream,

Like a twig of lilac,
This girl floats past me,
And quietly moves away, away,
Toward the broken bamboo-fence
And lost in the alley in the rain.

In the sad refrain of the rain,
Has disappeared her color,
Has disappeared her fragrance,
Has disappeared even her
Sigh-laden glance,
The lilaclike melancholy.

Holding an oil-paper umbrella, alone
I hesitate in a long, long,
Sparse, quiet alley in the rain.
Would that I encountered
A girl, sorrow-laden,
Like a lilac.

（Wai-lim Yip　译）

2) 卞之琳《距离的组织》

简介:《距离的组织》是卞之琳《鱼目集》中的一篇，也是卞之琳的诗中比较难懂的一首诗。原诗附有以下注解: 1934 年 12 月 26 日,《大公报》国际新闻版伦敦 25 日路透电:“两个星期前索佛克业余天文学者发现北方大景座中出现一新星，兹据哈华德观象台纪称，近两日内该星异常光明，估计约距地球一千五百光年，故其爆发而致突然灿烂，当远在罗马帝国倾覆之时，直至今日，其光始传至地球云。”卞之琳将本诗的主题解释为:“整诗并非讲哲理，也不是表达什么玄秘思想，而是沿袭我国诗词的传统，表现一种心情或意境，注重展现存在与觉识的关系。”这首诗在时空距离中反复穿梭，交叉运行，以此展现诗人的心情与联想。

距离的组织

卞之琳

想独上高楼读一遍《罗马衰亡史》，
忽有罗马灭亡星出现在报上。
报纸落。地图开，因想起远人的嘱咐。
寄来的风景也暮色苍茫了。
（醒来天欲暮，无聊，一访友人吧。）
灰色的天。灰色的海。灰色的路。
哪儿了？我又不会向灯下验一把土。
忽听得一千重门外有自己的名字。
好累呵！我的盆舟没有人戏弄吗？
友人带来了雪意和五点钟。

The Composition of Distances

Mount a high tower alone to read *The Rise & Decline of the Roman Empire*,
Rome's comet suddenly appears in the newspaper.
Newspaper falls. Map opens. And remember a distant friend's request.
The landscape sent here is already vague with dusk.
(Wake up: sky about to darken. Tedious! Perhaps go see a friend.)
Grey sky. Grey sea. Grey road.
Where now? And I know not how to verify some soil under the lamp.
A friend brings here snow and 5 o'clock.

（Wai-lim Yip 译）

5.6 翻译家：叶维廉

叶威廉（Wai-lim Yip, 1937 年—）是美国著名华裔学者、诗人、诗歌翻译家、文学批评家，中国文学与比较文学教授，长期从事比较文学和文学翻译研究。半个多世纪以来，叶维廉一直活跃在世界文坛上，在中国古典诗歌以及现代诗歌英译、中国诗学、中西比较诗学等领域成就卓著，在西方学术界，特别是英语世界有很大影响。

叶维廉于 1937 年出生于广东省中山县濒海的一个小村庄，父亲常年瘫痪在床，母亲是乡间的助产士。他从小家境穷困，又逢日寇入侵，常惊恐于炮火，每折磨于饥饿。他的童年生活艰苦，一边捕鱼砍柴，一边努力阅读。1948 年，叶维廉渡海去了香港，1955 年考取台湾大学外文系。他学习之余，热爱写诗，毕业后入台湾师范大学研究所，1961 年获英语硕士学位。1963 年到美国艾奥瓦大学写作班学习并获艺术硕士，次年到普林斯顿大学攻读比较文学，1967 年获比较文学博士学位。之后，他一直在加州大学圣迭戈校区从事比较文学、现代诗歌方面的教学和研究，并主持比较文学系前后几十年。1970 年到 1974 年以客座教授身份返台湾大学，协助建立比较文学博士班。1980 年到 1982 年，任香港中文大学英文系首席客座教授，并协助该校建立比较文学研究所。20 世纪 80 年代以来，他数度回到中国大陆，在中国社会科学院、北京大学、清华大学、中国作家协会等处讲授比较文学和传释学。1985 年，倡导和成立了中国比较文学学会。

叶维廉的主要成就包括诗歌创作、中西诗学和比较诗学研究、中国诗歌翻译等。叶维廉从学生时代即开始创作诗歌，是创世纪诗社成员之一，被认为是“一个真正的诗人”，1978 年与余光中、洛夫等一起获选台湾十大诗人。他的第一本诗集《赋格》于 1963 年出版，后陆续出版诗集《三十年诗》《留不住的航渡》等。叶先生说：“我写诗以来，很幸运地，曾有机会接触 60 年来每一个阶段的作品，而享受了某种程度的持续感，而且曾无阻地受过闻一多、卞之琳、艾青、臧克家、冯至、辛笛、穆旦、袁可嘉、吴兴华等人的启迪。我极其重视这种历史的整体性和持续感。”在台湾大学读书时，他也写英文诗，发表在美国的《脚迹》诗刊和《得克萨斯季刊》。20 世纪 50 年代末至 60 年代初，他发表大量的诗作刊登在台湾的《创世纪》、《现代文学》和香港的《新思潮》上。

叶维廉更多以诗学理论、中西比较诗学研究著名，研究成果丰硕，最突出的贡献是提出了东西比较文学的研究方法。他肯定中国古典美学特征，质疑西方将其固有文学理论应用于中国文学研究的可行性及其危机，提出了中西文学模子的“互照互省”，为更合理的文学共同规律建立多方面的理论架构。1983 年出版的《比较诗学》和 1992 年出版的《中国诗学》成为比较诗学的经典著作。其他比较重要的中文著作包括《现象·经验·表现》（1969）、《东西比较文学模子的运用》（1974）、《与当代艺术家对话》（1985）、《寻求跨中西文化的共同文学规律》（1986）、《道家美学与西方文化》（2002）等，中英文著述 50 余种。英语著作有《论庞德的〈华夏集〉》（*Ezra Pound's Cathay*, 1969）、《距离之消解——中西诗学对话》（*Diffusion of Distance: Between Chinese and Western Poetics*, 1983）等，他对中国现代小说也有精深研究，著有《中国现代小说的风貌》。

作为诗歌翻译家，叶维廉既翻译中国古典诗歌，也翻译现代新诗，对中国诗歌在美国的传播做出了突出贡献。中国古典诗歌译作包括：1976 年出版的《汉诗英华》（*Chinese Poetry: Major Modes and Genres*），包含自《诗经》到元曲的 150 多首中国诗的英译，被美国多所大学选作教材。其他译作还有 1972 年出版的王维诗选集《藏天下：王维诗选》（*Hiding the Universe: Poems of Wang Wei*）。

叶维廉为中国现代新诗的英译做出了突出贡献，编选并翻译了两部中国新诗选集:《中国现代诗选 1955—1965：中华民国诗人二十家》(*Modern Chinese Poetry: Twenty Poets of the Republic of China*, 1955–1965）和《防空洞抒情诗：现代中国诗歌，1930 —1959 年》(*Lyrics from Shelters: Modern Chinese Poetry*, 1930–1950），这两部诗集在美国及世界比较文学界都有重要影响。叶维廉同时还出版有汉译外国诗歌，他青年时期翻译了 T. S. 艾略特的《荒原》，是台湾地区最早出版的中文译本。《众树唱歌》收录了 12 位西方诗人作品的中文译本，涉及意大利、德国、西班牙、法国和希腊等国的诗人。

叶维廉作为诗人、翻译家、学者，对中西比较诗学和中国诗的英译功勋卓著，正如乐黛云教授所言，“他是著名诗人，又是杰出的理论家。他非常‘新’，始终置身于新的文艺思潮和理论前沿；他又非常‘旧’，毕生徜徉于中国诗学、道家美学、中国古典诗歌的领域而卓有建树……他的创作冲动、对文字的敏感、作为一个诗人所特有的内在的灵视，决定了他无可取代的学术研究特色。他对中国道家美学、古典诗学、比较文学、中西比较诗学的贡献至今无人企及。”

5.7 补充资源

参考书目

叶维廉 . 中国诗学 . 北京：人民文学出版社，2006.

朱辉 . 中国诗歌在英语世界 . 上海：上海外语教育出版社，2009.

海岸 . 中西诗歌翻译百年论集 . 上海：上海外语教育出版社，2007.

Michelle Y. *Anthology of Modern Chinese Poetry*. New Heaven: Yale University Press, 1994.

Harold A, CHEN Shih-hsiang. *Modern Chinese Poetry*. London: Duckworth, 1936.

Herbert B, Sheldon Z. *The Flowering of Modern Chinese Poetry*. Montreal: McGill-Queen’s University Press, 2016.

中国著名诗刊:《诗刊》《星星》《绿风》《诗歌月刊》《诗选刊》《诗潮》《诗林》《扬子江》等。

网络资源

中国诗歌网：http://www.zgshige.com/tjsg/

中国作家网：http://www.chinawriter.com.cn

中国诗人网：http://www.chinapoet.net/forum.php

国际短诗网：http://www.minipint.com/portal.php

中国诗歌流派网：http://www.zgsglp.com/portal.php

中华情诗词学会：http://www.zhscxh.com/index.asp

第六单元　中国古代诗歌

6.1 阅读欣赏:《古诗十九首》

【说明】 请欣赏下列古诗及其三个译文，体会原诗特点、翻译思路及三个译本的差异。

简介:《古诗十九首》是在汉代民歌基础上发展起来的五言诗，具体作者不详，作为一个整体收录于《文选》卷二十九，代表了汉代文人五言诗创作的最高成就，其著者绝大多数都是漂泊在外的游子，他们身在他乡，胸怀故土，满怀乡愁。其中“思妇”主题较为突出，如这首《青青河畔草》，以思妇的视角，表现思妇的精神苦闷、担心游子的离弃和自己的真情不被对方省察、期盼游子归来的心绪。原诗十九首，分别以首句为标题，此处三个译本分别从不同的角度另取题目。翟理斯以“思妇的心情”为题，译为 *Neglected*（冷遇）；庞德选取“思妇”的粉饰为题，译为 *Beautiful Toilet*（漂亮的装扮）；韦利在其编译的诗集《汉诗一百七十首》（*A Hundred and Seventy Chinese Poems*）中，选取了《古诗十九首》中的十七首（未选第八首《冉冉孤生竹》和第十八首《客从远方来》），因而取名为 *Seventeen Old Poems*（2）（《古诗十七首》其二）。

古诗十九首

其二　青青河畔草

青青河畔草，郁郁园中柳。
盈盈楼上女，皎皎当窗牖。

娥娥红粉妆，纤纤出素手。
昔为倡家女，今为荡子妇。
荡子行不归，空床难独守。

译文一

Neglected

Green grows the grass upon the bank,
The willow-shoots are long and lank;
A lady in a glistening gown
Opens the casement and looks down.
The roses on her cheek blush bright
Her rounded arm is dazzling white;
A singing-girl in early life,
And now a careless roué’s wife…
Ah, if he does not mind his own,
He’ll find some day the bird has flown!

（Herbert A. Giles　译）

译文二

The Beautiful Toilet

Blue, blue is the grass about the river
And the willows have overfilled the close garden.
And within, the mistress, in the midmost of her youth,
White, white of face, hesitates, passing the door,
Slender, she puts forth a slender hand.

And she was a courtezan in the old days,
And she has married a sot,
Who now goes drunkenly out

And leaves her too much alone.

（Ezra Pound　译）

译文三

Seventeen Old Poems (2)

Green, green,
The grass by the river-bank.
Thick, thick,
The willow trees in the garden.
Sad, sad,
The lady in the tower.
White, white,
At the casement window.
Fair, fair,
Her red-powdered face.
Small, small,
She puts out her pale hand.
Once she was a dancing-house girl,
Now she is a wandering man's wife.
The wandering man went, but did not return.
It is hard alone to keep an empty bed.

（Arthur Waley　译）

6.2 翻译热身:《静夜思》

【说明】 请将下列诗翻译为英语，参照“阅读欣赏”的译文体会古诗英译的思路。

简介:《静夜思》是李白的一首著名五言诗，大约创作于唐玄宗开元十四年（公元 726 年）9 月 15 日的扬州旅舍。在一个月明星稀的夜晚，诗人抬头望见天空的一轮皓月，思乡之情油然而生，写下了这首传诵千古的名诗。该诗写得清新朴素，内容简单，却让人读来意味深长，耐人寻味。

静 夜 思

李白

床前明月光，疑是地上霜。
举头望明月，低头思故乡。

6.3 翻译技巧：中国古诗英译

6.3.1 中国古诗的特点

中国古诗指与现代诗、新诗相对的一种诗歌体裁，又称古典诗歌，一般指现代白话新诗出现以前中国古代人创作的诗。作为古典诗歌的泛称，古诗也包括现代人按照古体诗风格创作的诗。广义的古诗涵盖诗、词、散曲等古代文学形式，分为古体诗和近体诗。古体诗又称古风，这个名称始于唐代。唐人把当时新出现的格律诗称为近体诗，而把产生于唐以前、较少格律限制的诗称为古体诗。后人沿袭唐人的说法，把唐以前的乐府民歌、文人诗以及唐以后文人仿照它的体式而写的诗歌统称为“古体诗”。

古体诗的主要形式有“诗经”“楚辞”“汉乐府”“南北朝乐府”等。古体诗不受格律限制，一般也要押韵，形式相对自由，按照诗句的字数，有四言（如《诗经》）、五言（如“汉乐府”诗）、七言（如曹丕《燕歌行》）、杂言（如李白《蜀道难》）等，其中五言和七言古体诗较多，简称“五古”“七古”。古体诗也可以杂用长短句，随意变化，称为杂言体。

近体诗也称今体诗，是相对于古体诗而言的格律诗。近体诗在南北朝时期初现，至唐代发展成熟。近体诗有四个基本特征：一是行数、每行字数固定；二是按规定的韵部押韵；三是上句和下句各字之间平仄对仗；四是某些句子之间用词对仗。近体诗主要包括律诗和绝句两类。律诗由八句组成，每句五字的称为五律，每句七字的称为七律。一般偶数句押韵，首句可入韵，也可不入韵。律诗每两句为一联，分别称为首联、颔联、颈联、尾联，颔联和颈联必须对仗。绝句由四句组成，每句五字的称为五言绝句，每句七字的称为七言绝句。律诗格律极严，篇有定句（除排律外），句有定字，韵有定位（押韵位置固定），字有定声（诗中各字的平仄声调固定），联有定对（律诗中间两联必须对仗）。

古诗总体上有以下特点：（1）句子整齐。除词和曲以外，古诗多数都是每句长短整齐，如《诗经》基本上是四言，《楚辞》大体上是六言加“兮”字。（2）平仄及对仗。古诗中的近体诗和词、曲都对字的平仄有严格规定，在特定的位置必须用规定的平声或仄声。中国古诗利用平仄有规律的变化，构成音调的和谐优美。古诗的平仄规律主要有四条：一句之中平仄相间；一联之内上下两句平仄相对；下联的上句与上联的下句平仄相粘；句末不可出现三平或三仄。总体的原则就是“寓变化于整齐之中”。如杜甫的《春望》：

国破山河在，城春草木深。
感时花溅泪，恨别鸟惊心。
烽火连三月，家书抵万金。
白头搔更短，浑欲不胜簪。

其平仄律如下：

仄仄平平仄，平平仄仄平。
仄平平仄仄，仄仄仄平平。
平仄平平仄，平平仄仄平。
平平平仄仄，平仄仄平平。

需要注意的是，诗句中的平仄以古音认定，部分字古音与现代音存在差异，如“国”“别”“白”现代音是平声，而古音为入声，所以属仄声。另外，平仄的规定也不是僵硬的规则，也会有变通。如此处《春望》第三句的“感”字，本应用平，实际变通为仄；第五句的“烽”字本应用仄，实际变通为“平”；第八句的“浑”本应用仄，变通为平。

不过，严格的平仄规定主要体现于律诗，很多古诗（比如绝句等）都不受此限制，如李白的《静夜思》。古诗的对仗指诗的一联中上下句相同位置上用词性相同、意义相对的词，如李白《送友人》中的一联：青山横北郭，白水绕东城。“青山”与“白水”、“横”与“绕”、“北郭”与“东城”都是词性相同、意义相对的词。（3）节奏和韵律。从句子形式看，古诗的节奏根据每句字数划分，一般四言诗为“二、二”顿，如“窈窕淑女，君子好逑”；五言诗为“二、三”或“二、一、二”顿，如“青青河畔草，郁郁园中柳”为“二三”式停顿，“举头望明月，低头思故乡”为“二、一、二”式停顿；七言诗为“二、二、一、二”顿，《春江花月夜》的“春江潮水连海平，海上明月共潮生”等。古诗一般都要押韵，使音调和谐优美，一般偶数句句末入韵，有的首句也入韵，如《静夜思》的一、二、四句的尾字“光、霜、乡”都押 ang 韵。

6.3.2 中国古诗英译思路

据史料记载，中国古诗最早的英译从 16 世纪末已经开始，距今已有 600 多年的历史。自英国传教士理雅各（James Legge）翻译的《中国经典》（1861 年至 1886 年陆续出版）以来，汉诗英译的历史也有至少 300 多年，先后有无数的中国翻译家和海外汉学家为中国古诗提供了多个英译本，并提出了不同的中国古诗翻译主张。

许渊冲（1994）曾总结中国古诗英译的具体策略：直译、意译、仿译、改译、逐字译、散体译法等。从形式角度看，中国古诗的英译主要有诗化译法和非诗化译法两类。

（一）诗化译法

诗歌翻译研究专家卓振英（2011）提出，诗化译法主要包括韵体译法（rhymed versification）和非韵体译法（unrhymed versification）。韵体译法的典型代表为许渊冲的“三美”主张。许渊冲（1984）认为，诗与散文不同，散文是井然有序的文字，而诗是井然有序的绝妙好词。所谓绝妙好词就是具备意美、音美、形美的文字。因此，翻译中国古诗也应力求意美、音美、形美。所谓意美，即在译文中尽可能地保留或传达原诗的意义、意境、内容之美，用许渊冲的话来说，是原文深层结构之美，而非表层的意似。中国古诗常用赋、比、兴等修辞手段，采用排比、比喻和以物言情的手法，再加上用典，使得很多词汇的意义不能做表层理解，而应探求其深层意义。如李白《送孟浩然之广陵》中的“故人西辞黄鹤楼，烟花三月下扬州”，“烟花”一词容易被误解，庞德将后半句译为：“The smoke-flowers are blurred over the river”。显然，“烟花”并非指“有烟之花”，而是指“柳絮如烟，繁花似锦”的春天景象，许渊冲译为：“My friend has left the west where the Yellow Crane towers; For Yangzhou in spring green with willows and red with flowers.”。

音美是诗化译法的重要体现。音美主要可通过押韵和重叠来体现。首先是押韵。许渊冲认为，押韵并不一定要追求与原诗“音似”，即原诗一、二、四行押韵，译诗也一、二、四行押韵。可根据译者的理解和选择进行每行或每两行押韵，主要目的是增加诗歌音韵上的整体和谐和回环共鸣效果。如许渊冲译的《静夜思》：

Before my bed I see a silver light,
I think the ground is covered with hoar frost.
Raising my head, I find the full moon bright;
And bowing down, in thoughts of home I'm lost.

译文保留与原诗一样的四行，并隔行押韵，相当于仿照英诗 abab 式押韵。也有一二行和三四行分别押韵的，即参照英诗的 aabb 式。如《登鹳雀楼》：“白日依山尽，黄河入海流。欲穷千里目，更上一层楼。”许渊冲的译文为：

On the Stork Tower

The sun beyond the mountains glows;
The Yellow River seawards flows.
You can enjoy a grander sight,
By climbing to a greater height.

音美的另一个方面是复沓重叠，即叠字。《古诗十九首》中的《青青河畔草》一共十句，其中有六句用了叠字，“青青河畔草，郁郁园中柳。盈盈楼上女，皎皎当窗牖。娥娥红粉妆，纤纤出素手。昔为倡家女，今为荡子妇。荡子行不归，空床难独守。”特别是形容词叠字，如“青青、郁郁、盈盈、皎皎、娥娥、纤纤”等，既增强了生动的艺术效果，也增加了音乐美感。翟理斯（Herbert A. Giles）将前两句翻译为：

Green grows the grass upon the bank,

The willow-shoots are long and lank.

译文并没有再现原诗的叠字，“青青、郁郁”重叠回环的声音效果没有了。不过首句 green grows the grass 选取了头韵 gr，并在两句尾押韵，对原诗的音美有一定的补偿。韦利将这两句诗翻译为：

Green, green,

The grass by the river-bank.

Thick, thick,

The willow trees in the garden.

韦利利用 green 和 thick 的重叠，模仿和再现了原诗的叠字效果。不过，需要注意的是，原诗的叠字是与节奏和平仄对仗结合起来使用的。不管是翟理斯的头韵、尾韵代替原诗的叠字，还是韦利的重叠译法，都有其优劣，都是为再现音美所选取的翻译策略。

非韵体译法主张翻译诗歌不用韵，林语堂认为，“只要文字好，仍有抑扬顿挫，仍可保存风味”，而如果用韵，则不仅颇费周折，而且容易失真。非韵体译诗不受韵的限制，避免因韵害意，可采用韦利提倡的弹性节奏来译，即用英语译诗的一个重读音节代表一个汉字，使每行译诗中都有一定数量的重读音节和不定数量的非重读音节。非韵体译法要追求译诗的意境再现，常常通过选词来传神。如林语堂翻译的《西江月 · 梅花》末两句“高情已逐晓云空。不与梨花同梦”：

Flesh of snow, bones of jade,

Dream thy dreams, peerless one,

Not for this world thou art made.

林语堂用字与原文虽不相同，但以“咏梅”转指对其侍妾“朝云”的悼念之意已经表达出来，而且意境颇为传神。

（二）非诗化译法

非诗化译法即在译诗时不拘泥于原诗的格律限制，而是在再现原诗意象的前提下有伸缩变化。非诗化译法也指散体译法，在无法用格律诗来翻译时（比如无法找到合适的韵脚等），运用自由诗体来翻译。正如刘重德（1996）所说，只要“能表原诗之意，达原诗之情，传原诗之神，尽管未能存原诗之形，它仍不失为佳作”。主张自由体或散体译法的典型代表是英国汉学家韦利和中国翻译家翁显良。王佐良评价韦利的译诗说，韦利抛弃了脚韵和诗歌用语的老套，而用自由诗体和白描手法，着重形象、意境和气氛的移植，于是译诗显得十分新鲜。

非诗化译诗需要注重意象再现。中国古诗的意象具体而且精练，意蕴深远，而英语诗歌具有更多抽象的意象，理想的译诗应该是尽量保留原诗的意象，或者至少以具有相似联想意义的意象进行替换。如陶潜《饮酒二十首之九》的两句“褴褛茅檐下，未足为高栖”，韦利的译文为：

You live in rags under a thatched roof,

And seem to have no desire for a better lot.

在此例中，韦利采用自由体译法，没有用韵，译诗具有现代英语诗风格。在形式上，韦利采用了他所称的“弹性节奏”，用英语的一个重读音节来代表原诗的一个汉字，轻重音节交替出现。此处的两句都是五个重读音节，对应于原文的五个汉字，很好地再现了原诗的节奏感。

非诗化译法的另外一种方式是散体译法，即散文化译法。译诗不分行，不押韵，也不将就原诗的格律和节奏，重在达意和传达神韵，如翁显良所译的《登鹳雀楼》：

Westward the sun, ending the day’s journey in a slow descent behind the mountains. Eastward the Yellow River, emptying into the sea. To look beyond, unto the farthest horizon, Upward! Upward another storey!

翁显良在这首诗里以散体译法来翻译，形式上比韦利的自由体更加自由，全诗不分行。不过，散体译诗并非普通的散文，而是诗化的散文，译者采用多种修辞手段来弥补和补偿原诗的效果，比如押头韵（sun, slow, sea）、押尾韵（westward, eastward, upward）、重复（upward, upward another storey）、平行和排比（westward the sun, Eastward the Yellow River）等。

总之，英译中国古诗的主要思路包括诗化译法和非诗化译法。诗化译法又根据对格律和音韵的忠实程度分为韵体译法和非韵体译法。理想的译法是韵体译法，不过韵体译法容易因韵害意，为了将就节奏或其他形式特征而影响措辞造句，造成僵硬的译诗。非韵体译法选取诗歌的部分形式特征，以现当代英语诗歌（特别是自由诗）的形式来翻译，相对较为灵活，容易实现，既具有可读性，也能传达部分原诗“诗味”的译文。非诗化译法虽然从表面看与原诗在形式上相去甚远，但译者可通过其他补偿手段，以诗化散文来翻译，最终目的还是要体现原诗的诗味。诗歌翻译要在承认“诗歌翻译不容易”“难以完全呈现原诗特征”的前提下，争取做到“译诗须像诗”。

6.4 翻译实战：《送别》《送友人》

【说明】 参照“阅读欣赏”“翻译热身”的译文特点和“翻译技巧”中有关中国古典诗歌的特点及翻译思路，从以下两首有关“离别”的诗中选取一首翻译为汉语。

(一)《送别》

简介：王维（701年—761年），盛唐时期诗人，唐代山水田园诗人的代表，有“诗佛”之称，兼擅书画，多才多艺，也精通音乐，苏轼评价其为“味摩诘之诗，诗中有画；观摩诘之画，画中有诗”，重要诗作有《相思》《山居秋暝》等。这首《送别》是题赠友人归隐的五言诗，以问答方式从友人口中说出归隐的原因，也表现了诗人复杂的感情。该诗语言看似平淡，实则情谊深厚，词浅情深，意蕴深刻，成为千古传诵的著名送别诗。

送　别

王维

下马饮君酒，问君何所之？
君言不得意，归卧南山陲。
但去莫复问，白云无尽时。

(二)《送友人》

简介：《送友人》为李白创作的一首充满诗情画意的送别诗，也是李白的名篇之一。诗人与友人策马辞行，情意绵绵，动人肺腑。首联点出送别友人的地点，中间两联切题，写出离别的深情，尾联两句更深刻地表达出不愿离别又不得不离别的真情。全诗以青山、白水、落日、浮云相互映衬，色彩斑斓。班马长鸣，形象鲜活，自然美与人情美交织在一起，有声有色，气韵生动。诗的节奏明快，感情真挚而又豁达乐观，为李白送别诗最鲜明、最受赞誉的特点。

送友人

李白

青山横北郭，白水绕东城。
此地一为别，孤蓬万里征。
浮云游子意，落日故人情。
挥手自兹去，萧萧班马鸣。

6.5 译文荟萃

1. 短语

中国古诗 classical Chinese poetry

《古诗十九首》*Nineteen Old Poems*

《诗经》*Book of Poetry / Classic of Poetry / Book of Songs / Book of Odes*

《楚辞》*Chu Ci / Verses of Chu*

《全唐诗》*Complete Tang Poems*

《唐诗三百首》*Three Hundred Tang Poems*

绝句 *Jueju*/ Chinese Quatrain

田园诗 fields and gardens poetry

山水诗 *Shanshui* poetry / landscape poetry

子夜歌 midnight songs poetry

诗节 stanza

《神州集》/《华夏集》*Cathay*

意象 imagery

2. 句子翻译

1) 古代送别诗自《诗经》滥觞始，其后逐渐演绎并发展为诗歌创作的重要题材和类别之一。

Having originated from *The Book of Songs*, send-off poems have evolved into one of the main themes in poetic creation.

2) 在文词语言上，本歌剧希望使古文复活，融汇诗经、辞、府等，赋予古诗词的形式以鲜丽的生命。

The lyrics of this opera utilize all types of Chinese classic poems; the mandate is to make this archaic form reborn with fresh breathes and its own heartbeat.

3) 杜甫是我国著名的诗坛圣手。

Du Fu was the renowned master of Chinese poetry.

4) 李白、杜甫、王维以及其他诗人的诗词兀立在荣光宝殿之上。

Poems by Li Bai, Du Fu, Wang Wei among others stand out in the halls of glory.

5) 昔我往矣，杨柳依依。今我来思，雨雪霏霏。(《诗经 · 采薇》)

译文 1：At first, when we set out, / The willows were fresh and green; / Now, when we shall be returning, / The snow will be falling clouds. (James Legge 译)

译文 2：When I set out so long, / Fresh and green was the willow. When now homeward I go, / There is a heavy snow. (汪榕培 译)

6) 悠哉悠哉，辗转反侧。(《诗经 · 关雎》)

译文 1：Long he thought; Oh! Long and anxiously; / On his side, on his back, he turned, and back again. (James Legge 译)

译文 2：That his thoughts by day and his dreams by night. / Have had but her as his sole delight. (C. F.

R. Allen　译）

译文 3：Long thoughts, oh, long unhappy thoughts, / Now on his back, now tossing on to his side.（Arthur Waley　译）

7) 月光如水水如天。（赵嘏　《江楼有感》）

译文 1：While the moonbeams dance on the tops of the waves where the waters touch the sky.（Herbert A. Giles　译）

译文 2：The moonbeams join the water; the water meets the sky.（W. J. B. Fletcher　译）

8) 海上生明月，天涯共此时。（张九龄　《望月怀远》）

译文 1：Over the sea the round moon rises bright, / And floods the horizon with its silver light.（Herbert A. Giles　译）

译文 2：The clear moon uprises, new-born from the sea. / This hour is the same through the bourne of the skies.（W. J. B. Fletcher　译）

译文 3：The moon, grown full now over the sea, / Brightening the whole of heaven.（Witter Bynner　译）

9) 寻寻觅觅，冷冷清清，凄凄惨惨戚戚。（李清照　《声声慢》）

译文 1：Search. Search. Seek. Seek. / Cold. Cold. Clear. Clear. / Sorrow. Sorrow. Pain. Pain.（Kenneth Rexroth　译）

译文 2：I pine and peak / And questless seek / Groping and moping to linger and languish / Anon to wander and wonder, glare, stare and start.（John A. Turner　译）

译文 3：I look for what I miss; / I know not what it is. / I feel so sad, so drear, / So lonely, without cheer.（许渊冲　译）

10) 明月几时有，把酒问青天。（苏轼　《水调歌头》）

译文 1：When did this glorious moon begin to be? / Cup in hand, I asked of the azure sky.（John A. Turner　译）

译文 2：How long will the full moon appear? / Winecup in hand, I ask the sky.（许渊冲　译）

3.《天净沙·秋思》五个译本

简介：马致远的《天净沙·秋思》是一首小令，属于元代散曲的一种。小令最早作为词的一种，大约初现于初唐时期，在唐、五代和两宋时期得以蓬勃发展。随着宋词在南宋中期的衰落，逐渐兴起了一种源于民间小调的文学形式“散曲”，这便是元曲的雏形。元曲与唐诗、宋词并称中国古典文学的三座高峰。这首小令内容简单，语言凝练，以质朴的笔触，寥寥数笔就勾勒出了一幅悲凉肃穆的秋思画面，淋漓尽致地刻画了旅人浪迹天涯、思念故土的情感，是中国诗歌史上最为脍炙人口的名篇，被称为“思秋之祖”。元曲分为小令和套曲两种，小令是单个的曲子，相当于一首单调的歌，但可以重复，每首的韵可不同。散曲的小令如词的小令一样，有其曲牌和乐曲，有韵律、行数和字数的要求。小令专用的曲牌包括“黄钟”“正宫”“仙侣”等十种，《天净沙》是其中的一种小令曲牌，属于“越调”，单调二十八字，五句四平韵、一叶韵。在许多以《天净沙》为曲牌名的小令中，马致远的《秋思》最为著名。

天净沙·秋思

马致远

枯藤老树昏鸦，
小桥流水人家，
古道西风瘦马。
夕阳西下，
断肠人在天涯。

译文一

Tune to "Sand and Sky"
—Autumn Thoughts

Dry vine, old tree, crows at dusk,
Low bridge, stream running, cottages,
Ancient road, west wind, lean nag,
The sun westering,
And one with breaking heart at the sky's edge.

（Wayne Schlepp　译）

译文二

Tune: "Clear Sky over the Sand" Autumn

O'er old trees wreathed with rotten vine fly evening crows;
'Neath tiny bridge beside a cot a clear stream flows;
On ancient road in western breeze a lean horse goes.
Westwards declines the setting sun;
Far, far from home is the heart-broken one.

（许渊冲　译）

译文三

Autumn Thoughts

Withered vines, olden tree, evening crows;
Tiny bridge, flowing brook, hamlet homes;
Ancient road, wind from west, bony horse;
The sun is setting,
Broken man, far from home, roams and roams.

（赵甄陶　译）

译文四

Tian Jing Sha: Qiu Si

Dried vines, an old tree, evening crows;
A small bridge, flowing water, men's homes;
An ancient road, west winds, a lean horse;
Sun slants west;
A heart-torn man at sky's end.

（叶威廉　译）

译文五

Autumn

Crows hovering over rugged trees wreathed with rotten vine — the day is about done. Yonder is a tiny bridge over a sparkling stream, and on the far bank, a pretty little village. But the traveler has to go on down this ancient road, the west wind moaning, his bony horse groaning, trudging towards the sinking sun, farther and farther away from home.（翁显良 译）

6.6 翻译家：韦利

阿瑟·大卫·韦利（Arthur David Waley, 1889 年—1966 年）是英国著名的东方学家、汉学家和翻译家，精通汉文、满文、蒙文、梵文、日文和西班牙文等语种，一生撰著和译著共 200 余种，被称为 20 世纪上半叶最伟大的英国汉学大师。他因翻译了大量中国和日本诗歌而受到普通大众和学者的敬仰，影响了英语世界很多汉学工作者。他在汉学研究和中国典籍英译方面成就卓著，但却从未到过中国。韦利从未担任过任何学术职务，其主要成就也主要是向普通大众翻译和传播东方文化，被称为“向普通英语读者传播中国和日本经典文学的伟大翻译家，20 世纪上半叶向西方介绍东方的文化大使”。他一生从未受过正式的中文训练，而是通过自学熟练掌握汉语，并翻译了大量中国和日本诗歌，1953 年获得“女王诗歌金奖”（Queen's Gold Medal for Poetry），1952 年和 1956 年被授予“大英帝国爵士”（Companion of the British Empire）和“荣誉爵士”（Companion of Honour）。

韦利于 1889 年 8 月 19 日出生于英格兰肯特郡滕布里吉韦尔斯（Turnbridge Welss）一个犹太家庭，出生时取名为阿瑟·大卫·史洛斯（Arthur David Schloss）。史洛斯家族是 1725—1765 年间来到英国定居的犹太人中的一支。韦利的父亲大卫·弗雷德里克·史洛斯曾是大律师和经济学家。由于当时反犹太主义的氛围甚浓，韦利的母亲将德语意味甚浓的“史洛斯”改为英语味更浓的“韦利”（Waley, 有的中文著作翻译为“威利”）。

1903 年，韦利入读拉格比学校（Rugby School），后因古典文学成绩优异获得奖学金进入剑桥大学国王学院学习古典文学，1920 年因眼疾退学。在剑桥大学学习期间受迪金森（G. L. Dickinson）和摩尔（G.E. Moore）仰慕东方文明思想的影响，立志研究东方文化。离开剑桥大学时，韦利已掌握 11 种语言，包括拉丁语、希腊语、法语、德语、西班牙语、意大利语以及希伯来语和梵语。1913 年，韦利被聘为大英博物馆助理馆员，作为英国著名诗人、学者劳伦斯·宾扬（Laurence Binyon）的助手，在大英博物馆的东方版画与绘画部工作，接触了许多中国和日本的绘画作品。基于工作的需要，韦利开始自学古代汉语和古代日语。韦利极具语言天赋，很快就掌握了日语和汉语，在大英博物馆工作期间，翻译和发表了多部中国和日本文学作品，包括:《中国诗选》《汉诗一百七十首》《日本诗歌》《日本能剧》《源氏物语》《枕草子》《爱虫女》等。大英博物馆为韦利学习和研究东方语言文化提供了绝佳的条件和理想的工作环境，他在这里可以尽享所有的馆藏资源，并能与来自世界各地的学者进行交流。更重要的是，他与宾扬一起工作，深受宾扬的启发和影响。

1929 年，韦利辞去大英博物馆的工作，专心从事翻译和著述。第二次世界大战期间，曾在英国情报部门日文组做了四年检审员，此后再也没有担任过公职。韦利作为剑桥大学和伦敦大学亚非学院的荣誉讲师，偶尔应邀做一些学术讲座或指导研究生论文。韦利对于大学教职或其他公职并不感兴趣，据其学生莫里斯（Ivan Morris）回忆，剑桥大学曾有意聘请他做中文教授，接替刚刚去世的哈伦教授，但韦利却表示“我宁愿死掉”也不愿意接受这一让许多人梦寐以求的职位，而更愿意潜心于自己的翻译与文化研究。离开大英博物馆后，韦利一直住在伦敦，还经常到大英博物馆查阅资料，然后翻译了《道德经》《诗经》《论语》《西游记》《九歌》等中国经典作品，还向英语读者介绍了李白、白居易、袁枚等中国古代诗人。韦利对中国文化在英语世界的传播做出了杰出贡献，1958 年中国文化代表团访问英国，专程前往拜访韦利，并邀请他访问中国，却被他婉言谢绝，他的回答是:“我想在心目中永远保持中国唐代的形象。”1966 年，韦利在英国去世，安葬于伦敦的海格特公墓（Highgate Cemetry）。

韦利倾其一生专注于中国思想史、中国绘画史、中国文化和日本文学的研究、翻译与传播，成果丰硕，影响深远。据统计，他共著书 40 余种，翻译中、日文化作品 46 种，撰文 160 余篇。多部诗歌翻译作品被收入牛津版《现代诗歌 1892—1935》、牛津版《20 世纪英文诗》和企鹅版《当代诗歌 1918—1960》中。

韦利翻译和撰写的作品包括：

1.《中国诗选》(*Chinese Poems*)，1916 年。

2.《汉诗一百七十首》(*A Hundred and Seventy Chinese Poems*)，1918 年。

3.《汉诗选译续编》(*More Translations from the Chinese*)，1919 年。

4.《诗人李白》(*The Poet Li Po*)，1919 年。

5.《郊庙诗集及其他》(*The Temple and Other Poems*)，1923 年。

6.《中国画研究引论》(*Introduction to the Study of Chinese Painting*), 1923 年。

7.《长春真人西游记》(*The Travels of an Alchemist: The Journey of the Taoist Ch'ang Ch'un from China to the Hindukush at the Sumons of Chingiz Khan*)，1931 年。

A HUNDRED AND SEVENTY
CHINESE POEMS

TRANSLATED BY
ARTHUR WALEY

NEW YORK
ALFRED · A · KNOPF
MCMXIX

8.《〈道德经〉研究及其在中国思想中的地位》(*The Way and Its Power: A Study of the Tao Te Ching and Its Place in Chinese Thought*)，1934 年。

9.《英译中国诗选》(*Select Chinese Verses*)，与翟理斯合译，1934 年。

10.《诗经》(*The Book of Song*s)，1937 年。

11.《论语》(*The Analects of Confucius*)，1938 年。

12.《古代中国的三种思维方式》(*Three Ways of Thought in Ancient China*)，1939 年。

13.《汉诗英译》(*Translations from the Chinese*)，1941 年。

14.《猴》(*Monkey*)(《西游记》节译)，1942 年。

15.《白居易的生平及其时代》(*The Life and Times of Po Chu-yi*)，1949 年。

16.《大招》(*The Great Summons*)，屈原著，1949 年。

17.《李白诗歌与生平》(*The Poetry and Career of Li Po*)，1950 年。

18.《真实的三藏及其它》(*The Real Tripitaka and Other Pieces*)，1952 年。

19.《九歌:古代中国萨满教研究》(*The Nine Songs: A Study of Shamanism in Ancient China*),1955 年。

20.《十八世纪中国诗人袁枚》(*Yuan Mei: Eighteenth Century Chinese Poet*)，1956 年。

21.《中国人看鸦片战争》(*The Opium War Through Chinese Eyes*)，1958 年。

22.《敦煌曲子词与变文选集》(*Ballads and Stories from Tun-huang: An Anthology*)，1960 年。

23.《蒙古秘史》(*The Secret History of the Mongols*)，1964 年。

韦利的很多翻译作品都产生了重要影响。他所翻译的《诗经》《论语》《道德经》等以既忠实又流畅的译文深受读者喜爱，成为西方的翻译名著。他所翻译的中国诗歌、小说、词曲和经论以及对著名诗人、中国古代思想和绘画等的介绍，促进了西方世界对中国历史和文化的了解。韦利的第一部汉诗英译选集是 1916 年出版的《中国诗选》。当时，由于没有出版商愿意接受这部译稿，韦利只好自费请伦敦洛厄兄弟公司印刷一百册。这本诗集收入从先秦到宋代的 53 首诗。他最为著名的汉诗英译集是《汉诗选译一百七十首》，该书于 1918 年由伦敦康斯特布尔出版公司首次出版，由于广受欢迎，同一年就出版了修订版，在随后几十年里数次再版，至 1946 年已印刷二十多次，并被转译成德语和法语版。诗集中的一些译诗还被谱成歌曲，产生了很大影响。

韦利在传播东方文化，尤其是中国文化方面的成就举世公认。《不列颠百科全书》在介绍他的词条里说："他是本世纪前半个世纪最杰出的东方学家，也是将东方文学译为英文的最杰出的翻译家。……他是一位诗人和诗歌的创新者。由于他的译作，中国文学易于为西方读者接受了。"

6.7 补充资源

参考书目

吕叔湘 . 中诗英译比录 . 北京：中华书局，2002.

许渊冲 . 中诗英韵探胜 . 北京：北京大学出版社，2010.

朱光潜 . 诗论 . 北京：人民文学出版社，2010.

袁行霈 . 中国诗歌艺术研究 . 北京：北京大学出版社，2009.

汪榕培，王宏 . 中国典籍英译 . 上海：上海外语教育出版社，2009.

萧涤非等 . 唐诗鉴赏辞典 . 上海：上海辞书出版社，2004.

理雅各 . 中国经典（第四卷，《诗经》）. 上海：华东师范大学出版社，2010.

网络资源

古诗文网：https://www.gushiwen.org

中华诗词：http://www.zhsc.net

Chinese Poems: http://www.chinese-poems.com/index.html

Chinese classics in English: http://bs.dayabook.com

China Knowledge: http://www.chinaknowledge.de/index.html

Chapter 4

第四章　哲理故事翻译

- 第七单元　中国现代哲理故事
- 第八单元　中国古代哲理故事

第七单元　中国现代哲理故事

7.1 阅读欣赏:《聪明人和傻子和奴才》

【说明】 阅读下列故事及译文，体会故事中的象征意义、所蕴含的道理以及译文如何再现这种象征意义和其中的道理。

简介:《聪明人和傻子和奴才》是鲁迅创作于 1925 年的一首散文诗，最初于 1926 年 1 月 4 日发表于《语丝》周刊第 60 期。当时，语丝社同“现代评论派”展开了激烈的论战。林语堂在《语丝》上发文说:“华北大学诸君子不曾骂人，正是因为他们对执政的谦恭，并不使我十分起敬，但是由他们方面却正以为谦恭于执政是学者的态度，肆口漫骂者正是一号流氓，由此我们更明白冯文炳所说的‘我们的不干净也是干净，否则世上到那里去找干净!’所以有人说《语丝》社尽是土匪,《猛进》社尽是傻子。”鲁迅针对当时的社会斗争创作了这个寓言故事，创造了聪明人、傻子和奴才三种人物形象，展示了他们对待主子压迫下的悲苦生活的不同态度。《聪明人和傻子和奴才》后来选入鲁迅的散文诗集《野草》。

聪明人和傻子和奴才

鲁迅

奴才总不过是寻人诉苦。只要这样，也只能这样。有一日，他遇到一个聪明人。

“先生!”他悲哀地说，眼泪联成一线，就从眼角上直流下来。“你知道的。我所过的简直不是人的生活。吃的是一天未必有一餐，这一餐又不过是高粱皮，连猪狗都不要吃的，尚且只有一小碗……”

“这实在令人同情。”聪明人也惨然说。

“可不是么！”他高兴了。“可是做工是昼夜无休息的：清早担水晚烧饭，上午跑街夜磨面，晴洗衣裳雨张伞，冬烧汽炉夏打扇。半夜要煨银耳，侍候主人要钱；头钱从来没分，有时还挨皮鞭……。”

“唉唉……”聪明人叹息着，眼圈有些发红，似乎要下泪。

“先生！我这样是敷衍不下去的。我总得另外想法子。可是什么法子呢？……”

“我想，你总会好起来……”

“是么？但愿如此。可是我对先生诉了冤苦，又得你的同情和慰安，已经舒坦得不少了。可见天理没有灭绝……”

但是，不几日，他又不平起来了，仍然寻人去诉苦。

“先生！”他流着眼泪说，“你知道的。我住的简直比猪窠还不如。主人并不将我当人；他对他的叭儿狗还要好到几万倍……”

“混帐！”那人大叫起来，使他吃惊了。那人是一个傻子。

“先生，我住的只是一间破小屋，又湿，又阴，满是臭虫，睡下去就咬得真可以。秽气冲着鼻子，四面又没有一个窗……。”

“你不会要你的主人开一个窗的么？”

“这怎么行？……”

“那么，你带我去看去！”

傻子跟奴才到他屋外，动手就砸那泥墙。

“先生！你干什么？”他大惊地说。

“我给你打开一个窗洞来。”

“这不行！主人要骂的！”

“管他呢！”他仍然砸。

“人来呀！强盗在毁咱们的屋子了！快来呀！迟一点可要打出窟窿来了！……”他哭嚷着，在地上团团地打滚。

一群奴才都出来了，将傻子赶走。

听到了喊声，慢慢地最后出来的是主人。

“有强盗要来毁咱们的屋子，我首先叫喊起来，大家一同把他赶走了。”他恭敬而得胜地说。

“你不错。”主人这样夸奖他。

这一天就来了许多慰问的人，聪明人也在内。

“先生。这回因为我有功，主人夸奖了我了。你先前说我总会好起来，实在是有先见之明……。”他大有希望似的高兴地说。

“可不是么……”聪明人也代为高兴似的回答他。

The Wise Man, the Fool and the Slave

What a slave did was just to look for someone to listen to his own grievances. That was the only thing he wanted to do and also the only thing he could do. One day he came across a wise man.

“Sir!” said he sadly, tears trickling down from the corners of his eyes. “As you can see, I lead a subhuman life. I'm not even assured of a single meal a day. If I have one, it's only a small bowl of kaoliang husks, which even a pig or dog would disdain to eat ...”

“What a wretched life you lead!” the wise man replied with pity.

“Isn't it?” the slave followed up with exaltation. “And I toil day and night without rest. I carry water at dawn and cook dinner at dusk. I run errands all morning and grind wheat at night. I wash the clothes when it's fine and hold an umbrella for my master when it's rainy. I take care of the heating stove in winter and keep cooling my master with a fan in summer. I boil white fungus for him late at night. I wait on him at his gambling table without ever getting a tip. Instead I sometimes get a good thrashing ...”

“Oh, dear!” the wise man said with a sigh, the rims of his eyes looking somewhat red as if he were about to shed tears.

“Sir! I can't put up with it any more. I've got to find a way out. But what can I do? ...”

“I'm sure you'll pull through sooner or later …”

“Really? I hope so. But sir, I already feel much better now as you've given me sympathy and encouragement after listening to my grievances. It's thus clear that Heaven always upholds justice ...”

A few days later, however, he again began to grumble and look for somebody to listen to his complaints.

“Sir!” he cried out tearfully. “You know, I live in a place even lousier than a pigsty. My master treats me like dirt. He treats his Pekinese ten thousand times better …”

“Damn it!” the listener swore in such a loud voice as to make the slave start. This man was a fool.

“Sir, I live in a run-down small hut which is wet, dingy, stinking and full of bedbugs. They bite me all over when I lie down to sleep. And the place doesn't even have a single window ...”

“Why not ask your master to have a window made?”

“How can I do that? ...”

“Ok, you show me around!”

As soon as they came to the slave's dwelling, the fool started to pound its mud wall.

"What the hell are you doing, sir?" the slave yelled with alarm.

"I'm trying to knock a hole to make a window for you."

"No, you can't do that! The master will be mad at me!"

"To hell with your master!" the fool continued pounding away.

"Help! A robber is breaking down our house! Hurry up, or he'll knock a big hole in the wall!..." sobbing and shouting at the top of his voice, the slave rolled round and round on the ground.

Thereupon, a whole troop of slaves arrived on the scene and drove away the fool.

The last one that came out unhurriedly on hearing the commotion was the master.

"A robber came to smash up our house," the slave spoke respectfully and smugly. "I was the first to shout the alarm. We together drove him away."

"You did well," the master praised him.

A great many people came that day to express their solicitude, among them the wise man.

"Sir, I've just been praised by my master for my meritorious service," the slave said to the wise man very happily and hopefully. "I remember you said the other day that I would pull through sooner or later. So you're really a man of foresight ..."

"Oh, yeah …" replied the wise man as if he, too, were happy for the sake of the slave.

（张培基　译）

7.2 翻译热身：《老人和他的三个儿子》（一）

【说明】 参照"阅读欣赏"的译文思路，将下列故事翻译为英语。

简介：《老人和他的三个儿子》是中国现代作家冯雪峰创作的一首寓言故事。冯雪峰（1903 年—1976 年）是中国现代著名诗人、翻译家、文艺理论家，1927 年加入中国共产党。1928 年结识了鲁迅，编辑出版《萌芽》月刊，并与鲁迅共同编辑《科学的艺术论丛书》。1929 年参加筹备中国左翼作家联盟，后任"左联"党团书记、中共上海文化工作委员会书记。1950 年任上海市文联副主席，鲁迅著作编刊社社长兼总编。后调北京，先后任人民文学出版社社长兼总编、《文艺报》主编、中国作协副主席、党组书记。冯雪峰不仅是著名诗人，还创作了不少现代寓言故事。从 20 世纪 40 年代开始，冯雪峰与张天翼、天戈等作家一起，将中国现代寓言推向了兴盛，其中冯雪峰的寓言创作成就最大，形成了中国现代寓言的顶峰。

老人和他的三个儿子（节选一）

冯雪峰

一位老人有三个儿子。大儿子是一个非凡的水手：坚强、勇敢、尽职，而且富于冒险精神。老人真的爱他，认为这是个做父亲的值得骄傲的光荣。可是，在一次暴风雨中，这个儿子以他的大胆的勇猛，葬身于大海的狂涛骇浪里了。

二儿子是一个不知道辛苦和疲劳的、力气比一般伙伴都大的在职壮健的矿工，又很诚实和守信用，乐意帮助伙伴和朋友，所以矿工们，尤其是青年们，都和他做朋友，以得到他的友谊为快乐。那父亲也真爱他，尤其是在大儿子死了以后，更认为这是上天给他的最大的弥补。可是，不久，二儿子也殉身于自己的勇敢和自我牺牲的行为了。因为这一天他在煤矿中工作，矿坑因为支柱损坏而崩坍，他英勇地撑住一根支柱，救出了许多伙伴，而他自己却被压死了。

7.3 翻译技巧：汉语连动式和文化负载词的翻译

7.3.1 汉语连动式的翻译

汉语是倾向于动态的语言。与英语相比，汉语句子中动词的使用更为频繁，而连动式的使用正是这一特征的突出表现。汉语的连动式是指两个或两个以上谓语动词共用一个主语的结构，其特点是多个动词连用，其间不必通过关联词来连接就可组成几个句段或小句。相比之下，英语更为倾向于静态，多数句子仅包含一个谓语动词，多个谓语动词连用的情况并不多见。在英语句子中，谓语动词以外的其他动作概念往往会以非谓语动词、介词短语或从句等形式出现。

连动式动词之间的关系多样，既有并列、先后关系，也有从属关系。具体可分为以下几类：

（一）并列和先后关系

并列关系是指行为或动作在其发生时间以及语义功能上没有先后、主次之分；而先后关系指的是动作行为在发生的时间上具有先后关系。在翻译这两类关系的“连动式”时，可以考虑将几个连续出现的动词均译成谓语动词，并以 and 等关联词来连接。如下例所示：

例 (1)：他接过钢笔，在书的封面上写下了几个字。

译文：He took the pen and wrote down a few words on the cover of the book.

例 (2)：我打开门看见他躺在沙发上。

译文：I opened the door and saw him lying on the sofa.

（二）目的关系

翻译具有目的关系的“连动式”时，通常可用不定式或介词短语来表达。如下例所示：

例 (3)： 我将和弟弟回乡去探望父母。

译文： I will go home with my brother to visit our parents.

例 (4)： 他回办公室取钥匙。

译文： He went back to his office for the key.

（三）伴随关系

如果连动式中的一个动词与另一个动词是伴随关系，可用分词或介词短语来翻译其中某个动词。如下例所示：

例 (5)： 他静静地躺着，茫然地望着天空。

译文： He lay still, staring blankly at the sky.

例 (6)： 他手里握着手枪，一步步向敌人逼近。

译文： He advanced to his enemy, with a pistol in his hand.

除了上述几种关系以外，汉语连动式的动词之间可能还具有因果关系、方式关系等等。在这些情况下，可根据具体情况灵活使用不定式、分词、介词短语，甚至从句等手段来翻译。另外，如果原文句子较长、连用多个动词或以流水句的形式出现，为将事件交代清楚，我们在翻译时应当考虑对原文句子进行适当拆分，并将上述方法综合起来使用。如下例所示：

例 (7)： 探家归来，他左手提着旅行包，右手擎着盛了大半清水、插了一束嫩绿柳枝的玻璃瓶，在街上缓缓地走着。

译文： Returning from a visit to his hometown, he walked slowly along the street in a chilly drizzling rain, a traveling bag in his left hand, and in his right hand a half-filled glass water bottle with a bunch of green tender willow twigs stuck in it.

例 (8)： 她的眉舒展了，带着一丝不易觉察的笑，慢慢地松开了手，眼睛虽然还看着她，却没有了往日的晶亮的闪耀。

译文： Her brows smoothed, and, with a smile that could hardly be detected, she slowly loosened her hand. Her eyes still watched her, but lacked their usual luster.

在例 (7) 中，除了“缓缓地走着”被译作谓语动词以外，其他动词分别使用了分词和介词短语来翻译；而在例 (8) 中，译者则对原文句子进行了拆分，并使用连接词 and、but 和 -ing 分词来体现动作之间的先后关系和逻辑关系。再看如下几例：

例 (9)： 这群市大学生摄影协会会员准备捕捉大自然恩赐的美妙镜头，心情舒畅地说笑着，渐渐地走近这棵倾斜的龙柏。

译文： These members of the town's College Photographers Society had come out to capture the beautiful scenery endowed by nature. Laughing and talking merrily, they were approaching the leaning cypress.

例 (10)： 刚巧小光手持长矛从外面冲了进来，发现自己的"作品"被擦了，立刻大闹起来："你干吗擦我的画？臭爸爸！"哭喊着用长矛向老纪刺过来。

译文： Just then his son, Xiao Guang, rushed in with a long spear in hand. Seeing that his "masterpiece" was cleaned off, he flared up. "Why did you clean off my picture? What a beastly dad you are!" he cried, pointing his spear at Lao Ji.

例 (11)：（我）有些诧异，忙看前面，是一所巡警分驻所，大风之后，外面也不见人。

译文： I was surprised. When I looked ahead, I saw a police station. Because of the high wind, there was no one outside.

例 (12)： 这位美术爱好者凝视片刻，灵感的火花映亮心窗，他立刻打开速写本，捏着炭精棒，勾勒这棵龙柏的体态轮廓，准备回宿舍精心画一幅漫画，连画名也想好了，就叫做《一株龙柏的控诉》。

译文： The amateur artist was staring at the bent cypress when inspiration flashed into his mind. He quickly opened his sketch book and drew an outline of the cypress with his charcoal pen. He planned to develop the sketch into a cartoon. When he got back to the dormitory, he had even figured out a title for it, "A Cypress Complains."

与例 (8) 类似，例 (9) 和例 (10) 同样使用断句的方法和分词形式来翻译篇幅较长的连动式；而在例 (11) 和例 (12) 中，译者不仅作了断句的处理，还将句中某些动词短语译作时间状语从句，从而使得译文层次分明，逻辑关系更为清晰。可见，在翻译汉语的连动式时，我们首先要判断多个动作行为之间的先后关系和逻辑关系，在必要的情况下对原文句子进行恰当的拆分，并基于语境选择合适的语法形式来翻译连动式中的各类动词，以符合英语的行文特点。

7.3.2 文化负载词的翻译

文化是一个内涵极其丰富，最具人文意味的概念。早在 1971 年，Tylor (1871:1) 就给出了如下定义 "Culture, or civilization, taken in its broad, ethnographic sense, is that complex whole which includes knowledge, belief, art, morals, law, custom, and any other capabilities and habits acquired by man as a member of society."。可见，文化包括群族的历史地理、风土人情、传统习俗，生活方式、宗教信仰、神话故事、文学艺术、法律规范，制度组织、思维方式、价值观念、审美情趣，精神图腾等等。语言和文化息息相关，一方面语言是文化的一部分，语言内部的词汇时时反映着文化；另一方面，文化影响着语言的表达、发展和变化。

翻译涉及两种语言和文化的转换。原文中存在的某些单词和短语，有可能在目标语文化系统中不存在对应项目或者与该项目有不同的内涵，因此在翻译时，很难将这些词汇的功能和含义转移到译文中。这样的项目被西班牙学者艾克西拉定义为“文化专有项”（culture-specific items），也被称作“文化负载词”（culture-loaded words）。文化负载词是在语言系统中，最能体现语言承载的文化信息、反映人类社会生活的词汇。

在翻译文化专有项时，我们可以选择异化或者归化的策略，甚至可以两者结合起来使用。概括而言，异化策略要求译者向作者靠拢，采取相应于作者所使用的源语表达方式，来传达原文的内容。异化翻译在一定程度上保持原文的异域性，保留原文的语言和文化差异；同时故意打破目标语言的常规，偏离目标文化主流价值观，因此可以丰富目的语文化和目的语的语言表达方式。

归化策略则要求译者向目的语读者靠拢，采取目的语读者所习惯的目的语表达方式，来传达原文内容。归化是一种采用透明、流畅的风格，最大限度淡化原文陌生感的翻译策略。

例 (1)：凤姐儿听了，眼圈儿红了半天，半晌方说道：“真是‘天有不测风云，人有旦夕祸福’。这个年纪，倘或就因这个病上怎么了，人活着还有甚么趣儿！”（曹雪芹 《红楼梦》第十一回）

译文 1：Xifeng's eyes became moist. After a pause she exclaimed, “Truly, ‘Storms gather without warning in nature, and bad luck befalls men overnight.’ But life is hardly worth living if such an illness can carry off one so young!”（杨宪益、戴乃迭 译）

译文 2：Xifeng's eyes became moist and for a moment she was too overcome to speak. I know “the weather and human life are both unpredictable,” she said at last, “but she's only a child still. If anything should happen to her as a result of this illness, I think all the fun would go out of life!”（David Hawkes 译）

译文 1 运用了异化的翻译策略，将“不测风云”译为“Storms gather without warning”，“旦夕祸福”译为“bad luck… overnight”，并且将汉语的对仗句式转化成英语的并列句式，这种翻译方法以原文为中心，保留了汉语的修辞方法、文化意味和句型结构，为异化策略。

译文 2 将“不测风云”和“旦夕祸福”合译为“weather and human life are both unpredictable”，采用了释义的方法，并且将原文中的对仗句式简化为一个单句。这种翻译方法以译文读者为中心，省去了汉语的修辞方法、文化意味和句型结构，为归化策略。归化翻译一般可读性较强。

由于归化翻译必然忽视源语的文化语境，可能会造成“文化失真”。从文化视角来看，特别是对于经典文学的翻译来说，文化特色不宜“归化”，应当尽可能保留再现源语的文化信息。因此，有的学着提倡要采用异化翻译，传达原文的文化内涵，使得异域文化得以保真，来维护文化间的平等传播。

当然，值得注意的是，异化和归化翻译各有特点，各有侧重，任何极端的翻译策略可能都会有损文化的传播。例如，极端的异化翻译可能会导致译文晦涩难懂，失去了可读性，丧失读者群，从而达不到文化交流的目的。因此，我们在翻译时，尽量以异化为主，在某些具体情况下，辅以归化翻译，以维持传播异域文化和保证可读性之间的平衡。

文化负载词有不同的翻译方法。学界对此有不同的分类，下面按照异化、归化以及异化和归化相结合的策略，对常见翻译方法做简单归纳介绍。

（一）异化策略

1. 音译法

异化策略中最为常用的翻译方法是音译，将外来文化词汇的读音直接引入译文。比如：

例 (2)：祥子生在北方的乡间，最忌讳随便骂街。可是他不敢打张妈，因为好汉不和女斗。（老舍《骆驼祥子》）

译文：Xiangzi had been brought up in a northern village where cursing was taboo. However, he dared not strike Nanny Zhang because no decent man will hit a woman.（施晓菁　译）

祥子是老舍笔下一个生动的人物形象，他是旧中国北平城里一个人力车夫，具有不可替代的特点。本例中，将他的名字直接音译为 Xiangzi，保留了其人物的异域色彩。

例 (3)：孔乙己是站着喝酒而穿长衫的唯一的人。（鲁迅《孔乙己》）

译文：Kong Yiji was the only long-gowned customer who used to drink his wine standing.（杨宪益、戴乃迭　译）

孔乙己是鲁迅同名短篇小说中的著名人物形象，他代表了受到封建腐朽思想和科举制度毒害的读书人。译文中 Kong Yiji 也是采用了音译方法。

2. 直译法

直译法是指译文既与原文内容一致，又与原文形式相同的翻译方法。直译可以对号入座，字字翻译，但很多时候必须在句子某些成分上作些调整或变动。

例 (4)：“祥子你等等走！”虎妞心中打了个闪似的，看清楚：自己的计划是没多大用处了，急不如快，得赶紧抓住祥子，别鸡也飞蛋也打了！“咱们俩的事，一条绳拴着两蚂蚱，谁也跑不了！”（老舍《骆驼祥子》）

译文：“Wait, Xiangzi! Don’t go yet!” Like a flash Tigress saw her way clearly. Her old plan was no use now. She must act fast to keep hold of Xiangzi otherwise she’d lose the hen and the egg would be broken too. “We’re like grasshoppers tied to one cord; neither can get away!”（施晓菁　译）

本例中，汉语成语“鸡飞蛋打”被译为“lose the hen and the egg would be broken too”，歇后语“一条绳拴着两蚂蚱，谁也跑不了！”被译为“We’re like grasshoppers tied to one cord; neither can get away!”就是采用了直译的方法，保留原文的文化意象和表达方式，生动形象，清新贴切。

例 (5)：贤弟比来比去，比到对牛弹琴，岂非把我当作牛了？（《梁山伯与祝英台》第四章）

译文：Are you saying that talking to me is like playing the flute to a water buffalo?（Thomas Shou　译）

本例中，“对牛弹琴”被直译为 playing the flute to a water buffalo。水牛是东西方文化中都有的动物。可是，这种直译法需要读者认真体会其中的真实含义。在汉语中，有不少以动植物为喻体的成语、谚语和歇后语，由于中西方对于一些动物及其文化内涵有着相似的感受与共同的认识，因此在不影响读者理解和接受的前提下，可以尽可能运用直译再现汉语谚语中的形象。

（二）归化策略

1. 意译法

例 (6)：贾政也撑不住笑了。因说道：“哪怕再念三十本《诗经》，也都是掩耳盗铃，哄人耳目。”（曹雪芹 《红楼梦》第九回）

译文：Even Jia Zheng himself could not help smiling. “Even if he studied another thirty volumes, it would just be fooling people.” He retorted.（杨宪益、戴乃迭　译）

例 (7)：后又附助着薛蟠图些银钱酒肉，一任薛蟠横行霸道，他不但不去管约，反助纣为虐讨好儿。（曹雪芹 《红楼梦》第九回）

译文：In return for money, drinks, he had lately given Xue Pan a free hand in his nefarious activities — had, indeed, not only refrained from interfering with him, but even aided the tyrant in his tyranny.（David Hawkes　译）

纣是历史上的暴君，后泛指恶人，“助纣为虐”就成了帮助坏人做坏事的代称，意译即能准确表达这一含义。

2. 替换法（substitution）

替换法就是指选用译文读者较熟悉、更易接受的另一个文化专有项来替代或套用。例如，翻译汉语的典故和成语时，有时也可以套用英语的典故和惯用语，巧妙传达文本的含义。这种方法的优点在于地道自然，便于理解；但是其中显著的缺点就是，容易引起文化误读。

例 (8)：谋事在人，成事在天。

译文：Man proposes, God disposes.

中西方的宗教观念不同，中国人信仰佛教和道教，而西方国家信仰基督教，这里的“天”在中华文化中是最高主宰，而上帝则是西方国家的最高信仰。

例 (9)：只有破釜沉舟地跟他们拼，还许有翻身的一天。

译文：All you can do is to burn your boats and fight them in the hope that one day you’ll come out on top.

英语 burn one’s boat 与汉语“破釜沉舟”无论从字面意思还是文化内涵都极为相似。欧洲古罗马的恺撒将军（Julius Caesar，公元前 100—公元前 44 年）曾率领大军乘船横渡卢比孔河（the

Rubicon)，登岸之后，即刻下令把自己部队所乘的船只全部焚毁，自断退路，以示只进不退、非决一死战不可的决心。现在人们借此表达在做一件事时不惜牺牲、孤注一掷的决心。

（三）异化和归化相结合

1. 音译加注

在一些情况下，音译文化专有项的同时可以对其加上注释，明确地阐述其意义，交代其出处，有助于译文读者的理解。注释可以采用“文内注释”(in-text note)的方式，即将注释以括号形式置于文内；也可以采用“脚注”(footnote)的形式，即将注释放置于每页的底端；或者采用“尾注”(endnote)，将注释集中放在文末。

例 (10)：我听到从高高的大堂上，从那高高大堂上的辉煌烛光里，传下来阎王爷几近调侃的问话：“西门闹，你还闹吗？”(莫言 《生死疲劳》)

译文：Then, from high in the hall above me, somewhere in the brilliant candlelight in the hall above, I heard a mocking question from Lord Yama himself: “Ximen Nao, whose name means West Gate Riot, is more rioting in your plans?” (Howard Goldblatt 译)

西门闹是莫言小说《生死疲劳》中的主人公。此处描写西门闹在阎罗大殿受审的情形。西门闹的字“闹”一语双关。译文中，首先采用音译 Ximen Nao, 接着用 whose name means West Gate Riot 这一文内加注的方式进行解释，既保留了人物姓名的独特性，又传达了言外之意。

例 (11)：水车“吱格”地停住，雪癞子转过身来，只见“招白眼”傻乎乎地笑。雪癞子也懵了，好像眼前不是日日开门相见的“招白眼”，而是从月亮上飘下来的嫦娥。(姚景文 《田水哗啦》)

译文：The waterwheel came to a stop with a creak and Scabby-headed Xue saw Black-browed Zhao gazing at him with a foolish smile. He felt dazed as if she were not the Black-browed Zhao he met day in and day out, but rather, Chang Er, the Moon Fairy coming down from the moon. (琥珀 译)

译文在“嫦娥”后加上 Moon Fairy 的补充释义，可以让不了解“嫦娥奔月”传说的英语国家读者理解嫦娥在中国文化中的身份与所代表的意向。

2. 直译加注

一些历史或典故并不为目标语言的读者所广泛熟知，在翻译的时候可以采用“直译加注”的方式。一方面，将文化专有项直译出来；另一方面，采用注释的方法，明示文化专有项的真实含义。

例 (12)：两府中都换了门神，联对，挂牌，新油了桃符，焕然一新。(曹雪芹 《红楼梦》)

译文：In both mansions, new door-gods had been pasted up on all the doors, the inscribed boards at the sides and over the tops of gateways had been repainted, and fresh “good luck” slips — auspicious couplets written in the best calligraphy on strips of scarlet paper — had been pasted up at the sides of all the entrance.

(David Hawkes 译)

例 (13)：“难道这也是个痴丫头，又像颦儿来葬花不成？”因又自叹道：“若真也葬花，可谓‘东施效颦’了；不但不为新特，且更可厌了。”（曹雪芹 《红楼梦》）

译文：“Can this be another absurd maid come to bury flowers like Taiyu?” he wondered in some amusement. “If so, she's 'Tung Shih imitating Hsi Shih'*, which isn't original but rather tiresome.”

（*Note：Hsi Shih was a famous beauty in the ancient kingdom of Yueh. Tung Shih was an ugly girl who tried to imitate her ways.）（杨宪益、戴乃迭 译）

例 (14)：心较比干多一窍，病如西子胜三分。（曹雪芹 《红楼梦》）

译文：She looked more sensitive than Pikan*, more delicate than Hsi Shih.

（Note: *Pikan was a prince noted for his great intelligence at the end of the Shang Dynasty.）（杨宪益、戴乃迭 译）

本例中，杨宪益、戴乃迭采用了异化翻译，并附加了两个注释来确保译文读者准确理解意图，让译文读者能体会到在比干和西施的映衬下林黛玉的聪明和美貌。

例 (15)：螳螂捕蝉，黄雀在后。

译文：The mantis stalks the cicada, unaware of the oriole lurking behind itself.

译文中 unaware of 的意思在原文字面并未提及，属于隐含意思，翻译时首先直译了“螳螂捕蝉，黄雀在后”，然后增添了文内注释（lurking behind itself），将原文的意思更好地表达出来。

7.4 翻译实战:《老人和他的三个儿子》(二)

老人和他的三个儿子（节选二）

冯雪峰

老人的伤痛是不用说的，他马上变成了一个非常衰败的软弱的人了。不过，还剩下一个小儿子，这是做父亲的唯一的安慰。老人改变了主意，决心不让小儿子成为一个出众的英雄好汉的人物，因为他实在不能再忍受那种折损儿子的痛苦。他叹着气说：“唉，与其因为他有才能而被夺，我宁愿他是一个一无所长的没有出息的人呵。”这样，老人就亲自教育这个小儿子，采取了一种连那些老婆婆们教育女娃娃都很少采用的教育方法。而这个小儿子，也真孝顺，果然没有叫父亲失望。就是说，他让自己成为一个又懦弱又自私而真的一无用处的人了。可是，真没有想到，到了这个时候，这个老人感到从来没有过的悲哀和不幸了。他一边痛悔自己的错误，一边憎恨而又可怜自己的小儿子说：“这就叫做废物，这就叫做脓包，是我一向所痛恨的。现在因为我自私，亲手把他制造出来了！嗳，嗳，这样一个海淹不死、山压不死的人，他活着到底做什么的？”

这个老人实在无法爱他的小儿子，因为他只能爱波澜壮阔的海和巍峨坚实的山以及像他大儿子二儿子那样的人。因此，他现在做父亲的心，不得不无限地痛苦，这是他一度错误的想法和他亲手毁坏了小儿子这件事情的一个惩罚。

7.5 译文荟萃

1. 短语与术语翻译

1) 文学评论家 literary critic
2) 民间盛行 prevail among populace
3) 痛定思痛 bring home a lesson painfully learned
4) 花钱阔气 extravagant with money
5) 跑生意 travel around doing business
6) 马后炮 second guess
7) 混为一谈 be mentioned in the same breath
8) 怦然心动 one's heart went pitter-patter
9) 混日子 drift along
10) 失之交臂 let slip a good chance
11) 金婚纪念日 golden wedding anniversary
12) 慷他人之慨 be generous with other people's money
13) 打长工 work as a long-term laborer
14) 三长两短 unexpected misfortune
15) 塞北 north of the Great Wall
16) 对音乐的朦胧向往 hazy aspiration for music
17) 退避三舍 retreat into seclusion
18) 吊脚楼 stilt house
19) 龙舟节 Dragon-boat Festival
20) 防患于未然 nip the problem in the bud before it gets out of hand

2. 句子翻译

1) 我只乞求您写一篇义正词严的文章把我批一个狗血淋头！积数十年之经验，我深知凡被您批了的，都可以风行全国，名震环球！(王蒙 《互助》)

I only beg you to write a very severe criticism against me. From my years of experience, I have come to the conclusion that all articles you criticize will become popular not only in our country but also in the world.

2) “针尖大的洞，也会刮进斗大的风。咱党员干部，那歪门邪道不要搞。”他停了一下，朝烟波迷茫、水天一色的湖面瞧去。(徐光兴 《枪口》)

“A tiny opening will let in a gust of wind. We Party cadres should not engage in any under-the-counter business.” Yang stopped to glance over the misty lake where the water joined the sky.

3) 他本来是一副铜筋铁骨，黑皮肤衬着那一套大布之衣，看去像个乡下人。他什么苦都吃得，从不晓得享用，也像乡下人。他心里那一团火，也像乡下人。那一团火是热，是力，是光。(朱自清 《哀互生》)

He was as strong as a man of steel, his dark complexion set off by clothes of coarse cloth, looking like someone from the countryside. He could withstand any hardship and never sought ease and comfort. In this respect he was like a countryman, too. Again like a countryman, he had a heart as warm as fire radiating warmth, power and light.

4) 我的邻居老纪，是位消息灵通人士。每天下班，总要带回几条新闻：大至国内外大事，小到谁家夫妻吵架、婆媳不和……他发布新闻，是大家都在做饭的时候，地点自然以厨房居多。(宋连昌 《“孺子马”》)

My neighbor Lao Ji was well informed. Every day when he got off work, he would bring several pieces of news from big events at home and abroad down to small strifes between husband and wife, or between mother-in-law and daughter-in-law. The time for his news broadcast was usually dinner time, so the best place for it was naturally the shared kitchen.

5) 这类事情在体坛司空见惯，但是这些英雄的悲剧场景不仅使失败的英雄热泪盈眶，而且使观众为之落泪。(亦云 《运动员的情操》)

Those are common occurrences in the athletic world but they are scenes of tragic heroism bringing tears to the eyes of the outgoing heroes as well as the audience.

6) 我从小就对自己没有信心，这是问题的根子。这种情绪使我受到一点点表扬都会感到难为情，使我怎么也说不出一个“不”字。也使我不敢向父母多要一分钱。此外，这种缺乏信心的情况也影响了我对钢琴的热爱。(在美 《爱梦想的羞怯女孩》)

At the root of it is my diffidence by which I have been enslaved since childhood. It embarrasses me at the mildest flattery, crushes my utmost efforts to say “no,” and prevents me from asking my parents for one cent more than necessary. Among other things, diffidence has wormed its way into my love of piano.

7) 我循着这上帝的召唤来到附近的一所教堂，一进教堂我就被那钢琴的乐音吸引住了，简直不能自拔。可是我父母哪儿买得起钢琴呀。(在美 《爱梦想的羞怯女孩》)

Tracing that call of God into a neighboring church, I found myself inexorably attracted by the melody of a piano — something beyond the means of my parents.

8) 探家归来，他左手提着旅行包，右手擎着盛了大半清水、插了一束嫩绿柳枝的玻璃瓶，在街上缓缓地走着。这时，清风拂面，凉雨漫洒，叫人忧伤……（贾宝泉 《撷自那片芳洲的清供》）

Returning from a visit to his hometown, he walked slowly along the street in a chilly drizzling rain, a traveling bag in his left hand, and in his right hand a half-filled glass water bottle with a bunch of green tender willow twigs stuck in it. A light wind touching his face called for painful memories of the past …

9) 那天一早，一辆古老的独轮车推着姐姐和他走上了村头那条弯弯曲曲的蛋黄色小路。（贾宝泉 《撷自那片芳洲的清供》）

That morning saw an ancient one-wheeled pushcart, with both his sister and him sitting on it, rolling along the yolk-yellow winding path stretching away from the end of the village.

10) 她的眉舒展了，带着一丝不易觉察的笑，慢慢地松开了手，眼睛虽然还看着她，却没有了往日的晶亮的闪耀。（贾宝泉 《撷自那片芳洲的清供》）

Her brows smoothed, and, with a smile that could hardly be detected, she slowly loosened her hand. Her eyes still watched him, but lacked their usual luster.

11) 前面就是他的住所了。他一边回思着那段回弯曲折的历史，一边极小心地用脚试探着凸凹不平的路面，他想起曲折的路心里就酸楚得难以自抑，虽然他并不是不知道，世界总是在曲折中前进的……（贾宝泉 《撷自那片芳洲的清供》）

Ahead of him was his house. As his feet carefully probed the uneven surface of the road, his mind kept pondering on that part of history, a tortuous path they had gone by. He could not help feeling grief, even with an awareness that history never followed a straight forward course...

12) 西风，秋水，雁阵，衔着落日的远山，交融在一起，更增添打猎者的无限兴致。（徐光兴 《枪口》）

An autumn stream ruffled by the west wind, and the lines of wild geese set against the background of distant mountains embracing the sinking sun, harmoniously merged to enhance the joy of the hunters.

3. 篇章翻译

维护团结的人

王蒙

艾团结悄没声息地走进了老王的家，他压低了声音，对老王说:“老王，不要理他。宰相肚子里撑大船，不跟他一般见识。”

老王莫名其妙，眨了眨眼睛，由于他正忙着打家具，顾不上回答老艾的话。

“其实你也早知道了，你不会计较的，你的水平不一样嘛。”

老王低下头，拾掇刨子。

艾团结弯下腰，凑过身去说：“你知道，老周说你的鼻子是假的。”

老王鼻子哼一下，没言语。

艾团结把脸凑得更近一些，哈出来的热气冲到老王的耳朵上：“老周说，你的鼻子是从他家的垃圾堆里找出来的，用猪皮胶粘在脸上的。”

老王抬起了头。

“老周还说，你把你原来的鼻子卖给走私商了，没有缴纳赋税。

老王皱起了眉。

艾团结说：“不必生气，不必生气，我们都知道嘛，你的鼻子是一等品，是珍品，是原作，他那样说，只能证明他的无知。你是不会计较的，你是不会计较的……”

老王又低下了头，同时开始琢磨：“老周背后讲我的坏话究竟是什么意思呢？”

艾团结临走的时候强调说：“一定要以团结为重，一定要以团结为重。”

艾团结离开了老王，又去找老周“维护团结”去了。

A Man Upholding Unity

Ai Tuanjie stole into Lao Wang's home quietly and whispered surreptitiously to him, "Lao Wang, just ignore him. As the saying goes, a Prime Minister's heart is big enough for a boat to sail. So you needn't bother to reason with him."

Lao Wang blinked his eyes in bewilderment. He was busy making furniture and so he didn't have the time to make any response.

"In fact, you must have heard about it," he continued. " But you didn't pay any heed to it, I am sure. You are above all gossip."

Lao Wang stooped to fix the plane.

Ai Tuanjie bent closer and went on, "You know, Lao Zhou said your nose is artificial."

Lao Wang let out a snort through his nose but kept silent.

Ai Tuanjie moved still closer, breathing hot air into Lao Wang's ear, "Lao Zhou said your nose was picked up from among the rubbish heap in front of his house and stuck on to your face by the adhesive made of pig skin."

This remark finally made Lao Wang look up at him.

He then added, "Lao Zhou also said that you have sold your own nose to a profiteer without paying tax."

Lao Wang knit his brows.

"Don't get upset. Don't, please!" Ai Tuanjie hastened to console him.

"We all know that your nose is first-rate. It is a rarity, an original one. What Lao Zhou said only proves his utter ignorance. You wouldn't mind, would you?"

Lao Wang lowered his head again and began to wonder, "What on earth prompted Lao Zhou to talk behind my back like that?"

Ai Tuanjie emphasized, "We must first of all uphold unity. Unity comes before anything else."

With these remarks, Ai Tuanjie left Lao Wang and went to "uphold unity" at Lao Zhou's.（琥珀　译）

7.6 翻译家：张培基

张培基是我国当代著名的翻译家，他不仅在翻译理论与实践方面有着突出的成就，在翻译教育方面也做出了重要的贡献。张培基于 1921 年出生于福建，1945 年毕业于上海圣约翰大学英国文学系。毕业之后他曾担任过英文报刊的记者和撰稿人，并在第二次世界大战结束之后赴东京远东国际军事法庭任英文翻译。新中国成立后，张培基先生先是任职于北京外文出版社，从事编译工作；后于 1955 年开始从事英语教学工作，先后在洛阳解放军外国语学院和对外经贸大学执教，直至退休。张培基先生还曾担任过中国译协理事、外文出版社英文翻译顾问和《英语世界》杂志社顾问等。

张培基先生从 20 世纪 50 年代开始从事文学翻译，他的译作涵盖小说、戏剧、传记和散文等。

其主要作品有柔石的《为奴隶的母亲》、曹禺的《明朗的天》、杨植霖的《王若飞在狱中》、王士菁的《鲁迅传》、廖静文的《徐悲鸿一生》和《英译中国现代散文选》。在他的各类译作中，《英译中国现代散文选》最为知名，影响范围也最大。这套丛书共有四册，分别于 1999 年、2003 年、2007 年和 2012 年出版。它收录了五四运动以来的诸多名家名作，以汉英对照的形式呈现，并附有详细的注释及对原作者的介绍，而对于翻译过程中可能遇到的语言难点、翻译方法和历史背景等，作者也做了分析和讲解。该书面世以来已多次再版，成为许多英语学习者和翻译从业者的必备书籍。

张培基先生基于自己长期的翻译实践探索，撰写了《英汉翻译教程》、《英语声色词与翻译》和《习语汉译英研究》等著作。在《英汉翻译教程》中，张培基详细阐发了自己的翻译思想，其中包括他对翻译的标准、直译与意译的关系、翻译过程、翻译教学和译者素养等几个方面的看法。例如在翻译标准方面，他认为翻译最重要的是做到“忠实”和“通顺”。“忠实”既指忠实于原作的内容，又指保持原作的风格，即“原作的民族风格、时代风格、语体风格和作者个人的语言风格”，而“通顺”是指译文语言“通顺易懂，符合规范”，这样才能避免“死译”和“硬译”的现象。在他看来，忠实与通顺相辅相成，“忠实而不通顺，读者看不懂，也就谈不到忠实；通顺而不忠实，脱离原作的内容与风格，通顺也失去了作用，使译文成为编纂、杜撰或乱译”；而在对待直译和意译这两种翻译方法的态度上，他认为两者“都是为了忠实表达原作的思想内容和文体风格，互不排斥”，因此“任何译作都是既有直译又有意译”，两者需结合起来运用；在论及翻译的过程、译者素养和翻译教学几个方面时，他从翻译的理解、表达和校核这三个层面对译者提出了非常细致的要求。另外，他在《习语汉译英研究》一书中还对汉英习语进行了深入的比较研究，并提出了系统的翻译方法；在《英语声色词与翻译》一书中，他又从词汇学、音韵与修辞角度比较了英汉语声色词的异同，并使用大量的实例探索了英语声色词的翻译规律。张培基先生在翻译领域默默耕耘数十载，他通过自己的著作向翻译学习者系统地介绍了文学翻译的理论知识和实践技巧，同时又以自己严谨的翻译态度和丰硕的翻译成果，为中国现当代文学的对外传播做出了十分重要的贡献。

7.7 补充资源

参考书目

张培基．英译中国现代散文选．上海：上海外语教育出版社，1999.
钱歌川．翻译的基础知识．长沙：湖南科学技术出版社，1981.
张庆年．佛经故事一百篇．北京：中国对外翻译出版公司，1995.
江蓝生．禅宗语录一百则．黎翠珍，张佩瑶，译．北京：中国对外翻译出版公司，1999.
杨立义．中国成语故事一百篇．北京：中国对外翻译出版公司，1991.
张慈赟．中国成语故事．上海：上海译文出版社，2015.

网络资源

美文网（故事）：https://www.wenjiwu.com/gushi
瑞文网（寓言）：http://www.ruiwen.com/wenxue/yuyan
短文学网（哲理故事）：https://www.duanwenxue.com/jingdian/zheli

第八单元　中国古代哲理故事

8.1 阅读欣赏：《西僧》

【说明】仔细阅读下列故事及其译文，体会原文体现的哲理以及英译思路。

西　僧

两僧自西域来，一赴五台，一卓锡泰山。其服色言貌，俱与中国殊异。自言历火焰山，山重重气熏腾若炉灶，凡行必于雨后，心凝目注，轻迹步履之，误蹴山石，则飞焰腾灼焉。又经流沙河，河中有水晶山，峭壁插天际，四面莹彻，似无所隔。又有隘可容单车，二龙交角对口把守之。过者先拜龙，龙许过，则口角自开。龙色白，鳞鬣皆如晶然。僧言途中历十八寒暑矣。离西土者十有二人，至中国仅存其二。西土传中国名山四：一泰山，一华山，一五台，一落伽也。相传山上遍地皆黄金，观音、文殊犹生。能至其处，则身便是佛，长生不死。

听其所言状，亦犹世人之慕西土也。倘有西游人，与东渡者中途相值，各述所有，当必相视失笑，两免跋涉矣。（蒲松龄　《聊斋志异》）

Arrival of Buddhist Priests

Two Buddhist priests having arrived from the West, one went to the Wu-t'ai Hill, while the other hung up his staff at T'ai-shan. Their clothes, complexions, language, and features were very different from those of our country. They further said they had crossed the Fiery Mountains, from the peaks of which smoke was always issuing as from the chimney of a furnace; that they could only travel after rain, and that excessive caution was necessary to avoid displacing any stone and thus giving a vent to the flames. They also stated that they had passed through the River of Sand, in the middle of which was a crystal hill with perpendicular sides and perfectly transparent and that there was a defile just broad enough to admit a single cart, its entrance guarded by two dragons with crossed horns. Those who wished to pass prostrated themselves before these dragons, and on receiving permission to enter, the horns opened and let them through. The dragons were of a white colour, and their scales and bristles seemed to be of crystal. Eighteen winters and summers these priests had been on the road; and of twelve who started from the West together, only two reached China. These two said that in their country four of our mountains are held in great esteem, namely, T'ai, Hua, Wu-t'ai, and Lo-chia. The people there also think that China is paved with yellow gold, that Kuan-yin and Wen-shu are still alive, and that they have only come here to be sure of their Buddhahood and of immortal life. Hearing these words, it struck me that this was precisely what our own people say and think about the West; and that if travelers from each country could only meet half-way and tell each other the true state of affairs, there would be some hearty laughter on both sides, and a saving of much unnecessary trouble.（Herbert Giles 译）

8.2 翻译热身：《邹忌比美》

【说明】请将下列篇章翻译为英语，注意体会古文翻译的基本特点。

邹忌比美

邹忌修八尺有余，而形貌昳丽。朝服衣冠，窥镜，谓其妻曰：“我与城北徐公孰美？”其妻曰：“君美甚，徐公何能及君也！”——城北徐公，齐国之美丽者也。忌不自信，而复问其妾曰：“吾与徐公孰美？”妾曰：“徐公何能及君也！”旦日，客从外来，与坐谈，问之：“吾与徐公孰美？”客曰：“徐公不若君之美也。”明日，徐公来。孰视之，自以为不如；窥镜而视，又弗为远甚。暮寝而思之曰：“吾妻之美我者，私我也；妾之美我者，畏我也；客之美我者，欲有求于我也。”（刘向《战国策》）

8.3 翻译技巧：汉语四字格和重复结构的翻译

8.3.1 汉语四字格的翻译

在汉语中，四字格是构成词语和句子的重要手段。它的优点在于能使文章在意义上言简意赅，形式上工整匀称。然而，由于汉语和英语在句法结构、词汇搭配和修辞功能上存在较大差异，我们在汉译英时不可能对四字格进行字面上的直译。

值得注意的是，汉语四字格常常以并列或排比的形式出现，且不必借助语言形式手段（如关联词）来连接。从语音层面而言，它可以给读者以抑扬顿挫、朗朗上口、一气呵成的阅读感受，从而提升文本的艺术表现力。应当注意的是，由于汉语重意合，词语和分句间即使不使用语言形式手段进行连接，句子的语法意义和逻辑关系也大多可以通过词语或分句的自身含义来表达；而英语重形合，句中的词语或分句间多用语言形式手段进行连接，以表达语法意义和逻辑关系。我们在翻译汉语四字格的并列结构时，应当充分意识到这一差异。如果将汉语四字格的并列结构字对字、词对词、句对句地进行直译，会使英语译文出现大量短句、简单句和并列句，这显然不符合译入语的语言习惯，在一定程度上将影响译文的质量。

以 8.5.2 部分的句子翻译为例，我们发现，在翻译汉语四字格及其并列结构时，往往需要通过添加介词、连接词，或使用其他语法手段来衔接词句，从而使得篇章更为连贯。试读下面的句子及其译文，注意体会译者在措辞方面的增补以及句式上的重组：

例 (1)：一道士坐蒲团上，素发垂领，而神观爽迈。

译文：A priest sat on the dais, his white hair reaching down to his shoulders, and he looked hearty and good-spirited.

在此例中，译者使用了独立主格结构 his white hair reaching down to his shoulders 来翻译原文的“素发垂领”这一外貌特征，从而避免了分句的简单罗列。

例 (2)：百年老屋，尘泥渗漉，雨泽下注，每移案，顾视无可置者。又北向，不能得日，日过午已昏。

译文：As it was nearly one hundred years old, dust and flakes of plaster fell and the roof let in rain. When I moved my desk, I could find no place to keep it off the rain. It faced the north and the sun could not get inside. Soon after noon it turned dusky.

在例 (2) 中，译文对句子进行重组，并通过添加关联词将“尘泥渗漉，雨泽下注”和“百年老屋”译作主 – 从结构，将原文的三个四字格单独合为一句，这既避免了同一句话所涉信息过于繁杂，又增加了句子的层次感。

例 (3)：三五之夜，明月半墙，桂影斑驳，风移影动，珊珊可爱。

译文：On the fifteenth night of the lunar month the bright moon flooded half of the wall. When a gentle breeze arose, laurel leaves shimmered flecks of moonlight on the wall and it was pleasing to see the shadows dancing and hear the leaves rustling in the wind.

在例 (3) 中，译者先将“三五之夜，明月半墙”断作一句，并通过添加介词将“三五之夜”译作时间状语；接下来将“桂影斑驳，风移影动，珊珊可爱”另起一句，通过添加关联词 when 和 and 把三个四字格结构译为并列复合句，与例 (2) 所举译文具有同样的效果。

8.3.2 汉语重复结构英译

重复在汉语中是十分常见的现象，这种现象在词、句子和篇章层面均有体现。在连淑能看来，“汉语的重复倾向与其语音文字的特点有密切的关系”。汉语的单音节词与单音节词相配，双音节词与双音节词相配，往往给读者以匀称整齐、平稳舒畅的感觉；其次，汉语讲究均衡美的特点也促成了句子的重复倾向。通过重复相同或相似的词语或句式，既可突出作者想要表达的思想，又可增添文采，令读者阅读时有朗朗上口之感；相较而言，英语对于重复的使用频率较低。除非有意强调或出于修辞的需要，英语极少出现不必要的重复。

重复既包括同一词句的多次使用，也包括相同或相似意义成分的反复出现。以本章《邹忌比美》这则故事为例，“吾与徐公孰美？”这句话重复了两次，这既是故事情节安排所需，也是出于对篇章结构工整、对称的考虑。然而，如在英译时过于忠实于原文形式，译文容易给目的语读者以啰唆繁复之感。

又如，在《西僧》一文里，在形容外国僧人途径火焰山小心翼翼的状态时，作者使用了“心凝目注，轻迹步履之”这一表达。在这里，“心凝目注”和“轻迹步履”体现了汉语在音韵上的节奏感和形式上的工整感，然而其表达的意义实际有所重复。如在英译时亦步亦趋地照字面翻译，译文必然会显得冗长繁复。

我们不妨参照两个故事的参考译文，体会译者对这两处重复做出了何种处理：

例 (4)：……谓其妻曰：“我与城北徐公孰美？”其妻曰：“君美甚，徐公何能及君也！”——城北徐公，齐国之美丽者也。

忌不自信，而复问其妾曰：“吾与徐公孰美？”妾曰：“徐公何能及君也！”

旦日，客从外来，与坐谈，问之：“吾与徐公孰美？”

译文：“Which is more handsome,” he asked his wife, “Lord Xu of the north city or I?”

“You are ever so handsome,” replied his wife. “How can Lord Xu compare with you?”

Since Lord Xu of the north city was famed for his good looks throughout the state, Zou Ji did not altogether believe his wife. He repeated his question to his concubine.

“How can Lord Xu compare with you?”cried the concubine.

Later that morning a protégé came in, and Zou Ji put the same question to him.

“You are by far the more handsome,” replied this man.

不难发现，译者先后使用了 repeated his question 和 put the same question 来替代前文的“Which is more handsome, Lord Xu or I?”这一问题，从而避免了重复。原文接连三次使用了“吾与徐公孰美”这一句式，而译文换用了不同的表达方式，通过恰当的替代使得文章更为流畅自然。

而在《西僧》的译文中，译者将“心凝目注，轻迹步履之”译作“excessive caution was

necessary”。这种简化的处理将“心凝”、“目注”和“轻迹步履”进行了合并，从而使译文更为简洁易懂。

除此之外，在《邹忌比美》一文的结尾，邹忌“暮寝而思之曰：‘吾妻之美我者，私我也；妾之美我者，畏我也；客之美我者，欲有求于我也。’”这里“……之美我者”这一结构使用了三次，译者使用 said so 替代了前面出现的“said I was more handsome”，从而避免了后两次的重复，使得文字更为轻快干练。

又如在《愚公移山》这则寓言故事中，“虽我之死，有子存焉；子又生孙，孙又生子；子又有子，子又有孙；子子孙孙，无穷匮也。”这段文字以排比的方式充分体现了汉语词句重复这一特征。而杨宪益和戴乃迭在翻译时使用了省略的方法来达到简化译文的效果：

Though I shall die, I shall leave behind me my son, and my sons' sons, and so on from generation to generation.

由上述例子可见，在翻译汉语文章中的重复词句时有三种方法可供借鉴：替代法、合并法和省略法。其中，替代法可借助代词、同义词或近义词来实现；合并法往往将意义相近的字、词、句进行合并；省略法则是略去汉语中并列句或排比句中反复出现的表达方式。汉语和英语在重复的使用上存在较大差异，我们在翻译过程中应当充分考虑英语的行文特点，对汉语中出现的重复现象进行适当处理，以便符合目的语读者的阅读习惯。

8.4 翻译实战：《画蛇添足》

【说明】 请将下列篇章翻译为英语，并思考如何运用本单元介绍的翻译技巧。

画蛇添足

楚有祠者，赐其舍人卮酒。舍人相谓曰：“数人饮之不足，一人饮之有余。请画地为蛇，先成者饮酒。一人蛇先成，引酒且饮之，乃左手执卮，右手画蛇，曰：“吾能为之足！”未成，一人之蛇成，夺其卮，曰：“蛇固无足，子安能为之足？”遂饮其酒。为蛇足者，终亡其酒。（刘向 《战国策》）

8.5 译文荟萃

1. 短语翻译

1) 才高八斗 possess immense knowledge

2) 东施效颦 blindly copying others and making oneself look foolish

3) 负荆请罪 make an apology for one's wrongdoings

4) 邯郸学步 slavishly imitate others and lose one's own originality

5) 狐假虎威 bully people by flaunting one's powerful connections

6) 毛遂自荐 recommend oneself to a post

7) 杞人忧天 make a fuss over sth.

8) 完璧归赵 return things to its owner intact

9) 卧薪尝胆 nurse vengeance through bearing hardships

10) 揠苗助长 Haste makes waste.

11) 目不识丁 not know one's ABC

12) 夜郎自大 play the great man

13) 班门弄斧 teach one's grandmother how to suck eggs

14) 半斤八两 six of one and half a dozen of the other

15) 逼上梁山 He must need swim that is held up by the chin.

2. 句子翻译

1) 虽我之死，有子存焉；子又生孙，孙又生子；子又有子，子又有孙；子子孙孙，无穷匮也。(《愚公移山》)

Though I shall die, I shall leave behind me my son, and my son's sons, and so on from generation to generation.

2) 转为蚊虻之声、孤犊之鸣，即掉尾、奋耳，蹀躞而听。(《对牛弹琴》)

Then he struck up some different notes, which sounded like mosquitoes droning and calves bleating. Whereupon the ox flicked its tail, pricked up its ears, and began frisking round and round, evidently absorbed in the music.

3) 或百步而后止，或五十步而后止。以五十步笑百步，则何如？（《孟子·寡人之于国也》）

Suppose one man runs a hundred yards and another man fifty, is the one who has fled only fifty right to laugh at the one who has fled a hundred?

4) 愚者千虑，必有一得。

Even a fool occasionally hits on a good idea.

5) 鹬蚌相争，渔翁得利。

If a snipe and a clam are locked in fight, it is the fisherman who is in delight.

6) 宁为玉碎，不为瓦全。

Better be a piece of broken jade than an unbroken tile.

7) 塞翁失马，焉知非福。

Loss sometimes spells gain.

8) 一言既出，驷马难追。

What is said cannot be unsaid.

9) 己所不欲，勿施于人。

Do not do to others that which you do not wish to be done to yourself.

3. 篇章翻译

黔之驴

柳宗元

黔无驴，有好事者船载以入。至则无可用，放之山下。虎见之，庞然大物也，以为神。蔽林间窥之。稍出近之，慭慭然，莫相知。他日，驴一鸣，虎大骇，远遁；以为且噬己也，甚恐。然往来视之，觉无异能者，益习其声，又近出前后，终不敢搏。稍近，益狎，荡倚冲冒，驴不胜怒，蹄之。虎因喜，计之曰："技止此耳！"因跳踉大㘎，断其喉，尽其肉，乃去。噫！形之庞也类有德，声之宏也类有能，向不出其技，虎虽猛，疑畏，卒不敢取。今若是焉，悲夫！

译文一

The Donkey of Guizhou

There were no donkeys in Guizhou until an eccentric took one there by boat; but finding no use for it he set it loose in the hills. A tiger who saw this monstrous looking beast thought it must be divine. It first surveyed the donkey from under cover, then ventured a little nearer, still keeping a respectful distance however.

One day the donkey brayed, and the tiger took fright and fled, for fear of being bitten. It was utterly terrified. But it came back for another look, and decided this creature was not so formidable after all. Then, growing used to the braying, it drew nearer, though it still dared not attack. Coming nearer still, it began to take liberties, shoving, jostling, and charging roughly, till the donkey lost its temper and kicked out.

"So that is all it can do!" thought the tiger, greatly pleased.

Then it leapt on the donkey and sank its teeth into it, severing its throat and devouring it before going on its way.

Poor donkey! Its size made it look powerful, and its bray made it sound redoubtable. Had it not shown all it could do, even the fierce tiger might not have dared to attack. But the donkey gave itself away!

（杨宪益、戴乃迭 译）

译文二

There was no ass in Kweichow, and somebody brought in one by boat. But when it arrived, he found he could make no use of it, so he left it at the foot of a mountain. Seeing it, a tiger thought such a tremendous thing must be none other than a god. At first he peered at it from behind the woods, and then moved timidly towards it; but still he dared not get in touch with it. One day the ass brayed, and the tiger was so frightened that he ran far away from it fearing it was going to eat him up. Later on he came back to look at it from all quarters, and found it possessing no particular ability. Though he, being more accustomed to its braying, was no longer afraid to come near it, yet he dared not attack it. He ventured to tease it more and more with a view to testing its abilities. Being irritated, the ass gave him a kick. At this time the tiger was very glad as he found it was all its wit's end and had no other ability than this. Therefore he pounced upon it, first breaking its neck and then eating up all its flesh, and went away. Alas! those with a huge form appear to be powerful, and those with a loud voice appear to be capable. No matter how fierce the tiger was, he would not be bold enough to grapple the ass, so long as it did not show off its ability. What a pity that it should have done thus!（钱歌川 译）

狐假虎威

虎求百兽而食之，得狐。狐曰："子无敢食我也！天帝使我长百兽。今子食我，是逆天帝命也！子以我为不信，吾为子先行，子随我后，观百兽之见我而敢不走乎？"虎以为然，故遂与之行。兽见之，皆走。虎不知兽畏己而走也，以为畏狐也。（刘向 《战国策》）

译文一

The Fox Who Profited by the Tiger's Might

While hunting for prey, the tiger caught a fox. "You can't eat me," said the fox. "The emperor of Heaven has appointed me king of the beasts. If you eat me, you'll be disobeying his orders. If you don't believe me, follow me. You'll soon see whether the other animals run away at the sight of me or not."

Agreeing to this, the tiger accompanied; and when all the beasts saw them coming they dashed away. Not realizing that they were afraid of him, the tiger thought they were afraid of the fox.（杨宪益、戴乃迭 译）

译文二

A tiger went about in search of other weaker animals for food. Once in his hunting, he happened to find a fox. "You won't dare to eat me," said the fox, "as I am head of all animals appointed by God. It is against the will of God, if you eat me now. In case you don't believe what I say, let us go together. You just follow me as I go ahead to see if there is any animal that does not run away when I pass." The tiger agreed and went with the fox. Certainly he saw all the animals run away on seeing the fox. He thought they were afraid of the fox without knowing it was he himself that they feared.（钱歌川 译）

8.6 翻译家：翟理斯

翟理斯（Herbert Allen Giles, 1845 年—1935 年）是 19—20 世纪英国著名汉学家、翻译家，西方现代汉学奠基人之一，曾被誉为英国汉学三大星座之一。他终生为传播中国语言、文学和文化而努力，研究和翻译了大量中国历史、文学、哲学和宗教典籍，汉学成就影响深远。

翟理斯的父亲约翰·翟理斯（John Giles）是一位编辑和翻译，翟理斯自小便对语言文字有着浓厚的兴趣。1867 年，翟理斯来到中国，先后在天津、宁波、汉口、广州、上海等地的英国领事馆担任翻译、助理领事和领事等职。在华期间，他将大量精力投入到中文典籍翻译以及汉语教材和汉英词典的编撰工作中。1893 年，他返回英国，并于 1897 年开始在剑桥大学担任汉学教授。此后他仍笔耕不辍，研究范围遍及中国文学、历史、宗教、哲学、绘画等诸多领域。他的译作和著述对于中国语言、文学和文化在西方世界的广泛传播起到了十分重要的作用。

翟理斯在翻译方面的成就最为突出。在其翻译生涯前期，他较有代表性的作品有《三字经》和《千字文》。他在《三字经》的序言中指出，该作品在中国是启蒙读物，对于希望掌握中国书面语、养成汉语思维习惯的外国人而言不可不读。次年，他又翻译了《闺训千字文》和《洗冤录》，发表于《中国评论》；1877 年，他翻译了东晋名僧法显所著的游记《佛国记》(又名《法显传》)，以纠正前人对该作品的误译；1878 年，他选译了蒲松龄《聊斋志异》中的 164 则故事，该译本是迄今为止《聊斋志异》最全的英译本，很受西方读者欢迎，曾多次再版。1883 年，他编译了《古文选珍》，收录了不同时期中国散文家的作品片段，向西方读者展示了中国数千年来散文、诗歌的独特魅力；五年后他又编译了《古今诗选》，选取了从《诗经》到清代的诗歌近两百首。该译本文字优美，简洁干练，可读性强，对中国诗歌在西方的传播起到极大的推动作用。除了小说和诗歌，翟理斯还于 1889 年翻译了《庄子》。该译本包括引言、庄子哲学札记和译文三部分。翟理斯对《庄子》极为看重，他在 81 岁高龄还重新修订了此译本，为西方汉学界的庄子相关研究提供了极为重要的参考。除此之外，他的翻译作品还有 1911 年出版的《中国神话故事》和 1925 年出版的《中国笑话选》等。

翟理斯勤于著述，其研究涉及中国文学、历史、宗教、哲学、绘画等诸多领域，同时还有不少语言教材行世。他撰写了第一部英文中国文学史、第一部中国绘画史、第一部英文中国人物传记词典，他所编撰的《华英字典》影响了几代外国学生，经他修改和确立后的威妥玛－翟理斯式拼音方案风行 80 余年而不衰。

翟理斯的个人著述较少论及具体的翻译方法和技巧，但他对自己翻译中国古代典籍的选材标准和译介动机有着明确的认识。正如他在《古文选珍》的译序中所言，“余习中华语，因得纵观其古今书籍，于今差十有六载矣。今不揣谫陋，采古文数篇，译之英文，以便本国士人诵习。观斯集者，

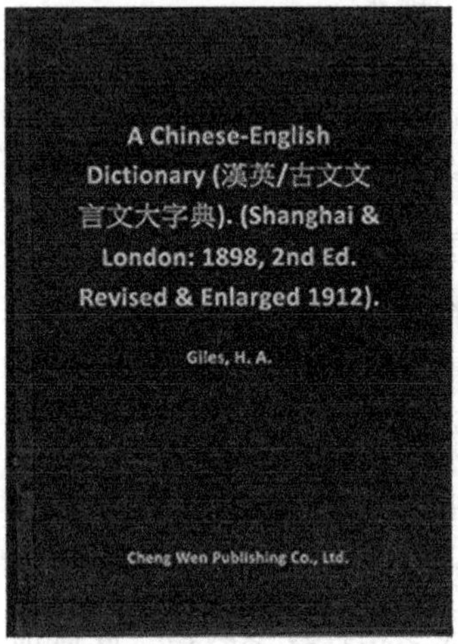

应念恍然于中国文教之振兴、辞章之懿铄，迥非吾国往日之文身断发、茹毛饮血者所能仿佛其万一也。”他的译介主张和翻译成就得到了西方社会的充分认可。1922 年，77 岁的翟理斯获得了皇家亚洲文会金奖，成为第一位获此殊荣的英国汉学家。在颁奖礼上，前英国外交官金璋（Lionel Charles Hopkins）指出，“翟理斯通过自己的著作，让越来越多的英语读者加深了对中国的了解，对中国的物质文化的了解，对中国人所珍爱的一切的了解。正因为翟理斯，人们对于中国人的精神、中国人的能力和成就，有了更好、更真切的了解。在这一点上，翟理斯的成就超过了其他任何一位学者。”他的评价充分肯定了翟理斯对中国文化在西方世界的传播与接受所做出的重要贡献。

8.7 补充资源

参考书目

杨宪益，戴乃迭，译 . 中国古代寓言选 . 北京：外文出版社，2006.

卢允中，周晓宇，译 . 中国幽默故事选（汉英对照）. 北京：中国对外翻译出版公司，2007.

乔车洁玲，译 . 中国古代寓言一百篇 . 北京：中国对外翻译出版公司，1991.

PU Sung-ling. *Strange Stories from a Chinese Studio*. Herbert Giles, Trans. New York: Boni and Liveright, 1927.

Ding Wangdao, Trans. *Stories of Chinese Wisdom*. Beijing: Foreng Language Press, 2007.

ZHANG Ciyun. *Chinese Idioms and Their Stories*. Shanghai: Shanghai Translation Publishing House, 2015.

网络资源

成语故事网：http://www.chengyugushi.net

成语网：http://www.chengyuwang.com

古诗文网：https://www.gushiwen.org

5

Chapter

第五章　历史翻译

- 第九单元　中国现代历史
- 第十单元　中国古代历史

第九单元　中国现代历史

9.1 阅读欣赏：《中国历史概要》（一）

【说明】 阅读下列历史介绍的原文和译文，体会历史材料翻译的特点。

简介：由翦伯赞、邵循正、胡华编写的《中国历史概要》是新中国成立后在马克思列宁主义、毛泽东思想指导下编撰的一部完整记述中国古代、近代和现代历史的通史著作。该书编纂于新中国从新民主主义走向社会主义的时代，体现了当时中国史学界对于中国历史发展的总体认识，提出了革命化的中国历史叙事模式，揭示了中国人民真正走向新时代的思想文化保障。中国是世界上文化发展最早的国家之一，有悠久的历史。《中国历史概要》的编写目的在于简要地介绍中国历史，从而展示中国社会发展过程的轮廓。

中国历史概要（节选一）

日本帝国主义强占东北，全国人民为反对日本侵略而斗争。

1929年末，世界资本主义国家爆发了经济危机。垄断资产阶级用建立法西斯专政的方法，镇压工人阶级；又挑起重新分割殖民地及势力范围的战争，来摆脱经济危机。日本帝国主义本着它一贯的侵略政策——先侵占满蒙，进而侵占全中国、再进而侵占全亚洲的所谓“大陆政策”，在1931年9月发动了强占中国东北的事变。9月18日，日本帝国主义进攻沈阳，蒋介石国民党采取不抵抗政策，使中国东北的辽宁、吉林、黑龙江三省200万平方里领土和3 000余万同胞在3个多月内全部沦于敌手。日本后来在那里组成了一个“满洲国”傀儡政府。日本强占东北的事变激起了中国人民民族民主运动的新高涨。中国共产党和工农红军首先提出抗日的号召，要求反抗日本的侵略。东北人民纷纷组织抗日义勇军进行抵抗。上海、广州、香港等地的工人举行了反日大罢工，全国各地人民自动起来抵制日货，许多城镇都举行了反日集会和游行示威。日本的侵略引起了国内阶级关系的新变化，原来投靠蒋介石国民党的民族资产阶级，这时也开始对蒋介石国民党的对日不抵抗政策表示不满。1931 年 12 月，上海、北平、天津、南京等地学生 3 万人在南京集合，抗议国民党出卖东北，遭到蒋介石国民党的血腥屠杀。这一流血事件，更引起了各阶层广大人民的愤慨。

A Concise History of China (Excerpt)

The Occupation of Northeast China by Japan and the People's Struggle Against Japanese Aggression

Towards the end of 1929, the capitalist world was plunged into the throes of an economic crisis. The monopoly bourgeoisie seeking a way out, resorted to fascist dictatorships and intensified its repression of the working class and unleashed new wars for the redistribution of colonial holdings and spheres of influence. Japanese imperialism, in pursuance of its "continental policy" (which aimed at occupation first of Northeast China and Mongolia, then the whole of China and the rest of Asia), began its aggressive campaign for the occupation of China's Northeast. On September 18, 1931, Japanese forces launched a surprise attack on Shenyang. Chiang Kai-shek's Kuomingtang adopted a policy of "non-resistance," with the result that the three northeastern provinces of Liaoning, Jilin and Heilongjiang with two million square kilometres of territory and a population of more than thirty million were lost to the Japanese in three months' time. The following year, the Japanese imperialists set up a puppet "Manchukuo" government to control this area.

Japan's seizure of northeast China caused a new upsurge in the people's movement for national independence and democracy. The Communist Party and the Workers' and Peasants' Red Army were the first to raise the slogan of resistance against Japan. The people took up this call and demanded action against Japanese aggression. In the Northeast they organized anti-Japanese volunteer corps to carry out resistance. In Shanghai, Guangzhou, Hongkong and other centers, workers staged anti-Japanese strikes, and there was a nation-wide voluntary boycotting of Japanese goods. Anti-Japanese rallies and demonstrations were organized by the people in numerous cities and townships.

Japan's aggression against China brought about changes in the relationship between various classes within the country. The national bourgeoisie which had hitherto depended on Chiang Kai-shek's Kuomintang, began to express dissatisfaction with its policy of "nonresistance" to Japan. In December 1931, thirty thousand students from Shanghai, Beiping, Tianjin and Nanjing gathered in the latter city to protest against the Kuomintang's sell-out of Northeast China and to demand resistance to Japan. They were suppressed by Chiang Kai-shek's Kuomintang. This sanguinary action aroused great anger among people in all sections of society.

9.2 翻译热身：《中国资本主义发展史》

【说明】请将下列历史材料翻译为英语。

中国资本主义发展史（节选）

第一卷 中国资本主义的萌芽

许涤新 吴承明

一个比较发展的封建社会，在晚期产生资本主义生产关系的萌芽，是许多民族历史的共同现象。中国资本主义的产生问题，在1930年前后关于中国社会性质的论战中，曾经涉及。1936年，吕振羽同志在所著《中国政治思想史》中，首先提到“布尔乔亚工场手工业”的出现。1939年，毛泽东同志在《中国革命和中国共产党》中明确指出：“中国封建社会内的商品经济的发展，已经孕育着资本主义的萌芽，如果没有外国资本主义的影响，中国也将缓慢地发展到资本主义社会。”但长时间内，学术界对此缺少专门的研究。新中国建立后，1955年，以讨论《红楼梦》一书的时代背景为契机，史学界和经济学界对我国资本主义萌芽问题展开了广泛的、深入的研究和讨论，发表了大量著作。十年动乱期间，正常研究中断，但一些同志仍在艰难条件下努力发掘新的资料，探讨新的问题。1977年以后，又深入一步，不断有新的研究成果问世。

9.3 翻译技巧：历史语篇翻译

9.3.1 历史文本类型及特点

有文字记载的历史象征着一个国家和民族的文明。中华民族具有几千年的文明史，中国拥有从不同角度记载的丰富史籍、史料。将中国历史书籍资料译成英语有助于对整个中华民族灿烂悠久的历史进行深入探讨和研究，也有助于世界其他国家了解中国、认识中国。

从文化层面看，历史学是一门独特的人文学科，它较哲学特殊，较文学真实，较其他学科综合。在人类社会的发展过程中，各国史学研究成果的交流必不可少，不管是中国史学著作的英译，还是西方史学著作的汉译，都显得尤为重要。从文本层面看，历史作品的写作方式可分为虚构与非虚构两类，虚构是指历史小说，至于非虚构，无论是单纯地讲述历史，还是延伸出议论，只要遵循真实要义基本均属此类。历史文本通常注重事实，语言较为严谨，也有历史文本运用大量的文学手法来描写史实。

9.3.2 历史著作英译思路

历史著作翻译是一种介绍史实、以信息传递为主要功能的文本，英译历史著作要做到史实准确、术语和表达准确，特别是对于历史人名、事件名或其他历史术语，应遵循国际上已约定俗成的英语译法。

英译历史著作时，除了常用的翻译工具外，对于有疑惑、不确定表达的翻译，可参阅涉及中国历史的英语在线百科全书或用英语撰写的中国历史著作、词典或百科全书，在线百科全书如 Wikipedia 的 History of China 词条或其他更具体的词条；英语撰写的中国历史著作包括:《剑桥中国史》(*The Cambridge History of China*，费正清、崔瑞德编)、《哈佛中国史》(*History of Imperial China*，卜正民编) 等。

翻译历史书籍关键要坚持"认真负责"四个字，也就是以严谨的科学态度对待这项工作。史籍翻译不同于文学翻译，文学翻译在保证原文基本含义的基础上可以适当发挥；历史书籍资料的翻译则必须切切实实地忠实于原文，不得随意发挥，这样才不失其历史的真实感和科学性。有学者提出，翻译历史书籍必须坚持四个字:"看""查""问""核"。

"一看"。我国史书如云，浩如烟海。翻译史书，必须有丰富的历史知识，需经常浏览史书，熟悉历史，特别是多参阅与所译史籍有关的史书。鉴于历史还涉及地理、政治、经济、军事、外交，特别是风俗人情等吕叔湘先生谓之"杂学"的东西，译者更需广泛涉猎，才能对原文有深刻的理解。这是译好历史书籍资料的基本要求。

"二查"。翻译离不开词典，这是千真万确的。鲁迅先生谈译《死魂灵》的体会时说:"里面却没有电灯和汽车，然而十九世纪上半期的菜单、赌具、服装，也都是陌生家伙，这就势必至于字典不离手，冷汗不离身……"可见，翻译任何不是自己经历的时代的内容，凡是有陌生感的词语，都要有"字典不离手，冷汗不离身"的刻苦精神，坚持勤查字典。

"三问"。词典并不是万灵药，包罗万象的大千世界和纵贯数千年的历史并非词典所能完全容纳阐明的。要多向专业人士或原作者请教，多方征询，切不可望文生义，闹出笑话。

"四核"。在史籍史料翻译中，"想当然"是为大忌，往往会歪曲原文本意，失去历史价值。凡无根据的、译者拿不准或查问结果不一的，必须不厌其烦地找有关典籍、书籍资料或该方面专业人士核对，确定无疑后再译，这样才做到对翻译工作"认真""负责"，才能保证译文在史学研究中的真正价值。

9.3.3 历史著作中的术语翻译

中国历史著作中包含很多人名、地名、官职名、机构名等专用术语，在英译时需特别注意，通常可采用音译、解释或两者相结合的方式。以官职名词为例:中国自周朝开始直到清朝末年均有"三公”这样的最高官位。但实际上不同朝代的“三公”往往所指不同。比如周代“三公”指司徒、司马和司空；后来又将辅佐国王的太师、太傅、太保尊为“三公”。秦汉时代则以丞相、太尉、御史大夫为“三公”（汉代后期改为“大司徒、大司马、大司空”）。这些都是具有强大实权的官职。唐、宋以来直到清末，虽然仍有“三公”官衔，但已非实职，名列“三公”者为太师、太傅、太保，一般只是朝廷为大臣额外加封的荣典。因此，在翻译此类专用名词术语时应根据时代背景仔细分辨其内涵，给出相应的译法。

译者还需深入了解不同历史时期的民情，厘清词义出处，不能简单地望文生义。由于中国历史悠久、地域辽阔，各地风俗民情大不相同，词语的含义更趋繁杂，历史书籍关涉不同的时代，更是增加了这样的繁杂性。比如：鸦片战争中，林则徐看到沿海人民对英国侵略者同仇敌忾，曾招募了一些渔民、蛋户加以训练。“蛋户”本是东南沿海对水上居民的谑称，把蓬船形状喻为“蛋”形，把常年生活其中的船民成为“蛋户”。如果有译者不了解上述民情，望文生义，则会译为 egg-sellers（卖蛋的），这既脱离了历史条件（当时沿海尚无专业经营蛋品的生产者和商人），又忽视了地理环境（海边），令读者费解。另举一例，清末河南巡抚吴昌寿奏章中谈到官军被捻军打得焦头烂额时说：“当此之时，虽韩白复生，无所用其勇，良平复出，无所用其智。”其中，“韩白”是指汉时名将韩信和秦时名将白起，“良平”指的是汉高祖刘邦的著名谋士张良、陈平。这是读过历史古书的读者都熟悉的常识，但倘若有译者不知道这些史情，将四个人凑成两个人的名字“韩白”“良平”，则会贻笑大方，失去了历史性和真实性。请看下列例子：

例 (1)： 天子死曰崩，诸侯死曰薨，大夫死曰卒，士曰不禄，庶人曰死。（《曲礼下第二》）

译文： The death of the son of Heaven is expressed by pang (has fallen); of a feudal prince, by hung (has crashed); of a Great officer, by zû (has ended); of an (ordinary) officer, by pû lû (is now unsalaried); and of a common man, by sze (has decreased).（理雅各　译）

在上例中，“天子、诸侯、大夫、士、庶人”这些社会不同阶层等级的专用术语以解释的方式进行翻译，而对于死亡的不同称呼，仅释义不足以看出地位尊卑，因此采用音译加解释的方式，让读者既能通过原音了解汉语文化中对不同阶层的人死亡的表述方式，也能通过释义了解不同表述方式的具体意义。

再以近代史国际关系为例，十九世纪对我国西藏垂涎已久的英国固然也插手西藏问题，但更多是“英印政府”，这个“英印政府”不能翻译为 British and Indian governments。当时的所谓印度政府其实是以英国派遣的总督为首，加上印度的傀儡组成，所谓“英印政府”就是“英国操纵的印度政府”或者“英国属下的印度政府”，故 British government in India 这样的译法更能体现“英印政府”所包含的宗主国控制下的殖民地的含义。

请看“阅读欣赏”中的例子：

例 (2)： 日本帝国主义本着它一贯的侵略政策——先侵占满蒙，进而侵占全中国、再进而侵占全亚洲的所谓“大陆政策”，在 1931 年 9 月发动了强占中国东北的事变。

译文： Japanese imperialism, in pursuance of its “continental policy” (which aimed at occupation first of Northeast China and Mongolia, then the whole of China and the rest of Asia), began its aggressive campaign for the occupation of China’s Northeast.

这个例子中的“大陆”其实是指整个亚洲，而不是相对台湾而言的中国大陆，故不能用 mainland 这样的表述，而应该用 continent。

9.3.4 历史著作英译中的断句处理

汉语句子多为流水句，即由各个小句构成，句间多由逗号或分号隔开，小句按事情发展顺序排列。这些小句可共用一个主语，也可在句子中间变换主语。汉语中多存在有松散短句构成的长句，这导致汉语长句英译困难，解决的方法是合理断句。李长栓指出，断句实质上就是核心句分析和句子重组。要通过句子本身的内在逻辑和译者的知识储备找到各个动作的逻辑主语，并依照逻辑关系对汉语文本进行重组。

例 (3)： 此前，传教士在南洋一带活动，虽然西学书刊也能传到中国大陆，学校中也有不少华人，但毕竟水路迢迢，对中国影响有限。

译文： Before this period, the missionaries had mainly stayed in the Southeast Asia. Although many Chinese students in their schools there could be affected by their activities, and the western books published by them spread to China, the influence of them over China was limited due to the long distance.

原文是典型的流水句，每小句主语分别是“传教士”“西学书刊”“学校”“传教士”，且句间结构松散。英译时采用断句将这部分分成两个句子，前一句为短句，后一句通过 although 一词连接，显得干净利落，且逻辑分明。

9.4 翻译实战：《中国历史概要》（二）

中国历史概要（节选二）

第一次世界大战以后，帝国主义国家为争夺中国而展开了激烈的争斗，主角是美、日、英三国。美国在大战中，通过卖军火、贷款大发战争财，战后成为资本主义世界的最大资本输出国。它对于太平洋上的霸权，是势在必争的。日本利用大战机会在中国夺到的利益最多。巴黎和会承认了日本在中国的特殊权利，就使日本有进一步独占中国的趋势。美、日两国竞相掠夺中国，成为帝国主义争夺中的要角。英国向来在中国保有最大的势力，在第一次世界大战后，比起美、日两国显得有些停滞不前，而日本在华势力日益膨胀，也损害了它的利益。这种形势使美、英有可能联合起来，共同对付日本。

1921 年 11 月，由美国发起在华盛顿召开太平洋会议。在这次会议上，美、英联合起来对日本施加压力，在 1922 年 2 月签订了美、比、英、中、法、意、日、荷、葡的《九国公约》。公约在名义上“尊重中国主权完整”，实际上是各个帝国主义国家共同宰割中国的一个协议。它以“各国在华机会均等”和“中国门户开放”的侵略原则为基础，取消了日本在大战时暂时取得的对中国的垄断地位，而代之以美国做首领和英、日等国共同控制中国的局面。

9.5 译文荟萃

1. 短语与术语翻译

1) 中国革命同盟会 Chinese Revolutionary League
2) 三民主义（民族、民权、民生）The Three People's Principles — the Principle of Nationalism, the Principle of Democracy, and the Principle of the People's Livelihood
3) 北洋军阀 Beiyang warlords
4) 五四运动 the May 4th Movement
5) 买办 compradors
6) 革命统一战线 Revolutionary United Front
7) 小资产阶级 petty bourgeoisie
8) 民族资产阶级 national bourgeoisie
9) 右倾投降主义倾向 Right capitulationist deviation
10) 康乾盛世 Age of Prosperity of the Kangxi - Yongzheng - Qianlong reigns
11) 闭关锁国政策 a policy of closure of the country
12) 南京条约 Treaty of Nanjing
13) 天津条约 Treaty of Tianjin
14) 太平天国 Taiping Heavenly Kingdom
15) 天朝田亩制度 the Land System of the Heavenly Dynasty
16) 洋务运动 the Westernization Movement
17) 资产阶级政治改良运动 The Bourgeois Political Reform Movement
18) 保皇派 monarchist-liberals
19) 义和团农民运动 The Yi He Tuan Peasant Movement
20) 八国联军 the combined forces of the eight powers

2. 句子翻译

1) 同盟会提出“驱除鞑虏、恢复中华之外，国体民生尚当变更，虽经纬万端，要其一贯之精神则为‘自由’‘平等’‘博爱’。故前代为英雄革命，今日为国民革命。”

The Tong Meng Hui issued a manifesto in which it pointed out that “in addition to the expulsion of the Manchus and the restoration of China, the form of the state and the livelihood of the people must be changed, and although many complications are involved, the underlying spirit should be ‘Liberty, Equality and Fraternity.’ In the past there were heroes’ revolutions; today we need a people’s revolution.”

2) 国家欲自强，以多译西书为本；学子欲自立，以多读西书为功。

If China wants to become strong, it is of primary importance to translate as many Western books into Chinese as possible; if the student wants to accomplish anything, he must read as many Western books as possible.

3) 毛泽东驳斥反动派污蔑农民革命“糟得很”的叫嚣，指出：豪绅地主阶级是几千年专制政治的基础，是帝国主义、军阀、贪官污吏的墙脚；而农民起来革命，打翻这个封建势力，乃是国民革命的真正目标。

Mao Zedong refuted and denounced the clamour of the reactionaries who slandered the peasant movement as being “terrible.” He pointed out that the local tyrants, evil gentry and lawless landlords had formed the basis of autocratic government for thousands of years and were the cornerstone of imperialism, warlordism and the corrupt officialdom. The overthrow of this feudal power by the peasants who had risen in struggle was the real objective of the national revolution.

4) 清朝对被征服的汉人采取严格的镇压政策：一方面，在全国各要冲的地方都驻扎八旗和绿营的军队，实行全面的军事控制；另一方面，又屡兴文字狱，压制汉人的反清思想。

An extremely repressive policy was carried out against the conquered Han people. Garrisons of the Eight Banners (Manchu troops) and Green Battalions (of Han origin) were stationed at all strategic points and military control was established throughout the country. The Qing government tried to suppress anti-Manchu ideas by persecuting many Han writers on the pretext that they used improper language against the Manchus.

5) “普天之下，莫非王土。”在古代，依据儒家的经典，中国皇帝为“天子”，代表“天”来统治地上的一切。

The line from the *Classic of Poetry* “Under the wide heaven, all is the king’s land,” indicated that the emperors of China were referred to as the “Son of Heaven,” a term found in the Confucian classics. They were supposed to be the representatives of Heaven and bearers of its mandate to rule the earth.

6) 由于文化背景的不同，英国最先进的事物，经过儒家教义的折光，顿时变为最荒谬不堪的东西。

Due to different cultural backgrounds, many of Britain's most advanced technologies and ideas looked ridiculous when transplanted into a new culture and in the refracted light of Confucian teaching.

7) 君主立宪，在皇权至上面前，有如大臣擅权；经商贸易，在农本主义面前，显为舍本求末；追逐利润，在性理名教面前，只是小人之举；至于女王主位、男女不辨，更是牝鸡司晨之类的“夷俗”。

To those accustomed to an emperor holding supreme power, constitutional monarchy smacked of officials overstepping the bounds of their authority. In the face of an ideology that held agricultural production as the foundation of state power, the British attention to trade seemed like neglecting one's core business to focus on trivia. According to Confucian ethics, only the vulgar were motivated by profit. Being ruled by a queen, as if there were no difference between men and women, was a cardinal sign of a savage society.

8) 林则徐以丁忧在籍的前江苏按察使的身份，被“夺情”而监督江苏高家堰河工。

Lin had been in his hometown after his mother's death, before which he had been the provincial judge of Jiangsu. He cut short the usual period of bereavement to respond to an imperial summon for him to go to Gaojiayan (in Jiangsu) to oversee the repair of dykes after a flood.

9) 以纪传体为正宗的中国传统史学，过多地注重了人物的褒贬，历史著作中登场的历史人物，身上都带着明显的标签。

In works of history in the orthodox style, composed primarily of annals and biographies that identified who was to blame and who was to be praised, key figures were clearly labeled.

10) 历史学家生来具有的无可排遣的民族情结，不应当演化为历史研究中对本民族的袒护。

Historians' sense of attachment to their country should never lead them to create alibis for it.

11) 英军已处于初步发展的火器时代，而清军仍处于冷热兵器混用的时代。

The British military belonged to the gunpowder age, while the Qing forces straddled the era of gunpowder and pre-gunpowder armies.

12) 强兵悍卒从来就是专制王朝的心头大患，而以少数民族入主中原的清朝，对于一支兵力强于本族武装（八旗）的汉族武装（绿营），更是多加防备。

Powerful armies were one of the great sources of anxiety for the dynastic rulers of China. The Qing Dynasty, an ethnic minority in China, was particularly nervous about the numerical superiority of the Han Green Standard army over the Manchu-dominated Eight Banners.

13) 清代的科举，分文、武两途。武科如同文科，分童试、乡试、会试、殿试 4 级考试，考中者也有武童生（武秀才）、武举人、武进士的称号。

The Qing examination system was divided into military and civil routes, both of which had the same progression through four exam levels: the junior examination (*tong shi*), the provincial examination (*xiang shi*), the metropolitan examination (*hui shi*) and palace examination (*dian shi*). Candidates for each exam in the military system were known as *tongsheng* ("juniors"), *wu xiucai* ("martial flourishing talents"), *wu juren* and *wujinshi*.

14)《海国图志》是一部介绍外部世界的史地著作，在人们普遍不知"英吉利"为何的"天朝"，其功能和意义非今日同类著作能比拟。

Hai Guo Tu Zhi was an introduction to foreign countries' history and geography. In the land of the "Heavenly Dynasty," where most people did not know what "Yingjili" (England) was, it was a work of incomparably greater importance than similar works today.

15) 一个民族战败了并不可怕，但战败引出的不是"制夷"而是"顺夷"时，就直接葬送了一切前程。

A nation's defeat is nothing to be afraid of. But when defeat elicits nothing more than a choice between "controlling" or "appeasing" the *yi*, prospects for progress are wasted.

3. 篇章翻译

简介：《天朝的崩溃：鸦片战争再研究》是澳门大学历史系教授茅海建撰写的历史学著作。鸦片战争在中国近代史上的影响重大，也是中国百年国耻的开端，给中华民族带来巨大的精神创伤。《天朝的崩溃》一书使用中国第一历史档案馆所藏清朝奏折和英国所藏中英交涉文件、日本学者汇编资料集等珍贵历史文献，详尽考订并重建了与战争相关的大量基本史实。本书抓住几个主要人物为线索展开叙述，从武器装备、防御工事、兵员训练到作战战术的运用，从后勤、兵力动员、兵员调动到军费的来源、筹集与分配，更涉及交战国可用于战争的经济实力、负责运筹帷幄人员的心态、他们的战争观（从文化层面言）、战术观（从军事角度言）等等。本书对当时的人和事的评价，均从事实认定来加以判断，尤其严肃检讨清朝奏折中呈现的天朝心态，直指中国战败的深层原因。本书展现的严谨论证破除了过去之误谬，避免了再蹈历史错误之覆辙，读之令人震撼动容。

天朝的崩溃：鸦片战争再研究（节选）

茅海建

5月30日的三元里抗英之战所以获此战绩，主要原因在于天时地利。那天的大雨，打湿了英军的燧发枪和火药，使之不能发射，这就使民众在兵器上提升至与英军同等的水准，皆为冷兵器。

又由于英军不谙地理，纵深追击，结果一个连迷路而被民众团团包围。如果离开了这些条件，像5月31日那样，以万余民众去攻打英军据守的四方炮台，局势完全会两样。

世界各国民众反对侵略的历史已经表明，他们最为有利有效的战法是游击战，即凭借地理环境的熟悉，抗敌斗志的高昂，设计消灭单独活动的敌军小部队，切忌使用正规的阵地战。以装备落后、缺乏训练、组织指挥不严密的三元里等北郊各乡的民众，强攻拥有先进武器的英军阵地，其结果将会与民众在宣言中的说法完全相反。

我们今天所能见到的三元里等处民众的各种长红、檄文，都是写于英军退出广州之后的。这种事后的张大其词，很有可能就是鼓动民众的宣传，原本不必一一引用而作检讨。但是，这种宣传，不仅使广州地区以外的官绅民众所深信不疑，写入其他官私文献，为这场极有可能获胜的抗争被扼制而叹息；而且随着时间的推延，宣传次数的增加，宣传者本身似乎也相信了这种说法，这可见证于1843至1849年广州民众反入城斗争时的各种官私言论；到了1858年底第二次鸦片战争中广州陷落，相信这种宣传的咸丰帝，竟然命令在籍官绅组织民众收复广州并攻占香港！

The Qing Empire and the Opium War: The Collapse of the Heavenly Dynasty

(Excerpt)

The reason for the success of the resistance at Sanyuanli lay mostly in the weather. The heavy rain on 30 May made the gunpowder in the British flintlocks wet so they would not fire, which put them on the same level as the cold weapon the villagers had. The British were also pursuing their enemy over unfamiliar territory, with the result that one company got lost and was surrounded by the villagers. Had these conditions not applied, as they did on 31 May when the locals surrounded the British at Sifang, the outcome would have been completely different.

The most effective way for the masses to resist an invader, as demonstrated by the history of many countries, is through guerrilla warfare; that is, by depending on familiarity with the terrain, a determined will to resist, the establishment of small units capable of eliminating enemy units operating away from their main bases, and completely forgetting about regular positional warfare. If the ill-equipped, untrained and disorganized locals from Sanyuanli and other villages north of Guangzhou had charged at the modern weapons of British soldiers defending Sifang fort, the result would have been the opposite of what popular wisdom maintained.

The unofficial accounts of Sanyuanli that survive today were written after the British withdrew from Guangzhou. The exaggeration in them was likely the result of their role as propaganda intended to inspire locals; it is not necessary to examine every claim they made in detail. This sort of propaganda was uncritically accepted by officials, gentry and common people of other provinces, who sighed at the thought of a resistance movement that was choked on the cusp of victory. As time passed, and the number of tellings increased, even the propagandists themselves began to believe it. This is shown in the official and private writings produced between 1843 and 1849, a time of popular resistance to the British taking up residence in Guangzhou. By the end of 1858, when Guangzhou fell in the Second Opium War, the Xianfeng emperor, believing in the sort of propaganda, ordered officials and gentry in the region to organize the masses to recapture the city and take Hong Kong!（Lawson Joseph 等　译）

9.6 翻译家：倪豪士

倪豪士（William H. Nienhauser, Jr. 1943 年—）是美国著名汉学家、中国历史研究专家，专注中国古代文学作品和历史著作的英译。倪豪士 1968 年毕业于美国印第安纳大学，获硕士学位，1972 年在该校获博士学位。倪豪士是美国唯一一份专门研究中国文学的杂志《中国文学》（*Chinese Literature: Essays, Articles, Reviews*，i.e. CLEAR）的创立者，并长期担任主编（1979—2010）。2003 年由于他在中国古典文学领域的突出贡献，获得 Humboldt Foundation 终身成就奖。

倪豪士对中国的兴趣产生于高中时期。在高中时他热衷于历史，读了很多传记与传记文学。其中一本书叙述了一个美国船长如何在 18 世纪初和满清政府做生意，另一本书描述了 20 世纪前半叶驻华的几位美国军人的故事。倪豪士在这两本书里看到，中美两国及两国人民，虽然不一样的地方很多，但还有不少地方双方可以彼此了解，彼此尊重。中学毕业以后，倪豪士就读于一所科技大学，但倪豪士志不在此。有一次倪豪士在电视里看到了一则面向中学毕业生的陆军征兵广告，就这样他顺利进入了陆军语言学校。进校后，斟酌再三，他选了中文，因为学中文可以满足他对中国历史的兴趣。倪豪士说："此后我也一直没有后悔。"

陆军语言学校一年的中文课程为倪豪士打下了良好的中文基础，并使他对中国文化的兴趣不断增强。三年兵役退伍后，倪豪士于 1965 年进入印第安纳大学东亚语言文学系，专修中国文学，师从柳亚子之子柳无忌。在柳先生的指导下，倪豪士决定重点研究唐代文学，并于 1968 年请假一年去德国波恩大学进修。1969 年回到印第安纳大学后，倪豪士请柳无忌先生开一门"柳宗元研究"课程。后来他把为其中的研究课题所写的论文编辑整理，写成一本专著《柳宗元》于 1973 年出版。在此同时也完成了博士论文《〈西京杂记〉中的文学和历史》。

获得博士学位后，倪豪士赴威斯康星大学教授中国文学。1983 年，他应邀担任台湾大学外文系客座教授。倪豪士认为这是他第二次深入学习中文，并进一步了解中国文化和学习汉语。

20 世纪 80 年代末，倪豪士在台湾文建会等机构的资助下开始翻译《史记》，他与郑再发、Robert Reynolds、陈照明、吕宗力等组成了翻译团体。到目前为止，他们已先后出版了《史记 · 汉以前的本纪》（1995）、《史记 · 汉以前的列传》（1995）、《史记 · 汉本纪》（2002）、《史记 · 汉以前的

世家（上）》（2006）、《史记·汉代的列传（上）》（2008）等五卷。倪译《史记》的注解具有史学研究的严谨性，是注释详尽的学术性著作，没有太多的功利性，扎扎实实，采用直译的方式逐字逐句逐篇逐卷地翻译，力求做到忠实于原文。译本保留了《史记》本纪、世家、列传等的排列顺序，内容包括“序言、使用说明、纪年说明、度量衡对照表、缩写表、译文”几个部分；译文的页下，附有详尽的歧义考证、地点考证、相关章节成书说明、互文考证说明、文化背景知识注释及资料依据、词汇对照表等；在每章译文后面，附有译者在翻译过程中遇到的问题的相关评注和说明，以及西文和日文译本书目、关于该卷的中外研究成果等。

倪译《史记》参考了大量相关史籍及中国历代评点、西方研究成果，且以协同方式翻译，一人或两人译一卷。一人翻译一卷可以保持翻译的统一与流畅，两人协同翻译又有两种情况：一种是一人先有初稿，另一人加工润饰；另外一种是两人各翻译一半，然后统一语言与注释。翻译组成员有美国、德国、中国的学者，如果是由母语非英语的学者进行翻译，通常会有一个英语水准较好的学者相互协作，以确保成书的英语水准。因此，倪译《史记》具有非常高的学术价值和准确性。

该译本一出版，就受到西方学者的纷纷称誉：卜德认为是“汉学的一项伟大成就”；加里·阿巴克尔（Gary Arbuckle）亦认为“是一项非常了不起的成就，并对各领域的读者都将有帮助”；张磊夫（Rafe de Crespigny）称赞“翻译是可靠的，注释是清晰而有帮助的……译著将使更多英语世界读者感知《史记》的学术性……通过这些著作，西方的学术界和文学界将对早期中国的辉煌和浪漫有更多了解，并对由伟大史家所展现出来的人类教训有更好理解”；葛朗特·哈代（Grant Hardy）在对比华兹生的《史记》译本后，评价倪豪士领衔英译的《史记》说：“从文学视角来看，华兹生生动的译本作为愉悦和悠闲阅读至今仍无人超越……但华兹生按照年代编排他的翻译时，他歪曲了司马迁的原始构想，读者将不能察觉司马迁结构的意义。与之相对照，倪豪士保留了《史记》的形式，允许读者尽可能猜想司马迁编撰的决心……倪的译注在朝着尽可能使英语读者理解司马迁所要求读者具有的这种留意、批判解释的漫长道路前行。我对华兹生的翻译保有一种亲密感，我仍旧欣赏。但是我认为倪的译著将更为值得仔细反复阅读。如果他和他的团队能够一直坚持到终点，他的翻译将是一个世纪以来或更长时间里最终的英译本。”

9.7 补充资源

参考书目

罗新璋，陈应年．翻译论集（修订本）．北京：商务印书馆，2009.

叶子南．高级英汉翻译理论与实践．北京：清华大学出版社，2001.

范存忠．漫谈翻译．北京：中国对外翻译出版公司，1980.

Levefere A. *Translating Literature: Practice and Theory in a Comparative Literature Context*. Beijing: Foreign Language Teaching and Research Press, 2006.

Munday J. *Introducing Translation Studies: Theories and Application*. London: Routledge, 2001.

网络资源

近代史研究：http://www.jdsyj.org/

国际汉学研究：http://www.sinologystudy.com/

译网情深：http://bbs.translators.com.cn/forum/index

我爱翻译论坛：http://5icat.cn/

中国翻译研究院：http://www.catl.org.cn/

第十单元　中国古代历史

10.1 阅读欣赏：《史记》（一）

【说明】 阅读下列《史记》选段及英译，体会古代历史著作的表达特点及英译思路。

简介：《史记》是西汉史学家司马迁撰写的纪传体史书，是中国历史上第一部纪传体通史，记载了上至上古传说中的黄帝时代，下至汉武帝太初四年间共3 000多年的历史。《史记》被列为“二十四史”之首，与后来的《汉书》《后汉书》《三国志》合称“前四史”，对后世史学和文学的发展都产生了深远影响。其首创的纪传体编史方法为后来历代“正史”所传承。《史记》还被认为是一部优秀的文学著作，在中国文学史上有重要地位，被鲁迅誉为“史家之绝唱，无韵之《离骚》”，有很高的文学价值。《陈涉世家》为《史记》中的一篇，是秦末农民起义领袖陈胜、吴广的传记。公元前209年，以陈胜、吴广为首的戍卒九百人在大泽乡（今安徽宿州东南）举行了中国历史上第一次大规模的农民起义，揭开了反对秦王朝残暴统治的序幕。

史记·陈涉世家（节选一）

司马迁

陈胜者，阳城人也，字涉。吴广者，阳夏人也，字叔。陈涉少时，尝与人佣耕，辍耕之垄上，怅恨久之，曰：“苟富贵，无相忘！”庸者笑而应曰：“若为庸耕，何富贵也！”陈涉太息曰：“嗟乎！燕雀安知鸿鹄之志哉！”

二世元年七月，发闾左适戍渔阳，九百人屯大泽乡。陈胜吴广皆次当行，为屯长。会天大雨，道不通，度已失期。失期，法皆斩。陈胜、吴广乃谋曰："今亡亦死，举大计亦死，等死，死国可乎？"陈胜曰："天下苦秦久矣。吾闻二世少子也，不当立，当立者乃公子扶苏。扶苏以数谏故，上使外将兵。今或闻无罪，二世杀之。百姓多闻其贤，未知其死也。项燕为楚将，数有功，爱士卒，楚人怜之。或以为死，或以为亡。今诚以吾众诈自称公子扶苏、项燕，为天下唱，宜多应者。"吴广以为然。乃行卜。卜者知其指意，曰："足下事皆成，有功。然足下卜之鬼乎？"陈胜、吴广喜，念鬼，曰："此教我先威众耳。"乃丹书帛曰"陈胜王"，置人所罾鱼腹中。卒买鱼烹食，得鱼腹中书，固以怪之矣。又间令吴广之次所旁丛祠中，夜篝火，狐鸣呼曰："大楚兴，陈胜王。"卒皆夜惊恐。旦日，卒中往往语，皆指目陈胜。

现代汉语译文

陈胜是阳城人，字涉。吴广是阳夏人，字叔。陈涉年轻的时候，曾经与别人一道被人家雇佣耕种，累了就停止耕作站在田埂上，感慨恼恨了好一会儿，说："如果谁将来富贵了，大家相互不要忘记。"同他一起耕作的伙伴们笑着回答说："你是被雇佣耕种的，会有什么富贵呢？"陈涉叹息说："唉，燕子、麻雀怎么能知道大雁、天鹅的志向呢！"

秦二世元年（公元前 209 年）七月，征发贫民百姓去守卫渔阳，有九百人驻扎在大泽乡。陈胜、吴广都被编在守卫的队伍之中，作了领队的屯长。正赶上天下大雨，道路不通，估计已经不能按期到达守卫的地点。秦朝规定，误了日期，依照法律都要处斩。陈胜、吴广就商议说："如今逃跑也是死，举事起义也是死，同样都是死，为国而死可以吗？"陈胜说："天下百姓遭受秦国残暴统治的苦害已经很久了。我听说二世是始皇的小儿子，不应当即位，应当即位的是公子扶苏。扶苏因为多次劝谏的缘故，皇上派他到外地带兵去了。如今有的人听说他没有罪，二世竟然杀死了他。百姓大都听说他是个贤德的人，不知道他已经死了。项燕是楚国的将军，多次立功，爱护士兵，楚国人都爱戴他。有的人认为他已经死了，有的人认为他逃跑了。现在假使我们冒用公子扶苏、项燕的名义，号召天下人起义，响应的人一定很多。"吴广认为很对。于是就去占卜吉凶。占卜的人知道他们的意图，说："你们的事情都能办成，是有功业的。可是你们问卜过鬼神吗？"陈胜、吴广很高兴，考虑借助鬼神的事情，说："这是教导我们首先借此取得威望。"于是就用朱砂在白绸子布上写上"陈胜王"三个字，塞进别人用鱼网捕来的鱼肚子里。戍卒们买鱼回来煮着吃，得到鱼肚子里的帛书，感到很奇怪。陈胜又暗中派吴广到驻地旁边一座草木丛生的古庙里，在夜里点起篝火，学着狐狸的声音叫唤道："大楚兴起了，陈胜做大王。"戍卒们在深夜听到这种叫声都很惊恐。第二天，戍卒们谈起这件事，都指点和注视着陈胜。

译文一

Selections from Chen She in *Records of the Historian*

(Excerpt I)

Chen Sheng, whose other name was She, was a native of Yangcheng. Wu Guang, or Wu Shu, was a native of Yangxia. Chen She was a farmhand when young. One day when resting from his labours he climbed up a mound and brooded morosely for some time.

"If I become rich and noble, I will not forget the rest of you," he said.

The other farmhands laughed.

"How can a farm labourer become rich and noble?" they asked.

"Ah!" said Chen She with a deep sigh. "Can a sparrow know a wild swan's ambition?"

In the seventh month of the first year of the Second Emperor of Qin, nine hundred men from the poor end of their village were conscripted for garrison service at Yuyang. On the way they stopped at Dazexiang. Chen She and Wu Guang, who were among the conscripts, were camp leaders. There was heavy rain, the roads were impassable, and they saw that they could not arrive on time. The penalty for delay was decapitation. Chen She and Wu Guang took stock of the situation.

"Desertion means death and so does revolt," they argued. "Since the risk is the same, why not die for our country?"

"The people have groaned long enough under Qin," said Chen She. "I have heard that the Second Emperor is a younger son and not the rightful heir. Prince Fusu was the rightful heir, but because he often disagreed with his father he was given a frontier command. Now they say the Second Emperor has killed him, although he had done no wrong. Many of the common folk have heard well of him, but do not know of his death. Then there is General Xiang Yan of Chu, who is popular there for his many deeds of daring and the good care he takes of his men. Some say he is dead and some that he may have gone into hiding. If we pretended to be Prince Fusu and Xiang Yan and called on the people to rise, many would respond."

Wu Guang agreed with him and they consulted a diviner, who, knowing what they had in mind, declared, "You will succeed in all you undertake and achieve great deeds. But why not ask aid from the spirits?"

Chen She and Wu Guang, pleased with this suggestion, said, "He means us to awe men first."

So they wrote "Chen She will be king!" in vermilion on silk and placed it in the belly of a fish someone had caught. When the conscripts bought the fish and cooked it, they were amazed to find this writing in its belly.

Chen She secretly sent Wu Guang at night with a lantern to the forest shrine near their camp, to cry like a fox, "Great Chu will rise again! Chen She will be king!"

The conscripts were terrified at hearing this cry at night. The next day they kept talking among themselves with many a side-long glance at Chen She.（杨宪益、戴乃迭　译）

译文二

Records of the Grand Historian: Han Dynasty I

(Excerpt)

Chen Sheng, whose polite name was Chen She, was a native of Yangcheng; Wu Guang, or Wu Shu, was from Yangxia. When Chen She was young, he was working one day in the fields with the other hired men. Suddenly he stopped his ploughing and went and stood on a hillock, wearing a look of profound discontent. After a long while he announced, "If I become rich and famous, I will not forget the rest of you!" The other farmhands laughed and answered, "You are nothing but a hired labourer. How could you ever become rich and famous?" Chen She gave a great sigh. "Oh, well," he said, "how could you little sparrows be expected to understand the ambitions of a swan?"

During the first year of the Second Emperor of Qin (209 BC), in the seventh month, an order came for a force of 900 men from the poor side of the town to be sent to garrison Yuyang. Chen She and Wu Guang were among those whose turn it was to go, and they were appointed heads of the levy of men. When the group had gone as far as Daze County, they encountered such heavy rain that the road became impassable. It was apparent that the men would be unable to reach the appointed place on time, an offence punishable by death. Chen She and Wu Guang accordingly began to plot together. "As things stand, we face death whether we stay or run away," they said, "while if we were to start a revolt we would likewise face death. Since we must die in any case, would it not be better to die fighting for our country?"

"The world has long suffered under Qin," said Chen She. "From what I have heard, the Second Emperor was a younger son and ought never to have succeeded to the throne. The one who should have been made ruler was Prince Fusu. But because Fusu several times remonstrated with the former emperor, he was sent to lead the armies in the field. Someone has told me that though Fusu was guilty of no crime, he has been murdered by the Second Emperor. The common people have heard much of Fusu's worth, but they do not know that he was dead. Xiang Yan was a general of Chu who many times distinguished himself in battle. He took good care of his troops and the people of Chu thought fondly of him. Some say that he is dead, but others say that he is only in hiding. Now with the group we have, if we could deceive people into thinking that I am Fusu and you are Xiang Yan, we could lead the world in our own tune, and there are sure to be many who will join in the chorus!"

Wu Guang approved of this idea, and they went to consult a diviner. The diviner guessed what the two were planning, and replied, "Your undertakings will all meet with success. But might you not seek your fortune with the spirits?"

Chen She and Wu Guang were delighted with the idea of enlisting supernatural aid in their scheme. "It must mean that we should first do something to overawe the men in our group!" they declared and proceeded to write with cinnabar on a piece of silk: "Chen She shall be king." They stuffed the silk into the belly of a fish someone had caught in a net. When one of the soldiers bought the fish and boiled it for his dinner, he discovered the message in the fish's belly and was greatly astonished. Also Chen She secretly sent Wu Guang to a grove of trees surrounding a shrine which was close to where the men were making camp. When night fell, Wu Guang lit a torch and, partly concealing it under a basket, began to wail like a fox and cry, "Great Chu shall rise again! Chen She shall be king!" The soldiers were filled with alarm, and when dawn came they talked here and there among themselves, pointing and staring at Chen she.（Burton Watson 译）

10.2 翻译热身:《史记》(二)

【说明】 参照“阅读欣赏”部分的翻译思路，将下列《史记》选段翻译为英语。

简介:《秦始皇本纪》出自《史记·卷六·秦始皇本纪第六》。这篇本纪以编年记事的形式，记载了秦始皇及秦二世一生的主要活动和所发生的重大事件，条理清晰，内容丰富，真实地反映了秦朝建立前后四十年间风云变幻的历史场面。以下选段介绍了秦始皇的身世以及始皇即位时秦国攻占其余诸国的情况。

史记·秦始皇本纪（节选二）

司马迁

秦始皇帝者，秦庄襄王子也。庄襄王为秦质子于赵，见吕不韦姬，悦而取之，生始皇。以秦昭王四十八年正月生于邯郸。及生，名为政，姓赵氏。年十三岁，庄襄王死，政代立为秦王。当是之时，秦地已并巴、蜀、汉中，越宛有郢，置南郡矣；北收上郡以东，有河东、太原、上党郡；东至荥阳，灭二周，置三川郡。吕不韦为相，封十万户，号曰文信侯。招致宾客游士，欲以并天下。李斯为舍人。蒙骜、王崎、麃公等为将军。王年少，初即位，委国事大臣。

现代汉语译文

秦始皇帝，是秦庄襄王的儿子。庄襄王继承王位以前，在赵国做人质，见到吕不韦的侍妾，很喜欢就娶了她，生了始皇。在秦昭王四十八年（公元前259年）正月生于邯郸。出生后，取名为政，姓赵。十三岁时，庄襄王死，赵政代立为秦王。当时，秦国土地已兼并了巴、蜀、汉中，越过宛占有了郢，设立了南郡；向北攻占了上郡以东，设有河东、太原、上党郡；东到荥阳，灭了二周，设置三川郡。吕不韦为相国，分封十万户，号为文信侯。招致宾客游士，想利用他们兼并天下。李斯为门客。蒙骜、王崎、麃公等为将军。秦王年幼，刚即位时，国事委托给大臣。

10.3 翻译技巧：古代历史著作的翻译

10.3.1 中国古代历史文本翻译策略

中国古代历史著作大多以文言文写成，文言文原是先秦时的口头语言，后代逐渐演变为书面语言。要了解中国文化和中国历史，很有必要掌握和熟悉文言文的特点。

就古籍英译而言，把文言文翻译成英语较之现代文英译多了一道汉语内部转换过程，即把文言原文译为现代汉语的过程。也就是说，中国古代历史文本的翻译涉及两个环节：语内翻译（Intralingual Translation）和语际翻译（Interlingual Translation）。

中国古代历史文本关涉古代中国的历史、社会、军事、外交、风俗等方面的内容，经历了悠久的历史沉淀，蕴含着丰富的文化内涵，具有强烈的华夏民族特色和风格。译者的任务就是运用各种翻译手段，译出合格并且承载文化内涵的译文，在时空界限上为读者搭建起沟通的桥梁。中国古代历史文本英译主要涉及两方面：文言语句理解与历史文化背景传递。历史典籍英译质量的优劣首先取决于译者对古文的理解，即对古文内容、词义、成语典故和风格、意境等方面的理解。精通原文语言被列为译者的必备条件之首。此外，中国古代历史文本中富含传统文化内涵，涉及的范围千差万别，这就要求译者具有丰富的知识储备和查阅资料的能力，综合运用多种翻译方式，尽量完整准确地传递原文中蕴含的传统文化信息。以下从文化负载词、句子文体特征和篇章策略几个方面来讨论中国古代历史文本的英译。

（一）历史文本中文化负载词的英译

历史典籍中包含很多中国特有的文化负载词（culture-loaded terms）。文化负载词是标志某种文化中特有事物的词、词组和习语，这些词汇反映了特定民族在漫长的历史进程中逐渐积累的有别于其他民族的独特的活动方式。中国文化负载词是中华传统文化的集中体现，是传统文化最为核心的外在表现形式。在对外翻译时，译者应谨慎处理这类词语，努力将中国传统文化的精髓准确传播至国外，达到中国文化走出去的目的。中国文化负载词包罗万象，涉及政治、经济、宗教、文化、艺术等方面。

在历史典籍中涉及最多、最难翻译的文化负载词当属古代官职。官职名称翻译之所以困难，有以下几方面原因：1）各朝代所设官职名称及职能变化很大。以中央官职系统为例，秦代设丞相、太尉和御史大夫，组成中枢机构。汉朝大体上沿袭秦制称为三公，下设九卿，分管各方面政务，后世又演变为三省六部制。宋代中书省职权扩大，同枢密院分掌文武大权，门下、尚书省遂废。明代内阁为最高政务机构，清代有军机处，掌握政府大权。各朝代所设官职名称及职能变化如此之大，翻译的时候出现错误在所难免。2）不同时期同一官职的职责不同。比如魏晋时“学士”是掌管典礼、编撰诸事的官员。唐朝后指翰林学士，为皇帝的秘书、顾问，到了明清时，林学士则包括承旨、侍读、侍讲、编修。3）特定历史时期特设的官职。根据客观需要，政府会设置一些特殊的职位。如唐代为镇压农民起义和讨伐叛逆设立了招讨草贼使，清代末年为了开展洋务运动设置了三口通商大臣（后改北洋通商大臣）和五口通商大臣（后改南洋通商大臣）这些历史时期设置的新职位给翻译也带来了新的困难。

鉴于这些复杂情况，要把古代官职正确地翻译成英语，译者必须认真对待，可参考以下思路和策略。

（1）根据读者对象确定翻译策略

德国功能派翻译学家 Reiss、Vermeer 和 Nord 等提出的目的论指出：只要能达到翻译的目的，对原文既可以采用逐字直译的方法，也可以采用完全改写的方法，或者采用介于两者之间的任何翻译策略。如果翻译作品的预期读者是一般的读者，他们只把这些古代典籍的译文当成普通的文学读物，那么对于官职的翻译要求就没有必要过分严格。读者们不会去关心把“大将军”译成 general 和 general-in-chief 有什么区别。但是如果以传播和推广中国文化为目的，预期读者是研究中国文化的学者，译文的准确性要求就必须提高。一般的将军可以译成 general，但是“大将军”必须翻译为 general-in-chief（大将军在先秦、西汉时是将军的最高称号）。

（2）对应译法

对应是官职翻译中常见的一种方法。Charles O. Hucker 也提道：“The ideal is a rendering that reveals both the actual function of the office and the literal sense of the Chinese title.”。官职翻译最理想的境界就是，在传达官职功能的同时把汉语的字面意义也表达出来。对应就是能同时实现这两个目

标的最好方法，但是也要注意两点：

一是采用英国官职系统的词语。在翻译古代官职名称时，我们需要面对英美两个官职系统的选择。英国是一个君主立宪制国家，实现了由君主制向虚君共和制的渐进变化。英国的变化是内部变了，外表照旧。所以语言系统保留了君主制的传统。英语中有很多和我国古代君主专制政体下的词汇相似，如国王、王后、大臣等。美国是从英国殖民地分离出来，倡导独立自由的民主国家。虽然英语也是母语，但是为了体现与曾经统治过他们的英国的区别，创造了很多标榜民主和独立的词汇。这些和我国古代词汇体系是无法对应的，所以古代官职系统英译时最好采用英国官职系统的词语。

例 (1)：黄龙元年，对于汉太子刘莳来说，是一段悲喜交加的难忘岁月。

译文：This year was a period of mixed sorrow and joy for the crown prince, Liu Shi.

“太子”一词在美国政治体系词汇中是没有的，而英国有，他们称为“王储”，即 prince，故可以借用。

二是不宜采用易引起误解的对应。虽然有些英文的官职和汉语的官职在一定程度上接近，但是实际上还是有差别的。如果不加甄别进行简单对应，很可能引起误解。

例 (2)：复有呼曰：“右相且至。”

译文：Presently it was announced that the Prime Minister had arrived.

“百度百科”对“左右丞相”的解释为：“春秋末齐景公置左、右相各一人。战国时秦武王始置左、右丞相各一人。秦统一后，仍以丞相为百官之长，有两人时，分为左右，以右为上。西汉惠帝、高后时亦有左右丞相，文帝后只置丞相一人。北齐、北周也有左右丞相。唐武后曾改尚书左右仆射为文昌左右相。玄宗开元时又改左右仆射为左右丞相，但不理政事，并不是宰相。天宝时仍恢复仆射原名。而改侍中为左相，中书令为右相，后亦复旧。南宋、元及明洪武十三年（1380）前，都有左右丞相，为执政的真宰相。”

中国古代的封建制王朝，皇帝是真正当权者，拥有至高无上的权力，丞相只是按照皇帝指令办事的大臣。另外，丞相位在不同历史时期的职能和权限是完全不同的。原文《南柯太守传》源于《唐代传奇》。当时设丞相两个，但不理政事。而英国的 prime minister 是行政首脑，只有一个，是真正的掌权者，国王没有实权。Prime minister 与丞相的职能差别很大。用 prime minister 直接对应“丞相”显然是不合适的，根据语境可译为 imperial chancellor。

（3）解释法

中国与英国的古代政治制度不同，官制上也相差甚远，想要找到对应词汇非常不易，这时需要进行阐释性翻译。具体方法有以下几类：

一是汉语拼音加解释。“汉语拼音 + 解释”的方法在文化因素的翻译中很常见，如地名和中国阴阳五行等。官职翻译也可以采用这种方法。一则可以让目的语读者知晓该词的字面读音和文化意义；二则其后的解释有助于读者对文本的理解。

例 (3)：廷尉是当时掌典刑狱之官。

译文： The Tingwei officer was in charge of interrogating and punishing erring officials.

这个例子采用的就是拼音法，读者通过后面的解释可以了解“惩办贪官污吏的官员”在古汉语里称为“廷尉”。

二是职能加官职泛称。所谓官职泛称是指如 officer、commander、minister、magistrate 等很多官职的通称。“职能 + 官职泛称”是目前古代典籍翻译的较普遍用法。如“高堂尉”的“尉”是主管司法的官员，可以翻译为 judicial official of Gaotang。

三是直接阐释法。部分官职或有故事渊源，或有时代背景，采用直接阐释性翻译，使读者能更好地理解。在杨宪益、戴乃迭英译的《史记·李将军列传》中“左贤王”译为 Eastern Prince，“贰师将军”译为 conqueror of Osrouchana。这两个例子是译文中很典型的阐释性翻译。“左贤王”是匈奴贵族官职，仅次于单于，匈奴以左为贵，故称之为左贤王；其封地应该在单于王庭之东方，故译者直接翻译为 Eastern Prince，不需要把“左”译出，避免了不必要的解释；与此原理相同的是“贰师将军”的翻译，这是李广在攻打大宛贰师城后获得的称号，贰师城就是今天吉尔吉斯斯坦境内的奥什，所以翻译成 conqueror of Osrouchana，既可以避免加注的麻烦，还可以暗示称号的来源。

（二）历史典籍中的句子英译

由于古代汉语在句法上与现代汉语有诸多不同，因此译者在翻译时需要灵活变通，以求意思的通达。文言文以简约为显著特色，经常省略各种语法成分，尤以省略主语为多见。这就要求译者根据上下文所叙述之主题，厘清文意，辨识省略的成分。

例 (4)： 修贻书责之，谓其不复知人间有羞耻事。若讷上其书，坐贬夷陵令。

译文： Xiu wrote a letter to Ruona blaming his absence of consciousness of shame. The letter was presented by Ruona to the Emperor, thus Xiu was exiled out of the capital and was degraded as the magistrate of Yiling County.

上例中，“坐贬夷陵令”承接上文“若讷上其书”，如果仅据此二句理解，认为主语是若讷，似乎也可说通：欧阳修写信给高若讷予以谴责，若讷因恨，把信上交给仁宗，仁宗斥责若讷的做法，把若讷贬至夷陵。然而查阅前文可见，范仲淹被贬乃仁宗授意，高若讷正是为了迎合仁宗之意，才不惜冒得罪其他大臣之险，独自一人反对赦免范仲淹。仁宗看了欧阳修的信之后，责其多事，故贬其为夷陵令。因此，“坐贬夷陵令”的主语应该是欧阳修。

另外，文言文句式短小，用词凝练，省却繁芜，含义多在语与不语之间，需要译者综合分析其字面与背景含义。

例 (5)： 每进见，帝延问执政，咨所宜行。既多所张弛，小人翕翕不便。修虑善人必不胜，数为帝分别言之。

译文： At each meeting, Renzong would consult Xiu about the new policies appropriate to implement. Xiu analyzed the situations: reforms in various fields produced different effects, which were taken as excuses by opponents who launched groundless attacks to the reformers for their own benefits. The officials who implemented the new policies perhaps could not withstand the attacks.

上例中仁宗向欧阳修咨询政事，欧阳修为之条析时局。当时正是庆历新政推行初期，仁宗询问“宜行”之政事，即是询问哪些新政适宜采纳推广。所以“帝延问执政，咨所宜行”可译为“Renzong would consult Xiu about the new policies appropriate to implement”。“多所张弛”，如果仅依其中的“多”字，理解为“在多个领域实行新政”，甚至根据“既”字反推理解为“新政之前的既有政策效果不一”，则与原文有所偏颇。此句实指新政实施后产生的效果不同，有松有紧，有好有坏，反应褒贬不一。事实上，庆历新政的改革措施触犯了大官僚大地主的利益，遭到他们的强烈反对，正如文中所言之“小人翕翕不便”。“小人”实指新政反对者，“善人必不胜”之“善人”实指范仲淹等新政推行者，因此此处分别译为 opponent 和 reformer，表达清晰，胜于按照字面意思意译为 the means 和 the righteous。“胜”可理解为“取胜”或“抵挡得住”。按原文，欧阳修担心在反对者的攻击下，新政夭折，范仲淹等人被罢免。因此理解为“抵挡得住”更为合适，译为 withstand the attacks。

同时，通过句子重组和变换句型的方式最大程度重现原文的文体特点。文言文虽句子短小，但意思全面生动，翻译成英语后往往冗长，失去了原文的文体特征，达不到预期的效果。这时需通过重组句子、变换句型等方式，尽量重现原文的文体特点。以下以杨宪益和戴乃迭译《史记》的部分内容作为例子说明。

例 (6)：陵军五千人，兵矢既尽，士死者过半，而所杀伤匈奴亦万人。且引且战，连斗八日……

译文：He had only five thousand men, and soon their arrows were exhausted and more than half of them had fallen; yet they killed and wounded over ten thousand of the enemy, fighting a running battle for eight days as they withdrew.

这段话描写李陵与匈奴作战，最后寡不敌众，被匈奴俘虏的情景。字里行间体现了司马迁对李陵遭遇的同情以及对他在绝境坚持战斗精神的钦佩。这段文字包含两个句子，在翻译时，译者将两句划入同一个句子，中间用分号连接，保持了战斗经过的连续性；同时，译者还对原句顺序进行了调整，将最难翻译的“且引且退”放置在“连斗八日”之后，符合读者的逻辑思维习惯，并保持了原句的连贯性。

（三）历史典籍英译的篇章策略

在篇章结构方面，历史典籍英译文不必死板地照搬原文段落划分方式，可根据英文写作要求和行文方式进行相应调整。仍以《史记》英译本为例来说明。《史记》具有文学和史学的双重价值，可究其根本来说，《史记》是史书，是我国历史上第一本正史，具有严谨正规的特点。所以，其行文特点是文字简洁凝练，段落内部信息量大，但关联程度低。

在《史记》原书中，《李将军列传》一篇共有 19 段，而杨宪益和戴乃迭的译文却有 61 段，如此大的差别正是译者在翻译时考虑到中英行文的不同而采用的一种归化翻译策略。

《李将军列传》作为历史记录，作者首先考虑的是如何在有限的篇幅内叙述李广的一生及其后代的事迹。由于原文每段的信息量较大，段落内事件衔接不明显，因此有必要在翻译时根据其段落衔接情况进行重新分段，以符合英美的行文习惯。译者在面对原文中典型的中文历史典籍叙述时，采取了归化的手段，以英美人熟悉的行文和段落规则译出，增强了译文的可读性。

例如，原文第一段：

李将军广者，陇西成纪人也。其先曰李信，秦时为将，逐得燕太子丹者也。故槐里，徙成纪。广家世世受射。孝文帝十四年，匈奴大入萧关，而广以良家子从军击胡，用善骑射，杀首虏多，为中郎将。广从弟李蔡亦为郎，皆为武骑常侍，秩八百石。尝从行，有所冲陷折关及格斗猛兽，而文帝曰："惜乎，子不遇时！如令子当高帝时，万户侯岂足道哉！"

General Li Guang, a man of Chengji in Longxi, was descended from Li Xin, the general of Qin who pursued and captured Dan, the crown prince of Yan. His family originated in Huaili but later moved to Chengji, and the men of each generation were trained in archery.

In the fourteenth year of Emperor Wen, a strong force of Huns rode through the Xiao Pass. Then Li Guang, as the son of a good family, joined the army to resist the enemy. A brilliant mounted archer, he killed and captured many Huns and was made a palace guard. He and his cousin Li Cai, another palace guard, served as mounted guards with a stipend of eight hundred piculs of grain.

Li Guang often accompanied the emperor on his trips, and his skill in attack and defence or in grappling with wild beasts made Emperor Wen remark, "What a pity you weren't born at a different time! Had you lived during Emperor Gaozu's reign, you would easily have won a fief with ten thousand households."

原文第一段篇幅虽不大，但却包含了三个重要的信息点：李广及其家族的来历、李广的发迹以及汉文帝对李广的评价。假如这三个信息点在译文中都被译作一段之中，会使外国读者产生迷惑，且不符合英文的行文习惯，所以译者很巧妙地将这个段落分为三段译出。第一段从"李将军广者"处开始译，到"广家世世受射"结束，主要交代了李广及其家族的来历；第二段从"孝文帝十四年"处开始到"秩八百石"结束，是李广荣耀的开始；从"尝从行"到原文最后是译文的第三段，通过汉文帝对李广的评语来显示李广的军事功绩，同时也揭示了他的一生：生不逢时。

10.4 翻译实战：《史记》（三）

【说明】 参照"阅读欣赏"、"翻译热身"和"翻译技巧"讲解，将下列《史记》选段翻译为英语。

简介：《项羽本纪》出于《史记》中第七卷，是关于楚霸王项羽的本纪。《项羽本纪》通过叙述秦末农民大起义和楚汉之争的宏阔历史场面，生动而深刻地描述了项羽的一生。他既是一个力拔山、气盖世、"近古以来未尝有"的英雄，又是一个性情暴戾、优柔寡断、只知用武不谙机谋的匹夫。司马迁巧妙地把项羽性格中矛盾的各个侧面，有机地统一于这一鸿篇巨制之中，虽然不乏深刻的挞伐，但更多的却是由衷的惋惜和同情。《史记》中，本纪所记录的大都是皇帝，其中项羽并没有成为皇帝，司马迁把他归入本纪则表现了对他的尊重。

史记·项羽本纪（节选三）

司马迁

原文

项籍者，下相人也，字羽。初起时，年二十四。其季父项梁，梁父即楚将项燕，为秦将王翦所戮者也。项氏世世为楚将，封于项，故姓项氏。项籍少时，学书不成，去学剑，又不成。项梁怒之。籍曰："书，足以记名姓而已。剑，一人敌，不足学。学万人敌。"于是项梁乃教籍兵法，籍大喜；略知其意，又不肯竟学。项梁尝有栎阳逮，乃请蕲狱掾曹咎书，抵栎阳狱掾司马欣，以故事得已。项梁杀人，与籍避仇于吴中。吴中贤士大夫皆出项梁下。每吴中有大徭役及丧，项梁常为主办，阴以兵法部勒宾客及子弟，以是知其能。秦始皇帝游会稽，渡浙江，梁与籍俱观，籍曰："彼可取而代也！"梁掩其口，曰："毋妄言，族矣！"梁以此奇籍。籍长八尺余，力能扛鼎，才气过人，虽吴中子弟皆已惮籍矣。

秦二世元年七月，陈涉等起大泽中。其九月，会稽守通谓梁曰："江西皆反，此亦天亡秦之时也。吾闻先即制人，后则为人所制。吾欲发兵，使公及桓楚将。"是时桓楚亡在泽中。梁曰："桓楚亡人，莫知其处，独籍知之耳。"梁乃出，诫籍持剑居外待。梁复入，与守坐，曰："请召籍，使受命召桓楚。"守曰："诺。"梁召籍入。须臾，梁眴籍曰："可行矣！"于是籍遂拔剑斩守头。

现代汉语译文

项籍，是下相人，字羽。刚起家时，二十四岁。他的叔父是项梁，项梁的父亲就是楚军将领项燕，是被秦将王翦杀掉的。项氏世世代代为楚将，封在项，所以姓项。项籍年少时，学习读书认字没有成就，就去学剑，又没学成。项梁很生他的气。项籍说："文字，只能记姓名罢了。剑能对付一个人，不值得学。我要学习能对抗万人的本事。”于是项梁就教项籍兵法，项籍大喜，略知其意，又不肯学下去了。项梁曾被栎阳官吏追捕，就请蕲县狱掾曹咎写信给栎阳狱掾司马欣，因此事情才了结。项梁杀了人，同项籍到吴中躲避仇人。吴中的贤士大夫才能都在项梁之下。每当吴中有大徭役及丧事，项梁经常主办，暗中用兵法管理约束宾客及年轻人，以此了解他们的才能。秦始皇游会稽，经过浙江，项梁与项籍一起去观看。项籍说："那人我们可以取而代之！”项梁捂住他的嘴，说："别胡说，会灭族的！”项梁因此认为项籍是奇才。项籍身高八尺多，力能扛鼎，才气过人，连吴中子弟也都畏惧项籍。

秦二世元年七月（公元前 209 年），陈涉等在大泽乡起兵。这年九月，会稽郡守殷通对项梁说："江西地区都已反叛，这是上天要灭亡秦朝的时候啊。我懂得先下手就能制伏别人，后下手就会被别人制伏。我想发兵，让您和桓楚为将。”当时桓楚逃亡在沼泽之中。项梁说："桓楚逃亡，没人知道他在哪里，只有项籍知道。”项梁于是出去，嘱咐项籍持剑在外等候。项梁又进去，同郡守坐在一起，说："请召见项籍，让他接受命令去召回桓楚。”郡守说："好。”项梁招呼项籍进来。一会儿，项梁给项籍使眼色说："可以行动了！”于是项籍就拔剑斩了郡守的头。

10.5 译文荟萃

1. 短语与术语翻译

中侍郎 Captain of the Imperial
郎中令 Chief of the Palace Guard
相国 the Chancellor
大司马 the Commander-in-Chief
束帛之币 rolls of silk
《大学》*The Great Learning*
《论语》*The Analects of Confucius*
《春秋》*The Spring and Autumn Annals*
《诗经》*The Book of Songs / The Book of Odes*
《礼记》*The Book of Rites*
安史之乱 the An Lushan-Shi Siming Rebellion
开元盛世 Flourishing Age of Kaiyuan Reign
贞观之治 Excellent Governance during the Zhenguan Reign
《山海经》*The Classic of Mountains and Rivers*
御史大夫 Chief Counselor
太史公 the Grand Historian
左丞相 Junior Prime Minister
天子玺符 the Imperial Seal
《三字经》*The Three-Character Scripture*
《中庸》*The Doctrine of the Mean*
《孟子》*The Mencius*
《史记》*Historical Records*
《易经》*The Book of Changes*
《孝经》*The Book of Filial Piety*

《资治通鉴》*Comprehensive History Retold as a Mirror for Rulers*

2. 句子翻译

1) 在《史记》之前，《尚书》《春秋》《左传》《国语》《战国策》等史书所记载的史事范围较狭窄，且各史所记只是一段时代的史事。

Previous history books, such as the *Book of History*, *Spring and Autumn Annals*, *Zuo Qiuming's Commentary on the Spring and Autumn Annals*, *Historical Anecdotes* and *Intrigues of the Warring States*, recorded selected events taken from comparatively narrow periods of history.

2)《史记》是中国第一部纪传体通史，记述了上起黄帝，下迄汉武帝几千年间的历史。

The Records of the Historian was the first general history in the form of a series of biographies to appear in China, recording all that was known at that time of historical events from Huangdi in prehistoric times to the reign of Emperor Wu of the Han Dynasty.

3)《史记》全书 130 篇，由五部分组成，即十二本纪、十表、八书、三十世家和七十列传。

The 130 chapters are divided into five categories: 12 chapters of *Benji* (biographies of prominent rulers), ten chapters of *Biao* (timelines of events), eight chapters of *Shu* (governance and cultural records), 30 chapters of *Shijia* (biographies of dukes and princes) and 70 chapters of *Liezhuan* (biographies of important figures).

4) 十二本纪用编年的形式来记载帝王的言行，反映朝代变迁的大势。十表用表格的形式把历史的轮廓及发展的主要线索纳入尺幅之中。八书则是从礼、乐、律、历、天官、封禅、河渠、平准八个方面，分专题载述司马迁认为的经国大政。三十世家按年月编年记事，主要是给诸侯王作传。七十列传则是以专传、合传、类传、附传等形式给上至公卿大臣下至平民百姓的社会各阶层的人士作传。

The *Benji* record the words and deeds of kings and emperors in chronological order reflecting the trends of dynastic changes, The *Biao* give the historical and developmental outlines in tabular form. The *Shu* record the development of what Sima Qian considered important governance in eight aspects, including rituals, music, law and the calendar. The *Shijia* are mainly biographies of dukes or princes in chronological order. The *Liezhuan* are accounts of people of different social strata, from ministers and officials to commoners, in the forms of special biography, joint biography, categorized biography and attached biography.

5) 咨尔国王远在重洋，倾心向化，特遣使恭赍表章，航海来庭，叩祝万寿，并备进方物，用将忱悃。

You, O King, live beyond the confines of many seas, nevertheless, impelled by your humble desire to partake of the benefits of our civilization, you have dispatched a mission respectfully bearing your memorial. Your Envoy has crossed the seas and paid his respects at my Court on the anniversary of my birthday. To show your devotion, you have also sent offerings of your country's produce.

6) 朕批阅表文，词意肫恳，具见尔国王恭顺之诚，深为嘉许。所有赍到表贡之正副使臣，念其奉使远涉，推恩加礼，已令大臣带领瞻覲，赐予筵宴，叠加赏赍，用示怀柔。

I have perused your memorial: the earnest terms in which it is couched reveal a respectful humility on your part, which is highly praiseworthy. In consideration of the fact that your Ambassador and his deputy have come a long way with your memorial and tribute, I have shown them high favour and have allowed them to be introduced into my presence. To manifest my indulgence, I have entertained them at a banquet and made them numerous gifts.

7) 其管船官役人等六百余名，虽未来京，朕亦加以赏赐，俾得普沾恩惠，一视同仁。

I have also caused presents to be forwarded to the Naval Commander and six hundred of his officers and men, although they did not come to Peking, so that they too may share in my all embracing kindness.

8) 尔至国王表内，恳请派一尔国之人住居天朝照管尔国买卖一节，此则与天朝体制不合，断不可行。

As to your entreaty to send one of your nationals to be accredited to my Celestial Court and to be in control of your country's trade with China, this request is contrary to all usage of my dynasty and cannot possibly be entertained.

9) 向来西洋各国，有愿来天朝当差之人，原准其来京，但既来之后，即遵用天朝服色，安置堂内，永远不准复回本国。此系天朝定制，想尔国王亦所知悉。

It is true that Europeans, in the service of the dynasty, have been permitted to live at Peking, but they are compelled to adopt Chinese dress, they are strictly confined to their own precincts and are never permitted to return home. You are presumably familiar with our dynastic regulations.

10) 今尔国王欲求派一尔国之人住居京城，既不能若来京当差之西洋人，在京居住不归本国，又不可听其往来常通信息，实为无益之事。且天朝所管地方，至为广远。凡外藩使臣到京，译馆供给行止出入俱有一定礼制，从无听其便之例。

Your proposed Envoy to my Court could not be placed in a position similar to that of European officials in Peking who are forbidden to leave China, nor could he, on the other hand, be allowed liberty of movement and the privilege of corresponding with his own country; so that you would gain nothing by his residence in our midst. Moreover, our Celestial dynasty possesses vast territories, and tribute missions from the dependencies are provided for by the Department for Tributary States, which ministers to their wants and exercises strict control over their movements. It would be quite impossible to leave them to their own devices.

11) 今尔国若留人在京，言语不通，服饰殊制，无地可以安置。若必似来京当差之西洋人，令其一例改易服饰，天朝亦从不肯强人以所难。设天朝欲差人常住尔国，亦岂尔国所能遵行。

Supposing that your Envoy should come to our Court, his language and national dress differ from that of our people, and there would be no place in which to bestow him. It may be suggested that he might imitate the Europeans permanently resident in Peking and adopt the dress and customs of China, but, it has never been our dynasty's wish to force people to do things unseemly and inconvenient. Besides, supposing I sent an Ambassador to reside in your country, how could you possibly make for him the requisite arrangements?

12) 交戟之卫士欲止不内，樊哙侧其盾以撞，卫士仆地，哙遂入。披帷西向立，瞋目视项王，头发上指，目眦尽裂。

Sword and shield in hand, Fan Kuai entered the gate. Guards with crossed halberds tried to bar the way, but he charged and knocked them down with his tilted shield. Bursting into the tent, he lifted the curtain and stood facing west, glaring at Xiang Yu. His hair bristled, his eyes nearly started from his head.

13) 大行不顾细谨，大礼不辞小让。如今人方为刀俎，我为鱼肉，何辞为?

Where big issues are at stake you cannot trouble about trifles. In matters of consequence you cannot observe the minor courtesies. They are the chopper and board, we the fish and meat. Why should we take our leave?

14) 汉有天下太半，而诸侯皆附之。楚兵罢食尽，此天亡楚之时也。不如因其机而遂取之。今释弗击，此所谓"养虎自遗患"也。

Han now has the greater half of the empire and the support of all the states, while the army of Chu is exhausted and has no food. Heaven has decreed Xiang Yu's downfall. You should seize this opportunity to crush him. To let Xiang Yu go now would be like bringing up a tiger — simply asking for trouble in future.

15) 力拔山兮气盖世，时不利兮骓不逝。骓不逝兮可奈何，虞兮虞兮奈若何！

My strength uprooted mountains,
My spirit overtopped the world;
But the times are against me,
And Zhui can gallop no more.
When Zhui can gallop no more,
What can I do?
And what is to become
Of Lady Yu?

3. 篇章翻译

史　记（节选四）

司马迁

吴广素爱人，士卒多为用者。将尉醉，广故数言欲亡，忿恚尉，令辱之以激怒其众。尉果笞广。尉剑挺，广起夺而杀尉。陈胜佐之，并杀两尉。召令徒属曰："公等遇雨，皆已失期，失期当斩。藉弟令毋斩，而戍死者固十六七。且壮士不死即已，死即举大名耳，王侯将相宁有种乎！"徒属皆曰："敬受命。"乃诈称公子扶苏、项燕，从民欲也。袒右，称大楚。为坛而盟，祭以尉首。陈胜自立为将军，吴广为都尉。攻大泽乡，收而攻蕲。蕲下，乃令符离人葛婴将兵徇蕲以东。攻铚、酂、苦、柘、谯皆下之。行收兵。比至陈，车六七百乘，骑千余，卒数万人。攻陈，陈守令皆不在，独守丞与战谯门中。弗胜，守丞死。乃入据陈。数日，号令召三老、豪杰与皆来会计事。三老、豪杰皆曰："将军身被坚执锐，伐无道，诛暴秦，复立楚国之社稷，功宜为王。"陈涉乃立为王，号为张楚。

当此时，诸郡县苦秦吏者，皆刑其长吏，杀之以应陈涉。乃以吴叔为假王，监诸将以西击荥阳。令陈人武臣、张耳、陈余徇赵地，令汝阴人邓宗徇九江郡。当此时，楚兵数千人为聚者，不可胜数。

葛婴至东城，立襄强为楚王。婴后闻陈王已立，因杀襄强，还报。至陈，陈王诛杀葛婴。陈王令魏人周市北徇魏地。吴广围荥阳。李由为三川守，守荥阳，吴叔弗能下。陈王征国之豪杰与计，以上蔡人房君蔡赐为上柱国。

译文一

Selections from *Records of the Historian*

(Excerpt IV)

Wu Guang was good to his men, all of whom obeyed him. One day when the commanding officers were drunk, he persuaded the conscripts to run away and goaded the officer to punish him and thus enrage the men. Sure enough, the officer had Wu Guang flogged. But when one of them drew his sword, Wu Guang snatched it away and killed him. Chen She came to his aid and killed the other officer too.

Then they called their men together and said, "This rain has already made all of us late, and the penalty for this is decapitation. Even if we do not lose our heads, seven out of ten will die at the frontier. If a stout fellow must die, let it be for some great cause. How can our birth prevent us from becoming princes and barons, generals and ministers?"

"We will do whatever you say," responded the men.

To win popular support they gave out that their leaders were Prince Fusu and General Xiang Yan. Being their right arms, they called themselves the army of Great Chu. They built an altar and made an oath, using the officers' heads as sacrifice. Chen She made himself general with Wu Guang as his chief commander. After storming Dazexiang they took the county of Ji and sent Ge Ying of Fuli with troops to take the districts east of Ji. Zhi, Guo, Ku, Zhe and Jiao all fell to them. As they advanced, their ranks swelled. By the time they reached Chen they had about seven hundred chariots, more than a thousand cavalrymen and several tens of thousands of infantry. When they attacked the county seat of Chen the magistrate was away and the deputy magistrate held the city gate against them. But they defeated the defenders, killed the deputy magistrate and occupied the city. A few days later they summoned the elders and chief citizens to a conference.

"My lord," said these men, "you have come wearing armour and carrying sharp weapons to attack an unjust government, to punish the Qin tyranny and re-establish the kingdom of Chu. Your achievements fit you to be our king."

So Chen She made himself king, calling himself the Magnifier of Chu. Thereupon all in the provinces and counties who hated the rule of Qin rose against their governors and magistrates and killed them in order to follow Chen She's lead. Wu Guang, made vice-regent over the other general, advanced west against Xingyang. Chen She also ordered Wu Chen, Zhang Er and Chen Yu, all natives of Chen, to conquer Zhao, and Deng Zong of Ruyin to take the province of Jiujiang. By this time Chu had countless bands of troops, each several thousand strong.

When Ge Ying reached Dongcheng he set up Xiang Qiang as king of Chu. Later, hearing that Chen She had proclaimed himself king, he killed Xiang Qiang and went back to report. But when he reached Chen, Chen She had him executed. Then Chen She sent Zhou Shi, a native of Wei (403 B.C. – 225 B.C.), to conquer Wei in the north. Wu Guang laid siege to Xingyang but the city was defended by Li You, governor of Sanchuan, and he could not take it.

Chen She summoned all the chief citizens of his kingdom to a conference and appointed Cai Ci, lord of Fang a native of Shangcai, as his chief minister.（杨宪益、戴乃迭　译）

译文二

Records of the Grand Historian: Han Dynasty I

(Excerpt II)

Wu Guang had always been kind to others and many of the soldiers would do anything for him. When the officer in command of the group was drunk, Wu Guang made a point of openly announcing several times that he was going to run away. In his way Wu Guang hoped to arouse the commander's anger, get him to punish him, and so stir up the men's ire and resentment. As Wu Guang had expected, the commander began to beat him. When the commander's sword slipped out of its scabbard. Wu Guang sprang up, seized the sword, and killed the commander. Chen She rushed to his assistance and they proceeded to kill the other two commanding officers as well. Then they called together all the men of the group and announced: "Because of the rain we encountered, we cannot reach our rendezvous on time. And anyone who misses a rendezvous has his head cut off! Even if you should somehow escape with your heads, six or seven out of every ten of you are bound to die in the course of garrison duty. Now, my brave fellows, if you are unwilling to die, we have nothing more to say. But if you would risk death, then let us risk it for the sake of fame and glory! Kings and nobles, generals and ministers — such men are made, not born!"

The men of the garrison all replied, "We'll do whatever you say!" Then, in order to win the loyalty of the people, Chen She and Wu Guang falsely proclaimed themselves to be Prince Fusu and Xiang Yan. Baring their right shoulders, they raised the cry of "Great Chu!" and built an altar and swore an oath before it, offering as a sacrifice the heads of the commanding officers. Chen She set himself up as commander of the army, with Wu Guang as his colonel, and together they attacked Daze County. After capturing Daze County, they proceeded to attack and capture Qi. They dispatched Ge Ying, a man of Fuli, with a force to seize control of the area east of Qi, while they themselves attacked Zhi, Zan, Ku, Zhe, and Qiao, all of which submitted. Recruiting soldiers as they went along, they were able by the time they reached the city of Chen to build up a force of 600 or 700 chariots, over 1,000 horsemen, and 20,000 or 30,000 infantry.

When they attacked Chen, neither the governor of the province nor any of the magistrates of the districts under him were in the city. Only one of the governor's aides was present, who engaged them in battle at the Qiao Gate but was defeated and killed. They entered the city and quartered there for several days, sending out an order summoning all the village heads and important men of the region to meet with them and plan a course of action. To this the village heads and distinguished men replied, "The general has buckled on armour and taken up his weapons to attack the unrighteous and punish the violence of Qin, then he may restore once more the sacred altars of the state of Chu. Because of the glory he has won, he deserves to be made a king."

Chen She accordingly was made king and given the title "Magnifier of Chu," whereupon men in many of the other provinces and districts who had suffered under the Qin officials overpowered and murdered their governors and magistrates and allied themselves with Chen She.

Chen She made Wu Guang an acting king with supervision over the other leaders of their band, and sent him west to attack Xingyang. Chen She ordered Zhang Er, Chen Yu, and Wu Chen, to seize the region of Zhao, while he sent Deng Zong, a native of Ruyin, to seize the province of Jiujiang. By this time a countless number of bands consisting of several thousand men each had been formed throughout Chu. When Ge Ying, who had been sent by Chen She to seize the land east of Chi, reached Dongcheng, he set up Xiang Qiang as king of Chu. Later, hearing that Chen She had already become king himself, he murdered Xiang Qiang and returned to report what he had done to Chen She. Chen She executed him, and dispatched Zhou Shi, a native of Wei, to march north and seize the region of Wei.

Meanwhile Wu Guang surrounded the city of Xingyang, but Li You, the Governor of Sanchuan, held the city, and Wu Guang was unable to conquer it.

Chen She summoned the distinguished men of the state of Chu to meet with him and plan the next move. He appointed Cai Ci, the lord of Fang, a man of Shangcai, as his chief minister.（Burton Watson 译）

10.6 翻译家：华兹生

伯顿·华兹生（Burton Watson，1925 年—2017 年）是美国著名汉学家、翻译家，美国笔会翻译终身成就奖得主。华兹生于 1925 年 6 月 13 日出生在纽约州新罗谢尔市（New Rochelle, New York），是 20 世纪美国汉学界和翻译界代表人物之一，也是继韦利（Arthur Waley）之后，译介中国文学到英语世界最多的翻译家之一。华兹生的汉学译著囊括了中国古代典籍、诗歌、传记、佛经等诸多类别，而且还广泛涉猎典籍评论、文学论述等领域，多部专著、译著入选联合国教科文组织《中国代表性著作选集系列丛书》，成果斐然。

1943 年，17 岁的华兹生在新罗谢尔市高中毕业。此时正值第二次世界大战后期，华兹生自愿选择加入美国海军，驻扎在位于日本东京湾的横须贺海军基地（Yokosuka Naval Base in Tokyo Bay）。日本的服役生涯使华兹生对东亚文化，尤其是中国文化心驰神往，服役结束后华兹生申请到了哥伦比亚大学的本科生院——哥伦比亚学院。哥大汉语教授富路特（Luther Carrington Goodrich, 1894 年—1986 年）经常在课堂上介绍唐诗，这激发了华兹生对译诗的热情，他经常在课后试图翻译这些诗作。在富路特的指导下，华兹生的汉语阅读能力得到了迅速提升。本科毕业后，华兹生选择继续留在哥大修读中文专业的研究生，师从著名学者王际真（Chi-Chen Wang, 1899 年—2001 年）

教授。当时，哥大东亚系鼓励学生采用自己的译作作为硕士论文，在王际真的指导下，华兹生以自己翻译的《史记》与《汉书》有关“游侠”的章节提交了硕士论文。此外，华兹生还在哥伦比亚大学结识了当时尚在修读汉学硕士和博士学位的狄百瑞（William T. Debary），并与之结成了学术挚友，这为他后来的翻译生涯埋下了伏笔。

1951 年，华兹生获得哥伦比亚大学汉学硕士学位，并前往同是东亚文明古国的日本。战后的日本依然是世界汉学研究的重镇，一大批从事中国古典文化研究的汉学家活跃于日本学术界。华兹生在朋友的帮助下，申请到了两份工作，一份是同志社大学的英语外教的职位，另一份工作是充任京都大学中文学系教授、著名中国古代文学专家吉川幸次郎的学术助手。当时，吉川幸次郎的学术兴趣主要是中国古诗，包括唐诗与宋词，正从事中国文学中的对偶研究。作为其学术助手，华兹生的主要任务是将他的学术成果翻译成英文。由于该项目中有较大篇幅论述了杜甫诗歌中的对偶，使得华兹生第一次较深入地了解并学习了中国古典诗歌，并对其产生了极大的兴趣。

由于硕士期间曾翻译《史记》的缘故，他选择了《史记》作为研究课题。两年后，华兹生的研究已取得初步成果，写成了一套学术专著初稿，于 1955 年夏返回哥伦比亚大学，以该课题注册入学攻读博士。在完成了一年的博士学分课程后，华兹生凭借博士论文《司马迁：伟大的历史学家》（“Ssu-ma Ch’ien: Grand Historian of China”）于 1956 年 6 月获得汉学博士学位。经修改后，其博士论文于 1958 年由哥伦比亚大学出版社正式出版，并荣获哥伦比亚大学克拉克 · 费希尔 · 安斯利杰出著作奖（Clarke F. Ansley Award）。

除此以外，华兹生先后译出了《墨子概要》（*Mo Tzu: Basic Writings*, 1963）、《荀子概要》（*Hsün Tzu: Basic Writings*, 1963）、《韩非子概要》（*Han Fei Tzu: Basic Writings*, 1964）、《庄子概要》（*Chuang Tzu: Basic Writings*, 1964）等四部先秦哲学著作。华兹生还就五位中国著名诗人的近 1 000 首古诗，出版了 7 本诗人专辑译著。1971 年，华兹生又陆续出版了介绍东汉至南宋抒情诗的著作：《中国抒情诗风：公元 2 世纪至 12 世纪的诗歌》（*Chinese Lyricism, Shih Poetry from the Second to the Twelfth Century*）和《中国赋文：从两汉到六朝》（*Chinese Rhyme-Prose: Poems in the Fu Form from the Han and Six Dynasty Periods*）。1984 年，哥伦比亚大学出版社出版了华兹生主编的《哥伦比亚中国诗选》（*The Columbia Book of Chinese Poetry: From Early Times to the Thirteenth Century*）。

华兹生的翻译成就使其蜚声学界。国际权威亚洲研究专业杂志《亚洲研究学刊》（*Journal of Asian Studies*）盛赞其译文，“任何出自华兹生之手的古典名著新译本都应被当作一次大事件来对待，对其应满怀敬意地欢迎”。美国汉学家、耶鲁大学东亚系教授傅汉思（Hans Frankel）认为：“在当今还健在的人群中，没有第二个人可以像华兹生那样用优雅的英文为读者翻译这么多中国文学、历史与哲学作品。从这位孜孜不倦的翻译家笔下译出的每一本新书，都让人感到如此地欣慰。”这点也得到了著名翻译家、美国《唐学报》（*T'ang Studies*）主编、科罗拉多大学中文教授柯睿（Paul W. Kroll）的赞同：“毫无争议，华兹生是本世纪在中国文学英译领域最高产的翻译家。他出版的书籍的名录很长，包括近两千年的中国文学史中哲学、历史和诗歌。他堪称我们时代的奥古斯特·费茨梅尔。”当代诗人温伯格（Eliot Weinberger）也曾经做过些文学翻译，但对翻译实践，尤其是面对华兹生这样的译者时，他显得格外谦虚，“我曾经翻译过一些东西，大多翻译是在许多年前做的，正如世界上有钢琴家与会弹钢琴的人之分一样，世界上有翻译家和从事翻译活动的人。华兹生正是一位翻译家，而我却最多算是个半吊子”。

10.7 补充资源

参考书目

陈福康．中国译学理论史稿．上海：上海外语教育出版社，1992.

谢天振．当代国外翻译理论导读．天津：南开大学出版社，2008.

邹振环．影响中国近代社会的一百种译作．北京：中国对外翻译出版公司，1996.

Baker M. *Routledge Encyclopedia of Translation Studies*. Shanghai: Shanghai Foreign Language Education Press, 2004.

Gentzler E. *Contemporary Translation Theories*. London: Routledge, 1995.

Twitchett D, Loewe M. *The Cambridge History of China* (Vol. 1): *The Ch'in and Han Empires, 221 BC–220 AD*. Cambridge: Cambridge University Press, 1986.

(*The Cambridge History of China* 目前已经出版 15 卷，涵盖从公元前 221 年秦朝建立到 1982 年的中国历史，是英语世界有关中国历史最为重要的英语著述。中国社会科学出版社自 1992 年开始陆续出版中文翻译版。)

Loewe M, Shaughnessy E. *The Cambridge History of Ancient China*: *From the Origins of the Civilizations to 221 B.C.*. Cambridge: Cambridge University Press, 1999.

网络资源

译网：http://www.translators.com.cn/

同文译馆：http://www.oktranslation.com/

爱问共享资料：http://ishare.iask.sina.com.cn/

百度百科：https://baike.baidu.com/

必应学术：http://cn.bing.com/academic/

Chapter 6

第六章 哲学翻译

第十一单元 中国现代哲学

第十二单元 中国古代哲学

第十一单元　中国现代哲学

11.1 阅读欣赏：《中国哲学》

【说明】 对照金岳霖有关中国哲学论述的中文和英文文本，体会哲学著作的翻译思路。

简介：金岳霖（1895年—1984年）是中国现代著名哲学家、逻辑学家，美国哥伦比亚大学博士，曾任清华大学文学院院长、北京大学哲学系主任、中国科学院哲学社会科学部委员等，主要著作有《逻辑》《论道》《知识论》《罗素哲学》等，部分著作收入《金岳霖文集》(4卷)。金岳霖一生用英语撰写了许多重要论著。2005年，刘培育组织中国社会科学院、北京大学等单位的十多名学者将这些论著翻译成中文，编撰为《道、自然与人：金岳霖英文论著全译》在生活·读书·新知三联书店出版。

《中国哲学》的原文是金岳霖1943年在昆明用英语撰写的一篇论文，英文题目为"Chinese Philosophy"，1980年首次公开发表于《中国社会科学》英文版 *Social Sciences in China* 创刊号（第1卷第1期），后收入《金岳霖文集》第2卷。钱耕森将其译为中文《中国哲学》，刊于《哲学研究》1985年第9期，后收入《道、自然与人：金岳霖英文论著全译》。此处的中文选段为钱耕森中文译文第一、二段，英语选段为金岳霖英语原文的第一、二段，编选时编者对中文译文略有修改。

中国哲学（节选）

金岳霖 原著，钱耕森 汉译

在三大哲学思想主流中，人们曾经认为印度哲学是“来世的”，希腊哲学史“出世的”，而中国哲学则是“入世的”。哲学从来没有干脆入世的；说它入世，不过是意图以漫画的笔法突出它的某些特点而已。在懂点中国哲学的人看来，“入世”的说法仅仅是强调中国哲学与印度、希腊的各派思想相比有某些特点；但是对于那些不懂中国哲学的人，这个词却容易引起很大的误解。它的本意大概是说，中国哲学是紧扣主题的核心的，从来不被一些思维的手段推上系统思辨的炫目云霄，或者推入精心雕琢的迷宫深处。正像工业文明以机器为动力一样，哲学是由理智推动的，这理智不管是否把我们赶进死胡同，总可以把我们引得远离阳关大道、一马平川。而在理智方面，中国哲学向来是通达的。

人们习惯于认为中国哲学包括儒、释、道三家。这三家在单提的时候又往往被说成宗教。在早期，儒家和道家本是地道的哲学，即先秦百家争鸣的两家，那个时期的学派纷纭是中国历史上无与伦比的。由于词语未尽恰当，我们不打算对此进行任何描述。把一些熟知的哲学用语加之于西方哲学足以引起误会，用于中国哲学则更加不妙，例如有人可以说先秦有逻辑家，这样说就会引得读者以为那时有一些人在盘算三段推论，研究思维律，甚至进行换质换位了。最近有一篇文章把阴阳家说成科学的先驱，这也不是全无道理，但是这样一来阴阳家就成了某种严格来说从未实现的事业的先驱；读者如果根据描述把阴阳家想象成古代的开普勒或伽利略，那便是对一大批思想家的曲解。

Chinese Philosophy

(Excerpt)

Of the three main flows of philosophical thought, it has been maintained that the Indian is otherworldly, the Greek unworldly and the Chinese worldly. No philosophy is ever plainly worldly; to say that it is so is merely an attempt to caricature it in order to bring out certain features into striking relief. To those who know something of Chinese philosophy the word “worldly” merely emphasizes certain features in comparison with the Indian and the Greek schools of thought; but to those who do not know anything about it, that word is liable to be quite misleading. What is meant is probably that Chinese philosophy sticks to the kernel of its subject matter; it is never propelled by the instruments of thinking either into the dizzy heights of systematic speculation, or into the depth of a labyrinth of elaborate barrenness. Like machines in industrial civilization, intellectuality in philosophy drives; and whether it drives us into blind alleys or not, it may lead us far away from the wide boulevards or spacious squares. Intellectually, Chinese philosophy has always been in the open air.

We are accustomed to think of Chinese philosophy as consisting of Confucianism, Buddhism and Taoism. It is rather as religions that these are exclusively mentioned. In the early stages both Confucianism and Taoism were only philosophies, and as such they were in the pre-Qin periods members of a whole democracy of different schools of thought, the variety of which during that period was unparalleled in Chinese history. Since terms are inadequate, we shall refrain from any attempt at description. It is misleading enough to apply the familiar philosophical terms to Western philosophy. It is much worse to apply them to the Chinese. One might say for instance that there were logicians in the pre-Qin period; but if so, readers might be led to think that there were people who brooded over syllogism, or the laws of thought, or even obversion and conversion. The Ying-Yang-ists have been described in a recent article as the precursors of science, and not without foundation either, but then they were precursors of something which strictly speaking never arrived; and if as a result of this description readers imagine them to be ancient Keplers or Galieos, they entertain a distorted view of a whole brand of thinkers.

11.2 翻译热身:《自然和人》

【说明】 翻译下面的文字，然后将自己的译文与所提供的参考译文对比，体会其中的差异，并进一步思考翻译哲学著作的思路和方法。

简介:《自然和人》选自金岳霖 1943 年—1944 年访问美国期间所写的英文著作 *Tao, Nature and Man*（《道、自然与人》）。该英文稿后收入《金岳霖文集》第 2 卷第 568—749 页。胡军将其译为中文，收入刘培育编撰的《道、自然与人:金岳霖英文论著全译》中。关于《自然和人》的写作背景,金岳霖在《道、自然与人》的序中有以下说明:“(在《论道》一书之外),我增加了“论自然和人”一章。这一章在原来的书中是没有的，增加它的目的是使本书的思想容易为人接受。”

自然和人（节选）

金岳霖

中国哲学中有这样的一种理论，我们可以把它概括为“自然与人合一”这一命题。这一思想在某些哲学中得到了更多的强调。但是这一思想不只是一种技术性的思想，它几乎为每一个普通接受过教育的人所信仰。它是一个很复杂的意念图案，我们不打算在此运用系统阐述的方法来处理这一思想，我们也不能说我们在下面所说的一切是完全准确地表达了历史上的思想家或某些思想流派的思想家所接受的这一思想。再次，我们的目的是多多少少用我们现在语言中的某些术语，并通过在前几章已经显示出的推论方法来介绍类似的思想。我们不是从思想历史的角度来介绍一历史上的思想，来追踪它的源头或来描绘它的发展线索，我们也不打算根据提出这一思想的思想家的自然环境来介绍它的发展原因。

11.3 翻译技巧：中国现代哲学的翻译

11.3.1 中国现代哲学特点

中国现代哲学通常是指从 1919 年五四运动到 1949 年中华人民共和国成立之间的中国哲学。中国现代哲学产生的历史背景较为复杂，既与中国当时内忧外患的社会现实有关，也与自 17 世纪以来“西学东渐”的中西文化交流进程有关。1840 年的中英鸦片战争开启了中国近代受屈辱的历史。在帝国主义列强不可一世的耀武扬威和清政府的不堪一击中，救亡图存逐渐上升为整个时代的主题。“中国向何处去？”“中国该怎么办？”成为中国近代最首要的问题。面对亡国灭种的危险，各种力量都在试图作出自己的回应。与此同时，明末清初以来“西学东渐”的整个进程此时已发展到第二阶段。在经历了第一阶段的中西文化碰撞之后，部分中国人已经开始掌握以逻辑为核心的西方理性思维，为清末民初的中西对话奠定了可靠的基础。在中西文明的比较中，中国文明在器物、制度以及文化上的不足日益明显。正是在这样的背景下，洋务派、资产阶级维新派以及资产阶级革命派开始以西方文化的启蒙理念来反对封建专制主义和弥补中国传统文化的先天缺陷，引发中国人对西方哲学思想的关注。此后，西方哲学思想开始在中国全面盛行，并在政治、经济和文化等各个方面产生重大影响。

以“五四”新文化运动为标志，“西学东渐”进入高峰期。这个阶段的中国哲学既介绍与引进西方哲学，又立足于中国哲学的“自创”，呈现出中西哲学融合的趋势。中国现代哲学就形成于这一时期。这个时期，中西哲学和文化的会通融合达到前所未有的高度，主要体现在部分学者开始尝试运用西方理性分析的方法去探索和研究中国哲学问题，取得的成果既深刻又富有创造性。其主要成果之一就是诞生了中国现代哲学中的新儒学。新儒学作为一个哲学流派之所以出现和形成于“五四”新文化运动时期，就是因为面对强势的西学东渐以及“五四”激进反传统和普遍流行的科学主义思潮，中国传统文化及其价值认同陷入了严重危机。新儒学的主旨就是维护传统文化，其第一部具有奠基意义的哲学著作是梁漱溟于 1921 年出版的《东西文化及其哲学》。梁漱溟在该书的序言中明确提出，“今天的中国西学有人提倡，佛学有人提倡，只有谈到孔子羞涩不能出口。若非我出头提倡，可有哪个出头？”（参见梁漱溟《东西文化及其哲学》，商务印书馆 1922 年版第 2 页）另一部具有定位意义的奠基之作是张君劢于 1923 年所写的《人生观》。张君劢主张人生观是主观的、直觉的、综合的、自由意志的、单一的，而科学则是客观的、论理的、分析的、因果律的、统一的。科学是相对自然现象而言，它受因果律的支配。人生观则属于社会现象，它不受因果律的支配，而为自由意志所支配，科学不能支配人生观。他的这一基本主张和基本思路为后来的几代新儒家共同遵循。第三个具有重要意义的新儒学论述是1941年贺麟所写的《儒家思想新开展》，这篇文章对儒学的现代开展颇有影响。贺麟提出，“民族复兴的本质应是民族文化的复兴。民族文化的复兴，其主要潮流，根本的成分，就是儒家思想的复兴、儒家文化的复兴。假如儒家思想没有新的前途，新的开展，则中华民族以及民族文化也就没有新的前途，新的开展。”“儒学是合诗教、礼教、理学三者为一体的学养，是艺术、宗教、哲学三者的和谐体。因此，新儒家思想之开展，大约将循艺术化、宗教化、哲学化途径之迈进。”（参见贺麟《文化与人生》，商务印书馆1947年版第5页）具体而言，贺麟所谓的新儒家思想之开展，“就是以西洋之哲学发挥儒家之理学，吸收基督教之精华以充实人类之礼教，领略西洋之艺术以发挥儒家之诗教。”（参见张文儒、郭建宁《中国现代哲学》，北京大学出版社2001年版第7页）也就是说，新儒学不是简单意义上的回归儒学，而是运用现代西方哲学的一些理论观点来阐释儒学，并把它和儒学融合在一起，从而形成了一种中西合璧式的哲学体系，使儒家哲学现代化。熊十力的新唯识论、冯友兰的新理学以及贺麟的新心学、金岳霖的新实在论等都是借用现代西方哲学的基本范畴、基本概念、基本观点对儒学思想进行系统化阐释的结果。

“西学东渐”第三阶段的第二个重要成果就是马克思主义在中国的传播及其中国化。马克思主义哲学产生在西方，以西方哲学特别是德国古典哲学为重要理论来源。马克思主义哲学与现代西方哲学处于同一历史时代，具有共同的科学和文化背景。因此，尽管两者作为不同性质的哲学具有原则区别，但共同的时代背景又使两者必然存在重要的共通之处，其基本范畴、概念、术语等在内涵和外延上是基本一致的。20世纪初，马克思主义在中国的发展经历了以下几个阶段：一是陈独秀、李大钊与马克思主义哲学在中国的初步传播阶段，其重点是马克思主义的唯物史观；二是瞿秋白与马克思主义哲学在中国的全面传播阶段。瞿秋白是第一个比较全面地介绍马克思主义辩证唯物主义和历史唯物主义的人；三是艾思奇与马克思主义哲学的大众化阶段。四是李达与马克思主义哲学的系统化阶段；五是以毛泽东为首的中国共产党人与马克思主义哲学的中国化阶段。中国化了的马克思主义哲学正是中国现代哲学的主要组成部分，是运用马克思主义基本原理来研究和解决中国革命和社会发展所存在的实际问题的实践中逐步形成的。马克思主义中国化仍然没有脱离中国传统哲学和文化的影响，它辩证化地融合中国传统哲学的精华，吸取了中国历史上优秀的哲学思想，对中国古代哲学遗产在理论上进行了改造，常常借用中国古代文化典籍和民间成语故事、神话、寓言、谚语、俗语等来阐释深刻的唯物辩证法原理。马克思主义哲学中国化最重要的、最具代表性的成果就是毛泽东思想，主要体现在毛泽东《实践论》《矛盾论》等哲学著作以及他提出的实事求是思想路线和实际工作中的辩证法思想，如军事斗争辩证法、统一战线辩证法和领导方法辩证法等。

11.3.2 中国现代哲学的翻译思路及方法

中国现代哲学是在西方哲学的影响下产生的，它在吸收西方哲学精髓的同时，又融合了中国传统哲学的一些基本哲学理念，是中国哲人论古今中西、求自强图新之道，引入西学，会通中西，形成一种影响至今的亦中亦西的新文化。因此，对中国现代哲学著作的英译，必须考虑到上述特点。

（一）借自西方哲学的范畴、概念以及术语的英译策略

中国现代哲学中的许多理论范畴、概念和术语等实际上都是借用西方哲学，特别是马克思主义哲学，从英文直接转译而来，因此在英译过程中，将此类范畴、概念和术语进行回译即可。例如：

马克思主义：Marxism

科学社会主义：Scientific Socialism

矛盾的普遍性：the universality of contradiction

矛盾的特殊性：the particularity of the contradiction

伦理：ethics

唯物主义：Materialism

唯心主义：Idealism

实用主义：Pragmatism

本体论：Ontology

方法论：Methodology

认识论：Epistemology

解构主义：Deconstructionism

他者：the Other

（二）来自中国传统哲学的理念和术语等的英译策略

中国现代哲学著作（尤其是新儒家的某些著作）中的许多哲学理念、术语，往往由中国传统哲学继承和发展而来，在将此类哲学文本进行英译时，要注意这些哲学理念和术语同传统哲学理念和术语的传承关系，精确把握这些理念和术语的真正内涵。具体说来，可以从以下两个方面进行考虑。第一，对于那些在中西文化交流中已经有比较固定的对应英译文的中国传统哲学范畴、概念、术语或专有名词，只要其译文与相应的中文原文在内涵上没有太大的出入，出于尊重和继承传统以及出于减轻译文读者认知负担考虑，对于这类范畴可以直接沿用已有译文。当然，如果觉得译文不够明确，可以在采用既有对应译文的同时，对其内涵进行必要的解释（其中一种办法是加夹注），如：

道家（道教）：Daoist; Daoism

墨家：Mohist/ Moism

孔子：Confucius

孟子：Mencius

老子：Laozi

《论语》：*The Analects*

《大学》：*The Great Learning*

阴阳：yin and yang (the two opposing principles in nature)

知行合一：the unity of knowledge and practice

三纲五常：the Three Cardinal Guides and Five Constant Virtues

第二，对于那些在中西文化交流中已经有比较固定的对应英译文的中国传统哲学范畴、概念、术语或专有名词等，如果其译文与相应的中文原文在内涵上出入很大，甚至造成了对中国哲学范畴、概念、术语、专有名词的歪曲或误解，或者内涵阐释不够准确，给西方读者造成理解上的困难，应根据实际情况进行重新解读和翻译。例如：读到中国传统哲学中的“心”，很容易让人联想到其对应的英译文 mind 或 heart。很多从事中国文化译介的学者确实也试图在它们之间建立某种对应关系，把“心”与 mind 对应，并把“心学”译成 the school of mind；有的则试图糅合 mind 和 heart 来与“心”对应，并相应地把“心学”译成了 the Learning of the Mind-and-Heart、the school of heart-mind 等。而实际上，中国传统哲学中的“心”与英文中的 mind 或 heart 在内涵上有很大的差异。中国哲学中的“心”是一个融物质和精神于一体的、无所不包的概念，是中华思想文化中既有丰富内涵又最具代表性的文化符号之一。它不但与天、理、命、性、情通而为一，也包含思、虑、念、意、欲乃至天地万物。与此相对，mind 和 heart 基本上是两个平行概念。不仅如此，对二元论而言，它们在功能上也是截然分开的：人的思想和观点等理性功能源于脱离物质实体的 mind，而欲望和情感等感性功能则源于作为身体组成部分的 heart。Mind 虽然被赋予了认识论意义，主观唯心主义者还赋予了它本体论意义，但它缺乏“心”所具有的伦理意义；heart 虽然被《圣经》赋予了认识论意义和伦理意义，但又缺乏“心”所具有的本体论意义。总之，就内涵而言，不论哪一个都比“心”狭隘得多。因此，英译时把“心”简单而笼统地对应于 mind 或 heart 是不合理的。例如，《朱子语类》有“仁义礼智根于心”之说。此处的“仁”是情感，“义”是理性，“礼”是行为规范，“智”是智慧。既然仁、义、礼、智都根于心，此“心”就不可能单纯表理性、情感或智慧，而应是包括理智与情感等在内的多重精神意识活动。据此，无论把“心”译为 heart 还是 mind 都有失偏颇。实际上，“心”至大而又至微，既可以指天，也可以指一个人一时一会的情绪，还可以代指一切精神意识活动，且搭配不同，意思也可能大相径庭，mind 和 heart 却缺乏类似的广义性和张力。此外，在特定语境里，有时“心”并无具体所指，而是一种泛称。此时它不但可能涵盖 mind 和 heart 的全部内涵，还可能远远超出 head、brain、soul、spirit 等词汇内涵的总和。可以说，如果把上述所有词汇视为一个范畴的话，“心”实际上具备了该范畴的上义词性质。面对这种情形，即便是把 mind 和 heart 糅合起来也无能为力。因此，为了消除翻译时将“心”与 mind 或 heart 进行简单套用或对应可能给西方读者造成的误读或误解，可考虑把“心”的汉语拼音 xin 作为一个正式术语引入英语，并使之与 mind、heart、soul、spirit 等构成事实上的上下义关系，以作为“心”表示泛称时英译的对应词。这样就不但可以理顺上述词汇间内涵上的逻辑关系，使翻译更加准确，更重要的是传达出“心”的独特内涵，避免以偏概全，从而尽可能消除西方读者对“心”的误解和误读。（参见杨洁《中华思想文化关键术语“心”的内涵演变及其英译》，载《中国翻译》2016 年第 6 期）在中国传统哲学相关的现代哲学探究中，此类概念和术语比比皆是。因此，中国哲学文本的英译需立足于传统哲学的基本内涵，把握古今哲学思想观念流变的传承性和差异性，进行灵活而准确的传译。

11.4 翻译实战:《中国哲学简史》

【说明】根据文末的提示，将下文翻译为英语。

简介:《中国哲学简史》是冯友兰于 1947 年在美国宾夕法尼亚大学讲授中国哲学史的英文讲稿，后整理为 *A Short History of Chinese Philosophy* 于 1948 年由美国麦克米伦公司出版。1985 年，冯友兰的学生涂又光将其翻译为中文，由北京大学出版社出版。2004 年，中国社会科学院赵复三教授再次依据英文版将其翻译为中文，由天津社会科学院出版社出版。以下所选即为赵复三中文译本的节选。

中国哲学简史（节选）

冯友兰

中国哲学以为，一个人不仅在理论上而且在行动上完成这个统一，就是圣人①。他是既入世而又出世的②。中国圣人的精神成就，相当于佛教的佛、西方宗教的圣者的精神成就。但是中国的圣人不是不问世务的人③。他的人格是所谓“内圣外王”④的人格。内圣，是就其修养的成就说⑤；外王，是就其在社会上的功用说⑥。圣人不一定有机会成为实际政治的领袖。就实际的政治说，他大概一定是没有机会的。所谓“内圣外王”，只是说，有最高的精神成就的人，按道理说可以为王，而且最宜于为王。至于实际上他有机会为王与否，那是另外一回事，亦是无关宏旨的。

照中国的传统，圣人的人格既是内圣外王的人格，那么哲学的任务，就是使人有这种人格。所以哲学所讲的就是中国哲学家所谓内圣外王之道。

翻译提示

1. 如何理解①处的"圣人"？
2. 请注意②这句话的表达。想一想，"既入世而又出世"在英文中该如何处理？
3. ③中的"不问世务的人"是一些什么样的人？
4. 如何翻译④"内圣外王"？
5. 如何进行⑤⑥两句的逻辑衔接？

11.5 译文荟萃

1. 哲学术语翻译

1) 形而上学 metaphysics
2) 辩证法 dialectics
3) 辩证唯物主义 materialist dialectics
4) 历史唯物主义 historical materialism
5) 逻辑实证主义 logic positivism
6) 经验真理 empirical truth
7) 客观真理 objective truth
8) 主观真理 subjective truth
9) 自然辩证法 dialectics of nature
10) 量变到质变 transformation of quantity into quality
11) 对立统一 the unity and interpenetration of opposites
12) 否定之否定 the negation of the negation

2. 哲学段落翻译

1) 墨里曾说过，柏拉图是个好诗人，黑格尔是个坏诗人。根据这个说法，也许应该把庄子看成大诗人甚于大哲学家。他的哲学用诗意盎然的散文写出，充满赏心悦目的寓言，颂扬一种崇高的人生理想，与任何西方哲学不相上下。其异想天开烘托出豪放，一语道破却不是武断，生机勃勃而又顺理成章，使人读起来既要用感情，又要用理智。（钱耕森汉译自金岳霖所著 *Chinese Philosophy*）

John Middleton Murray has said that while Plato was a good poet, Hegel was a bad one. On some such basis, Chuang Tze should be regarded as a great poet perhaps even more than a great philosopher. His philosophy is expressed in exquisite poetic prose in delightful parables, extolling as lofty an ideal of life as any philosophy in the West. There is a certain whimsicality that yet manages to be robust, a kind of finality that is not dogmatism, together with that liveliness and graspability which appeal to the understanding as well as to the emotion of the readers.（金岳霖著 *Chinese Philosophy*）

2) 多数熟悉中国哲学的人大概会挑出“天人合一”作为中国哲学最突出的特点。“天”这个词是扑朔迷离的，你越是抓紧它，它越会从指缝里滑掉。这个词在日常生活中用得最多的通常意义，并不适于代表中国的“天”字。如果我们把“天”理解为“自然”和“自然神”，有时强调前者，有时强调后者，那就有点抓住这个中国字了。（钱耕森汉译自金岳霖所著 *Chinese Philosophy*）

Perhaps most people at all acquainted with Chinese philosophy will single out the unity of nature and man as its most distinguishing characteristic. The term “nature” is illusive and the more one grapples with it, the more it slips through one’s fingers. In the ordinary sense in which it is most often used in our everyday life, it is not adequate to stand for the Chinese term “tian.” Perhaps if we mean by it “both nature and nature’s God,” with emphasis sometimes on the one and sometimes on the other, we have something approaching the Chinese term.（金岳霖著 *Chinese Philosophy*）

3) 在社会底生活中，人之行为之最社会底者，是道德底行为。我们对于道德底行为，可有两种看法：一是从对于社会之观点看，一是从对于天之观点看。从对于社会之观点看，则人之道德底行为，是尽其社会的一分子的责任；从对于天之观点看，则人之道德行为，乃是尽其宇宙的一分子的责任，即是尽人道。若从此观点看，则人之行道德底事，即是“事天”。（冯友兰 《新理学》）

In social life man’s most social conduct is moral conduct. We can approach moral conduct in two different ways, one from the point of view of society and the other from the point of view of heaven. From the point of view of society, man’s moral conduct consists in fulfilling one’s social duty. From the point of view of Heaven, one’s moral conduct consists in fulfilling his universal duty, that is, fulfilling the way of man. From this point of view, in doing something moral, one is serving Heaven.（陈荣捷 译）

4) 认识的多元论虽采唯用论之说，却不主张知识是为了行动而始生的。以知识为行动的工具，这是唯用论的太极端处。知识固然与行为不能分离，甚且为行动所限制，但知识的自身却不是行动所产，亦非专为行动作工具。我主张知识与行为有密切关系，而不承认行为可以吸收知识。（张东荪《认识论》）

Although epistemological pluralism adopts the theory of functionalism, nevertheless it does not hold that knowledge is produced only because of action. To regard knowledge as an instrument of action is an extreme of functionalism. Although knowledge cannot be separated from action or even restricted by it, nevertheless knowledge itself is not the product of action nor does it exist solely as an instrument of action. I hold that knowledge and action are intimately related but do not admit that action can absorb knowledge.（陈荣捷 译）

3. 篇章翻译

简介：本选段“理气合一”源自熊十力所著《新唯识论》语体文本卷中第六章《功能下》。熊十力（1884年—1968年）是中国著名哲学家、现代新儒学开创者，著有《新唯识论》《原儒》《体用论》《明心篇》《佛教名相通释》《乾坤衍》等。陈荣捷在其所译著的《中国哲学文献选编》中称：“正如冯友兰之试图重建唯理的新儒学，熊十力则试图重建违心的新儒学。他在哲学方面，有八部著作。其整个思想，有系统地表达在《新唯识论》中。”此处的中文选段引自黄俊杰校阅、杨儒宾等所译《中国哲学文献选编》，该书原著由陈荣捷选取中国哲学典籍精要部分译为英语并补充论述编撰而成，于1963年以 *A Source Book in Chinese Philosophy* 为题由美国普林斯顿大学印行。此处的英语译文即选自该书。

理 气 合 一

熊十力

我以为，这气字只是一种生生的动势，或胜能的意思。此气是运而无所积的。动相诈现，犹如气分，故名为气。详核此所谓气，正是本论所谓用。至于万有或形气，唯依动转的迹象，假为之名，非离一切动势，有实形气。

理字，本具有调理或法则的意义，但不可如宋明儒说是气上的条理。宋明儒中，许多人把气说为实有的，因以为理者只是气上的条理。如此，则理的本身竟是空洞的形式，只气是实在的。明儒持这种见解的更多，即在阳明派下，也都如是主张。他们阳明后学一面谈良知，不得不承认心是主宰，一面谈气是实有，理反是属于气上的一种形式，颇似心物二元论，甚乖阳明本旨。我在此处，不欲多作评判，只说我对于理气的解释。我以为，理和气是不可截然分为二片的。理之一词，是体和用之同称；气之一词，但从用上立名，气即是用，前面解释气字的意义时，尽说得明白。

理之一词，何以是体用之通称呢？因为就体而言，此体元是寂然无相，而现似翕辟万象，即众理灿然已具。故此体，亦名为理。

The Unity of Principle and Material Force

In my opinion the word *ch'i* (material force) means the tendency to produce and reproduce, or energy. It operates universally without coming to a standstill. The character of activity falsely appears as if the material force is distributed. For this reason we call it material force. Please understand thoroughly what is called material force here is precisely what I have called function in this treatise. As to the myriad things or material force in physical forms, it is tentatively so called because it is the trace or manifestation of transformation. There is no material force in concrete, physical forms apart from the various tendencies.

The word *li* (principle) originally has the meaning of order or pattern. But we should not say, as Song (960–1279) and Ming (1368–1644) Neo-Confucianists said, that it is order within material force. Many of them considered material force to be real being, and consequently considered principle to be merely order within material force. According to this, principle itself is an empty form and material force alone is real. This view was more prevalent among Ming Neo-Confucianists. Even within the [idealistic] Wang Yang-ming School scholars generally held this view. On the one hand, they talked about innate knowledge of the good and necessarily admitted that the mind is the master. On the other hand, they said that material force is real being and principle is a form belonging to it. Their theory seems to be a dualism of mind and matter, which violates very much the fundamental teaching of Wang Yang-ming. Here I do not want to criticize them too much. I merely want to explain my idea of principle and material force. I believe they cannot be sharply divided into two pieces. The word "principle" is a general term for both substance and function, whereas the word "material force" refers only to function. When the meaning of the word *ch'i* was explained above, it was already made quite clear that material force is function.

Why is "principle" the general term for both substance and function? Because spoken from the point of view of substance, it is originally absolute quiet and without [distinguishing] character, but it manifests itself as the countless phenomena involved in closing and opening. It means that all principles are brilliantly present. Therefore this substance is also called principle.（陈荣捷　译）

11.6 翻译家：安乐哲

安乐哲（Roger T. Ames, 1947 年—），美国著名汉学家，夏威夷大学哲学系教授、北京大学人文讲席教授、夏威夷大学和美国东西方中心亚洲发展项目主任、《东西方哲学》主编、《国际中国书评》主编、世界儒学文化研究联合会会长、国际儒联副主席。

安乐哲于 1947 年出生于加拿大多伦多，曾在香港中文大学崇基学院和新亚书院学习，受教于劳思光、唐君毅、牟宗三等"新儒家"宗师。后离开香港，辗转于加拿大哥伦比亚大学、台湾大学、伦敦大学、剑桥大学等学府求学，先后受业于张佛泉、陈鼓应、方东美、葛瑞汉等著名学者。1978 年，安乐哲在刘殿爵指导下获得伦敦大学亚非学院博士，博士毕业后一直任教于夏威夷大学。

在夏威夷大学任教期间，安乐哲与郝大维、罗思文等人合作，陆续发表了一系列引起广泛关注的学术著作，翻译了多部中国哲学经典。他的《通过孔子而思》《期待中国：探求中国和西方的文化叙述》等著作，被认为纠正了几百年西方人对中国哲学思想的误会，清除了西方学界"中国没有哲学”的成见，开辟了中西哲学和文化深层对话的新路。2014年，安乐哲在夏威夷大学发起成立了世界儒学文化研究联合会，致力于儒学国际化，将儒学的价值向全球推广。同时，他从比较哲学角度出发，促进儒学与西方学术的交流，增进彼此的沟通与了解。2014年9月，在第五届国际儒联大会上，安乐哲当选为国际儒联副会长。

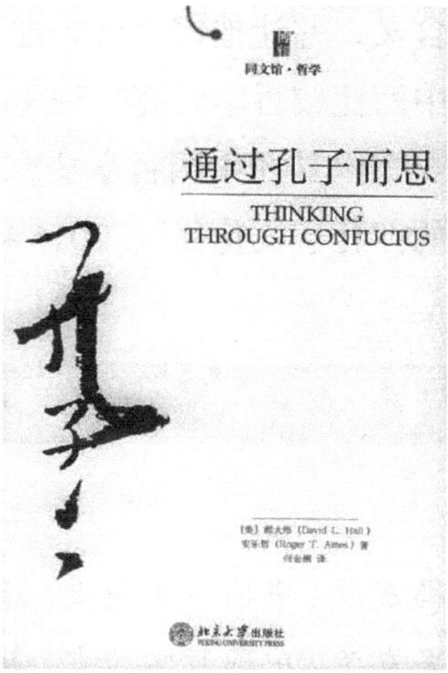

安乐哲的学术兴趣主要是中西比较哲学研究和中国哲学经典翻译。他的研究著作包括：

《通过孔子而思》（*Thinking Through Confucius*）（1987，与郝大维合著）；

《汉哲学思维的文化探源》（*Thinking from the Han: Self, Truth, and Transcendence in Chinese and Western Culture*）（1995）；

《期望中国：探求中国和西方的文化叙述》（*Anticipating China: Thinking Through the Narratives of Chinese and Western Culture*）（1998）；

《主术：中国古代政治思想研究》（*The Art of Rulership: A Study in Ancient Chinese Political Thought*）（1983）；

《先哲的民主：杜威、孔子和中国民主之希望》（*The Democracy of the Dead: Dewey, Confucius, and the Hope for Democracy in China*）（1999）；

《儒学角色伦理学：一套语汇》（*Confucian Role Ethics: A Vocabulary*）（2011）；

《安乐哲卷》（*Excerpted Roger T. Ames*）（孔子文化奖学术精粹丛书）（2015）等。

安乐哲多年致力于中国哲学经典英译，先后翻译出版了《道德经》《论语》《中庸》《孙子兵法》《孙膑兵法》《淮南子》等中国古典哲学著作。对于中国哲学的翻译，安乐哲提出了“自觉性诠释”（self consciously interpretive）的翻译策略。在发表于《孔学堂》2015年第1期上的《活着的中国哲学》一文中，安乐哲指出，传教士和汉学家的中国哲学翻译并没有从哲学的角度进行解读和阐释，因此他提出一个新的哲学翻译策略，即“搭建一个框架，通过前言解读背景、更新哲学术语表的关键词条、运用自觉性诠释的翻译方法，并提供重要语句的中文原文”。安乐哲认为：“西方人文主义者在解读中国经典哲学文献的过程中，不经意植入了他们的臆断，使表述中国哲学的词汇带有特定的色彩。西方读者所熟知的中国哲学，首先经过‘基督教化’的洗礼，然后又被渲染了‘东方化’玄妙神秘的色彩，这与我们所追求的理性启蒙是相悖的。”安乐哲指出，那些看起来最舒服的语言或译者乍看下认为最靠谱的目标语词汇，可能会人为地把我们原来并不了解的事物一下子变得似乎很熟悉。把“道”翻成 the Way，“天”译作 Heaven，“礼”译为 ritual，就是传统翻译中对中文改写太多的明显例子。因此，有必要对中国哲学原典的现有阐释提出挑战，还原中国哲学的本来意蕴，在对关键术语进行翻译时，让这些哲学术语发挥提示性“占位符”的作用，让读者回顾术语表，探寻其含义，并让他们自己去理解中文术语。这集中体现了安乐哲翻译中国哲学的基本主张，也是他进行中西比较哲学研究的理念基础。

因其在中国哲学研究和翻译方面的重要贡献，安乐哲于2013年荣获第六届世界儒学大会颁发的“孔子文化奖”，2016年荣获第二届“会林文化奖”。

11.7 补充资源

参考书目

冯友兰 . 中国哲学简史 . 涂又光，汉译 . 北京：北京大学出版社，1948/1985.

冯友兰 . 中国哲学简史 . 赵复三，汉译 . 天津：天津社会科学院出版社，1948/2004.

金岳霖 . 论道 . 北京：中国人民大学出版社，2010.

牟宗三 . 中国哲学十九讲 . 上海：上海古籍出版社，2005.

姜新艳 . 英语世界中的中国哲学 . 北京：中国人民大学出版社，2009.

网络资源

“Chinese Philosophy” at Routledge Encyclopedia of Philosophy:

https://www.rep.routledge.com/articles/overview/chinese-philosophy

“Chinese Philosophy” at The Internet Encyclopedia of Philosophy:

http://www.iep.utm.edu/chin-ovr/

“Chinese Philosophy” at Wikipedia: https://en.wikipedia.org/wiki/Chinese_philosophy

Translating and Interpreting Chinese Philosophy:

https://plato.stanford.edu/entries/chinese-translate-interpret/

Chinese philosophy at the Indiana Philosophy Ontology Project:

https://www.inphoproject.org/taxonomy/2420

第十二单元　中国古代哲学

12.1 阅读欣赏:《道德经》

【说明】 对照原文阅读译文，对比三个译文的异同，体会不同译者对原文句式的处理技巧以及对原文微妙含义的处理效果。

简介:《道德经》又称《道德真经》《老子》《五千言》等，据传说为春秋时期老子（李耳）所作，是中国早期最重要的哲学著作之一，是道家哲学思想的重要来源。《道德经》分上下两篇，上篇为《德经》，下篇为《道经》，总字数因为版本不同而有所差异，现代通行本为王弼所注，字数为 5 162 字。《道德经》以哲学意义的“道德”为纲，论述修身、治国、用兵、养生之道，文意深奥，包含广博，被誉为万经之王。《道德经》是中国历史上最伟大的名著之一，对传统哲学、科学、政治、宗教等产生了深刻影响。据联合国教科文组织统计，《道德经》是除了《圣经》以外被译成外国文字发布量最多的文化名著。

道　德　经（节选）

老子

道可道，非常道；
名可名，非常名。
无名天地之始，
有名万物之母。

故常无欲以观其妙，
常有欲以观其徼。
此两者同出而异名，
同谓之玄。
玄之又玄，
众妙之门。

译文一

The Wisdom of Laotse

(Excerpt)

The Tao that can be told of
Is not the Absolute Tao;
The Names that can be given
Are not Absolute Names.

The Nameless is the origin of Heaven and Earth;
The Named is the Mother of All Things.

Therefore:
Oftentimes, one strips oneself of passion
In order to see the secret of life;
Oftentimes, one regards life with passion
In order to see its manifest forms.

These two (the Secret and its manifestations)
Are (in their nature) the same;
They are given different names
When they become manifest.

They may both be called the Cosmic Mystery;

Reaching from the Mystery into the Deeper Mystery
Is the Gate to the Secret of All Life.

（林语堂 译）

译文二

Laws Divine and Human

(Excerpt)

The divine law may be spoken of,
But it is not the common law.
Things may be named,
But names are not the things.
In the beginning Heaven and Earth are nameless;
When named, all things become known.
So we should be free from desires
In order to understand the internal
Mystery of the divine law;
And we should have desires
In order to observe its eternal manifestations.
Come from the same origin,
But have different names,
They may be called essence.
The essential of the essence
Is the key to the understanding of all mysteries.

（许渊冲 译）

译文三

The Book of Tao and Teh

(Excerpt)

The Tao that can be expressed in words

Is not the true and eternal Tao;
The name that can be uttered in words
Is not the true and eternal name.
The word Nothingness may be used
To designate the beginning of Heaven and Earth;
The word Existence (Being) may be used
To designate the mother of all things.
Hence one should gain an insight into the subtlety
Of Tao by observing Nothingness,
And should gain an insight into the beginning
Of Tao by observing Existence (Being).
These two things, Nothingness and Existence,
Are of the same origin but different in name.
They are extremely profound in depth
Serving as the door of myriad secret beings.

（辜正坤　译）

12.2 翻译热身：《周易·系辞传》

【说明】翻译下面的文字，然后将自己的译文与所提供的参考译文对比，体会其中的差异。

简介：夏朝的《连山》、商朝的《归藏》和周朝的《周易》合称《易经》。《连山》《归藏》现已失传，传世的只有《周易》，因而现在的《易经》一般指《周易》。《周易》据传系周文王姬昌所作，内容包括《经》和《传》两个部分，《经》主要是六十四卦和三百八十四爻，卦和爻各有说明（卦辞、爻辞），作为占卜之用；《传》包含解释卦辞和爻辞的七种文辞共十篇，统称《十翼》。《周易》是中国传统思想文化中自然哲学与人文实践的理论根源，是古代汉民族思想、智慧的结晶，被誉为“大道之源”。《周易》内容丰富，对中国几千年来的政治、经济、文化等各个领域都产生了极其深刻的影响。

《系辞传》是《易传》的第4种，相传孔子做了七篇阐发和总结《周易》的论述，形成《易传》，而《系辞传》的思想水平最高。

周易·系辞传（上）

第一章

天尊地卑，乾坤定矣。卑高以陈，贵贱位矣。动静有常，刚柔断矣。方以类聚，物以群分，吉凶生矣。在天成象，在地成形，变化见矣。

是故刚柔相摩，八卦相荡。鼓之以雷霆，润之以风雨，日月运行，一寒一暑，乾道成男，坤道成女。乾知大始，坤作成物。

乾以易知，坤以简能。易则易知，简则易从。易知则有亲，易从则有功。有亲则可久，有功则可大。可久则贤人之德，可大则贤人之业。易简，而天下之理得矣；天下之理得，而成位乎其中矣。

12.3 翻译技巧：古代哲学经典的翻译

中国古代哲学经典的特点主要有两个：一是义理的玄妙性；二是词章的灵活性。对中国古代哲学经典的英译也可围绕这两点进行构思运营。下面将分开论述之。

12.3.1 中国古代哲学经典英译中义理的传译

中国古代哲学义理的表达，是与中国古代的文字表意方式密切相关的。众所周知，汉字为象形文字。现代人谈及作为象形文字的汉字，往往多指汉字的字形有模仿自然万物的特点，如山、水、马、鱼等。其实，这种说法有误，表现在以下两方面：

一方面，“文字”二字对现代人而言是一个概念，而对古人而言却是两个概念。在古人那里，单体字叫“文”，如日、月、木、目等；而合体字叫“字”，如明、相、汕、渔等。现代人笼统地称之为“文字”，就混淆了两者的细微差别。不过对于汉英翻译而言，这种混淆似乎无关大要。

另一方面，“象形”二字对现代人而言是一个概念，而对古人而言也是两个概念。在古人那里，“象形字”可分为“象字”和“形字”，其中“象字”多因《周易》的卦象而形成的字，具有抽象性的特征；而“形字”则由万物的外形而形成的字，具有具体性的特征。由此可见，“象”与“形”两者之间存在着相当大的差异，而在现代人这里，又将这两者混为一谈了。这种混淆将会阻碍我们把握古人的真意，会对中国古代哲学经典的英译产生较大的影响，因此不可掉以轻心。

根据“象字”和“形字”的差异，可以看出，中国古代文字的表意方式大致有两种：一、因象显意；二、因形显意。下面，就从中国古代哲学经典英译的角度，来探讨对这两类汉字意义的把握与传达。

（一）因象显意的传译策略

孔子曾言："书不尽言，言不尽意，是故圣人立象以尽意。"由此可见，"立象以尽意"是古代汉字表意的典型形式，今人在传译古代哲学典籍时，往往不自觉地用现代汉语中的字义去附会古文原意，这样就会发生一些理解错误，在翻译中就会以讹传讹而不自知。例如：

例 (1)： 加我数年，五、十以学易，则可以无大过矣。（选自《论语 · 述而》）

译文： Give me a few more years, so that I may have spent a whole fifty in study, and I believe that after all I should be fairly free from error.（Arthur Waley　译）

值得注意的是，原文中孔子所说的"大过"，不是"大的过错"（great error）的意思，而是《周易》第二十八卦"大过卦"的意思。见下图所示：

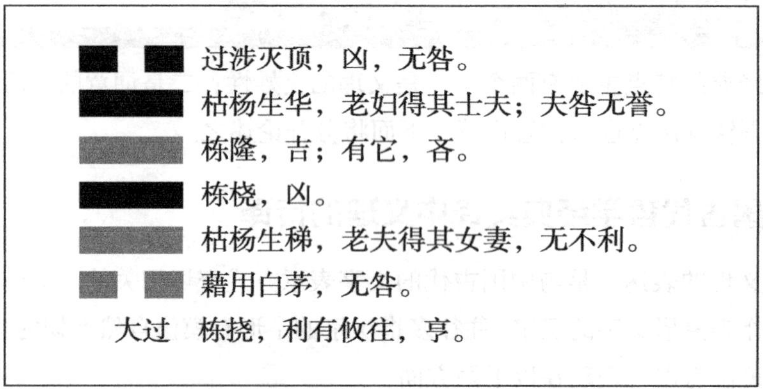

图 1 《周易》之"大过卦"卦象图

从该卦上下卦的卦象上来看，该卦上卦为兑卦，为泽；下卦为巽卦，为木。两卦叠加，形成"泽灭木"（灭顶之灾）的状态。若以该卦六爻对应天下家国，初爻为阴，喻民生疲敝；末爻亦为阴，喻圣道凌迟。一个国家出现了这种状态，无异于"灭顶之灾"。而孔子周游列国 14 年，就是要寻求明君、恢复周礼，改变这种礼乐崩坏、民不聊生的灭顶局面。如果像韦利所理解的那样，将"可以无大过"译为"I should be fairly free from error."这显然是不准确的。再如：

例 (2)：

是以圣人之治，
虚其心，
实其腹，
弱其志，
强其骨，
常使民无知无欲，

使夫智者不敢为也。
为无为，
则无不治。
（选自《道德经》第三章）

译文：

Therefore in the government of the sage:
He keeps empty their hearts,
Makes full their bellies,
Discourages their ambitions,
Strengthens their frames;
So that the people may be innocent of knowledge and desires.
And the cunning ones shall not presume to interfere.
By action without deeds
May all live in peace.

（林语堂　译）

老子在《道德经》第三章阐述圣君治国的无上理念的时候，实际上采用了以象显意的表述方式，文中所说的“心”“腹”“志”“骨”只有对应在《周易》的卦象上，才能显示出其真实的意义：按照《周易》六爻的构成原理，“心”（体）和“志”（用）对应着第五爻，“腹”分别对应着第三爻（下腹）和第四爻（上腹），“骨”分别对应着第六爻（头骨）、第二爻（四肢骨）和第一爻（手足骨）。按虚为阴、实为阳、弱为阴、强为阳的分类将上述各爻依次排列，我们就会得到《周易》的第十四卦：大有卦。如图所示：

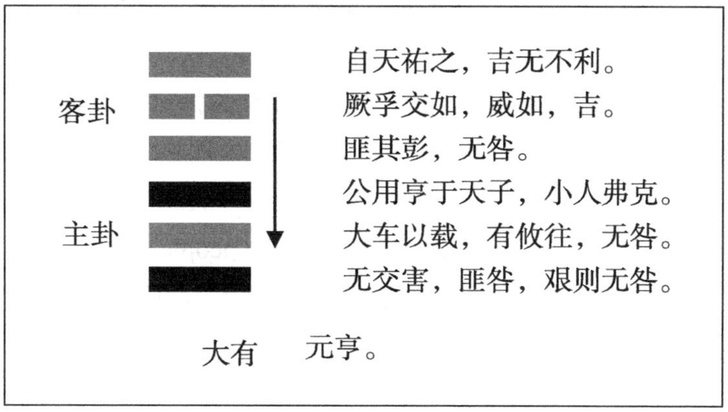

图 2 《周易》之“大有卦”卦象图

值得注意的是，我们按照人体各部位在卦象六爻的对应组合而得到大有卦之后，发现该卦卦辞爻辞的文字表述，似乎与“心”“腹”“志”“骨”没有明确的关联。这是因为《周易》的易象往往是以类取象的。意思是说，同一个卦象可以同时对应着多种事物。以上述《道德经》中所涉及的人体部位而言，《周易》之“大有卦”的爻象排列，既对应着身体各部，也对应着一个国家的各个层次。比如，第五爻在身体上对应着心志，在国中就对应着君王，其他各爻也各有其对应。如下表所示：

身体各部与国家各阶层在六爻上的对应图

爻次	身体	国家
第六爻	头	太上
第五爻	心	君王
第四爻	上腹	大夫
第三爻	下腹	士子
第二爻	四肢	平民
第一爻	手足	大众

从图 2 可以看出，《周易》之“大有卦”的卦辞和爻辞是从国家的角度对应附会的，讲的是“圣君无为”的治国理念：如果圣君恪守圣道，无为而治，就会产生“厥孚交如，威如，吉”的政治格局，而整个国家自然会呈现“元亨”的大好局面。若要达到这一政治佳境，圣君就要“治大国若烹小鲜”，就要“无知无欲”（不折腾），以役使民众。

可见，“虚其心，实其腹”等说法，只是运用人所共知的体相，来组合成一个特有的易象。易象一旦组成，就会具有易象语境下特有的意思，而与“心”“腹”“志”“骨”之间就没有直接的关联了。在中国古代的哲学典籍中，类似的表达比比皆是。如果我们忽略了这种特有的表意特征，望文生义，按字而传，肯定会出大错的。

若要避免此类翻译错误，就必须洞悉古汉语中因象显意的特点，确知中国古典哲学文本中特定字眼的特定意义，采取要么意译、要么直译加注释的方式，尽可能精确地表达原文的意义。

值得一提的是，如果我们从《周易》的古典语境把握了“圣君无为”的意蕴，那么“常使民无知无欲”就不是“经常使民众没有知识和欲望”（So that the people may be innocent of knowledge and desires）的意思，而是“常使民以无知无欲”的意思了。该句的语义把握属于“以形显意”的探究范畴，接下来我们将进一步探究。

（二）因形显意的传译策略

该小节中“因形显意”的形，即训诂学中“形训”之形，也就是字形之形。众所周知，汉字的字形是相对稳定的，但在数千年的华夏文化演变中，汉字的字形与字义之间也不可避免地发生了各式各样的演变，在不同的时代、不同的地域，同一个汉字往往会有不同的意思。在中国古代哲学典籍的英译中，往往存在着同字异义或异字同义的现象，往往给译者带来很大的挑战。例如：

例 (3)： 子曰：“学而时习之，不亦说乎？有朋自远方来，不亦乐乎？人不知而不愠，不亦君子乎？”（选自《论语·学而》）

译文 1： The Master said, “Is it not pleasant to learn with constant perseverance and application? Is it not delightful to have friends coming from distant quarters? Is he not a man of complete virtue, who feels no discomposure though men may take no note of him?”（James Legge 译）

译文 2： The Master said, to learn and at due times to repeat what one has learnt, is that not after all a pleasure? That friends should come to one from afar, is this not after all delightful? To remain unsoured even though one’s merits are unrecognized by others, is that not after all what is expected of a gentleman?（Arthur Waley 译）

译文 3： He said, study with the seasons winging past, is not this pleasant? To have friends coming in from far quarters, not a delight? Unruffled by men’s ignoring him, also indicative of high breed.（Ezra Pound 译）

译文 4： Confucius said, “Is it not a pleasure to acquire knowledge and, as you proceed, to put into practice what you have acquired? Is it not also a pleasure to have friends come from afar? The man who is not ruffled even when others pay no attention to him—is he not a gentleman?”（辜鸿铭 译）

上面四个译文虽然各有特色，但有一个共同的倾向，就是不自觉地用现代汉语的文义去附会古代语境下的原意。试简要分析如下：

第一，对“学而时习之”的语义训诂。

在现代汉语中，“学”字可以翻译成 to learn 或 to study，但在古代汉语、特别是先秦时期的汉语文本中，“学”字具有“修身成人”的意思。例如，孟子曰：“学者，所以明人伦也；……圣人，人伦之至也。”即便到了汉代，依然具有“学者，求为君子也”（郑玄语）的意思。

另外，在现代汉语中，“习”字往往有“复习”或“练习”的意思，但在古汉语中却不然。汉代许慎在《说文解字》中，将“习”字训为“鸟重飞也”。古人言“习”，多有“践行”之意，就由此衍生而来。

再者，在现代汉语中，“时”字多有“时时”或“时常”之意。但先秦时期的古汉语中确有“适时”、“合时”或“应时”的意思。如孔子曰“使民以时”，《尚书》曰“先时者杀无赦，不及时者杀无赦”，《中庸》曰“君子而时中”等，皆与现代汉语中“时”的意思不同。

通过以上分析，“学而时习之”应该具有“修身成人而超凡入圣，时机到时再推己及人，化育天下”的意思。如果将该句理解为“学了然后经常复习它”，就显得浅陋可笑了。

第二，对“有朋自远方来”的语义训诂。

中国古代汉语中，有“同门为朋、同志为友”之说，可见“朋”“友”是有所分别的。在原文语境下，“有朋自远方来”的“朋”字，应该具有“共同修学圣贤之道者”的意思。如果不假思索地将“朋”翻译成 friend，就与原意大相径庭了。

第三，对“人不知而不愠”的语义训诂。

在先秦时期的古汉语中，“人”与“民”是同义词，也可以“民人”或“人民”合称。另，“知”与“智”是通假字。故“人不知”就是“民不智”，即“民智未开”的意思。现在的人往往将该句理解成“别人不知道我”的意思，严重偏离了古文原意。

现在的译者，不管是外国译者还是中国译者，在翻译中国古代哲学典籍时，往往先在现代汉语的语境下去把握古代汉语的意思，然后把在现代汉语语境下附会出来的所谓的原意翻译成英语，这样，各种各样的谬误就在翻译中产生了。

为了避开这些谬误，就必须在翻译之初努力回到原文语境，并在原语境下精确把握原意，然后运用准确而灵活的翻译策略翻译之。

12.3.2 中国古代哲学经典英译中辞章的传译

在中国古代哲学经典的英译中，另一个比较大的挑战是古汉语文本中辞章的处理。

所谓辞章的传译，实际上就是古汉语特有的句式的传译。古汉语辞章的特色之一，在于古汉语的句读，换言之，古汉语原文本来没有标点。现在我们读到的古汉语文本，往往由今人以新式标点符号断句而成。由于古今汉语的文法及表意差异，译者往往在现代汉语语境下去把握古汉语文本的文法和句法。这样，因为对古汉语文法和句法的理解错误，在中国古代哲学经典的英译中，就会产生各种各样的辞章处理错误。例如：

例 (4)：此两者同出而异名。（选自《道德经》第一章）

译文 1：

These two (the Secret and its manifestations)
Are (in their nature) the same;
They are given different names
When they become manifest.

（林语堂　译）

译文 2：

(These two)
Come from the same origin,

But have different names,

（许渊冲 译）

从以上两个译文来看，林语堂与许渊冲对原文句读的处理是不同的：根据林语堂的译文，他对原文的断句应该是："此两者同、出而异名。"而根据许渊冲的译文，他对原文的断句却是："此两者、同出而异名。"不同的断句，其译文自然就产生了不同的意思。

到底哪种处理是正确的？这必须从老子对"道"与"名"、"无"与"有"的辩证关系的角度来理解：老子在该章中所论的是大道之流行：道之本体是难以言说的，但欲传此大道，必须强立名以言之。道之名为有，但道之本实无。因此，论道之时，所用的道体之"无"和道名之"有"，在形而上的层面是一致的，如果勉强进行分判，就会有名相上的差别。

依据以上分析，老子的真意是：道体之"无"和道名之"有"其实是一回事，是混同在道的统一体之中的，如果将此分判而言说之，就会产生"无"和"有"两种不同的名称。这样的话，该句的断句应该是："此两者同、出而异名。"

值得一提的是，该句中的"同"是"混同"的意思，翻译成英语，应该是"These two belong to the same unity of Tao"。可见，林语堂断句虽然无误，但他将该句译成了"These two are the same"，显然没有领会该句的微言大义。而许渊冲将该句译为"These two come from the same origin"，显然是由断句的问题而导致了翻译处理的错讹。又如：

例 (5)： 民可使由之，不可使知之。（选自《论语 · 泰伯》）

译文 1： The common people can be made to follow a path but not to understand it.（刘殿爵 译）

译文 2： The common people can be made to follow it; they cannot be made to understand it.（韦利 译）

由于古人历代曲解，加之今人望文生义，该句就产生了"可以使老百姓按照我们的意见去做，不容易使他们知道为什么要这样做"（孔令河 译）的意思，这无疑就让孔子屡遭诟病了。究其原因，这是汉语句读的模糊性导致的误读。

如果细读《论语》，把握住孔子先"富之"、后"教之"的化民理念，就会知道该句正确的句读应该是："民可使，由之；不可使，知之。"翻译成现代汉语，应该是：如果民众听从教化，就顺势而导之；如果不听从教化，就开启民众的智慧而引他们向善。（在古汉语中，"知"是"智"的通假字。）这样的文义处理，就免除了孔子"愚民"的嫌疑，与他所追求的"民无信不立"的理念相一致了。

此类句读错误在中国古代哲学的英译中比比皆是。要避免此类翻译失误，就必须精确掌握古汉语句读的基本知识，同时也要在文化哲学的高度贴近中国古代圣贤的文化境界，然后采取准确而灵活的翻译策略与技巧，方能对中国古代哲学的典籍进行准确无误的传译。

12.4 翻译实战：《道德经》（第二章）

【说明】根据文末的提示，把下文翻译成英文。

道德经（第二章）

老子

天下皆知美之为美，
斯恶①矣；
皆知善之为善，
斯不善矣②。
故有无相生，
难易相成，
长短相形，
高下相倾，
音声③相和，
前后相随。
是以圣人④
处无为之事，
行不言之教；
万物⑤作而弗始，
生而弗有，
为而不恃，
功成而弗居。
夫唯弗居，
是以不去⑥。

翻译提示

1. 如何理解①处的“恶”？
2. 请注意②这句话的真实意思：是“知道善之为善就是不善”，还是“人们知道善是善，就是因为有不善存在”？想一想，在英文中该如何处理？
3. ③中的“音声”与现代汉语中的“声音”是一回事吗？
4. ④之“圣人”和⑤之“万物”的逻辑关系是怎样的？
5. 如何理解句⑥“夫唯弗居，是以不去”？

12.5 译文荟萃

1) 子曰："弟子入则孝，出则弟，谨而信，泛爱众，而亲仁，行有余力，则以学文。"（《论语·学而》）

译文 1：The master said, "A young man should be a good son at home and an obedient young man abroad, sparing of speech but trustworthy in what he says, and should love the multitude at large but cultivate the friendship of his fellow men. If he has any energy to spare from such action, let him devote it to making himself cultivated."（刘殿爵　译）

译文 2：The Master said, "A young man's duty is to behave well to his parents at home and to his elders abroad, to be cautious in giving promises and punctual in keeping them, to have kindly feelings towards everyone, but seek the intimacy of the Good. If, when all that is done, he has any energy to spare, then let him study the polite arts."（韦利　译）

2) 有子曰："礼之用，和为贵，先王之道，斯为美，小大由之，有所不行，知和而和，不以礼节之，亦不可行也。"（《论语·学而》）

译文 1：Yu Tzu said, "Of the things brought about by the rites, harmony is the most valuable. Of the ways of the Former Kings, this is the most beautiful, and is followed alike in matters great and small, yet this will not always work: to aim always at harmony without regulating it by the rites simply because one knows only about harmony will not, in fact, work."（刘殿爵　译）

译文 2：Master Yu said, "In the usage of ritual it is harmony that is prized; the Way of the Former Kings from this got its beauty. Both small matters and great depend upon it. If things go amiss, he who knows the harmony will be able to attune them. But if harmony itself is not modulated by ritual, things will still go amiss."（韦利　译）

3) 子曰："不仁者，不可以久处约，不可以长处乐。仁者安仁，智者利仁。"（《论语·里仁》）

译文 1：One who is not benevolent cannot remain long in straitened circumstances, nor can he remain long in easy circumstances. The benevolent man is attracted to benevolence because he feels at home at it. The wise man is attracted to benevolence because he finds it to his advantage.（刘殿爵　译）

译文 2：Without Goodness a man cannot for long endure adversity, cannot for long enjoy prosperity. The Good Man rests content with Goodness; he that is merely wise pursues Goodness in the belief that it pays to do so.（韦利　译）

4)

道冲，
而用之或不盈。
渊兮，
似万物之宗。

挫其锐，
解其纷；
和其光，
同其尘；
湛兮，
似或存。
吾不知谁之子，
象帝之先。
（《道德经》第四章）

译文一

Tao is a hollow vessel,
And its use is inexhaustible!
Fathomless!
Like the fountain head of all things.
Its sharp edges rounded off,
Its tangles untied,
Its light tempered,
Its turmoil submerged,
Yet dark like deep water it seems to remain.
I do not know whose Son it is,
An image of what existed before God.

（林语堂　译）

译文二

The divine law is formless,
Its use is inexhaustible.
It is endless,
Whence come all things

Where the sharp is blunted,
The knots are untied,
The glare is softened,
All look like dust.
Apparent,
It seems to exist.
I do not know whence it came;
It seems to exist before God.

（许渊冲　译）

译文三

Tao is invisibly empty,
But its use is extremely plentiful.
It is profound like the originator
Of all things.
It shows no sharpness,
Stays away from entanglements,
Glows with veiled radiance,
Mingles with dust.
It is formless and invisible,
But indeed exists.
I do not know where it comes from.
It seems to have appeared
before the existence of God.

（辜正坤　译）

5)

道生一，
一生二，
二生三，
三生万物。
万物负阴而抱阳，

冲气以为和。
人之所恶，
唯孤、寡、不谷，
而王公以为称。
故物
或损之而益，
或益之而损。
人之所教，
我亦教之：
强梁者不得其死，
吾将以为教父。

（《道德经》第四十二章）

译文一

Out of Tao, One is born;
Out of One, Two;
Out of Two, Three;
Out of Three, the created universe.
The created universe carries the *yin* at its back and the *yang* in front;
Through the union of the pervading principles it reaches harmony.

To be "orphaned," "lonely" and "unworthy" is what man hate most.
Yet the princes and dukes call themselves by such names.
For sometimes things are benefited by being taken away from,
And suffer by being added to.

Others have taught this maxim,
Which I shall teach also:
"The violent man shall die a violent death."
This I shall regard as my spiritual teacher.

（林语堂　译）

译文二

One is the child of the divine law.
After one come two,
After two come three,
After three come all things.
Everything has a bright and dark side,
Co-exist in harmony.
People dislike to be
Lonely and worthless.
But rulers call themselves the sole and worthy.
So things may gain when they seem to lose,
Or lose when they seem to gain.
I will teach
What others teach me.
The brute will die a brute death.
I will teach this as a lesson.

（许渊冲　译）

译文三

Tao begets the One;
The One consists of Two in opposition (the Yin and Yang);
The Two begets the Three;
The Three begets all things of the world.
All things connote the Yin and Yang.
The Yin and Yang keep acting upon each other
And thus things keep changing and unifying themselves.
Words like "the solitary," "the few" and "the unkind"
Are usually detested by people,
Yet lords and kings
Use them to call themselves.
That is why

A thing is sometimes added to
When being reduced,
Or is reduced when being added to.
So I teach what I'm taught:
"The violent will not come to a good end."
This I will take as the first lesson when I teach.

（辜正坤　译）

12.6 翻译家：理雅各

理雅各（James Legge，1815 年—1897 年）是近代英国著名汉学家，伦敦布道会传教士。他是第一个系统研究、翻译中国古代经典的人，从 1861 年到 1886 年的 25 年间，他将“四书”“五经”等中国主要典籍全部译出，对西方思想文化界产生了深远影响。理雅各在中国办学和传教长达 30 年，返回英国后担任牛津大学汉学教授。他一生致力于中国儒家经典在西方的传播，对西方的哲学、伦理、文学和文化都产生了很大影响。他在西方世界传播和弘扬中华文明，让世界理解和认识中国，做出了巨大的历史性贡献。作为西方汉学界的奠基人之一，理雅各与法国学者顾赛芬、德国学者卫礼贤并称汉籍欧译三大师。

理雅各于 1815 年出生于苏格兰阿伯丁郡的杭特利城，自小就读于家乡的一所教区学校，曾从一位盲妇学习英国古典诗篇。1815 年至 1822 年间理雅各家与在马六甲传教的英国传教士米怜经常通信，这些信使理雅各初步接触了传教事业。1831 年理雅各考入阿伯丁英王学院，1836 年获文学硕士学位。在大学求学期间，他为当时英国的海外传教士事业所吸引，志愿当了传教士。1837 年进入希伯利神学院，接受系统神学教育。1838 年在伦敦大学师从吉德（Samuel Kidd）教授学习汉语。1839 年受伦敦传道会委派到南洋马六甲接管由首位来华新教传教士马礼逊创办的“英华书院”（Anglo-Chinese College）及伦敦传道会的印刷所，在教学之余开始研读中国典籍。英国占领香港后，理雅各将英华书院迁至香港，从此在香港定居 30 年。

1858 年，理雅各赴广州考察科举考试，亲身感受到了儒家经典在中国文化和中国社会所占据的重要地位，于是决定开始翻译中国典籍。理雅各在中国学者王韬和英国传教士湛约翰（John Chalmers）等的协助下翻译中国儒家经典著作。1861 年至 1872 年间，理雅各翻译了《论语》《大学》《中庸》《孟子》《诗经》《书经》《礼记》《易经》《道德经》《春秋》《左传》等，集合成《中国经典》（*Chinese Classics*），分五卷于 1861 年至 1886 年间在香港陆续出版。这套规模宏大的译著使理雅各闻名于世。1875 年，法国汉学界将以法国汉学大师儒莲（Stanislas Julien）命名的“儒莲奖”首次奖励颁发给理雅各。1976 年，英国牛津大学任命理雅各为该校历史上第一位汉学教授。理雅各在

此教职上工作了20年，直至1897年逝世。在这20年中，理雅各是西方汉学界的泰斗。他的中国典籍翻译和著述深刻地影响了19世纪末乃至20世纪的西方汉学研究，此间的西方汉学史被称为“理雅各时代”。

除了《中国经典》中的译著，理雅各从中国返回英国后还继续翻译出版了《尚书》、《诗经之宗教部分》、《孝经》、《庄子》、《离骚》和佛教文献《佛国记》等著作。翻译之余，理雅各还撰写了大量论及中国宗教、历史、文学方面的文章。其他主要著述包括:《中国人关于天神和鬼怪的概念》(*The Notions of the Chinese Concerning God and Spirits*)、《孔子生平及其学说》(*The Life and Teaching of Confucius*)、《孟子生平及其学说》(*The Life and Teachings of Mencius*)、《帝国入学讲稿四篇》(*Imperial Confucianism*)、《中国的宗教：儒教、道教与基督教的对比》(*The Religions of China: Confucianism and Taoism Described and Compared with Christianity*)、《法显行传》(*A Record of Buddhist Kingdoms*)等。其所翻译的《诗经》中部分具有宗教意义的诗篇收入了牛津大学麦克斯·缪勒（Max Müller）主编的《东方圣典》(*The Sacred Books of the East*)系列丛书第三卷《中国圣典：儒家卷》(*The Sacred Books of the East: Texts of Confucianism*)。

12.7 补充资源

参考书目

James L. 中国经典（*The Chinese Classics*，第1—5卷）. 上海：华东师范大学出版社，2010.
孔子. 大师经典文库：论语（汉英对照）. Arthur Waley，译. 北京：外语教学与研究出版社，1997.
老子. 大师经典文库：道德经（汉英对照）. Arthur Waley，译. 北京：外语教学与研究出版社，2013.
孙子. 大师经典文库：孙子兵法（汉英对照）. 袁士槟，译. 北京：外语教学与研究出版社，1998.
冯友兰. 中国哲学史. 上海：华东师范大学出版社，2011.
罗素. 西方哲学史. 马元德，译. 北京：商务印书馆，1997.

网络资源

中国古代哲学：https://www.ancient.eu/Chinese_Philosophy/
国际儒学网：http://www.ica.org.cn
耶鲁大学东亚研究中心：https://ceas.yale.edu
哈佛大学燕京学社：https://harvard-yenching.org

中国孔子网：http://www.chinakongzi.org

Chinese Classics in English: http://bs.dayabook.com/home

The Stanford Encyclopedia of Philosophy: https://plato.stanford.edu/index.html

Chapter 7

第七章 应用翻译（一）

第十三单元 发言与演讲

第十四单元 政府文件

第十三单元 发言与演讲

13.1《构建新型国际关系，打造人类命运共同体》

【说明】阅读下列译文，思考原文在用词、句式结构、语体色彩、篇章结构等方面有何特点。译文采取了什么样的总体翻译策略（归化、异化）？为什么？译文是如何处理时态的？

简介：2015年8月21日，澳大利亚联合国协会举办2015年全国大会，纪念联合国成立70周年。中国驻澳大利亚大使马朝旭应邀出席并发表了这篇题为《构建新型国际关系，打造人类命运共同体》的演讲。他全面回顾和阐述了中国在联合国政治安全、经济发展、人权社会、军控条法、维和、安理会改革等各领域发挥的积极重要作用，强调中国一贯坚持《联合国宪章》的宗旨和精神，坚定维护以联合国为中心、以《联合国宪章》为基础的战后国际秩序，坚持奉行独立自主的和平外交政策，坚持不懈地致力于国际和平、安全与合作，为维护世界和平、促进共同发展作出了重要贡献。本文选自该演讲的开头部分。

构建新型国际关系，打造人类命运共同体

——马朝旭大使在澳大利亚联合国协会2015年全国大会上的讲话

女士们，先生们：

上午好！很高兴出席澳大利亚联合国协会全国大会，感谢澳联协主席 Russell Trood 先生的盛情邀请。澳大利亚联合国协会在联合国成立70周年之际召开此次全国大会，具有特殊的重要意义。

70年来，联合国历经国际形势风云变幻，走过了一条不平坦的道路，取得了举世瞩目的成就。

《联合国宪章》倡导的主权平等、不干涉内政、和平解决争端等基本原则深入人心，奠定了当代国际秩序的基石。联合国在维护国际和平安全、推动共同发展和促进人权进步等方面的实践受到国际社会广泛支持。

人们不会忘记，联合国诞生于国际社会对战争教训的深刻反思之中。今年是世界反法西斯战争和中国人民抗日战争胜利 70 周年。中国人民抗日战争是世界反法西斯战争的重要组成部分，中国人民为世界反法西斯战争的最终取得胜利付出了巨大民族牺牲，作出了不可磨灭的贡献。为此，中国政府将于 9 月 3 日在北京举行隆重纪念活动，目的是铭记历史，开创未来。

Developing a New Type of International Relations and Building a Community of Common Destiny for Mankind

Address by Ambassador Ma Zhaoxu at the UNAA National Conference 2015

Ladies and gentlemen,

Good morning! I am very pleased to attend the UNAA National Conference. My sincere thanks go to Dr. Russell Trood for inviting me to this special event. It is most fitting and relevant to hold the event as this year marks the 70th anniversary of the founding of the United Nations.

The United Nations has traveled an extraordinary journey in an ever-changing world and made remarkable achievements over the past 70 years. The fundamental principles enshrined in the UN Charter — sovereign equality, non-interference in internal affairs and peaceful settlement of disputes — have since taken hold as the cornerstone of the current international order. The UN has secured extensive support for its practice in safeguarding international peace and security, promoting common development and human rights progress.

It is never to be forgotten that the United Nations was born out of profound reflections on the war. This year also marks the 70th anniversary of the victory of World Anti-Fascist War and Chinese People's War of Resistance Against Japanese Aggression, with the latter being an important part of the former. China has made tremendous national sacrifices and made significant contribution to the final victory of the World Anti-Fascist War. For this reason, China will hold special commemorative events to remember the history and create a better future.

13.2《人民日报社社长杨振武在人民日报英文客户端上线仪式上的致辞》

【说明】 请将下列段落翻译为英语，注意恰当处理具有中国特色的表述和古典名言的翻译问题，并正确使用英语时态。

简介：2017年10月15日，人民日报英文客户端上线仪式在人民日报社新媒体大厦举行。来自相关部委、部分驻华使节、新闻媒体及学界代表约百名嘉宾参加了当天的上线仪式。人民日报社社长杨振武发表了讲话。本文选自讲话的中间部分。人民日报社推出英文客户端，定位于“联结中外、沟通世界”，这是中国权威媒体为讲好中国故事、加强国际传播能力建设的又一次创新。英文客户端将成为全球用户了解中国新闻、中国观点、中国主张、中国理念的权威资讯类平台，同时还将突出“服务”功能，力争打造一个联结国外用户与中国的桥梁。

人民日报社社长杨振武在人民日报英文客户端上线仪式上的致辞

2017年10月15日

伴随着时代前进的步伐，当代中国呈现生机勃勃的发展局面，展现不可阻挡的发展势头，正前所未有地走近世界舞台中心。中国的发展是世界发展的巨大机遇，也离不开世界各国的共同发展；发展起来的中国需要更好向世界展示自己，剧变中的世界渴望更好地了解中国。介绍中国经验、阐述中国主张、提出中国方案、贡献中国智慧，已成国际社会期盼，实为中国发展必然。在这一进程中，媒体肩负着重要责任。

明者因时而变，知者随事而制。习近平总书记指示我们要“加强国际传播能力建设”“讲好中国故事，传播好中国声音”“联结中外，沟通世界”。近年来，人民日报认真贯彻落实习近平总书记重要指示精神和党中央决策部署，坚持统筹内宣外宣一体发展、传统媒体新兴媒体融合发展，努力用海外读者乐于接受的方式、易于理解的语言，讲好中国故事、传播好中国声音，在对外宣传和国际传播方面取得了显著成绩。

13.3 翻译技巧：发言与演讲的翻译

13.3.1 汉语发言与演讲的文体特点

第一，语体色彩方面，发言与演讲文体兼具口语体和书面体的特征，这是因为发言与演讲均是以口语为载体向受众传播的，但是许多时候又是经过事先准备的，以写好的讲稿为基础（王佐良、丁往道，1987）。不少发言与演讲，尤其是政治人物的讲话，常具有庄重、严肃的特点。

第二，词汇方面，常使用政治、军事、经济、金融等领域的专业术语，以凸显说话人的权威性与专业性，但不同于科技、法律等文体，发言与演讲文体往往将艰深、晦涩的术语排除在外，而且注意避免术语堆砌，因为其受众通常情况下为一般大众，而非专业人士。除术语之外，发言与演讲文体的其他用词一般也较为正式，而且还会使用一些生僻词。汉语时政类发言与演讲还常常使用一些别具中国特色的惯用语。

第三，句式特征方面，多用陈述句，偶尔会使用祈使句、疑问句和感叹句。句子结构较其他口语文体复杂，长句比较多。有时会使用简短的排比句增强语气、增加气势。句子主语常使用第一人称，以拉近演讲人与受众之间的距离；或使用某个团体、机构或组织的名称（如“我国”“中国共产党”“党中央”等），以突出该团体、机构或组织已经、正在或者将要采取的行动，因而句子多使用主动语态，较少使用被动语态。

第四，修辞方面，常使用明喻、暗喻、排比、拟人、转喻等修辞手段，以增强表达效果，吸引受众注意，一些演讲者，尤其是政治领袖还常常使用典故或古典名言来增强效果或引发思考。

与英语相比，汉语发言与演讲文体具有以下几个特别之处，翻译时须注意：

第一，汉语用词常具有很深的文化内涵，往往与英语形成词汇空缺，即在英文中找不到对等表达，比如时政类发言与演讲常常会有诸如“一国两制”“改革开放”“外来腐朽思想”“三个代表”“四个意识”“四个全面”这些具有中国特色的政治术语，还有“明者因时而变，知者随事而制”“司马昭之心路人皆知”这样的古典名言和典故。

第二，汉语发言与演讲中动词的使用频率相当高，尤其习惯使用一连串的动词来作谓语（即所谓的连动式），比如“我相信，有全国人民作坚强后盾，香港特别行政区政府和香港同胞一定能够管理和建设好香港，保持香港长期繁荣稳定，创造香港更加美好的未来”一句中，“香港特别行政区政府和香港同胞”这个主语之后就跟了四个谓语动词（“管理”、“建设”、“保持”和“创造”）。英语则多用名词、名词化结构、介词、形容词等来表达动作概念，而且不习惯使用一长串动词来作谓语，汉英转换时常需将一些谓语动词降格为非谓语动词或者介词、名词等非动词形式。

第三，汉语发言与演讲文体中会使用一些情态动词，如“可能”“会”“可以”“要”“应当”“必须”等，但其频率低于英语发言与演讲文体，而且在时政类发言与演讲文体中，汉语倾向于使用低量值情态动词（如“能”“能够”）和高量值情态动词（如“要”“必须”），英语则倾向于使用低量值情态动词（如 can）和中量值情态动词（如 will）（王和私、尹丕安、王芙蓉，2011）。

13.3.2 汉语发言与演讲的英译

（一）总体思路

Peter Newmark（1981）提出了语义翻译和交际翻译这两个概念，指出语义翻译就是“在语义和句法结构许可的情况下，尽可能切近地传递出原文准确的语境意义”；交际翻译则指“译文对译文读者产生的效果尽可能地接近原文对原文读者产生的效果”。他指出，语义翻译是“停留在源语文化内”，译者要做的只是“帮助读者理解其内涵”，因而译文读上去有翻译的痕迹（overtranslated）；交际翻译则只关注译文读者，使译文读起来没有困难或含混之处，异域元素被消解在读者自己的文化或语言之中，因而译文读起来少有翻译的痕迹（undertranslated）。在阐释语义翻译时，Newmark 还专门以戴高乐将军的一段演说词为例说明，类似演说词这样的文体，其语言（风格）与内容同等重要，就需要采用语义翻译，既须精确传递原文意思，又须保留原文语言风格（比如戴高乐的演说直白、朴实、不加修饰）。这么看来，汉语发言与演讲的翻译需要遵循“语义翻译”的原则，即从内容到形式均向源语靠拢。

另一方面，汉语发言与演讲的翻译属于外宣翻译的范畴。所谓“外宣翻译”，是指“在全球化背景下以让世界了解中国为目的，以汉语为信息源，以英语等外国语为信息载体，以各种媒体为渠道，以外国民众（包括境内的各类外籍人士）为主要传播对象的交际活动”（张健，2013）。为了“让世界了解中国”，就必须考虑译文的可接受性问题，如果一味强调“语义翻译”——即对原文的绝对忠实而忽略译文的可接受性问题，外宣翻译的目的就很难实现。为此，黄友义（2004）提出了“外宣三贴近”原则：“贴近中国发展的实际，贴近国外受众对中国信息的需求，贴近国外受众的思维习惯”。

综合考虑 Newmark 的语义翻译原则和黄友义的“外宣三贴近”原则，我们可以将汉语发言与演讲的翻译要点归结为一句话：兼顾原文内容与风格的忠实传递和译文的可接受性。以政府领导人的发言与演讲为例，这类文体往往传达的是中国政府的立场、方针与政策，其内容的准确性至关重要，否则会引发一系列不良后果。同时，每个领导人的语言风格不同，有的朴实、直白，有的含蓄、委婉，有的辞藻华丽，有的引经据典，翻译时忠实传递语言风格有利于读者更好地了解领导人的个性特点。但是，由于语言和文化差异，对原文内容与风格的忠实有时必然会导致它与译文可接受性之间的冲突，这时就需要采取变通策略，在忠实与可接受性之间找到一个平衡点。比如，汉语讲话者为了突出或强调某个意思，有时可能会采用同义反复的手法，即使用不同的词语、词组或句子表达相同的意思，如果照直翻译，就可能会令译文重复啰唆，不符合读者的文化预期，这时就可以删繁就简、加以变通，既确保意思忠实原文，又确保译文易于为读者所接受。

（二）时态问题

时态往往是汉英翻译学习者容易忽略的一个问题，这是因为与英语不同，汉语的时态往往不是体现在语言形式上，而是隐藏在字里行间，学习者翻译时受母语干扰，容易忽略对语言形式的选择。汉语发言与演讲中，说话人往往会回顾过去、谈论现在、展望未来，其时态富于变化，翻译时需要注意选择不同的语言形式来表达不同的时态。

以“阅读欣赏”的原文第三段为例，“联合国诞生于国际社会对战争教训的深刻反思之中”说的是过去发生的事情，故译文使用一般过去时；“今年是世界反法西斯战争和中国人民抗日战争胜利70周年”说的是目前的情况，因而译文使用一般现在时；“中国人民为世界反法西斯战争的最终取得胜利付出了巨大民族牺牲，作出了不可磨灭的贡献”强调发生在过去的动作对现在的影响，所以译文使用现在完成时；“中国政府将于9月3日在北京举行隆重纪念活动”说的是将来要做的事情，因此译文使用一般将来时。可见，短短一段话中就可能涉及几种时态。

（三）古典名言的翻译

我们先来看看以下三句古典名言的翻译：

例 (1)： 中华民族的昨天，可以说是“雄关漫道真如铁”。

译文： In the old days, the Chinese people went through hardships as grueling as “storming an iron-wall pass.”

例 (2)： 中华民族的今天，正可谓“人间正道是沧桑”。

译文： Today, the Chinese nation is undergoing profound changes, like “seas becoming mulberry fields.”

例 (3)： 中华民族的明天，可以说是“长风破浪会有时”。

译文： In the future, the Chinese nation will “forge ahead like a gigantic ship breaking through strong winds and heavy waves.”

从上述译文你发现什么规律了吗？根据上文提到的翻译要点——兼顾原文内容与风格的忠实传递和译文的可接受性，为了突出领导人的语言风格（喜欢用典），古典名言的翻译宜采取直译为主的策略，即在不影响译文可接受性的情况下尽量直译。直译时需注意三点：一是不能逐字逐句死译，否则读者难以理解；二是避免孤立地翻译古典名言，而是将其融入上下文中，使行文流畅；三是针对某些隐晦的古典名言要适当增词使其意义明晰化，如例 (1) 译文中的 went through hardships as grueling as、例 (2) 译文中的 undergoing profound changes、例 (3) 译文中的 forge ahead 都属于直译基础上的增词。

再如以下例子：

例 (4)： 两千五百五十年前诞生的中国古代杰出的教育家、思想家孔子说过：“逝者如斯夫！不舍昼夜。”时光流逝不可逆转。

译文： Confucius, an outstanding educator and thinker of ancient China who was born 2,550 years ago, once said, “The passage of time is just like the flow of water, which goes on day and night.” The Lapse of time is irreversible.

上述例子同样采取了直译法，由于原文本身意思就很明显，而且在行文中相对独立，所以翻译时既不需要增词加以阐释，也不需要刻意融入上下文，以直接引用的方式处理即可。

13.4 翻译实战：《崔天凯大使在美国中国总商会2018年年度晚宴上的讲话》

【说明】运用本单元学到的文体特点、翻译要点和翻译技巧翻译以下段落。

简介：美国中国总商会2018年年度晚宴于当地时间1月17日在纽约举行，中国驻美国大使崔天凯在晚宴上发表主旨演讲。崔大使表示，过去一年在双方共同努力下，中美关系总体保持稳定并取得重要进展。展望未来，他指出中美双方应高度警惕20世纪50年代以来的“冷战”思维和“零和”博弈再度回潮，决不允许其干扰双方增进相互了解和友谊的努力。本文选自这篇致辞的中间部分和结尾部分。

崔天凯大使在美国中国总商会2018年年度晚宴上的讲话

纽约

2018年1月17日

2018年是中国改革开放40周年。我们将继续坚持深化改革和扩大开放。习近平主席多次指出，改革开放是实现中华民族伟大复兴的必由之路，中华民族伟大复兴必将在改革开放的进程中得以实现。今年，我们将继续推出一系列改革开放新举措。例如，下半年我们将在上海举办首届中国国际进口博览会，欢迎美方积极参展。总之，中国正在正确的轨道上向前发展，我们有信心实现“两个一百年”奋斗目标，有信心实现中华民族伟大复兴的中国梦。

………

明年是中美建交40周年。孔子说，四十不惑。展望未来，我们要以中美关系过去40年的发展为基础，始终坚持正确方向，构建更加牢固的双边关系，造福两国和世界人民。我希望并相信中美两国工商界，特别是美国中国总商会会员企业，继续利用自身影响，为中美关系健康稳定发展进一步发挥积极作用。

13.5 译文荟萃

1. 短语与术语翻译

1) 共享经济	sharing economy
2) 无人超市	unmanned supermarket
3) 互联网 + 策略	Internet Plus strategy
4) 供给侧结构性改革	supply-side structural reform
5) 人均可支配收入	per capita disposable income
6) 精准扶贫	targeted poverty alleviation
7) 自贸试验区	free trade pilot zones
8) 数字经济	digital economy
9) 云计算	cloud computing
10) 物联网	Internet of things
11) 网络直播	live video streaming
12) 网红经济	Internet celebrity economy
13) 虚拟货币	virtual currency
14) 无人机	unmanned aerial vehicle
15) 实名登记	real-name registration
16) 国家大数据战略	national big data strategy
17) 货币政策	monetary policy
18) 乡村振兴战略	the strategy of rural vitalization
19) 生态保护红线	red lines for ecological protection
20) 冰上丝绸之路	Polar Silk Road

2. 句子翻译

1) 我谨代表中国出口商品交易会感谢大家今天莅临指导参观，首先请允许我简单地向大家介绍广交会的基本情况。

I would like to extend my gratitude for your coming today on behalf of Chinese Export Commodities Fair. Please allow me to begin with a briefing on the basic information of Canton Fair.

2) 非常荣幸来到杭州应邀参加“第三届全球化论坛”。请允许我代表中国教育部并以个人名义预祝本次论坛圆满成功！

I feel greatly honored to join you, at the invitation of the Third Globalization Forum. Please allow me, on behalf of the Chinese Ministry of Education, and in my own name, to wish this forum a complete success.

3) 很高兴时隔 5 年再次来到达沃斯，出席世界经济论坛 2015 年年会。

It gives me great pleasure to come to Davos again after five years to attend the World Economic Forum Annual Meeting 2015.

4) 很高兴与大家相聚在美丽的澳门，共同出席中国－葡语国家经贸合作论坛第五届部长级会议开幕式。

It gives me great pleasure to meet you in the beautiful city of Macao and attend the opening ceremony of the Fifth Ministerial Conference of the Forum for Economic and Trade Cooperation Between China and Portuguese-speaking Countries.

5) 罗斯柴尔德勋爵是中国人民的老朋友，曾多次访华，致力于推动中英合作，我对此表示赞赏。今天，罗斯柴尔德勋爵希望我谈谈中国经济和中英务实合作。我愿就上述问题谈几点看法。

Lord Rothschild is an old friend. I appreciate his continued support for China-UK cooperation, not least through his many visits to China. Lord Rothschild asked me to talk about China's economy and China-UK business cooperation. So let me share with you some of my views on this important issue.

6) 在此，我谨代表中国政府，对大会的召开表示热烈祝贺，对远道而来的各位嘉宾表示诚挚欢迎，对长期致力于全球旅游事业发展的各界人士致以崇高敬意！

On behalf of the Chinese government, let me offer warm congratulations on the opening of the conference. I also express sincere welcome to all guests coming from afar, and pay high tribute to those who have long been committed to the development of tourism in the world.

7) 中国地域辽阔，历史悠久，民族众多，有着壮美秀丽的自然风光、光辉灿烂的传统文化、各具特色的民族风情，发展旅游业的优势和潜力巨大。

China is a huge country. It has a long history, a splendid culture and enchanting natural scenery. The Chinese population is multi-ethnic, each with its own uniqueness. All this could be translated into advantage and potential for tourism development.

8) 当今世界仍不太平，地区冲突和热点问题此起彼伏，恐怖主义危害加重。和平与发展是各国人民的共同期盼。

The world today is not a tranquil place. In some parts of the world, conflicts and hotspot issues keep cropping up and the threat of terrorism simply gets more imminent. Peace and development are the shared aspiration of people of all countries.

9) 今后，我们将一如既往支持和参与联合国世界旅游组织的相关工作，加强与各国的交流与协作，共同推动承载着世界和平与发展希望的旅游之舟破浪前行，驶向胜利的彼岸！

China will continue to support and take an active part in the UNWTO's work, and will increase exchange and cooperation with other countries in tourism. Together, we can make sure that tourism, the ship of peace and development, will sail far and take us to a better future.

10) 非常感谢美国中国总商会今晚给我同大家一起交流的机会。我要特别感谢全国政协董建华副主席，他今天专程从香港赶来参加这场活动，他的演讲让我们很受启发。

Let me first thank the China General Chamber of Commerce (CGCC) for giving me the honor to speak tonight. I also want to take this opportunity to thank Chairman C. H. Tung for coming all the way from Hong Kong and giving us a most inspiring keynote speech just now.

11) 我们愿以此项白衣天使奖来表彰格林女士对我医院作出的巨大贡献。

We would like to acknowledge Ms. Green's enormous contribution to our hospital with this award of "Angel in White."

12) 我在这里代表上海市政府宣布本年度白玉兰奖的获奖者名单。

On behalf of the Shanghai Municipal Government, I hereby announce the recipients of this year's Magnolia Award.

13) 最后，预祝本届年会取得圆满成功！

To conclude, I wish this annual conference a complete success.

14) 我们再次受到了隆重热烈的接待和无限盛情的款待，我再次非常愉快地向我们的东道主表示深深的谢意。

It gives me great pleasure to express once again to our host my deep appreciation for the grand reception and boundless and generous hospitality we enjoy here.

15) 在我结束讲话之际，我请各位与我一起举杯，

为威廉斯副总统和夫人的身体健康，
为所有贵宾们的身体健康，
为我们两国之间持久的友谊与合作，
为世界和平与繁荣，
干杯！

In closing, I would like you to join me in a toast
To the health of Vice President and Mrs. Williams,
To the health of all our distinguished guests,
To the lasting friendship and cooperation between our two countries,
To the peace and prosperity of the world,
Cheers!

3. 篇章翻译

简介：2017 年 7 月 14 日，中国驻东盟使团与印尼大学东盟研究中心在印尼首都雅加达共同举办主题为“东盟成立 50 周年：中国 – 东盟关系新篇章”的研讨会。来自中国与东盟国家的专家学者围绕“东盟 50 周年的发展成就与挑战”“中国 – 东盟关系现状和展望”等议题进行了深入研讨。各方积极评价中国 – 东盟关系取得的成就，一致认为，在新形势下，双方应进一步加强战略沟通，妥善应对挑战，提升政治互信，深化务实合作，扩大人文交流，共同维护和平稳定与发展繁荣。中国驻东盟大使徐步在开幕式上发表了致辞。他表示，中国和东盟是陆海相连的亲密近邻。自 1991 年建立对话关系以来，双方政治关系不断加强，经贸合作飞跃发展，人文交流更加密切，各领域合作取得了丰硕成果。中国 – 东盟关系已发展成为东盟同对话伙伴关系中最强劲、最活跃的一组关系。本文选自该致辞的开头和中间部分。

携手建设更为紧密的中国 – 东盟命运共同体

——驻东盟大使徐步在东盟成立 50 周年暨中国 – 东盟关系研讨会开幕式上的讲话

2017 年 7 月 14 日，雅加达

尊敬的印度尼西亚外交部东盟事务高官何塞阁下，
尊敬的东南亚国家联盟副秘书长穆赫坦阁下，
各位使节，各位学者，朋友们，

欢迎大家应邀出席今天的研讨会。

今年是东盟成立 50 周年。半个世纪以来，东盟奉行独立自主、中立和不结盟外交政策，积极探索并坚持符合自身特点的发展道路，致力于加强内部团结，化解地区纷争，使东南亚从动荡走向稳定，从对抗走向合作，从贫穷走向繁荣。东盟已经成为本地区最重要的区域组织，成为不同社会制度和发展水平国家联合自强的典范。

……

2013 年，中国国家主席习近平在印尼国会发表重要演讲，倡议与东盟共建 21 世纪海上丝绸之路，携手建设更为紧密的中国 – 东盟命运共同体。中国愿与东盟国家一道，抓住难得的发展机遇，合力应对全球和地区挑战，实现共同发展与繁荣。习近平主席的倡议有其深刻的时代背景和现实意义，为中国 – 东盟关系发展勾画了美好蓝图。

当前，世界经济增长动力依然不足，保护主义和逆全球化思潮对地区一体化进程造成干扰。恐怖主义、宗教极端主义等非传统安全威胁日益突出，给地区的安宁稳定蒙上阴影。面对全球性挑战和地区性难题，任何一国均无法独善其身。建立合作共赢、安全共担、发展共享的中国－东盟命运共同体，承载了中国追求和平发展的愿望，顺应当今时代的潮流要求，也符合东盟国家的根本利益。

Towards a Closer ASEAN-China Community of Shared Future

Remarks by Ambassador Xu Bu at the Seminar on "ASEAN at 50: A New Chapter for ASEAN-China Relations"

14 July 2017, Jakarta

Your Excellency Mr. Jose Antonio Tavares, SOM Leader and Director General of ASEAN of the Ministry of Foreign Affairs of Indonesia,

Your Excellency Dr. AKP Mochtan, Deputy Secretary-General of ASEAN,

Excellencies,

Scholars from China and ASEAN countries,

Dear Friends,

Let me begin by warmly welcoming all of you to join us at today's seminar.

This year marks the 50th anniversary of the founding of ASEAN. In the half a century since, by upholding a policy of independence, neutrality and non-alignment, ASEAN has blazed a successful path of its own, and remains committed to strengthening unity and defusing conflicts, lifting Southeast Asia out of turbulence, confrontation and poverty to a region of stability, cooperation and great promise. Along the way, ASEAN has grown into the most important sub-regional organization in our region and a model of seeking strength and harmony among differences and diversity.

In 2013, Chinese President Xi Jinping delivered an important speech at the Indonesian Parliament, in which he called for joint efforts with ASEAN to build a Maritime Silk Road of the 21st century and proposed, for the first time, the concept of building a more closely-knit China-ASEAN community of shared future. This is an official statement that China will work with ASEAN to seize the opportunities and address common challenges so as to realize shared growth and prosperity for our people. This initiative takes roots in a vastly changing historic background and will exert rich implications for our region and beyond, laying out a blueprint for the future growth of China-ASEAN relations.

In the global context, the world economy still lacks momentum, and protectionism and anti-globalization sentiments have posed threats to regional integration process. Non-traditional security challenges such as terrorism and religious extremism are on the rise, casting a shadow over regional peace and stability. In the face of these challenges, no country can manage alone or stand aloof. By building a

China-ASEAN community of shared future, we work for common security and shared prosperity through win-win cooperation. It embodies China's pursuit for peace and development, answers the call of the time and serves the fundamental interests of ASEAN as well.

13.6 翻译家：程镇球

程镇球（1919 年—2007 年），江苏宜兴人，被誉为我国政治文献翻译研究首开先河者。精通英语，《毛泽东选集》英译组组长、定稿组成员，《香港特别行政区基本法》英译定稿组成员。曾长期参与重要外事活动和大型国际会议、党和国家重要文件的翻译工作。主编《新时代汉英大词典》。曾任外交部翻译室主任、中国译协常务理事、外事翻译委员会和中译外委员会副主任。著有《翻译问题探索》《论汉译英的几个问题》等。被中国译协表彰为首批资深翻译家。

庄绎传（1995）回顾程镇球自 1949 年以来在翻译事业上所取得的成就时这样说：

"1949 年 5 月，程镇球同志在新中国成立前夕从英国经香港回国，抵达北京（当时叫北平）。不久便分配到外事学校（即北京外国语大学的前身）英文部任教。由于新中国成立初期工作上的需要，程老多次借调到国内外担任口笔头翻译工作。如 1949 年夏世界青年联欢节（布达佩斯）、1950 年夏国际学联代表大会（布拉格）、1952 年亚太和大和世界和平大会（维也纳），以及 1956 年负责中共八大翻译处英文同声传译组工作，1959 年主持国庆十周年译员训练班，接着担任国庆十周年翻译处英文组组长。1960 年起，他参加《毛泽东选集》第四卷的英文翻译定稿工作，随后又参加对《毛选》前三卷英译本的全面修订。此外，他还主持了一系列'反修文章'的英译和定稿工作。1965 年程老调外交部参加外事翻译。'文化大革命'后期，又在中央编译局从事国家领导人文集，如《周恩来选集》的英译定稿工作。70 至 80 年代多次主持党代会、人代会文件的英译定稿工作，其间还为《邓小平文选》的英译文定稿。"

程镇球的翻译思想表现为（庄绎传，1995）：第一，政治文献翻译要突出政治。"由于原文内容涉及党和国家的方针政策或重要思想和理论问题，译文必须一丝不苟，忠实地传达其精神实质。"他认为，政治文献翻译要忠实于原文，必须既反对任意脱离原文的自由主义 (liberalism)，也反对死扣原文字面的机械主义 (literalism)，翻译可以说是在 continual tug of war between literalism and liberalism 中前进的。第二，运用唯物辩证法分析翻译问题。他在总结《毛选》英译的《翻译问题探索》（1980 年商务版）一书中写道："由此可见，翻译必须从原文的文字着手，离开原文的字句就无所谓翻译，这是翻译的唯物论。但是原文的文字和内容有时存在着矛盾，因而翻译不能完全受原文字面的束缚，而要透过字面，从文章通篇精神和上下文着眼，进行一番由此及彼、由表及里的分析和推敲，来抓住原文的思想实质。这是翻译的辩证法。"

13.7 补充资源

（1）人民网英文版（http://en.people.cn/）

（2）新华网英文版（http://www.xinhuanet.com/english/home.htm）

（3）常熟理工学院汉英政治平行语料库（http://pcpt.cslg.cn/）

（4）中国日报“英语点津”（http://language.chinadaily.com.cn/）

第十四单元　政府文件

14.1 阅读欣赏：《中国对拉美和加勒比政策文件》

【说明】 阅读下列译文，并回答：原文在用词、句式结构、语体色彩、篇章结构等方面有何特点？译文采取了什么样的总体翻译策略？为什么？译文在具有中国特色的政治表述和长句的翻译方面主要采用了哪些技巧？

简介：继国家主席习近平访问厄瓜多尔、秘鲁、智利等拉美三国后，2016 年 11 月 24 日，中国政府发布第二份对拉政策文件，全面阐述新时期中国对拉政策的新理念、新主张、新举措。文件称，中拉关系处于全面合作新阶段，中方致力于构建政治上真诚互信、经贸上合作共赢、人文上互学互鉴、国际事务中密切协作、整体合作和双边关系相互促进的中拉关系“五位一体”新格局，推动中拉全面合作伙伴关系再上新台阶，成为携手发展的命运共同体。本文为该文件的前言部分。

中国对拉美和加勒比政策文件

前言

当今世界正处在前所未有的历史性变革之中，多极化和全球化深入发展，新兴市场国家和发展中国家的崛起成为不可阻挡的历史潮流。同时，世界经济复苏进程艰难曲折，国际和地区热点问题频发，传统和非传统安全威胁相互交织，维护世界和平、促进共同发展仍然任重道远。

中国进入实现中华民族伟大复兴的关键阶段，正围绕到 2020 年全面建成小康社会、到本世纪中叶建成富强民主文明和谐的社会主义现代化国家的“两个一百年”奋斗目标，积极推进社会主义市场经济、民主政治、先进文化、和谐社会、生态文明建设。中国坚持独立自主的和平外交政策，坚定不移地实行对外开放，愿扩大同各国利益交汇点，推动构建以合作共赢为核心的新型国际关系，打造人类命运共同体。

中国的发展离不开包括拉美和加勒比在内广大发展中国家的共同发展。2013 年以来，中国领导人就加强中拉关系和各领域合作提出一系列重大倡议和举措，赋予中拉关系新的发展目标和发展动力。值此之际，中国政府发布第二份对拉政策文件，旨在总结经验，展望未来，全面阐述新时期中国对拉政策的新理念、新主张、新举措，推动中拉各领域合作实现更大发展。

China's Policy Paper on Latin America and the Caribbean

Preface

The world today is undergoing unprecedented historical changes, with multi-polarization and globalization gaining momentum. The rise of emerging markets and developing countries has become an irresistible historical trend. At the same time, the world economy is recovering amidst twists and turns. Global and regional hot-spot issues take place frequently. Traditional and non-traditional security threats are intertwined. Safeguarding world peace and promoting common development remains a daunting task.

China has entered a crucial stage in achieving the great rejuvenation of the Chinese nation. In order to fulfill the "two centenary goals" of building a moderately prosperous society in all respects by 2020 and turning the nation into a modern socialist country that is prosperous, strong, democratic, culturally advanced and harmonious by the mid-21st century, China has been actively promoting the construction of a socialist market economy, socialist democracy, advanced culture, a harmonious society, as well as ecological civilization. China adheres to the independent foreign policy of peace and is unswerving in its implementation of the opening-up policy. China stands ready to expand common interests with other countries, promote the construction of a new type of international relations with win-win cooperation at the core, and forge a community of shared future.

The development of China cannot be possible without the development of other developing countries, including countries in Latin America and the Caribbean. Since 2013, the Chinese leadership has set forth a series of major initiatives and measures on strengthening China's relations and cooperation with Latin America and the Caribbean in a wide range of areas, which has provided new development goals and new driving forces for the relations. Building on the previous achievements, the Chinese government hereby releases its second policy paper on Latin America and the Caribbean, to summarize experience, draw a blueprint for the future, provide a comprehensive explanation of the new ideas, proposals and initiatives in

China's Latin America and Caribbean policy for the new era, and promote China's cooperation with Latin America and the Caribbean in various areas.

14.2 翻译热身：《中国人权法治化保障的新进展》

【说明】 请将下列文件翻译为英语，注意恰当处理政治术语和长句的翻译问题。

简介：《中国人权法治化保障的新进展》是 2017 年 12 月 15 日国务院新闻办公室发表的白皮书。白皮书全文约 17 000 字，除前言、结束语外，共包括六个部分，分别为不断完善人权保障法律体系、依法行政保障公民合法权益、有效提升人权司法保障水平、夯实人权法治化保障的社会基础、加强党对人权法治化保障的领导和积极促进全球人权法治建设。本文选取的是该白皮书的“结束语”部分。

中国人权法治化保障的新进展（白皮书）

中华人民共和国国务院新闻办公室

2017 年 12 月

推进全面依法治国，不仅使建设社会主义法治国家迈出了重要步伐，也使中国的人权法治化保障达到了一个新的高度。事实表明，中国人民从来没有像今天这样享有如此充分的经济、社会、文化权利和公民及政治权利，中国人权事业的发展正如沐春风、充满生机。

社会主义初级阶段，是当今中国的基本国情和最大实际。坚持全面依法治国，建设法治国家、法治政府、法治社会，实现国家治理体系和治理能力现代化，实现更高水平的人权法治化保障，仍有许多工作要做，还有很长的路要走，需要作出长期不懈努力。

中国共产党第十九次全国代表大会已就深化全面依法治国实践作出重大部署。当前，在习近平新时代中国特色社会主义思想指导下，在以习近平同志为核心的党中央坚强领导下，中国人民正在为实现“两个一百年”奋斗目标和中华民族伟大复兴的中国梦而努力。在实现伟大梦想的征程上，社会主义法治国家建设必将取得更加丰硕的成果，中国的人权法治化保障水平必将得到更大提升，中国必将为发展人类政治文明作出新的更大的贡献。

14.3 翻译技巧：政府文件的翻译

14.3.1 汉语政府文件的文体特点

政府文件包括政府发布的各种公告、决议、通告、通报、宣言、法律法规、法令等。概括起来，汉语政府文件具有以下文体特点：

第一，语体色彩方面，政府文件属于书面体，具有庄严性、规定性、规范、严谨、简练、明确无歧义等特点。

第二，词汇方面，一是用词正式，力避口语化，以凸显其庄重性；二是多使用政治、军事、经济、金融、法律等领域的专业术语，以凸显其权威性与专业性；三是多使用程式化的表述，以代表政府的一贯立场。

第三，句式特征方面，几乎全部使用陈述句；复杂长句的使用频率很高；主语一般不用第一人称，其他人称代词的使用也十分少见，多用政府首脑、政府部门、机构、团体的姓名或名称等充当主语，也常用抽象名词、甚至动词词组充当主语；主动语态的使用频率远高于被动语态，以突出主语政府首脑、政府部门、机构、团体等的主体性和主观能动性。

第四，修辞方面，较少使用修辞格，多采用平铺直叙的手法，对政府立场、主张、决断、要求等进行客观阐述。

与汉语发言与演讲文体类似，汉语"政府文件"文体相对于英语同类文体，也具有以下几个特别之处，翻译转换时须加以注意：

第一，常使用具有中国特色的政治表述，这些表述烙上了很深的文化内涵，往往与英语形成词汇空缺，比如"高举中国特色社会主义伟大旗帜""'三个代表'重要思想""习近平新时代中国特色社会主义思想""全面建成小康社会"等。

第二，汉语政府文件中动词的使用频率同样相当高，尤其习惯使用连动式，比如"值此之际，中国政府发布第二份对拉政策文件，旨在总结经验，展望未来，全面阐述新时期中国对拉政策的新理念、新主张、新举措，推动中拉各领域合作实现更大发展。"（见"阅读欣赏"）这句话就使用了"发布""总结""展望""阐述""推动"等一连串的动词。汉英转换时同样常需将一些动词处理为非谓语形式或者介词、名词等非动词形式。

14.3.2 汉语政府文件的英译要点

政府文件属于公文文体。刘宓庆（1998）归纳了公文文体英汉翻译的几个要点，包括：抓住对原文的透彻理解；注意汉语语体，不宜使用口语词汇；注意研究材料所涉及的专业内容、了解专业词汇和术语的含义，最好具有有关专业的必要知识；注意形式问题，包括公文程式、格式、体例等；

译文所用词语应严格遵守“一贯性”原则，即在同一篇或同一类材料中避免一词数译，造成概念混乱。方梦之、毛忠明（2004）在阐述政论文（属于政府文件的一部分）的翻译时也指出，这类文体的译文预期功能是在译语语境中让读者了解原文论述的政策观点，保证原文含义的准确性，因此，“达意”是翻译这类文体的主要目的，其翻译要点就是“紧扣原文内容，做到语义精确，用词分寸把握得体”。

上述翻译要点在政府文件的汉英翻译时同样具有借鉴意义。但同时必须考虑这类文体的“外宣翻译”性质，“外宣三贴近”原则同样需要得到遵守，在精确传递原文内容、保持原文庄严性、规定性、规范性等风格特点的前提下，考虑译文的可接受性。在不曲解原文意义的情况下，为了“贴近国外受众的思维习惯”，有时也需要对原文作变通处理。但与发言与演讲的翻译相比，政府文件的翻译更强调准确性，切忌为了一味地迎合受众而歪曲原文的意思，这样可能会造成严重的后果。

14.3.3 汉语长句的翻译

我们先来看看“阅读欣赏”第二段中这个长句的译文：

①中国进入实现中华民族伟大复兴的关键阶段，|| ②正围绕到 2020 年全面建成小康社会、到本世纪中叶建成富强民主文明和谐的社会主义现代化国家的“两个一百年”奋斗目标，③积极推进社会主义市场经济、民主政治、先进文化、和谐社会、生态文明建设。

① China has entered a crucial stage in achieving the great rejuvenation of the Chinese nation. ② In order to fulfill the “two centenary goals” of building a moderately prosperous society in all respects by 2020 and turning the nation into a modern socialist country that is prosperous, strong, democratic, culturally advanced and harmonious by the mid-21st century, ③ China has been actively promoting the construction of a socialist market economy, socialist democracy, advanced culture, a harmonious society, as well as ecological civilization.

类似这样的长句在翻译时一般遵循以下程序：

首先反复阅读原文，充分理解原文，分析原文结构，提炼原文“骨架”，理顺骨架中各个分句之间的逻辑关系。比如，经过理解与分析，上述长句的骨架为：

①中国进入……关键阶段，②正围绕……“两个一百年”奋斗目标，③积极推进……建设。

我们发现，骨架共由 3 个部分组成，其中第二部分从属于第三部分，充当第三部分的目的状语；第一部分和第三部分是平级、并列关系。

其次，确定译文句子信息呈现的顺序——是保留原句顺序（原序译法），还是颠倒原句顺序（换序译法）？是把原句拆成几句（拆句译法），还是将原句的几个分句合并成一句（合句译法）？总体而言，汉语长句往往内容十分庞杂，一句话表达了若干层意思，意思与意思之间的关系并不十分紧密。英语中虽然长句也很多，但句子各个部分之间的语义联系十分紧密，若需表达关系松散的不同

意思，就需要使用另外的句子。因此，许多汉语的复杂长句往往需要采用拆句译法，翻译成两个或多个英语句子。上述长句就属于这种情况，译者需要根据原文的语义关系进行断句（见原文“||”处）。至于是否保留原句信息呈现的顺序，就要看原序是否符合译文的表达习惯或者是否符合读者的文化期待。上述长句在整体保留原序后不会影响二者，因此我们就可采用原序译法。但是第二部分“奋斗目标”前面有十分冗长的定语，我们必须在翻译时处理为后置定语才符合英语的表达习惯，因此，我们还得在局部地方采用换序译法。

第三，选择恰当的句型，确立译文句子的总体结构。比如上述句子在经过第一步的理解分析和第二步的策略制定之后，就可以先列出一个总体框架来。

① China has entered a crucial stage in ... ② In order to fulfill the “two centenary goals” of..., ③ China has been actively promoting the construction of ...

这个框架总体上遵循了原文信息的呈现顺序，对原文进行了拆分，局部地方对原文顺序进行了调整。

第四，完善译文信息，推敲措辞，注意词语间的搭配关系，完成译文句子的初稿。这一步是为译文添砖加瓦，完善细节。这时需要动用词典、网络搜索引擎等工具，仔细推敲措辞并验证词语间的搭配关系是否地道。

以上讨论的是汉语长句英译的程序问题，至于其翻译技巧问题，我们在第二步里已经提到了，即原序译法、换序译法、拆句译法和合句译法。这个需要学习者在反复实践中去摸索、体会，这里就不再赘述。

14.3.4 中国特色政治术语的翻译

汉语政府文件的一大特色就是广泛使用具有中国特色的政治术语，由于“具有中国特色”，也就意味着这些术语在英语中很难找到对等语，翻译时需要“再创建”（冯雪红，2014）。

中国特色政治术语的翻译需要遵循以下几个原则：准确性，即要忠实传递原术语的内涵；统一性，即相同的术语应有相同的译名，不然会造成概念混乱；可读性，即要考虑读者的接受度，一要易懂，二要简约，三要符合译语表达习惯；约定俗成，即对于那些已有定译且已被国际社会接受的术语就采用已有的译名，不再另行翻译。

中国特色政治术语常见的翻译技巧包括：

第一，直接借用，即直接使用英语中现成的表述，如：国家主席→ President，总理→ Premier，总书记→ General Secretary，部长→ Minister，等等（冯雪红，2014）。

第二，按字直译。这是政治术语“再创建”时经常用到的技巧。比如：

（1）中华民族的伟大复兴

the great rejuvenation of the Chinese nation

（2）习近平新时代中国特色社会主义思想

Xi Jinping Thought on Socialism with Chinese Characteristics for a New Era

（3）批评和自我批评

criticism and self-criticism

（4）新常态

new normal

第三，直译加阐释。如果直译后意思不明确，就需要进一步以简练的语言加以阐释，比如：

（5）三个代表

Three Represents (to represent the requirements for developing China's advanced productive forces, to represent the orientation of China's advanced culture and to represent the fundamental interests of the overwhelming majority of the Chinese people)

（6）严打

Strike Hard Operation, campaign to crack down relentlessly on criminal activities

第四，意译。有些术语直译后可能会令读者不知所云，这时就需要变通，采用意译法加以处理。比如：

（7）政治意识、大局意识、核心意识、看齐意识

consciousness of the need to maintain political integrity, think in big-picture terms, uphold the leadership core, and keep in alignment

如果直译为"consciousness of politics, overall situation, core and keeping in alignment"，就无法清晰而准确地传递原文意思，读者也会摸不着头脑，所以此处的译文抛开了原文的语言形式，将其深层内涵翻译了出来。

14.4 翻译实战：《愿景与行动》

【说明】 运用本单元学到的文体特点、翻译要点和翻译技巧翻译以下段落。

简介：2015 年 3 月 28 日，国家发展和改革委员会、外交部、商务部联合发布了《推动共建丝绸之路经济带和 21 世纪海上丝绸之路的愿景与行动》（以下简称《愿景与行动》），全文共分为 8 个部分：一、时代背景；二、共建原则；三、框架思路；四、合作重点；五、合作机制；六、中国各地方开放态势；七、中国积极行动；八、共创美好未来。"一带一路"倡议由习近平主席在 2013 年提出。推动共建"一带一路"的愿景与行动，阐明了坚持开放合作、和谐包容、市场运作和互利共赢等共建原则，政策沟通、设施联通、贸易畅通、

资金融通和民心相通是五大合作重点，完善多边双边合作机制是制度保障。该《愿景与行动》回应各界关切，为“一带一路”务实合作点亮了“航标灯”。（据国务院新闻办公室网站）本文选自该《愿景与行动》的前言部分。

推动共建丝绸之路经济带和21世纪海上丝绸之路的愿景与行动

国家发展和改革委员会、外交部、商务部

（经国务院授权发布）

2015年3月

2 000多年前，亚欧大陆上勤劳勇敢的人民，探索出多条连接亚欧非几大文明的贸易和人文交流通路，后人将其统称为“丝绸之路”。千百年来，“和平合作、开放包容、互学互鉴、互利共赢”的丝绸之路精神薪火相传，推进了人类文明进步，是促进沿线各国繁荣发展的重要纽带，是东西方交流合作的象征，是世界各国共有的历史文化遗产。

进入21世纪，在以和平、发展、合作、共赢为主题的新时代，面对复苏乏力的全球经济形势，纷繁复杂的国际和地区局面，传承和弘扬丝绸之路精神更显重要和珍贵。

2013年9月和10月，中国国家主席习近平在出访中亚和东南亚国家期间，先后提出共建“丝绸之路经济带”和“21世纪海上丝绸之路”（以下简称“一带一路”）的重大倡议，得到国际社会高度关注。中国国务院总理李克强参加2013年中国－东盟博览会时强调，铺就面向东盟的海上丝绸之路，打造带动腹地发展的战略支点。加快“一带一路”建设，有利于促进沿线各国经济繁荣与区域经济合作，加强不同文明交流互鉴，促进世界和平发展，是一项造福世界各国人民的伟大事业。
（原文选自求是网 http://www.qstheory.cn/2017-05/12/c_1120962775.htm）

14.5 译文荟萃

1. 短语与术语翻译

1) 全面从严治党

The Party shall exercise strict self-governance in every respect.

2) 富强民主文明和谐美丽的社会主义现代化强国

a great modern socialist country that is prosperous, strong, democratic, culturally advanced, harmonious, and beautiful

3) 不忘初心，方得始终

Remain true to your original aspiration, and you can accomplish your mission.

4) 坚定理想信念

deepen commitment to the ideals and convictions of the Party

5) 人类命运共同体

a community with a shared future for mankind

6) 加强对权力运行的制约和监督

strengthen checks on and oversight over the exercise of power

7) 食品安全战略

food safety strategy

8) 脱贫攻坚工程

the fight against poverty

9) 互联互通

connectivity

10) “四个全面”战略布局

Four-Pronged Comprehensive Strategy

11) “一带一路”倡议

the Belt and Road Initiative

12) 有权不可任性

Power is not to be used arbitrarily.

13) 宪法日

Constitution Day

14) 有法可依，有法必依，执法必严，违法必究

Ensure that laws are put in place, observed, and strictly enforced and that anyone who violates the law is held to account.

15) 政府权力清单

list of government powers

16) 重大决策责任倒查机制

mechanism for retroactive investigation into accountability for major decisions

17) 转变政府职能

transform government functions

18) 行政审批

government review and approval

19) 创新政府、廉洁政府和服务型政府

an innovative, clean, and service-oriented government

20) 市场准入负面清单

market access negative list

2. 句子翻译

1) 中国有 13 亿多人口，是世界上最大的发展中国家。发展是中国共产党执政兴国的第一要务，是解决中国所有问题的关键。

China, with a population of over 1.3 billion, is the largest developing country in the world. Development is the top priority of the Communist Party of China in governance and national revitalization, and the key to resolving all other problems.

2) 当前，国内外形势正在发生深刻复杂变化，我国发展仍处于重要战略机遇期，前景十分光明，挑战也十分严峻。

Both China and the world are in the midst of profound and complex changes. China is still in an important period of strategic opportunity for development; the prospects are bright but the challenges are severe.

3) 改革开放之初，我们党发出了走自己的路、建设中国特色社会主义的伟大号召。

In the early days of reform and opening up, the Party made a clarion call for us to take a path of our own and build socialism with Chinese characteristics.

4) 一百年前，十月革命一声炮响，给中国送来了马克思列宁主义。

A hundred years ago, the salvoes of the October Revolution brought Marxism-Leninism to China.

5) 中华民族有五千多年的文明历史，创造了灿烂的中华文明，为人类作出了卓越贡献，成为世界上伟大的民族。

With a history of more than 5,000 years, our nation created a splendid civilization, made remarkable contributions to mankind, and became one of the world's great nations.

6) 实现中华民族伟大复兴是近代以来中华民族最伟大的梦想。

National rejuvenation has been the greatest dream of the Chinese people since modern times began.

7) 中国共产党和中国政府始终坚持以人民为中心的发展思想，奉行人民至上的价值取向，牢牢把握人民群众对美好生活的向往，把增进人民福祉、促进人的全面发展作为发展的出发点和落脚点。

The Communist Party of China (CPC) and the Chinese government have always focused on the people's needs while seeking the development of the nation. Putting the people first, the Party and the government work to fulfill the people's aspiration for a better life, and strive to enhance the people's well-being and all-round development.

8) 多年来，中国坚持依法治国基本方略，努力建设社会主义法治国家，人权法治化保障不断迈上新台阶。

Over the years China has upheld the law-based governance of the country as a basic guideline, striving to put the rule of law in a socialist context and making new progress in legal protection of human rights.

9) 40 年来，中国坚持对外开放基本国策，打开国门搞建设，逐步形成了全方位多层次宽领域的对外开放格局，极大促进了中国与外部世界的交流交融，为人类和平与发展的崇高事业作出了重要贡献。

Over the past 40 years, China has been adhering to the fundamental national policy of reform and opening-up and pursuing development with its door wide open. A model of all-round, multi-level, and wide-ranging opening-up has gradually taken shape. China is closely connected with the outside world and has made a significant contribution to the noble cause of global peace and development.

10) 中国倡导构建人类命运共同体，是北极事务的积极参与者、建设者和贡献者，努力为北极发展贡献中国智慧和中国力量。

A champion for the development of a community with a shared future for mankind, China is an active participant, builder and contributor in Arctic affairs who has spared no efforts to contribute its wisdom to the development of the Arctic region.

11) 马克思列宁主义揭示了人类社会历史发展的规律，它的基本原理是正确的，具有强大的生命力。

Marxism-Leninism brings to light the laws governing the development of the history of human society. Its basic tenets are correct and have tremendous vitality.

12) 十一届三中全会以来，以邓小平同志为主要代表的中国共产党人，总结新中国成立以来正反两方面的经验，解放思想，实事求是，实现全党工作中心向经济建设的转移，实行改革开放，开辟了社会主义事业发展的新时期，逐步形成了建设中国特色社会主义的路线、方针、政策，阐明了在中国建设社会主义、巩固和发展社会主义的基本问题，创立了邓小平理论。

After the Third Plenary Session of the Eleventh Party Central Committee, the Chinese Communists, with Comrade Deng Xiaoping as their chief representative, analyzed their experience, both positive and negative, gained since the founding of the People's Republic of China, emancipated their minds, sought truth from facts, shifted the focus of the work of the whole Party onto economic development and carried out reform and opening to the outside world, ushering in a new era of development in the cause of socialism, gradually formulating the line, principles and policies concerning the building of socialism with Chinese characteristics and expounding the basic questions concerning the building, consolidation and development of socialism in China, and thus creating Deng Xiaoping Theory.

13) 本宪法以法律的形式确认了中国各族人民奋斗的成果，规定了国家的根本制度和根本任务，是国家的根本法，具有最高的法律效力。

This Constitution, in legal form, affirms the achievements of the struggles of the Chinese people of all nationalities and defines the basic system and basic tasks of the State; it is the fundamental law of the State and has supreme legal authority.

14) 一切法律、行政法规和地方性法规都不得同宪法相抵触。

No laws or administrative or local regulations may contravene the Constitution.

15) 国家在社会主义初级阶段，坚持公有制为主体、多种所有制经济共同发展的基本经济制度，坚持按劳分配为主体、多种分配方式并存的分配制度。

In the primary stage of socialism, the State upholds the basic economic system in which the public ownership is dominant and diverse forms of ownership develop side by side and keeps to the distribution system in which distribution according to work is dominant and diverse modes of distribution coexist.

（说明：以上译例选自新华网（http://www.xinhuanet. com/english/special/2017-11/03/c-136725942. htm）、中华人民共和国国务院新闻办公室网站（http://www. scio. gov. cn/zfbps）、中国网（http:// www. china. org. cn/chinese/18da/2012_11/19/content_27156212_2.htm）、中国人大网（http://www. ppc. gov.cn/englishnpc/Constitution/node_2825.htm）等网站。）

3. 篇章翻译

简介：2016年10月17日，国务院新闻办发表《中国的减贫行动与人权进步》白皮书。白皮书包括六部分，分别是：减贫促进了中国人权事业发展、保障贫困人口生存权、维护特定群体权利、改善贫困地区发展环境、合力推进减贫事业和减贫进入攻坚阶段。白皮书指出，改革开放30多年来，已有7亿多贫困人口摆脱贫困，中国的减贫行动是中国人权事业进步的最显著标志。白皮书系统阐述了中国的减贫发展与人权进步。白皮书指出，改革开放30多年来，农村贫困人口减少到2015年的5 575万人，贫困发生率下降到5.7%，有力促进了贫困人口基本权利的实现，为全面建成小康社会打下了坚实基础。白皮书说，联合国《2015年千年发展目标报告》显示，中国极端贫困人口比例从1990年的61%，下降到2014年的4.2%，中国对全球减贫的贡献率超过70%。中国成为世界上减贫人口最多的国家，也是世界上率先完成联合国千年发展目标的国家。本文选自该白皮书的开头部分。

《中国的减贫行动与人权进步》白皮书

中华人民共和国国务院新闻办公室

2016 年 10 月

消除贫困是人类梦寐以求的理想，是各国人民追求幸福生活的基本权利。多年来，中国共产党和中国政府从基本国情出发，把人民的生存权、发展权放在首位，致力于减贫脱贫，努力保障和改善民生，发展各项社会事业，使发展成果更多更公平惠及全体人民，保障人民平等参与、平等发展权利。2012 年中国共产党十八大以来，在全面建成小康社会、实现中华民族伟大复兴中国梦的伟大进程中，以习近平同志为总书记的党中央，坚持以人民为中心的发展思想，实施精准扶贫、精准脱贫基本方略，中国的减贫行动更加扎实有效，为世界减贫事业作出了重大贡献，创造了世界人权发展新奇迹。

一、减贫促进了中国人权事业发展

贫困的广泛存在严重妨碍人权的充分实现和享有。减缓和消除贫困，是人权保障的重要内容。多年来，中国政府坚持消除贫困、改善民生、逐步实现共同富裕，持续开展以农村扶贫开发为中心的减贫行动，努力实现脱贫致富。中国减贫行动涉及的范围十分广泛，既包括农村农业基础设施建设，提高贫困人口收入水平，也包括提供社会保障和卫生、教育、文化等公共服务。这些扶贫措施在全面保障贫困人口的经济、社会、文化权利的同时，也为进一步保障其他人权创造了条件。

China's Progress in Poverty Reduction and Human Rights

The State Council Information Office of the People's Republic of China

October 2016

Poverty eradication is and always has been a goal and a basic right of all peoples in their pursuit of a happy life. Over the years, based on the prevailing national conditions, the Communist Party of China (CPC) and the Chinese government have remained committed to a development concept that puts people's rights to subsistence and to development first. Committed to reducing and eliminating poverty, China has endeavored to guarantee and improve people's well-being, and developed a full range of social undertakings, so as to ensure that the results of development benefit all the people in a fairer way, and that all enjoy the rights to equal participation and equal development.

Since the 18th National Congress of the CPC in November 2012, in the great cause of building a moderately prosperous society and realizing the Chinese Dream of great rejuvenation of the Chinese nation, the CPC Central Committee led by General Secretary Xi Jinping has remained committed to a development concept that puts people first, and implemented the basic strategy of targeted poverty alleviation and elimination. China's poverty reduction actions, both solid and effective, have made a great contribution to the cause of international poverty reduction, and achieved remarkable results in world human rights development.

I. China's Poverty Reduction Program Has Promoted the Development of Human Rights

Poverty is so widespread that it has seriously hindered the fulfillment and enjoyment of human rights; reducing and eliminating poverty is therefore a major element of human rights protection.

Over the recent decades, the Chinese government has persevered in its attempts to eliminate poverty, improve people's well-being, and gradually realize common prosperity. It has made continuous development-oriented poverty-reduction efforts in rural areas to help those who are striving to escape from poverty and improve the quality of their lives.

China's poverty reduction actions are broad in extent; they include building rural and agricultural infrastructure, helping increase the incomes of impoverished population, and providing public services such as social security and health care, education and cultural services. While comprehensively safeguarding the economic, social and cultural rights of those living in poverty, these measures have created conditions for the protection of other human rights.

14.6 翻译家：黄友义

黄友义，当代资深翻译家，长期参与党政文献的对外翻译，曾为党政领导人担任口译。曾参加党政文件和领导人讲话的翻译和译文审定工作，包括《江泽民论三个代表》《习近平谈治国理政》（一卷、二卷）等文献，主持编写《汉英外事工作常用词汇》和《汉英翻译词典最新词汇》。

译著有美国文学名著《名利场大火》、《马歇尔传》和《无冕之王》；对外介绍中国各个方面的中译英图书，如《中国的社会保险制度》、《中国加入 WTO 与经济改革》、《千年古都西安》、《中国长城》、《中国旅游》、《中国玉器》以及《聊斋志异选编》等。此外还完成了《全景中国》、《全景中国》（浙江卷、广州卷）、《中国制造》、《21 世纪中国当代文学书库》、《我从新疆来》、《浦东故事》、《中国天机》、《到中流击水：经济全球化大潮与中国之命运》等数百万字的中译英书稿的核定工作。

黄友义现任中国经济社会理事会理事、国务院学位委员会委员、中国译协常务副会长、中国翻译研究院副院长、全国翻译资格（水平）考试英语专家委员会主任、全国翻译系列高级职称任职资格评审委员会主任、全国翻译研究生专业学位教学指导委员会主任委员、教育部外语中文译写规范和中华思想文化术语传播部际联席会议首席专家，《中国翻译》杂志主编、《公共外交季刊》编委会副主任、《大中华文库》副总编辑。

曾任中国外文出版发行事业局副局长兼总编辑和中国互联网新闻中心主任、国际翻译家联盟副主席、中国翻译协会秘书长。

14.7 补充资源

（1）人民网英文版（http://en.people.cn/）

（2）新华网英文版（http://www.xinhuanet.com/english/home.htm）

（3）中国人大网英文版（http://www.npc.gov.cn/englishnpc/news/）

（4）常熟理工学院汉英政治平行语料库（http://pcpt.cslg.cn/）

（5）中央编译局“中央文献重要术语译文发布”（http://www.cctb.net/bygz/zywxsy/）

（6）中国日报“英语点津”（http://language.chinadaily.com.cn/）

Chapter 8

第八章 应用翻译（二）

第十五单元 宣传与介绍

第十六单元 公示语

第十五单元　宣传与介绍

15.1 阅读欣赏:《北京老街·前言》

【说明】 对照欣赏下列原文和译文，体会介绍性文本翻译的特点，确认信息传达是否充分、准确，译文是否具有可读性。

> **简介:**《北京老街》是人民艺术剧院舞台设计专家陈永祥早年为了创作需要，在街头巷尾体验生活、收集素材创作的绘画作品，由社会科学文献出版社于2006年出版。该画册含有100余幅老北京的铅笔淡彩画，基本上再现了记忆中的故都面貌，堪称老北京建筑的缩影。书中文字简洁凝练，文笔朴实而不失流畅，对喜欢老北京的中外读者无疑具有较大的参考价值。以下为该画册前言节选。

北京老街·前言（节选）

老北京城的建筑多为砖木结构，无论城垣、店铺门面、牌楼和四合院民居，均体现着中国建筑的传统风格，营造出恬静、暗香的生活氛围。在当时的街道上，车辆稀少。除了公共交通工具有轨电车外，汽车很少见到，随处可见的只是自行车和人力三轮车。然而这样简单的交通工具，并未让北京市民感到出行如何不便。

值得一提的，是老城老街难以言表的味道。例如，老北京店铺特有的中国龙形象，虬龙木雕挑头，雕刻精美，造型生动；其他如雕工细致的挂檐板，油漆彩绘的木梁柱，变化多端的木质窗棂，屋顶上格式各异的朝天栏杆，古色古香的匾额等等，虽经雨打风吹，早已破旧不堪，但是浸透在里面的浓浓的北京味儿丝毫不减。那些耸立在街头巷尾的各式木结构的牌楼，以其五光十色、重重叠叠、镂空架起的斗拱而夺人眼目。这些历尽沧桑、行迹斑驳的艺术瑰宝，含蓄地诉说着当年的辉煌。

星罗棋布在北京各个区域的古建筑群，其布局也是颇讲章法的。记得在 1951 年，我曾聆听建筑大师梁思成先生所做的关于北京城市规划的报告，很值得一提。

其一是，北京城在世界都市规划中，有一条举世闻名、独一无二的南北方向的“中轴线”。它最南段的起点是永定门，向北依次经正阳门（即前门）、中华门、天安门、故宫端门、午门、前三殿（即太和殿、中和殿、保和殿）、后三殿、神武门、北山门、景山万春亭、寿皇殿、地安门、鼓楼，直至最北端的钟楼为终点。这条“中轴线”全长 7.5 公里，由明朝至今已历经数百年。所有皇家宫殿、坛庙、街署等古建筑均依附着这条中轴线，紧密相连在一起，依次昭示皇权至尊和一统全局的观念。

其二是，建筑群体的布局均为东西或南北对称排列。比如天坛在南，地坛在北；日坛在东，月坛在西；太庙（今日的劳动人民文化宫）在东；社稷坛（今日的中山公园）在西。又如，城垣布局也是对称的，内城东为东直门，西为西直门；东南为崇文门，西南为宣武门。紫禁城的安排更是对称的，东门为东华门，内为文华殿；西门为西华门，内为武英殿；城垣四角更有对称修建、遥相呼应的四座角楼。市井商贸中心地区的建筑群，布局亦复如是。比如东城有东四牌楼、东单牌楼，西城有西四牌楼、西单牌楼。

其三是，老北京的城墙，无论是外城、内城还是紫禁城，尽管其地基起伏不定，内外城墙高低有别，但各自的城脊却奇迹般地坐落在同一水平线上，无一例外。这在世界测量史和建筑史上都是一个奇迹。

Old Beijing

(Excerpt)

The constructions in Old Beijing were mostly made of wood and brick, displaying a style of traditional Chinese architecture and a life of tranquility and peacefulness. There was almost no other means of transport than buses and trams, though bicycles and rickshaws could be seen everywhere. Such simple means of transport, however, did not put the citizens into any inconvenience.

What is worth mentioning is the uniqueness of the streets, as seen in the vivid carvings of Chinese dragon figures on the facades of the shops, the painted beams, the variety of window frames, and so on. Despite the fact that they have long been worn, exposed to wind and rain, condensed in them is the flavor of Old Beijinger in the bygone times. The wooden archways standing in the streets are pleasant to the eye. These artistic treasures seem to be telling people about their past.

The old buildings in every part of Beijing follow regular patterns. I remember that in 1951 I attended a lecture given by Liang Sicheng, the renowned architect, on the planning of reconstructing Beijing, who said that for one thing, Beijing had a unique axis from south up to north, starting from Yongdingmen (the Gate of Lasting Peace), the southern terminal, there was successively Zhengyangmen(the Gate of Direct Sunshine, also known as Qianmen, the Front Gate), Zhonghuamen (the Gate of China), Tian'anmen (the Gate of Heavenly Peace), Duanmen (the Southern Gate of the Forbidden City), Wumen (the Meridian Gate), the Outer Court (the Hall of Supreme Harmony, Central Harmony and Preserving Harmony), the Inner Court, Shenwumen (the Gate of Spiritual Valor), Beishanmen (the Northern Gate of the Forbidden City), Wanchunting (the Pavilion of Springs on the Prospect Hill), Shouhuangdian (the Palace for Worshipping Ancestors), Di'anmen (the Gate of Earthly Peace), Gulou (the Drum Tower), and Zhonglou (the Bell Tower) at the very north. This central axis was built in the Ming Dynasty (1368–1644) and extended for seven and a half kilometers. All the imperial palaces, altars, temples and government offices clustered along the axis, making obvious the supreme authority and national unity.

The pattern of the buildings was purely symmetrical. For example, the Temple of Heaven was in the south, with the Temple of Earth in the north, the Temple of Sun in the east and the Temple of Moon in the west. The Altar of Ancestors and Gods was in the east (now the Working People's Cultural Palace) and the Altar of Earth and Harvests was in the west (now the Zhongshan Park). The arrangement of the city walls, the halls in the Forbidden City and the Corner Towers of the city walls was also symmetrical. Similarly, the trading centers were symmetrically arranged.

The third point was that although the old city walls were of different heights, the spine of the walls was miraculously on the same horizontal level, without any exception. Isn't it a miracle in surveying and architecture?（索毕成、史宝辉 译，部分译文略有改动。）

阅读提示

（1）有关老北京或者中国传统建筑的翻译，宜参照故宫博物院的主页中约定俗成的译法，也可查询西方友人参观北京之后的游记或者感受之类。换言之，需要译者充分利用相应的工具书和网络资源。

（2）译文尽量简明扼要，不宜拖泥带水。源文本部分语句存在反复拖沓的现象，译文根据行文安排将主要信息译出即可，同时，还要考虑国外游客或读者的接受习惯，不可想当然地直译硬塞给他们。比如：“北京老街独特的味道”不宜译作 the unique taste of the streets，应该译为 the uniqueness / unique quality of the streets；“夺人眼目”如果译为 appeal to the eyes of everyone，则会出现同义反复的问题，显然 appeal to everyone 或 pleasant to the eye 更为恰当。源文本中四字结构较多，而且语义重复现象比较明显，这样的修饰性结构宜简化处理，不可逐一照译。

15.2 翻译热身:《南京采风》《清华大学简介》

【说明】 请将下面两个篇章翻译为英语，体会如何在介绍性文字的翻译中根据文体特点、表达需要和翻译目的做到信息准确、功能恰当而又适当地“增、减、改”?

(1) 南京采风

南京市境内，东郊有中山陵、明孝陵、灵古寺;城南有夫子庙、中华门、雨花台;城西有莫愁湖、朝天宫；城东有梅园新村、总统府旧址；城北有玄武湖、鸡鸣寺，这些众多的旅游景点，形成了以历史古迹为核心的南京独特的旅游观光胜地。

梅园新村位于长江路东端，是一组欧式的建筑，尽管经历了岁月的风雨，但依然保持着当年的风采。这里就是中国共产党代表团办公原址。从 1946 年 5 月到 1947 年 3 月，周恩来同志率领中共代表团在这里与国民党政府进行了十个多月的和平谈判，写下了历史上光辉的一页。1961 年在这里建成中共代表团梅园新村纪念馆; 1990 年兴建了“国共南京谈判史料陈列馆”；同年 7 月 1 日周恩来全身铜像落成。

“南京 1912”是集文化、餐饮、娱乐、休闲观光为一体的时尚休闲商业区及知名品牌的展示地。“南京 1912”紧邻总统府西侧，呈 L 型环绕总统府，占地 3 万平方米，总建筑面积达 3 万平方米，由 20 余栋民国府衙式建筑及太平、博爱、共和、新世纪四大广场组成。“昔日总统府邸，今日城市客厅”，东西方时尚在这里交融汇聚，古典与现代文化也在这里前后传承。“南京 1912”文化休闲街区，提供了在保护城市记忆和文化遗产的前提下挖掘城市文化资源的成功模式。

梅花是南京的市花，它具有傲立风雪的顽强品质，是南京这座历尽沧桑的历史文化名城的象征。

南京小红花艺术团至今已有 50 多年的历史，是全国首创的集文化教育、艺术教育与舞台表演于一体的少儿艺术团体。

甘熙故居俗称“九十九间半”，始建于清嘉庆年间，现共有四组五进穿堂式建筑群，占地面积 9 500 多平方米，建筑面积 8 000 余平方米，是南京现存面积最大、保存最完整的清代私人住宅。建筑群在平面布局上为坐南朝北，中轴线由北向南建有门厅、轿厅、大厅、后厅和后堂等房屋，各进建筑多以墙垣隔成院落，整个故居内共有大小天井 35 个，且有假山、树木点缀，建筑装饰精细考究，各式题材的“吉祥”雕刻图案，内容丰富，刀笔细致，形象生动。

南京夫子庙是供奉和祭祀我国古代著名的大思想家、教育家孔子的庙宇，其全称是“大成至圣先师文宣王庙”，简称“文庙”。夫子庙始建于宋景祐元年（公元 1034 年），由东晋学宫扩建而成。如今的夫子庙焕然一新，是秦淮风光带核心景观区，也是蜚声中外的旅游胜地。

（2）清华大学简介（节选）

清华大学的前身清华学堂始建于1911年，1912年更名为清华学校。1928年更名为国立清华大学。1937年抗日战争全面爆发后南迁长沙，与北京大学、南开大学组建国立长沙临时大学，1938年迁至昆明改名为国立西南联合大学。1946年迁回清华园。

1952年全国高等学校院系调整后，清华大学成为一所多科性工业大学，重点为国家培养工程技术人才，被誉为“红色工程师的摇篮”。改革开放以来，清华大学逐步确立了建设世界一流大学的长远目标，进入了蓬勃发展的新时期。目前，清华大学共设20个学院、58个系，已成为一所具有理学、工学、文学、艺术学、历史学、哲学、经济学、管理学、法学、教育学和医学等11个学科门类的综合性、研究型大学。在校生25 900人，本科生13 100人，研究生12 800人。

清华大学一贯坚持“树德育人”的教育理念，建校以来为国家共培养了120 000名学生，有杰出的学者、出色的企业家和政治家。

面向未来，清华大学将秉持“自强不息、厚德载物”的校训和“行胜于言”的校风，为实现高等教育内涵式发展、建设高等教育强国做出新的更大的贡献。

15.3 翻译技巧：外宣翻译的思路与方法

外宣翻译，顾名思义，是以完成对外宣传材料的翻译任务为基本内容的翻译实践活动的总称。在我国，外宣翻译的主要任务是将中文译成英文，或者是其他外文，向世界传播来自中国的声音。这些翻译任务都是以“外宣”命名、以“外宣”为基本特征的翻译活动。在遵循翻译的共性原则的前提下，外宣翻译可以从广义和狭义的角度去理解。广义的外宣翻译包罗万象，几乎涵盖所有的翻译活动，包括各行各业、各级部门从事与对外宣传有关的翻译活动，即人们常说的“大外宣”的翻译概念。狭义的外宣翻译包括各种媒体报道、政府文件公告、政府及企事业单位的介绍、公示语、信息资料等实用文体的翻译。一般说来，外宣翻译常见或主要的文本类型大致可以分为：政治文献翻译（政府工作报告、党和国家领导人讲话等）、新闻文本翻译（新闻报道等）、公示语翻译（政治口号或标语等）、信息资料翻译（科技、旅游介绍等）、汉语典籍翻译（文学名著等）等。简而言之，外宣翻译是翻译的一种特殊形式，指在经济全球化背景下以让世界了解中国为目的、以汉语为信息源、以英语等外国语为信息载体、以各种媒体为渠道、以外国民众（包括境内的各类外籍人士）为受众对象的交际活动。

外宣翻译与文学翻译的主要区别在于翻译目的不同。文学翻译的目的主要是审美欣赏，唤起读者的艺术感受；外宣翻译的目的则是实现交流，沟通信息。从本质上讲，外宣翻译是信息性翻译，文学翻译是艺术性翻译；从功能上讲，外宣翻译是信息传播，文学翻译是美学审视；从审美视角来看，外宣翻译重在源文本朴实之美，文学翻译重在再现源文本绚丽之美。由此可见，与文学翻译相比，外宣翻译显然具有自身特色，它更关注目标受众接受情况和信息传达的完整性，旨在取得最佳传播效果。中西方（英语世界为主）在文化背景、价值观念及思维方式的区别较为明显，而且审美观和逻辑观也不尽相同，在语言形态上主要表现为：汉语表达过度修饰、言辞华丽、同义反复；英文行文讲究简洁明快、逻辑严谨、文风质朴；在汉译英中，尤其在外宣英译中，译者应充分考虑到这种差异，做出相应的调整，使英语译文受者能够顺利地获取我们所要宣传的内容和目的，否则容易给他们带来理解上的困难，甚至会引起误解，达不到宣传效果。

下面以南京大屠杀纪念馆馆长于 2001 年 12 月在美国旧金山圣玛利亚大教堂和平祈祷仪式上致辞的翻译为例，看看译者是如何处理源文本中辞藻华丽的表达和结构的。

“女士们、先生们、大主教：

当圣玛利亚大教堂的钟声在低沉回响的时候，当我们手中的蜡烛在幽幽燃烧的时候，美丽的旧金山已经经历了一天的喧嚣，笼罩上了浓浓的夜幕，无边的灯海穿透了城市向四周蔓延，与远处太平洋波涛拍岸的搏击声融为一体，旷古的自然与旧金山都市的文明交相辉映，使人们油然生成的联想飘向久远。

此时此刻，我，一个来自大洋彼岸、64 年前曾经遭受过侵华日军残暴蹂躏的古城南京的普通市民，在这里，与各位女士、先生们一起，共同感受着圣玛利亚教堂肃穆、凝重、庄严的氛围，在深邃、幽静的大殿下，让虔诚的心与历史一同呼吸，共同去追忆 64 年前发生在中国南京的那场血腥暴行，向被无辜杀戮的 30 多万遇难者寄予深深的怀念。……”

The most Reverent Archbishop, Ladies and Gentlemen,

In this beautiful city of San Francisco, amid the candlelight, we pray for peace and for the victims of the outrageous atrocities and terrorism.

I am an ordinary citizen from Nanjing, a Chinese age-old city situated across the Ocean, which the Japanese invading troops raped and devastated 64 years ago. I am here today to share with this solemn silence of St. Mary Cathedral the memories of the bloody atrocities committed 64 years ago during the Nanjing Massacre, extending our deep condolences to the over 300 thousand victims.（袁晓宁译，编者略有改动）

译者认为，原文虽讲究铺垫，渲染气氛，但如果全部译出，“势必会给讲究直观和简洁明快”的美国听众带来理解上的困难，无疑会大大降低祈祷仪式“庄严肃穆的气氛”，甚至引起他们的反感。因此在处理译文时，译者进行了语篇层次的调整，使译文简单明了，中心突出，在修辞上更加贴近译文受众的习惯。

外宣英译的目的是让英语世界的读者准确理解并获得译文所传递的信息要旨。要达到这一目的，译者应设法化解英汉这两种语言在逻辑、语体风格、文化等方面的差异而引起的理解上的困难，以目的语为归宿，使译文受者在获取信息的过程中不遇到障碍。英国当代翻译理论家纽马克认为，不同文体的文本翻译应采取不同的翻译策略。他将文本分成三种类型：表达型 (expressive)、信息型

(informative) 和呼唤型 (vocative)。以介绍源语文化为目的的表达型文体如小说、诗歌等文学作品应采取语义翻译，即力求传达原文的语义内容，保持作家个人的感情色彩、文学风格、结构形式等；对于以目的语文化为归属的信息型和呼唤型文体，如广告、通知、报告、旅游、宣传材料、技术资料等则应采取交际翻译方法，注重读者的理解和反应，在表达方式、格式、措辞等方面应尽可能符合该文体在译入语中的习惯 。纽马克这一理论对于我们从事不同类型、不同体裁文本翻译的指导意义是不言而喻的。奈达特别强调译文读者对译语的反应，尽管译文读者的反应不太可能与原文读者的反应一致。就外宣英译而言，如果以目的语为归宿，处理好英汉这两种语言所依附的不同民族文化、社会背景、思维习惯等方面的差异，使译文读者能大体理解并获取译文所要传递的信息，是译者不可推卸的责任。

事实上，在目前的外宣英译中，英语译文常常让读者不能理解，甚至产生误解，达不到对外宣传的目的。具体表现为译文带有很重的“死译和硬译”的翻译痕迹，虽然在外在形式上汉语转变成了英文，但在句子结构、语篇构成、语言民族风格、信息量的传递等层面上仍保留着汉语的特征，读起来很别扭、很难懂，即我们所说的中式英语。目前，国内学者基本上认同“外宣三贴近”原则，即：贴近中国发展的实际，贴近国外受众对中国信息的需要，贴近国外受众的思维习惯 。鉴于此，本节以《南京采风》翻译为例，从译文语篇结构的安排、句子形态的布局、语言风格的呈现和信息传递等四个方面探讨相关文本（如城市、景区和主页介绍）的翻译策略和方法。

（1）根据英语语篇构成安排译文的篇章结构

在语篇构成方面，汉语语篇往往是先分后总，即通常从具体或细节入手，由远及近，常在结尾时点题，文章段落以螺旋式形态发展。英语语篇开宗明义，直点主题。一般来说，翻译过程就是译者促成两种语言和文化之间的会通和融合过程。译文语篇的生成质量取决于译者两个方面的能力：一是译者对源语篇内容的掌控程度，二是对译文读者的思维和阅读习惯的了解以及译语语篇的建构能力。

原文第一、二段：

南京市境内，东郊有中山陵、明孝陵、灵古寺；城南有夫子庙、中华门、雨花台；城西有莫愁湖、朝天宫；城东有梅园新村、总统府旧址；城北有玄武湖、鸡鸣寺，这些众多的旅游景点，形成了以历史古迹为核心的南京独特的旅游观光胜地。

梅园新村位于长江路东端，是一组欧式的建筑，尽管经历了岁月的风雨，但依然保持着当年的风采。这里就是中国共产党代表团办公原址。从 1946 年 5 月到 1947 年 3 月，周恩来同志率领中共代表团在这里与国民党政府进行了十个多月的和平谈判，写下了历史上光辉的一页。1961 年在这里建成中共代表团梅园新村纪念馆；1990 年兴建了“国共南京谈判史料陈列馆”；同年 7 月 1 日周恩来全身铜像落成。

仔细阅读原文第一段后，我们可以发现，置于结尾的“这些众多的旅游景点，形成了以历史古迹为核心的南京独特的旅游观光胜地”是主题句，这是汉语语篇的构成习惯。但在翻译过程中，译者应该根据英文语篇构成模式，将该主题句放在语段的开头，起到开宗明义的作用，然后再对主题句进行一一阐释，提供背景信息。上面译文的第一句就是主题句，起到总提的作用，符合英文的表达习惯，因而层次清楚，读上去自然。原文第二段从结构上看，语义重心模糊，意义层次不够清楚，这种现象在汉语中比较普遍。但在英译时，就要顾及英文的直截了当、开宗明义的语篇构成特征。事实上，该段主题句为“梅园新村是中国共产党代表团办公原址，周恩来同志率领中共代表团在这里与国民党政府进行了和平谈判。”因此，在英语译文中就应将其放在语段开头的第一个主句中，起到点题作用。原文中“尽管经历了岁月的风雨，但依然保持着当年的风采”并不是语义重点，不能起到概括全文、开门见山的作用，在英语译文中不宜放在段落句首。换言之，翻译段落时，译者应根据源文本的语义信息和译文本的构成特征，对整个段落进行适当调整。另外，翻译中个别词语的英语表达需要注意，比如“同志”不宜译为 comrade，而应译为英语中常用的 Mr.。译文如下：

The plentiful travel destinations in Nanjing form her unique tourist resorts featuring cultural relics of historic interest. Situated on the eastern outskirts of the city are Dr. Sun Yat-sen's Mausoleum, Xiaoling Mausoleum of the Ming Dynasty, and the Spirit Valley; in the southern part of the city lie the Confucius Temple, Zhonghua City Gate, the Rain Flower Terrace (Yuhuatai); in the western part Mochou Lake, and Chao Tien Temple; in the eastern part Meiyuan New Village, and Presidential Palace; in the northern part Xuanwu Lake, and Jiming Temple.

Situated at the east end of Changjiang Road in Nanjing, Meiyuan New Village, a cluster of buildings of European architecture, is the former office of the CPC delegation. From May, 1946 to March, 1947, Mr. Zhou Enlai led the delegation in a successful 10-month-odd peace negotiation with the KMT government, thus leaving a splendid page in history. In 1961, the Memorial Hall to the CPC Delegation was set up on the basis of the Village. In 1990, it witnessed the establishment of the Exhibition Hall of Historical Data on the CPC-KMT Negotiation. On July 1 of that year, a full-length copper statue of Zhou Enlai was erected there. The Village, though exposed to rain and wind for decades, still remains as elegant as it was.

（2）在表达风格上根据译语行文习惯对源文本适当增删、调整甚至重构

从修辞角度来看，汉语表达往往存在过度修饰、言辞华丽、同义反复的现状；英语行文讲究简洁明快、逻辑严谨、文风质朴。因此，在汉译英中，如果只求英文译文的语言风格在表现形式上与原文一致，势必导致译文的文字诘屈、行文堆砌、逻辑混乱、语义传达失真，与英美民族的审美观、逻辑观及欣赏习惯相抵触。所以，在汉英翻译中，应遵守“贴近国外受众对中国信息的需要，贴近国外受众的思维习惯”的原则，对原文进行适当改写，包括删减、增添、调整、重构等，使译文受

众毫无障碍地通过译文摄取原文的意义要旨，达到对外宣传的目的。

原文第三段：

“南京 1912”是集文化、餐饮、娱乐、休闲观光为一体的时尚休闲商业区及知名品牌的展示地。“南京 1912”紧邻总统府西侧，呈 L 型环绕总统府，占地 3 万平方米，总建筑面积达 3 万平方米，由 20 余栋民国府衙式建筑及太平、博爱、共和、新世纪四大广场组成。“昔日总统府邸，今日城市客厅”，东西方时尚在这里交融汇聚，古典与现代文化也在这里前后传承。“南京 1912”文化休闲街区，提供了在保护城市记忆和文化遗产的前提下挖掘城市文化资源的成功模式。

这篇名为《南京 1912》的短文是较典型的汉语旅游宣传类语篇。该语篇虽然很短，但通篇充斥着套话，而具体介绍南京作为风景名胜的特色的语句并不多。如“集文化、餐饮、娱乐、休闲观光为一体的时尚休闲商业区及知名品牌的展示地”“昔日总统府邸，今日城市客厅”、“东西方时尚在这里交融汇聚，古典与现代文化也在这里前后传承”“提供了在保护城市记忆和文化遗产的前提下挖掘城市文化资源的成功模式”。这些语义笼统的套话如不加改写重构，直接译成英文，就成了翻译腔十足的中式英语语篇了，很难让译文受众看明白。原文中的“知名品牌展示地”并非指展览馆，而是指一些精品旅游商店，用这样似是而非的词语来描述具体的餐饮文化娱乐场所，不符合同类英语语篇简洁明了的表达习惯。为此，译者在保留原文主旨意义的前提下，对原文进行了改写，翻译如下：

Bordering the Presidential Palace on the west, Nanjing 1912 is a popular, L-shaped street block with a cluster of tourist shops, bars, restaurants, teahouses, cafes, as well as upmarket shops. With an area of 30,000 square meters and equally large floorage, the block boasts more than 20 mansions in distinctive architectural style of the Republic of China, and five squares known respectively as Taiping (Peace), Boai (Fraternity), Gonghe (Republic) and Xinshiji (New Century). It is about 1 000 meters away from the Xinjiekou business area, the city’s largest shopping mall. Nanjing 1912, so to speak, is the very place where vogues of the East and the West meet, and classic and contemporary cultures merge into each other.

（3）句法安排以译语语篇结构为归依，确保原文信息传递畅通，译语结构配置合理

在汉译英中常出现“英语词语，汉语结构 ”的现象，即英语译文在句子形态上看起来就像十足的汉语结构。在汉英句法对比研究中，人们常将英文句式比作树干结构，将汉语句式比作竹竿结构。英语的所谓的“树干结构”，就是指它的句式呈“主句 + 多个从属”结构，表现出“共干多枝”的外在形态，体现了从属关系；而汉语的句式呈竹竿结构，即缺少从属连接成分，在形式上由一个个逗号分开的并列分句组成，其语义层次主要靠语境来体现；而英语以形表意，即它的共干多枝结构是意义的外在表现形式，是其重要的表达语用意义的手段。根据英语修辞学，在英文的表达中，语义重心通常放在主句里，以表示其凸显强调的语用意义，非语义重心应置于从属结构中，以传递

其非凸显的次要地位。从属结构可以是一个限定分句、非限定分句或无动词分句，也可以是一个词组，主要是介词词组；就主句而言，已知信息应放到句首，新的信息或强调的信息应置于尾部，即所谓尾重。当两个或两个以上语义信息处在同一个语义层次上，可选择并列结构将其表达出来。在汉英翻译中，译者就应将汉语里通过上下文表现出的凸显等语用意义，通过英语的句法结构再现出来，这是在英文译文中去除不符合英语表达习惯现象的关键。再看该文接下来的几段和译文。

原文第四段：

梅花是南京的市花，它具有傲立风雪的顽强品质，是南京这座历尽沧桑的历史文化名城的象征。

译文： The plum blossoms, which are in full bloom in bitterly cold winter, are the Flower of Nanjing, symbolizing its tenacity and vitality.

在原文语段中，“梅花是南京的市花”是主题句，其他部分均围绕着此句或修饰或说明，因此，“梅花是南京的市花”应作为主句译出，其他应作为从属成分译出。另外，虽然原文中出现“南京这座历尽沧桑的历史文化名城”的句子，如果从上下文考虑，这部分可不用译出，因为“南京作为一个历史文化名城”是整个篇章所要传达的信息，自然融在字里行间，不必逐一翻译，否则必然产生叠床架屋、语义重复的蹩脚式译文，更不符合译文读者阅读习惯，翻译效果大打折扣。

原文第五、六段：

南京小红花艺术团至今已有 50 多年的历史，是全国首创的集文化教育、艺术教育与舞台表演于一体的少儿艺术团体。

甘熙故居俗称“九十九间半”，始建于清嘉庆年间，现共有四组五进穿堂式建筑群，占地面积 9 500 多平方米，建筑面积 8 000 余平方米，是南京现存面积最大、保存最完整的清代私人住宅。建筑群在平面布局上为坐南朝北，中轴线由北向南建有门厅、轿厅、大厅、后厅和后堂等房屋，各进建筑多以墙垣隔成院落，整个故居内共有大小天井 35 个，且有假山、树木点缀，建筑装饰精细考究，各式题材的“吉祥”雕刻图案，内容丰富，刀笔细致，形象生动。

以上汉语原文是较典型的“竹竿结构”，即典型的流水句，将这一“竹竿结构”转换成英语的“树干结构”，用结构形式来体现汉语原文中通过上下文隐含的意义层次，是译出地道英文的关键。以上汉语原文根据英文语段构成的习惯，大致可分为三个语义层次：第一层是总提全文的概括性的语句，即“甘熙故居俗称‘九十九间半’，是南京现存面积最大、保存最完整的清代私人住宅。”；第二层主要描述故居的外形结构和布局；第三层描述故居内部的结构和装饰等。翻译为英文时，可根据以上语义层次，选出表示主要意义的句子作为英语译文的主句，其他成分可以考虑为从属结构译出。如各句子处在同一个语义层次，可译为并列结构。请看译文：

With a history of 50 years, Nanjing Little Red Flower Art Troupe, which integrates cultural education, art learning with stage performing, is the first children's art troupe of its kind in China.

Built in the Qing Dynasty, the former Residence of Ganxi, known as "Ninety Nine and a Half Rooms," is the largest and best preserved private residence of the Qing Dynasty in Nanjing. With an area of 9,500 square meters and a floor space of 8,000 square meters, the Residence is made up of four southward integrated clusters of houses, with entrance halls, sedan chair porches, front living rooms, rear living rooms built from south to north along an axis running through the houses. The Residence contains as many as 35 walled-up courtyards with one such yard in each of the clusters. These courtyards are dotted with rockeries and trees, and decorated with carvings of various patterns, which are exquisite, vivid and rich in meaning, symbolizing good luck.

（4）在信息传递方面应以译语为归依，译出源文本的实质性内容

由于处在不同的文化和社会环境中，译文读者对信息的理解和接受能力肯定不如原文读者，在翻译时，如不根据具体情况，将适合原文读者的信息量进行变通处理，压缩、解释或两者兼而有之，而是亦步亦趋，将所有字词句统统翻译出来，就会造成内容繁杂、信息量过大，译文读者就无法理解、把握其意义要旨。汉语行文中常常含有无实质性内容的信息，这是因为汉语在表达上往往过度修饰、语义重复，一些修饰表达成分没有实质意义，主要在修辞上有押韵或构成对偶的作用，读起来朗朗上口；而英语行文则崇尚简洁明快、逻辑严谨，对语义重复、过度修饰则视为不可接受。因此，汉译英时一方面顾及译文受众对原文信息的接受能力，对超额信息进行变通处理，如压缩、解释等；另一方面，应对那些没有实质意义的表达修饰成分进行删除。

原文第七段：

南京夫子庙是供奉和祭祀我国古代著名的大思想家、教育家孔子的庙宇，其全称是“大成至圣先师文宣王庙”，简称“文庙”。夫子庙始建于宋景祐元年（公元 1034 年），由东晋学宫扩建而成。如今的夫子庙焕然一新，是秦淮风光带核心景观区，也是蜚声中外的旅游胜地。

以上原文中“大成至圣先师文宣王庙”、中国古代的纪年“宋景祐元年”不是主要信息，对一般的译文读者来说无实质意义，可略去不译，这是为了避免信息过于繁杂琐碎，从而影响译文读者对意义主旨的理解。另外，原文中的“如今的夫子庙焕然一新”，如果照字面翻译成“Now the Confucius Temple takes on a brand-new look”就会让英文读者以为夫子庙是完全新建的，因此将其改译为“Nowadays the Confucius Temple looks magnificent”。实际上，这样的译文与汉语原文所要表达的意义更加贴近。译文如下：

The Confucius Temple is a place to worship and consecrate Confucius, a great thinker and educator in ancient China. The Temple, also known as Wenmiao in Chinese, was first set up in 1034 A.D., on the basis of an extended study hall in the East Jin Dynasty. As a major scenic spot along the Qinhuai River, it has become a world famous tourist attraction.

15.4 翻译实战:《神话世界九寨沟》《北京大学简介》《香格里拉酒店》

【说明】 结合以上“翻译欣赏”、“翻译热身”和“翻译技巧”提供的宣传介绍材料的翻译思路，将下列篇章翻译为英语。

（1）神话世界九寨沟（节选）

蜀中山水，不知迷醉了多少古人和今人……

祖国山水，风格多样；多样的风格，相对应而存在，相比较而多姿。杭州西湖，水榭歌台，人工赋予它典雅美。蜀中仙山峨眉，飘浮于云涛雾海，呈秀色于烟雨浸漫的山林。誉满中华的桂林山水，水秀山奇，山水平分秋色。九寨沟风光，却又是另一番景象了。在那里，古树摇曳春秋，山花自谢自开，植被茸茸生烟，海子和瀑布随着季节的推移而变幻多姿；在那里，冰河时期遗留下来的星叶草、独叶草、先花后叶的领春树，以及熊猫、金丝猴、扭角羚、白马鸡、獐、鹿……组合成了奇异的“动植物王国”。当你步入沟中，便可见树正琼海淡荡生辉，瀑布舒洒碧玉。一到金秋，满山枫叶绛红。盛夏，湖山幽翠。仲春，树绿花艳……四时都呈现出它的天然原始，宁静幽深。日则沟里的镜湖、五花海，则查洼沟里的五彩池，虽缤纷艳丽，但令人迷醉的却是绚丽的和谐景色。这种独特的景观，只有在这个自然保护区才能见到。

（2）北京大学简介（节选）

北京大学位于北京市西郊的海淀区，创办于1898年，初名京师大学堂，是中国第一所国立综合性大学，也是当时中国最高教育行政机关。辛亥革命后，于1912年改为现名。

作为新文化运动的中心和五四运动的策源地，作为中国最早传播马克思主义和民主科学思想的发祥地，作为中国共产党最早的活动基地，北京大学为民族的振兴和解放、国家的建设和发展、社会的文明和进步做出了不可替代的贡献，在中国走向现代化的进程中起到了重要的先锋作用。爱国、进步、民主、科学的传统精神和勤奋、严谨、求实、创新的学风在这里生生不息、代代相传。

近年来，在“211工程”和“985工程”的支持下，北京大学进入了一个新的历史发展阶段，在学科建设、人才培养、师资队伍建设、教学科研等各方面都取得了显著成绩，为将北大建设成为世界一流大学奠定了坚实的基础。据不完全统计，北京大学的校友和教师有400多位两院院士，中国人文社科界有影响的人士相当多也出自北京大学。

今天的北京大学已经成为国家培养高素质、创造性人才的摇篮、科学研究的前沿和知识创新的重要基地和国际交流的重要桥梁和窗口。

（3）香格里拉酒店（节选）

总述

香格里拉的故事始于 1971 年，我们的第一家豪华酒店在新加坡开业。

香格里拉品牌灵感来自于詹姆斯·希尔顿在 1933 年出版的小说《消失的地平线》中的传奇之地。“香格里拉”这个名字代表着我们酒店及度假酒店享誉国际的宁静氛围与卓越服务。

今天，总部位于香港的香格里拉酒店集团已经成为亚太地区豪华酒店行业的领军企业。香格里拉也是世界上公认的最优秀的酒店集团和管理企业之一。集团目前拥有和 / 或管理超过 100 家酒店及度假酒店共 40 000 多间客房，范围覆盖亚太、北美、中东和欧洲等地区。此外，集团位于澳大利亚、巴林、中国内地、柬埔寨、印度尼西亚、马来西亚及沙特阿拉伯等地的酒店也正在开发中。

企业文化

我们一直以来的经营理念是“香格里拉热情好客，亲如家人”。香格里拉秉承独特的亚洲式热情好客之道。我们致力于为客人提供独具特色的亚洲待客之道和热情服务，这是我们有别于其他酒店业同行的关键所在，同时也是香格里拉赢得世界级酒店集团荣誉的基础。“自豪而不骄矜”极其重要，我们希望员工能够由衷地为我们所获得的成就而自豪，但在对待客人时仍表现出温良谦恭的品质。总之，真正的成功是不需要大肆宣扬的。在力求每时每刻令客人喜出望外的过程中，我们始终希望能够超越客人的期望，始终如一地为客人提供物有所值的优质产品和服务。这也正是我们要寻求那些勇于创新、追求卓越的潮流引领者和专业人士的原因。

我们的原则

我们要确保领导者具有追求经营业绩的魄力。

我们要将赢得宾客忠实度作为事业发展的主要驱动力。

我们要使同事能够在为宾客服务的现场及时做出果断决定。

我们要确保每家酒店乃至整个公司都取得最佳经营业绩。

我们要努力创造一个既有利于同事事业发展、又有助于实现其个人生活目标的环境。

我们要在与人相处时表现出诚挚、关爱和正直的品质。

我们要确保政策和程序简明易行，方便客人及同事。

我们始终坚持履行企业社会责任，为社区、环境、同事、宾客及经营伙伴做出积极贡献。

我们的愿景

成为客人、同事、股东和经营伙伴的首选。

我们的使命

以发自内心的待客之道，创造难以忘怀的美好经历，时刻令客人喜出望外。

15.5 译文荟萃

1. 句子翻译

1) 弘扬体育精神，促进国际往来。

Promote sportsmanship and international exchanges.（吴伟雄　译）

（比较：Spreading over the physical spirits and promoting international communications.）

2) 龙舟传友谊，重庆奔世界。

Friendship through dragon boats, Chongqing towards the world.（吴伟雄　译，编者略有改动）

（比较：Dragon boat delivering friendship, Chongqing facing the outside world.）

3) 携手合作，共创未来。

Prosperity through Partnership.（吴伟雄　译）

（比较：Cooperate hand in hand to create our common bright future!）

4) 创一流服务，迎四海嘉宾。

First class service to all guests.（吴伟雄　译）

（比较：Welcome our honored guests from all over the world with first-class service.）

5) 创优秀旅游城市，为名城争光。

Build a Top Tourist City of China for the honor of our famous city.（吴伟雄　译）

（比较：Build a China Best Tourist City to win honor for our famous city.）

6) 姑苏城外，湖泊河流，星罗棋布，河港纵横，各具特色的桥梁鳞次栉比，举目入画。建筑傍水而立，幽静雅逸，形成了水乡城市的独特风貌。

Outside Suzhou Rivers, lakes and artificial waterways spread all over the place. The canals are spanned with small bridges with distinct features. If you look round, you will enjoy the view of picturesque beauty. The quiet, elegant waterside buildings have assumed the unique feature of a water city.

7) 上海博物馆有馆藏珍贵文物 12 万件，包括青铜器、陶瓷器、书法、绘画、雕塑、家具、玉牙器、竹木漆器、甲骨、玺印、钱币、少数民族工艺等 21 个门类，其中青铜器、陶瓷器和书画为馆藏二大特色。

With bronze ware, ceramics and paintings and works of calligraphy as its distinctive collections, Shanghai Museum boasts 120,000 pieces of rare and precious cultural relics in 21 categories, including bronze ware, ceramics, calligraphy, paintings, sculpture, furniture, jade and ivory carvings, bamboo and wood carvings, lacquer ware, oracle bones, seals, coins, and handicrafts of ethnic art.

8) 尽管夏威夷地处热带，气候温和宜人，年均温度 24 摄氏度左右。岛上时时刮过的东北风，伴着太平洋吹来的阵阵海风，让人倍感凉爽舒适。

Although Hawaii is located in the tropical zone, its climate is comfortable because of the ocean currents that pass its shores and winds that blow across the land from the northeast. The temperature usually remains close to the annual average of 24 degrees Centigrade.

9) 发展才是硬道理。

译文 1: Development is the top priority.

译文 2: Development is of overriding importance.

译文 3: Development is the absolute principle.

译文 4: Development is the fundamental principle.

译文 5: Development is the absolute need.

译文 6: Development is the cardinal principle.

译文 7: Development leads to prosperity.

译文 8: Constant improvement is the sure way to progress.

译文 9: Development is always ironclad.

译文 10: Development is the only way.

译文 11: Development is the irrefutable fact.

译文 12: Development is the bottom line.

译文 13: Development is the most essential criterion.

译文 14: Socialism or capitalism, developing economy is the firstism.

10) 桂林山水甲天下。

译文 1: East or West, Guilin Landscape is best!

译文 2: The scenery of Guilin is world-renowned.

译文 3: Guilin's natural beauty is next to none.

译文 4: Natural scenery of Guilin is second to none.

译文 5: Scenery of Guilin, the finest under heaven.

译文 6: The scenery of Guilin is unparalleled in the world.

译文 7: By water, by mountains, most lovely, Guilin!

译文 8: Guilin's water and mountains captivate the world.

2. 段落翻译

1) 杭州的春天，淡妆浓抹，无不相宜；夏日荷香阵阵，沁人心脾；秋天桂枝飘香，菊花斗艳；冬日琼装玉琢，俏丽媚人。西湖以变幻多姿的风韵，令人心旷神怡。郁郁葱葱的峰岭之间，一条碧澄的玉带逶迤而过，这是美丽的富春江。溯源而西，便是有中国"第二漓江"之称的新安江。尽头处，有浩瀚的"千岛湖"。人们来到这里，无异于回到了大自然的怀抱，能充分享受纯朴的自然灵气。

译文：Sunny or rainy, Hangzhou looks its best in spring. In summer, lotus flowers bloom. Their fragrance gladdens people's hearts and refreshes their minds. Autumn brings with it the sweet scent of osmanthus flowers along with chrysanthemums in full bloom. In winter, snow scenes can be likened to an exquisite jade carving. West Lake's beauty is ever changing but never fails to entice and entrance. The picturesque Fuchun River stretches itself through the luxuriantly green hills and is said to resemble a clear jade ribbon. Traveling up to the Fuchun River, one may trace its source to the Xin'anjiang River, renowned as second only to the famous Lijiang River in Guilin of Guangxi Zhuang Autonomous Region. The journey is completed in the vast expanse of the Thousand-Islet Lake. In such scenic spots, tourists will fully enjoy the fresh air and natural beauty.（郭建忠　译）

2) 享受地利之便的北京红墙饭店与故宫博物院、景山、北海公园、北京最繁华的商业区王府井步行街仅几步之遥；周边的北大红楼（五四新文化运动发祥地）、老黄城根、四合院民居、老北京胡同环绕四周，宾客可乘坐饭店具有北京特色的三轮车前往游览和亲历感受普通北京居民的传统生活。入住本饭店的客人可在展间上皇家公园跑步，也可在夜幕时分驻足观赏皇城御河宫灯倒影，忙碌一天，情侣朋伴相约在饭店附近的什刹海酒吧一条街，把酒茗盏，享受这份承载皇族生活历史风韵下的宁静以及现代文明碰撞交汇的繁华。……北京红墙饭店秉承个性化的温馨服务理念，拥有严格专业的管理团队，饭店所有员工以热情诚挚的服务殷切期待您的光临！

译文：Just around the corner from the hustle and bustle of Beijing's shopping center—Wangfujing Street, you will find a haven of peace and comfort: Redwall Hotel. This excellently located hotel is ideally suited for travelers in the capital, with the Imperial Palace, the relics of the Imperial City and the former Royal Parks of Jingshan and Beihai only within a few minutes' walk of it. Staying at the Redwall turns a holiday into sheer delight. Whether touring typical Beijing hutungs by tricycle, watching the colorful reflections of lanterns on the Imperial Palace Canal at night or savoring refreshing drinks at Shichahai Bar Street, at the Redwall Hotel you will discover the essence of gracious living. …With Redwall's signature hospitality, the staff at our Beijing hotel looks forward to welcoming you.

3) 紫禁城北门。建于明永乐十八年（1420 年），初名玄武门，取古代“四神”中的玄武，代表北方之意，后因避康熙皇帝玄烨名讳改名神武门。台上为重檐庑殿顶门楼，内设钟鼓，与钟鼓楼相应，用以起更报时。但皇帝居宫中时，神武门上的钟不鸣。城台开有三门，帝后走中间正门，嫔妃、官吏、侍卫、太监及工匠等均由两侧的门出入。皇后祭先蚕，清代选秀女，将妃嫔迎入宫中均走此门。1924 年，逊帝溥仪被驱逐出宫即由此门离去。门外上方匾额“故宫博物院”为著名历史学家郭沫若于 1971 年题写。

Construction of the northern fortified gate of the Forbidden City was completed in 1420 during the Yongle reign of the Ming Dynasty (1368–1644). It was originally named Gate of the Dark Warrior (Xuan Wu Men) after a symbol for the north. Later, during the Qing Dynasty (1644–1911), because the personal name of the Kangxi Emperor (reign: 1662–1722) was Xuanye, the character *xuan* (dark, profound) was taboo and therefore was changed to *shen* (divine). On the high terrace stands a gate tower with double eaves that housed drums and bells; they were sounded at regular two-hour intervals to give the correct time — except when the emperor slept in the palace. Of the three passageways, the middle one was reserved for the emperor, and those on either side for Imperial concubines, officials, guards, eunuchs, and artisans. In the Qing Dynasty, this gate was used when the empress offered sacrifices to the Goddess of Silkworms, when the palace maidens were selected and Imperial concubines were welcomed. In 1924, when the last emperor Pu Yi was driven out of the palace, he and his retinue left through this gate. Above the gate's north face hangs a horizontal board which reads “Palace Museum,” written by the prominent historian Guo Moruo in 1971.

15.6 翻译家：林戊荪

林戊荪（1928 年—），著名翻译家，2011 年中国外文局和中国翻译协会“翻译文化终身成就奖”获得者，原外文出版发行事业局局长兼中国对外出版集团主席。曾任中国翻译工作者协会常务副会长、国际翻译家联盟理事、《中国翻译》杂志主编，现任全国翻译系列高级专业技术职务任职资格评审委员会主任、中国翻译协会顾问、欧美同学会理事、国际友人研究会理事。

林戊荪于 1946 年赴美国新泽西州劳伦斯威尔学校学习，1947 至 1950 年在新罕布什尔州达特茅斯大学主修哲学，期间参加中共地下党领导的留学生进步活动，1950 年归国参加祖国建设。20 世纪 50 年代初曾两次赴朝鲜，担任红十字小组和解释代表团翻译。1958 年参与创办《北京周报》，撰写国际问题专栏。在此前后还为亚太地区和平会议（1952 年）与中国共产党第八次代表大会（1956 年）从事同声传译。20 世纪 80 年代任《北京周报》副总编辑与临时负责人。林戊荪多次在《北京周报》、《中国日报》和 *US-CHINA REVIRW*（《美国季刊》）等刊物上发表文章，也曾多次率团参加世界翻译

大会。翻译作品绝大多数为中译英，为向世界介绍中国做出了重要贡献。主要译著有:《孙子兵法》《孙膑兵法》《论语》《南京大屠杀》《西藏》《布达拉宫珍宝》《丝绸之路》《江边对话：一个无神论者和一位基督徒的友好交流》《浦东奇迹》等。曾参与改稿及定稿《毛泽东外交文选》《国际形势与安全战略》《国际战略与新军事变革》等，于2012年荣获中国翻译协会颁发的“翻译事业特别贡献奖”。年近90岁的林戊荪先生最近在翻译《墨子·非攻》。近年来，林戊荪所推出《论语新译》(*Getting to Know Confucius — A New Translation of The Analects*)颇受国内学者的推崇，好评如潮。王宏印先生认为该译本体现了中国文化的内涵，能够和西方文明沟通，全文清晰可读，了无障碍；对话栩栩如生，语气和氛围清晰可见，场面描写真实可信，恢复了历史的环境，使人如临其境；译本整体行文风格简洁有力，文雅流畅，略有现代气息，而且表现手法多样，得体而丰富，不枯燥艰涩，有思想而无学究气，精彩译笔随处可见 。

林戊荪的主要翻译观点和思想包括:（1）做好翻译，首先要学好中文；两种语言和两种文化的功底都要深厚。做好翻译，就要做好跨语言和文化的传播。翻译质量的优劣取决于是否真实地表达了原作的意思以及相应的文化内涵。（2）必须树立精益求精的态度。林戊荪翻译《论语》时，十年时间内修改了五次。《论语新译》出版后，他发现按照原著翻译出的译文缺乏体系和逻辑，不便于外国读者理解和体会。因此，他又用三年的时间按体系对原译进行整理，于2017年年初出版了《论语新解全译》。他认为翻译的魅力在于不断地探索和发现新的领域，这个探索过程使人受益无穷、快乐无比。（3）译前的准备和译者的素养：翻译工作者必须是杂家，知识既要广博、又要精深。翻译前，首先要对原著的主题和主要思想有精准的了解；翻译过程中，不能离开原作，但又必须发挥译者最大的想象力和表达能力；翻译后，要反复推敲和修改，定稿后要梳理原文和译文，积累好的表达，形成自己的语料库。此外，要善于运用各种工具书和百科全书。（4）译者不仅要善于翻译，而且要善于运用两种语言写作，二者相互补充，相互促进。

15.7 补充资源

参考书目

黄友义．坚持“外宣三贴近”原则，处理好外宣翻译中的难点问题．中国翻译，2014 (6)：27-28.
郭建中．汉译英的翻译单位问题．外国语，2001 (6)：49-56.
吴伟雄．翻译是创造，是技术也是艺术——从“桂林山水甲天下”英译获奖谈起．中国科技翻译，

2007 (1)：1-3.

袁晓宁．外宣英译的策略及其理据．中国翻译，2005 (1)：75-78.

袁晓宁．语篇翻译中重构现象探讨．东南大学学报（社科版），2008 (2)：102-106.

Nida E A., Taber C R. *The Theory and Practice of Translation*. Leiden：E. J Brill, 1969.

Newmark P. *A Textbook of Translation*. Shanghai: Shanghai Foreign Language Education Press, 2001.

网络资源

故宫博物院官网：http://www.dpm.org.cn/Home.html

牛津大学官网：http://www.ox.ac.uk/

第十六单元　公示语

16.1 阅读欣赏：公示语英语示例

【说明】 英语公示语通常被视为是刚性表达，但也不乏文字优美、充满人文关怀的言辞，下面提供几种译文供学习者参考。

（1）禁止吸烟

译文 1: No smoking.

译文 2: You are now entering a non-smoking zone. Thank you for your assistance.

一般情况下，该公示语的英译为 No Smoking。而此处所给的英译较长，尤其是最后一部分“Thank you for assistance.”人情味十足，一下拉近了与受众的距离，从而使受众发自内心遵守这条要求。由此观之，公示语的表达并非绝对化，也可根据语境和受众心理灵活翻译。

（2）请勿入草地

译文 1: Keep off the grass!

译文 2: The Grass so Fair, needs your care!

目前很多公共绿地都有类似“小草青青，足下留情”这样的温馨提示，句子诗意盎然、不乏人文气息，然而英译文却较为别扭：“Mind you don't tread on the green meadow.”。英文最稳妥的译法就是 Keep off the grass。如果要再现原文的形式对仗、音韵和谐的语体特征，那么可以英译如下：“The grass so fair, needs your care!”这也是英美国家今年来在一些公共场所出现的类似公示语的缘由吧。

（3）爱心传递你我，文明就在身边。

译文： Where there is a love, there is a virtue.

（4）随地吐痰乞人恨，罚款一千有可能，传播肺痨由此起，卫生法例要遵行。

译文：No Spitting. Maximum Penalty $1,000.

上句为香港政府卫生当局在香港大街小巷张贴过的一则公示语，以打油诗方式教育市民，不要随地吐痰、触犯法律，否则给予罚款。若将这则偏长的公示语忠实通顺地译为英文，即便意思准确，韵律完整，效果也未必明显，因为来自英语世界的游客看了之后，往往以为是在开玩笑。若要起到原文警示之效，不妨简化处理，直接译为"No Spitting. Maximum Penalty $1,000."（周兆祥译）。这样翻译，一语中的，无须绕弯子。由此看来，公示语翻译并无"形到义随"之强求，必要时"得意忘形"不失为明智之举。

16.2 翻译热身：公示语英译练习

【说明】请将下列公示语翻译为英语。

（1）来也匆匆，去也冲冲！

（2）禁止在广场内私自摆摊设点、销售物品或从事其他经营性活动！

（3）严禁进入草坪、花坛和攀折毁坏树木花草！

（4）请为长者和残疾人士让座！

（5）谢谢惠顾（超市出口处）！

（6）欢迎再次光临（超市出口处）！

（7）公园内严禁遛狗！

（8）施工重地，闲人免进！

（9）禁止随意倾倒垃圾，违者罚款！

（10）请勿携带水酒！

16.3 翻译技巧：公示语英译

16.3.1　英语国家公示语表达特点

在讨论汉语公示语的翻译之前，我们有必要对英语公示语的语言文体特征做一简要的介绍和分析。通过各方收集的材料（特别是英语国家的公示语）来看，英语国家（以英国为主）常见的公示语具有以下构成与语体特征。

（1）大量使用核心词（动词、过去分词、形容词或名词）

推 / 拉门 Pull, Push

可回收再用 Recyclable

打烊 Closed

厕所有人 Vacant/Engaged/ Occupied

出口 Exit/Way Out

入口 Entrance /Way In

手动洗车 Hand Car Wash 意见箱 Complaint Box

（2）适当使用动词、动名词

请系好安全带 Fasten seat belts

请勿大声喧哗 Thank you for keeping your voices down

请在此等候 Wait for walk signal（过斑马线）

主动让行 Give way

保持通畅 Keep clear

请小心台阶 Mind the step

当心道槽 Mind the gap

严禁停车 No parking

禁止随地吐痰 No spitting

（3）多用词组、短语

因故停用 Out of order/ Not in service

短时停车 Short Stay

注意：正在维修 Caution: Maintenance in Progress

车载监视器在工作 Cameras in Operation

（4）多用一般现在时态，祈使句使用较频繁

英语公示语表达中祈使句使用较为频繁，能够有效地传递“言后之力”，句子形态使用一般现在时态，以传递信息的长期性。

在此付款 Please Pay Here（收银台 Pay Point）

请排队 Please wait here for service/ Please queue this way

请戴好护脚 / 手 Wear foot /hand protection

请戴好护脸 Wear face field/ mask

禁止张贴 Post No Bills

此座为老人、病弱者专用 These seats are particularly appreciated by the elderly and infirm.

如果警报拉响，请联系工作人员并寻求帮助 If the alarm sounds, please contact a member of staff for assistance.

（5）文字与图形标志共用

在部分公共场所，公示语常常和醒目的通用标志共同使用，能取得更好的效果。如下所示：

（6）用语简洁，措辞精确

英语公示语语汇和句法简洁、措辞准确，只要不影响公示语准确体现特定的功能意义，多用实词、关键词、核心词汇，而部分冠词、代词、助动词则省略。

未经许可货车禁止通行 No trade or business vehicle unless authorized

春节期间，暂停营业 Business suspended during the Spring Festival

紧急开门时，请使用此开关 Emergency use only

16.3.2 中文公示语英译思路

（一）汉语公示语英译原则

翻译公示语时须用词准确，不宜随意使用公示语中忌用的词语和冗长的句型，避免牵强和误会。由于公示语的语言和功能具有一定的特殊性，翻译时需要遵循一定的原则。有研究者提出了统一（consistency）、简洁（conciseness）和易懂（comprehensibility）作为公示语翻译的三原则，可简称为三 C 原则。

公示语汉英翻译的“统一原则”有三层含义：（1）如果英语国家有现成的惯用的公示语，英译时可直接借鉴，为我所用，参照国际惯例进行翻译。例如商场商品打 5 折，英国所有商场使用的几乎是 50% off，而不是 50% discount。（2）对于沿用至今、被广泛接受的译名，尤其是一些机构或者街道的名称，英译时须采用固定译名，即名从主人。例如，“上海交通大学”英译为 Shanghai Jiaotong University，而“华东师范大学”英译为 East China Normal University，前者音译，后者意译。遇到类似的翻译，需要遵循统一原则。（3）若既没有现成的英文公示语可以借鉴，也没有固定译名可以沿用，可以参照比较可靠的相关网站、报刊和辞典，最终寻求统一的译名。此处所说的“统一性”即指上文所言的“规范性”或“标准性”，即一旦固定下来，就不宜随意更改。公示语的目的是为满足公众的社会、行为和心理需求而提供的一种信息服务，信息服务的关键是信息准确与信息统一。对具有历史意义且为英语世界受众熟知的地名的翻译不宜采用新式表达，直接沿用即可。例如，“国泰电影院”应当为 Cathay Theater，而不是 Guotai Cinema；“百盛购物中心”应当为 Parkson Plaza，而不是 Baisheng Plaza 等等。如果不沿用，国外游客很容易认为是两个不同的地方，这样的翻译已经失去了其应有的社会功能。换言之，对于此类公示语的翻译应当给予特殊处理，才能有效地发挥公示语的提示、引导等职能。如果将上海著名的“南京路”译为 Nanjing Lu，那么外国旅游者很可能会认为上海还有一个与南京路一样繁华的商业购物街。既然这样，我们为什么不用现存的 Nanjing Road，而非要译为 Nanjing Lu 呢？

公示语英译“简洁原则”是指译文精练、清晰明了，无晦涩之词语，无复杂之长句。地道的公示语具有两个明显的特征：准确和简洁。基于英语公示语的语体特征，确立简洁为其英译的一条原则，不失为一种选择。例如，“贵宾候车室”原译为 Distinguished Guests Wait for a Bus at the Place，这是某汽车站候车室的一条公示语。原译把简明标识翻译成了一个完整的句子，这显然有悖公示语简明的语体特征。依照简洁原则，我们不妨译为：VIP Waiting Lounge, 也可以考虑使用 Reserved Waiting Lounge，“候车室”不宜使用 waiting room。原译中的 guests wait for a bus 和 at the place 皆为多余文字，更不应该译为一个完整的句子。既然该公示语醒目地挂在汽车站候车室门口，就没必要再强调旅客在此等汽车。由此观之，公示语英译如果遵循简洁原则，译文不仅言简意赅，词汇、句法简单，更容易达到传递信息的效果。

公示语英译的易懂原则是指英译文具有相当的可读性，容易被英语人士理解。避免使用中式英语，成为译者遵守易懂原则的首要任务。这条翻译原则对具有中国特色的公示语的英译尤其重要。译者因受到本土文化的影响，习惯上按自己熟悉的文化去理解，用中文的思维方式去翻译。结果，所译公示语虽无语言错误，但如果按照英语语言和文化模式的表达习惯，英语本族语者很难准确理解。这种中式英语公示语经常导致交际失败、信息中断。换言之，译者在翻译过程中应尽量消减翻译的痕迹，即积极参照英语公示语中类似的表达，并加以适当改造和创造。比如：“（火车）软座、硬座”的确带有中国特色，英国火车并无此区分。依照国家标准，可译作 Soft Seat 和 Hard Seat，国外乘客从字面和车票价格也能理解二者的区别。如果将二者分别翻译成 Cushioned Seat 和 Ordinary Seat，前者是指有垫子的座位，当然就是软席；后者则是普通的、没有垫子的座位。

从以上三个原则来看，汉英公示语的英译应当是三个原则合力的结果。英语表达既要统一，又要简洁易懂。只有英语行文清楚明了，符合英语表达习惯和思维模式，来自英语世界的受众方能明白所译公示语的真实意图，公示语也就能体现其应有的社会价值，发挥应有的宣传和交际功能。

（二）汉语公示语英译方法

根据英语公示语的语体特征，汉语公示语英译主要采用两种方法：借用（仿译）法和正反译法。

1. 借用法

由于英语世界的很多公共区域和其功能与我们中国的情况相似，最简便而实用的办法，莫过于直接使用国外的惯用公示语。英文公示语必须照顾到英语使用者的感受。而那些约定俗成的公共标识，最原汁原味，也最容易让外国人明白其中的内涵。请看下列译文在统一上的问题：

例 1： 小心碰头

这一公示语的英语译名可谓五花八门，应有尽有：

（1）Take Care of Your Head（北京新街口商贸百货商场电梯旁）

（2）Attention Your Head（南京地铁沿线站台）

（3）Be careful your head /Be careful to hit you r head（哈尔滨一商厦警示牌）

（4）Notice your head（重庆重百商场）

（5）Meet carefully

这五种译文均存在严重问题。Take Care of Your Head 这句英文在外国人看来就变成了“请照顾好您的头”。他们会感到纳闷：为什么要在这里照顾自己的头？译成 Attention Your Head，语法和译文都有问题，attention 是名词，即使要用 attention 来翻译也应该用它的动词短语 pay attention to, 即 Pay Attention to Your Head。即便如此，这样的译文仍然有问题，因为 pay attention to your head 按照字面意思应该解释为“注意 / 留意你的头部 / 脑袋”，让乘客感到不知所云。翻译成 Be careful your head / Be careful to hit your head，让人感到莫名其妙。Notice your head 显然未能传递公示语的基本信息。最后一种译文更是荒唐，中文理解明显有误。如果对英语公示语熟悉，那么自然就会选择这样的表达：Mind / Watch your head。

很多公共绿地都有类似于“青青绿草，请勿践踏”“小草有生命，足下留情”“请珍爱小草的生命”等公示语，而英文一般是 Grass and Flower, No Trampled Please；Grass has a life and please take good care of it；Please treasure grass’s life 等等。尤其是第一种翻译，口气非常生硬，踩在草地上就等同于践踏生命。这样的翻译错误百出，译犹不译也。之所以如此翻译，主要是由于译者对英语公示语不熟悉，而且缺乏精益求精的务实态度。因为“爱护小草”这类公示语在西方、尤其是英语世界极为平常，最常见的莫过于 Keep off the Grass。“保护一池碧水 营造一片宁静”译为 The protection of a pool of water, creating a quiet（其实可译为 Keep water clean）等类似的表达，不胜枚举。

汉语公示语翻译中借用最为成功莫过于“当心地滑”，国内大小商场包括超市几乎用 Caution Wet Floor。由于国情不尽一致，生活场景有别，加之英语公示语自身在“与时俱进”，翻译时需要因地制宜。尽管如此，英语公示语作为一种成熟的语体，具有自己特有的语言规范，即便是不能照搬，我们也可以依样画葫芦译写出适合中国语境的、自然地道的英语公示语。由于公示语范围非常广泛，本书不可能一一涉及，只能选取部分实例加以分析，在翻译思路方面为读者提供某些参考。下面以提示（提醒）类公示语为例。提醒或警示类公示语多用三种语言形态：Caution —, Beware of —, Danger —。

以 Caution 开头的公示语的主要作用是提醒公众注意某种情况，比如路滑等：

当心海浪 Caution Waves!

小心脚下 Caution: Mind Your Step

小心电缆 Caution Overhead Cables

小心地滑 Caution Wet Floor

注意：请勿攀爬墙体 Caution: No Climbing

以 Beware of 开头的公示语，暗示某地有某种危险：

当心有蛇 Beware of Snakes

当心低飞飞机 Beware of Low Flying Aircrafts

当心行进车辆 Beware of Moving Vehicles

当心坠落 Beware of Falling

当心扒手 Beware of Pickpockets

为了提醒过往行人注意极为危险的情况，英语公示语常用 Danger 开头：

危险！高度易燃物品！ Danger! Highly Flammable Material

危险！深水区 Danger! Deep Water

危险！薄冰 Danger! Thin Ice

当心触电 Danger! High Voltage

危险！不要在悬挂物下停留！ Danger! Stand Clear of Suspended Load!

另一类公示语可以套译为— Only，比如“旅客止步”在英语国家的通用说法是 Staff Only，而非“Tourists, Please Stop”之类的译文。Staff Only 这个译文是回译的结果。多数含有“专用”二字的汉语公示语几乎均可译为— only。类似表达还有“员工专用”Staff Only；“公交车专用”Buses Only,“贵宾专用”VIP Only / Distinguished Guests Only；“会员俱乐部”Members Only；“专用停车位”Authorized Cars Only；“警车专用停车位”Police Cars Only；“请绕行此路”Arrow Only；“超车道”Overtaking Only 或者 Overtaking Lane；“送客止步”Passengers Only；“残疾人通道（专用）”Handicapped Only。同样，“非公勿入”也可译为 Staff Only；“凭票入场”译为 Ticket Only。含有“仅限于”之意的公示语如“购物车仅限超市购物使用”The shopping cart is for store-use only，或者“此窗口对学生开放”译为 For Students Only。

表示禁止意义的汉语公示语可用 Do not —，No —等翻译，如：

请勿触摸展品 Do not touch exhibits

行车途中禁止与公交司机说话 Do not speak to the driver while bus in motion

严禁打扰 Do not disturb

严禁疲劳驾驶 Do not drive when Tired.

请勿挤靠车门 Please do not push or lean against the door.

禁止右转弯 No Right Turn

禁止照相 No Photography/Cameras

禁止张贴 No Bills

禁止入内 No Entry

谢绝入内 No Admittance

禁止烟火 No Fire

禁止钓鱼 No Fishing

禁止骑车 No Cycling

从以上实例来看，no 后面跟名词或动名词，均可表达禁止之意，往往能收到“言后之效”。

2. 正反译法

正反译法是翻译中常用的一种方法，该方法依然适用于公示语的翻译。有时候，一个汉语公示语译为正反两个或多个英语公示语，这样可以满足不同的场合需求，同样也为来自不同国家的受众提供了方便。以下举例分析：

严禁停车 No Parking

切勿挤压 Fragile / Handle with care

勿放潮湿处 Store in dry place

切勿倾倒 Keep Upright

请不要堵住入口 Keep Clear of Entrance

禁止小孩入内 No Children Allowed

这种表示禁止性的公示语的目的在于提示公众禁止做某事，重在信息的传递，并暗示“如果不按照该提示做，可能就要受到某种惩罚”之意。比如“严禁停车”不宜译作 Parking Forbidden，尽管没有语言问题。没有语言错误，并不意味着此公示语符合要求。“勿放潮湿处”提示公众应该把东西放在干燥的地方，故此译作 Store in dry place。同样，“禁止小孩入内”若译作 Children Forbidden，则命令性太强，受众会感到不舒服。因此在翻译公示语时应当考虑受众的接受心理，以确保译出语更像是源语的译入语。

除了上面这两种常用的翻译方法之外，译者还需依据语境灵活翻译，正所谓译无定法。“请勿随地乱扔烟头”通常可译作“Please don’t litter the floor with cigarette ends”。但如果有烟灰缸，那么这样翻译更符合英语表达习惯：Thank you for using ashtray。

以上实例表明，公示语翻译是一个国家对外交流水平和人文环境建设的具体体现。不论是建立国际化大都市，还是发展经济，都需要良好的语言生态环境。改善公示语翻译的质量，无疑是提升国家形象的有力举措之一。作为译者，首先要认真研究英语公示语的语言特点、功能意义，更要分析汉英公示语在文化和语言表达上的差异。对于公示语的翻译中存在的问题，要对症下药，不仅要分析问题的根源，还要提出具体解决方案。另外，译者必须加强自身的语言修养，养成严谨的治学和翻译态度。为保证翻译质量，必须做好充分准备，多查找资料，诚恳地向专家学者和外国友人寻求指导，甚至向外国游客咨询并及时获得反馈，在翻译过程中充分利用参考书籍和网站上的相关资源。一言以蔽之，只有精心准备、诚心咨询、细心斟酌，才能得到表达准确、言辞精当、地道自然的公示语译文，也才能真正为净化我国的语言生态环境尽一份绵薄之力。

16.4 翻译实战

【说明】 请结合上面介绍的翻译方法翻译以下公示语，注意语言表达的准确性和规范性。

（1）美容美发厅

（2）网上商城

（3）请勿使用手机！

（4）请勿遗忘随身携带物品！

（5）请在黄线外等候！

（6）儿童须由成人陪同！

（7）文字记者席！

（8）禁止在广场树木建筑雕刻及公共设施上留言刻字、随意张贴！

（9）果皮、纸屑、酒瓶等废弃物请扔进垃圾箱！

（10）严禁在广场内进行球类、轮滑、放风筝等有碍他人的活动。对违反本规定者，广场执法人员将依据有关规定进行处罚！

（11）为了您个人的安全，本站安装有闭路电子监视系统！

（12）火车开车前 20 分钟，旅客不准进入！

（13）您的安全，我们的天责！

（14）远离毒品，珍爱生命！

（15）本店二十四小时营业。

16.5 译文荟萃

1) 禁止吸烟！

译文：No Smoking

Smoke Free

No smoking Area

Non-smoking Area

This is a smoke free station

No Smoking beyond free facility

This is a non-smoking facility

2) 老弱病残孕者专座

译文：Priority Seats/Courtesy Seats

3) 酒后勿驾驶。

译文：If you drink, you can't drive.

4) 请勿乱丢宣传单张，违者可被检控。

译文：It is an offense to litter handbills.

5) 来也匆匆？去也冲冲！

译文：Come with a rush? Go with a flush!

6) 文明用餐，请勿喧哗

译文：Please help Maintain a Quiet Atmosphere

7) 请勿影响其他客人休息

译文：Please Do Not Disturb Other Guests

8) 请牵好狗！

译文：Dogs must be carried.

Dogs must be kept on a lead.

Dogs must be on a leash at all times.

Dogs are not allowed, except on a leash.

Dogs must be leashed. Owners must clean up after dogs.

9) 房屋出租

译文：To Let

For Rent

For Lease

10) 当心地滑

译文：Caution/ Slippery Floor

Caution/ Slippery Surface

Caution/ Uneven Surface

Caution/ Slippery When Wet

Caution/ Floor May Be Slippery

Caution/ Watch your steps. Floor May Be Slippery at times

16.6 翻译家：汪榕培

汪榕培（1942 年—2017 年），著名英语教育专家、翻译家、词典学家。1942 年出生于上海，1964 年本科毕业于上海外国语学院英语系，1967 年研究生毕业于复旦大学外文系。长期担任英语教学工作，1985 年 6 月到 2001 年 9 月担任大连外国语学院院长。曾获政府特殊津贴、陈香梅教育奖励基金一等奖、辽宁省优秀专家、大连市优秀专家等奖励。曾担任中国典籍英译研究会会长、中国英语教学研究会副会长、中外语言文化比较学会副会长、辽宁省外语教学研究会会长、辽宁省外国文学研究会副会长、辽宁省委省政府咨询委员、大连市委市政府咨询委员等；现任大连大学特聘教授，兼任苏州大学、大连理工大学等校博士生导师。

汪榕培教授在学术研究上也取得了丰硕的成果，至今已发表论文 60 余篇、论译著 50 余部，主审各类论译著和词典20余部，涉及英语语言文学的多个领域。他在英语词汇学等三方面取得了显著的成就，1983年出版的《实用英语词汇学》是我国在这一学术领域中的第一部专著，1997年出版的《英语词汇学教程》、1999年出版的《英语词汇探胜》和2000年出版的《英语词汇学研究》把这一领域的研究提高到一个新的水平。1992年出版的《八十年代国外语言学的新天地》和1997年出版的《九十年代国外语言学的新天地》则追踪了国外语言学研究的最新动态。

在中国古典文学英译和中西文化比较等方面，汪榕培也取得了突破性的进展，译著辉煌，先后完成了《英译老子》《英译易经》《英译诗经》《英译庄子》《英译汉魏六朝诗三百首》《英译孔雀东南飞·木兰诗》《英译陶诗》《英译牡丹亭》《英译邯郸记》《陶渊明集》《邯郸记》《吴歌精华》《评弹精华》《昆曲精华》《苏剧精华》等译著，其中多项已入选《大中华文库》；并撰写了一系列相关的论文，出版了专著《比较与翻译》和《陶渊明诗歌英译比较研究》，得到国内外学者的高度重视与好评。《人民日报》《人民日报·海外版》《光明日报》《辽宁日报》《大连日报》《大连晚报》等报刊都曾发表通讯和报道，介绍他的事迹。他一生主要从事典籍英译和研究工作，为中国文化走向世界做出了巨大贡献。

汪榕培认同“传神达意”的翻译原则，其主要译学思想或体会有以下四点：

（1）要有翻译热情，耐得住寂寞。只有真正发自内心的爱好才能帮助他们克服所面临的困境，全心投入。

（2）精选原作：尽量选择跟译者自己的特点和爱好相似的作品，这样翻译出来的文学作品才能既传神又达意。就像电影演员一样，有全能的演员，也有本色演员，出演跟演员本色性格比较符合的角色，观众看起来也比较自然。有些译者尽管一辈子从事文学作品的翻译工作，数量不少，理解不错，文字也规范，但就是缺那么一点“味道”，缺那么一点“感情”，达不到最佳境界。

（3）译者需提高自身的语言和文化素养：翻译文学作品与创作文学作品相通，需要译者有文学素质，甚至是天赋。

（4）对译作评论需谨言慎行：若未从事过翻译和认真研读原文和译文，对译作的优劣就没有发言权。

16.7 补充资源

参考书目

中国国家标准化管理委员会．公共服务领域英文译写规范（通则，交通，旅游等）．北京：中国标准出版社，2017.
刘季春 . 实用翻译教程 . 广州：中山大学出版社，2008.
王振国，李艳琳 . 新汉英翻译教程 . 北京：高等教育出版社，2014.
王欣，吕婷婷等 . 公共标识英语纠错指南 . 北京：中国书籍出版社，2010.

网络资源

云浮翻译网 http://www.yfta.net/view. asp? xxid=567

http://language. chinadaily. com. cn/trans/2008-12/29/content_7348744.htm

http://en. wikipedia.org/wiki/Road_signs_in_Canada

美国交通标识网：http://www.usa-traffic-signs.com/

英国公共场所标识（语）网：http://www.safetysignsandppe.co.uk/（该网站有各种类型的公示语，值得借鉴）

参考文献

曹雪芹，高鹗．红楼梦（汉英对照，共6卷）．杨宪益，戴乃迭，译．北京：外文出版社，2006.
曹雪芹，高鹗．红楼梦（范圣宇版本校勘　汉英对照）．闵德福，译．上海：上海外语教育出版社，2014.
陈毓贵．对翻译历史书籍资料的一点浅见．语言与翻译，1988（1）：23-26.
陈毓贵．再谈翻译历史书籍资料的一点浅见．语言与翻译，1994（2）：104-112.
陈荣捷．中国哲学文献选编．杨儒宾等，译．南京：江苏教育出版社，2006.
方梦之，毛忠明．应用翻译教程．上海：上海外语教育出版社，2004.
丰华瞻．诗歌翻译的几个问题．复旦学报（社会科学版），1978// 罗新璋，陈应年．翻译论集（修订本）．北京：商务印书馆，2009.
冯雪红．论中国政治术语英译再创建的三个维度．上海翻译，2014（1）：58-61.
何刚强．笔译理论与技巧．北京：外语教学与研究出版社，2009.
黄鸣奋．英语世界中国古典文学之传播．上海：学林出版社，1997.
黄友义．从翻译工作者的权利到外宣翻译．中国翻译，2005（6）：31-33.
黄友义．坚持“外宣三贴近”原则，处理好外宣翻译中的难点问题．对外传播，2004（6）：27-28.
翦伯赞，邵循正，胡华．中国历史概要．北京：北京大学出版社，2009.
金岳霖．金岳霖文集（第2卷）．兰州：甘肃人民出版社，1995.
金岳霖，刘培育．道、自然与人：金岳霖英文论著全译．北京：生活·读书·新知三联书店，2005.
李铁匠．谈谈历史著作翻译——以《波斯帝国史》和《伊朗历史》的翻译为例．常熟理工学院学报（哲学社会科学），2011（1）：98-102.
连淑能．英汉对比研究．北京：高等教育出版社，1993.
林语堂．论译诗 // 海岸．中西诗歌百年论集．上海：上海外语教育出版社，2007.
刘宓庆．文体与翻译．北京：中国对外翻译出版公司，1998.
刘重德．论译诗．现代外语，1996（2/3）// 海岸．中西诗歌翻译百年论集．上海：上海外语教育出版社，2007.
马迁．大中华书库 史记选．杨宪益、戴乃迭，译，安平秋，校译．北京：外文出版社，2008.
茅海建．天朝的崩溃：鸦片战争再研究．北京：三联书店，1995.
沈既济．唐代传奇选（汉英对照版）．杨宪益，戴乃迭，译．北京：外文出版社，2016.
施耐庵，罗贯中．水浒全传．长沙：岳麓书社，1988.

王和私，尹丕安，王芙蓉．中英文政治演说的情态对比研究．西安外国语大学学报，2011（2）：38-42.

王季春．实用翻译教程．广州：中山大学出版社，2007.

王林海，史玉姝，刘磊．语料库视角下中国古代经典外译中主要官衔的原型对等化处理——以《东周列国志》的英译为例．外语电化教学，2015（6）：47-53.

王绍祥．西方汉学界的“公敌”——英国汉学家翟理斯（1845—1935）研究．福州：福建师范大学，2004.

王振国，李艳琳．新汉英翻译教程．北京：高等教育出版社，2014.

王佐良，丁往道．英语文体学引论．北京：外语教学与研究出版社，1987.

吴芳，张龙宽．简论中国古代官职名称翻译．长春师范学院学报（人文社会科学版），2009（6）：114-118.

吴伏生．汉诗英译研究：理雅各、翟理斯、韦利、庞德．北京：学苑出版社，2012.

吴敬梓．大中华文库:儒林外史 （汉英对照,THE SCHOLARS Ⅰ/Ⅱ/Ⅲ 全 3 册）．杨宪益,戴乃迭，译．长沙：湖南人民出版社，2011.

习近平．习近平谈治国理政．北京：外文出版社，2014.

许涤新，吴承明．中国资本主义发展史 第一卷：中国资本主义的萌芽．北京：人民出版社，1985.

许渊冲．中诗英韵探胜．北京：北京大学出版社，2010.

许渊冲．意美、音美、形美．翻译的艺术（论文集）．北京：中国对外翻译出版公司，1984：52-61.

杨全红．高级翻译十二讲．武汉：武汉大学出版社，2009.

杨自俭，刘学云．翻译新论．武汉：湖北教育出版社，2003.

袁行霈．中国诗歌艺术研究．北京：北京大学出版社，2009.

张斌．杨宪益、戴乃迭英译本《史记·李将军列传》翻译技巧初探．英语教师，2016（7）：133-135，138.

张健．全球化语境下的外宣翻译“变通”策略刍议．外国语言文学，2013（1）：19-27, 43.

张培基．英汉翻译教程．上海：上海外语教育出版社，1980.

朱辉．中国诗歌在英语世界：英美译家汉诗英译研究．上海：上海外语教育出版社，2009.

庄绎传．程镇球——翻译政治文献的老专家．中国翻译，1995（4）：42-43.

卓振英．汉诗英译论纲．杭州：浙江大学出版社，2011.

Bassnett S. Translating the seed: Poetry and translation//Bassnett S, Lefevere A. *Constructing Cultures: Essays on Literary Translation*. Shanghai: Shanghai Foreign Language Education Press, 2001.

Cao Xueqin. Hawks D, Trans. *The Story of The Stone*. London: Penguin Classics, 1974.

Chan, Wing-tsit. A *Source Book in Chinese Philosophy*. Princeton, NJ: Princeton University Press, 1963.

Curven C A. *Chinese Capitalism, 1522-1840*. London: Macmillan Press, 1999: 1.

Ivan M. The Genius of Arthur Waley//Morris I. *Madly Singing in the Mountains: An Introduction and Anthology of Arthur Waley*. New York: Walker and Company, 1970.

JIAN Bozan, SHAO Xunzheng, HU Hua. *A Concise History of China*. Beijing: Foreign Languages Press, 1986.

MAO Haijian. *The Qing Empire and the Opium War: The Collapse of the Heavenly Dynasty*. Lawson Joseph et al, Trans. Cambridge: Cambridge University Press, 2016.

Newmark P. *Approaches to Translation*. London: Pergmon Press, 1981.

MAO Tse-tung. *Selected Readings from the Works of Mao Tse-tung*. Beijing: Foreign Language Press, 1967.

SIMA Qian. *Records of the Grand Historian: Han Dynasty I: Revised Edition.* Watson B, Trans. New York: Columbia University Press, 1961.

XI Jinping. *Xi Jinping: The Governance of China*. Beijing: Foreign Language Press, 2014.

主要参考网站：

人民网（http://www.people.com.cn/GB/shizheng/252/6688/6715/20011023/588430.html）

《中国日报》网“英语点津”栏目（http://language.chinadaily.com.cn/）

央视网（http://www.cctv.com/special/1068/3/89380.html）

中央编译局网站（http://www.cctb.net/bygz/zywxsy/）

马克思主义者网 (https://www.marxists.org/reference/archive/deng-xiaoping/1974/04/10.htm)

新华网（http://www.xinhuanet.com/english/special/2017-11/03/c_136725942.htm）

中华人民共和国国务院新闻办公室网站（http://www.scio.gov.cn/zfbps/）

中国网（http://www.china.org.cn/chinese/18da/2012-11/19/content_27156212_2.htm）

中国人大网（http://www.npc.gov.cn/englishnpc/Constitution/node_2825.htm）

图书在版编目（CIP）数据

汉英翻译教程 / 文旭总主编；肖开容，罗天主编. —北京：中国人民大学出版社，2018.9
全人教育英语专业本科教材系列
ISBN 978-7-300-25975-8

Ⅰ. ①汉…　Ⅱ. ①文…　②肖…　③罗…　Ⅲ. ①英语－翻译－高等学校－教材　Ⅳ. ①H315.9

中国版本图书馆 CIP 数据核字（2018）第 147474 号

全人教育英语专业本科教材系列
总顾问　刘润清
汉英翻译教程
总主编　文　旭
主　编　肖开容　罗　天
副主编　李　智　孟凡君　杨　洁
编写人员（按章节排序）
杨　洁　罗　天　肖开容　朱晓烽
刘　黎　孟凡君　李奉栖　李　智
Hanying Fanyi Jiaocheng

出版发行	中国人民大学出版社		
社　址	北京中关村大街 31 号	邮政编码	100080
电　话	010-62511242（总编室）		010-62511770（质管部）
	010-82501766（邮购部）		010-62514148（门市部）
	010-62515195（发行公司）		010-62515275（盗版举报）
网　址	http://www.crup.com.cn		
经　销	新华书店		
印　刷	北京捷迅佳彩印刷有限公司		
开　本	889 mm × 1194 mm　1/16	版　次	2018 年 9 月第 1 版
印　张	19.75	印　次	2024 年 7 月第 2 次印刷
字　数	416 000	定　价	45.00 元

中国人民大学出版社读者信息反馈表

尊敬的读者：

感谢您购买和使用中国人民大学出版社的 ______________________ 一书，我们希望通过这张小小的反馈表来获得您更多的建议和意见，以改进我们的工作，加强我们双方的沟通和联系。我们期待着能为更多的读者提供更多的好书。

请您填妥下表后，寄回或传真回复我们，对您的支持我们不胜感激！

1. 您是从何种途径得知本书的：
   □书店　□网上　□报纸杂志　□朋友推荐
2. 您为什么决定购买本书：
   □工作需要　□学习参考　□对本书主题感兴趣　□随便翻翻
3. 您对本书内容的评价是：
   □很好　□好　□一般　□差　□很差
4. 您在阅读本书的过程中有没有发现明显的专业及编校错误，如果有，它们是：

   ____

   ____

   ____

5. 您对哪些专业的图书信息比较感兴趣：

   ____

   ____

   ____

6. 如果方便，请提供您的个人信息，以便于我们和您联系（您的个人资料我们将严格保密）：

   您供职的单位：______________________________

   您教授的课程（教师填写）：______________________

   您的通信地址：______________________________

   您的电子邮箱：______________________________

请联系我们：黄婷　程子殊　王新文　王琼　鞠方安

电话：010-62512737，62513265，62515580，62515573，62515576

传真：010-62514961

E-mail：huangt@crup.com.cn　chengzsh@crup.com.cn　wangxw@crup.com.cn　crup_wy@163.com　jufa@crup.com.cn

通信地址：北京市海淀区中关村大街甲59号文化大厦15层　邮编：100872

中国人民大学出版社